PENGUIN BOOKS

BERLIN:

COMING IN FROM THE COLD

Ken Smith is the author of *Inside Time*, the apocryphal *A Book of Chinese Whispers*, and several collections of poetry. He was born in 1938.

BERLIN:
COMING IN FROM THE COLD

KEN SMITH

PENGUIN BOOKS

PENGUIN BOOKS

Published by the Penguin Group
Penguin Books Ltd, 27 Wrights Lane, London w8 5tz, England
Penguin Books USA Inc., 375 Hudson Street, New York, New York 10014, USA
Penguin Books Australia Ltd, Ringwood, Victoria, Australia
Penguin Books Canada Ltd, 2801 John Street, Markham, Ontario, Canada l3r 1b4
Penguin Books (NZ) Ltd, 182–190 Wairau Road, Auckland 10, New Zealand

Penguin Books Ltd, Registered Offices: Harmondsworth, Middlesex, England

First published by Hamish Hamilton 1990
Published in Penguin Books 1991
1 3 5 7 9 10 8 6 4 2

Printed in England by Clays Ltd, St Ives plc

CONTENTS

ACKNOWLEDGEMENTS

To many people in both cities of Berlin whose advice and practical help I acknowledge, and whose friendship I value, this book is dedicated: to Friedemann and Lucky and Tim and Heidi in East Berlin, and in the West to Thora, Tony, Maureen, John, Gesine, Katja. In particular I wish to thank Elke for the research and Joachim for his patience in reading the manuscript and the precision of his comments and suggestions.

i.m. Andrew Musgrave, 1964–1990

The sources of this book lie in reportage, anecdote, rumour, apocrypha, in what's heard on the street as much as what's read in the newspaper, in what's believed at the time, true or false. Acknowledgement is herewith made to sources in the *Berliner Morgenpost*, *BZ*, *Bild Berlin*, *Welt am Sonntag*, *Volksblatt Berlin*, *Tagesspiegel*, *Tageszeitung*, *Die Wahrheit*, *Neues Deutschland*, *Berliner Zeitung*, *Junge Welt*, *Die Welt*, *Die Zeit*, *Spiegel*, *Stern*, *Tip*, *Zitty*, and in the Amnesty International report on the GDR published in January 1989.

With the exception of 'Peter's *Arbeit*' (reproduced here by kind permission of Peter Unsicker/Wall Street Gallery) all photographs were taken by the author.

LIST OF ABBREVIATIONS

GDR/DDR   *Deutsche Demokratische Republik*, the German Democratic Republic

FRG/BRD   *Bundesrepublik Deutschland*, the Federal Republic of Germany

CDU   *Christlich-Demokratische Union*, the Christian Democrats

DA   *Demokratischer Aufbruch*, Democratic Awakening

DJ   *Demokratie Jetzt*, Democracy Now

DBD   *Demokratische Bauernpartei Deutschlands*, the Farmers

DBU   *Deutsche Biertrinker-Union*, the jokers

DSU   *Deutsche Soziale Union*

FDJ   *Freie Deutsche Jugend*, the Communist Youth

FDP   *Freie Demokratische Partei*, the Free Democrats

KPD   *Kommunistische Partei Deutschlands*, the Communist Party

LDP   *Liberale Demokratische Partei*, the Liberal Democrats

NDPD   *Nationale-Demokratische Partei Deutschlands*, the neo-Nazis

NF   *Neues Forum*, New Forum

PDS   *Partei des Demokratischen Sozialismus*, the Communists, formerly the SED

RAF   *Red Army Fraction*, the terrorists

SED   *Sozialistische Einheitspartei Deutschlands*, the Socialist Unity Party

SPD   *Sozialdemokratische Partei Deutschlands*, the Social Democrats

Note: 1 billion = 1,000,000,000

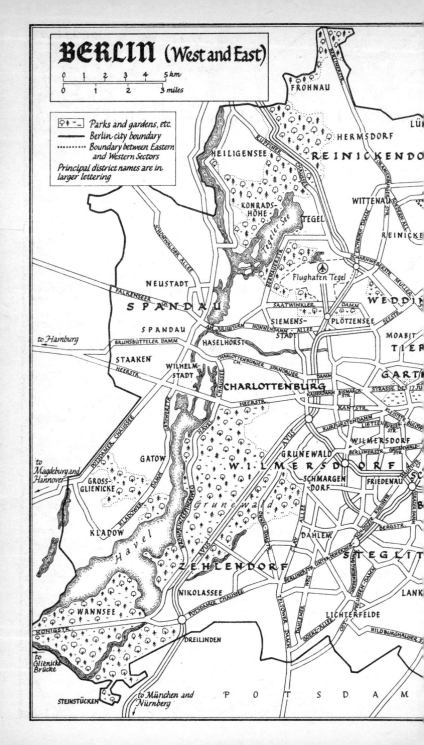

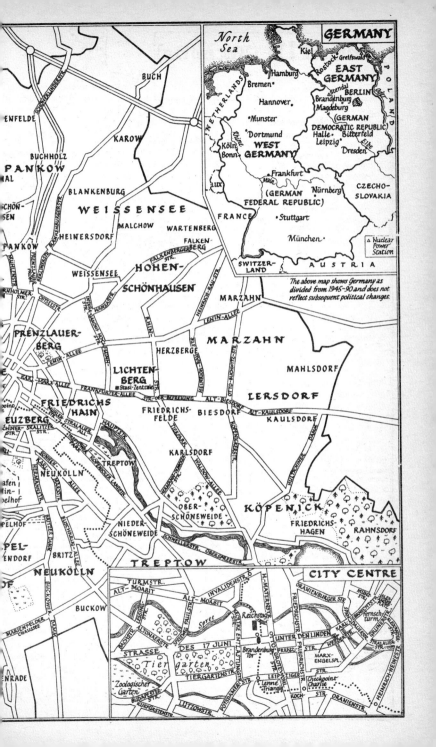

Wörter sind nur Schatten (Words are but shadows)
(graffiti, the Ararat Café, Kreuzberg)

I

CITY OF THE BEAR

Two cities. Two that were one and will again become one. Trains enter the East at Friedrichstrasse and Ostbahnhof, the West at Wannsee and Zoo. Traffic enters West Berlin via the long transit routes, down which West Berlin's supplies come. Coal comes in on the canals and waterways. Planes from the East fly into Schönefeld – Aeroflot and Lot and Interflug. From the West into Tegel fly British Airways and PanAm and Air France, all under Allied joint control from the Air Safety Centre at Schöneberg near Tempelhof, the only remaining area of co-operation between East and West since the death of Hess and the closure of Spandau prison. But the city split by a solid wall must still share its airspace. From the West the planes circle over East Berlin, and bank north across the Wall at Bernauer Strasse. From here, between tall blocks of flats East and West, the Wall looks like a long double row of heating pipes wandering across the city, but it is the sandy death strip and the line of watchtowers between that say that below on the approach is the cold barrier of the Berlin Wall. This is the city with a wall through it.

Split city. The two cities of Berlin, hemmed in by each other.

On either side of the city is the bear, sometimes brown, sometimes black, sometimes piebald, on flags fluttering from apartments and allotment cabins an upright black bear on a white background, the motif in statuary and reliefs, on beermats and shoulder flashes, in guidebooks, in trade and traffic logos. Shaggy, awkward, clumsy, but also funny, an animal that draws out humour, and noted for its endurance, the brown one: the bear.

For forty-five years there was not much else in common here, and for the last twenty-eight even less; what became two cities shared the same totem animal, the same dialect, the same mischievous humour, the Berliner Schnauze, the quick lip, cynical, deflating. They are still what Goethe called an 'audacious race', survivors of war and cold war, isolation and hostility, in both halves of the city. In the East they have survived forty years of the dictatorship of the leadership, 'socialism in one village'; before that, Russian occupation under the Russian bear; before that, World War II, Hitler, and then a common history with the city's Western half going back 750 years. If the East is deformed by the last half-century of its history in the service of ideologies of left and right, the West, on the other side of the city, has developed a genius for self-organization in awkward circumstances, where the Wall was always the absolute limit of jurisdiction, and then of the imagination. 'Over there' was a hostile country, and the same was said there to be true of here. In the West they shrugged, worked out a compromise, a way around difficulties, figured out how to live with impossibility. In Berlin, where the post-war conflict in Europe was keenest, and the cold the hardest, solutions were worked out, however compromised, however tenuous. Eventually agreements were worked out between states that did not even recognize each other.

Back in 1945, when the formerly Allied Occupying Powers became each others' enemies, they enlisted into their respective camps the Germans of their own sectors. What happened in Germany, divided into four by the then allied Russians, Americans, British and French, was intensified in the city of Berlin, divided into four zones. Where the original intention had been that the four powers together would administer Germany, the Russian sector became East Germany, the Russian zone of Berlin its capital. The rest became West Germany, of which Berlin is a part and not a part of the Federal Republic. The city split in 1948. What followed was the Cold War, an era of intense state paranoia on all sides, as the Soviets tried to dislodge the Western toehold in the East, and the West hung on, probing, waiting. In Berlin the conflict was fought out intimately and daily, in the early years in conditions of defeat and near-starvation through long cold winters after the war. It was fought out in currency and siege, sabotage, blackmail, intrigue, spying, betrayal; the Berlin Airlift, confrontations on the transit routes, tanks at Checkpoint Charlie, Russian ultimatums, spy swaps and the shooting of escapers form the flicker pictures of history in our time. Berlin held out. In 1961 came the Wall, and the city was closed in, the East within itself, West Berlin within the GDR. Thereafter the border froze, troops of both sides watching each other, paranoia, bullets, death.

Walled in, threatened, West Berlin became a hostage to the East. An isolated exclave 150 kilometres inside the GDR, surrounded by distance and hostility and concrete and Kalashnikovs, and by seventeen Soviet tank and motor rifle divisions, 350,000 men backed by twenty-nine non-Soviet Warsaw Pact divisions, it had a declining population through the fifties and sixties and was considered a dying city, failing to keep pace with the rest of West Germany. The Federal Republic, of which it is a *Land*, a province subject to conditions peculiar to its status as an island in the East and a city under Allied control, paid huge subsidies to keep the city alive and to encourage people to settle there. West Berlin became the showcase in the East; at the same time the GDR diverted resources to the capital at the expense of the provinces, and it too put on its best face to the West. In West Berlin there were tax concessions and travel subsidies, and for young men the attraction of exemption from military service. Berlin was always an immigrant city, and its position at the crossroads made it a target for refugees from all over the world. Students come to study at the Freie and the Technische in the West, at the Humboldt in the East. The result is a city with a strong cosmopolitan element and a vigorous counter-culture. Until now, West Berlin has invariably been a pleasant place to be, stay, live, work, walk, bike, eat out, drink, talk, dream, do business, love someone. The public transport systems of both sides are efficient and comprehensive, and heavily subsidized. East and West Berliners take the view that getting people to and from work, to and from the shops, quickly and efficiently, stimulates business and keeps the city alive. There are parks, lakes, rivers, canals, islands, forests. Both East Berlin as the capital and West Berlin as the satellite city have rich cultural lives; literature and theatre and painting and sculpture and music thrive here.

In West Berlin, because the population was declining, areas near the Wall were left derelict, or turned into parks. The city's mood was against planning. The areas around the Wall were unpopular for housing, left to the poor and to squatters. The city fell back on its old fashionable shopping centre around the Ku'damm (Kurfürstendamm) and Zentrum, and turned its back on the East. Not until the mid-eighties, with the Wall considered a permanent feature, were flats and offices built close to it, and the area came to have more life. In the East, houses near the Wall were demolished or abandoned or turned into barracks and offices for the border forces, and the result was a city dead through its middle, affording a more vigorous life in the suburbs. The Wall was ugly and obscene, though no uglier than other walls in Belfast and Cyprus and Beirut; no uglier, for that matter, than the miles of metal fencing along the southern border of the United States with Mexico, and certainly more flexible than the border kept tightly shut on both sides between the two Koreas. But the Berlin Wall stood in the spotlight, in centre stage, central Europe, at the one spot where the forces of NATO and the Warsaw Pact directly faced each other.

In the East the Wall cast a long shadow. Beyond it life was cold and grudging and dispirited, a country where in the end one third of the population informed on the rest. Closed in on itself, ultra orthodox, East Germany was a creation of the Russians, in the end left high and dry by their withdrawal from Eastern Europe. For years it resisted the inroads of *perestroika* and *glasnost*. East Berlin was a place for Westerners to visit the museums and wander, to drink a beer in the Nikolaiviertel and explore the S-Bahn and the dusty quarters of the city, and to go back home to the West, forgiving its shortcomings. It was old-fashioned; old customs survived, as I discovered when I found myself one night, with others, Easterners, hurling plates at the door of a bar in which a wedding was being celebrated. It seemed an incongruous thing to do in such a tight society that discouraged all excess or flamboyance. Eating out in East Berlin was invariably an unlovely experience, the sort to be had once and once only – the waiters unmotivated, the food uninspired, the cooking indifferent, choices few. People didn't talk much; they were afraid to, for the Stasi were always listening and foreigners, especially West German foreigners, were always dangerous. There are those East and West who say they recognize no difference between the two parts of the city, but the two sides of the Wall are in stark contrast with each other, each other's opposites, summer into winter.

The East is old-fashioned, they say. We are new-fangled, that is to say. Next door to East Berlin, West Berlin is flashy and prosperous. In the East life was consistently grim, and it won't get better for a while, if ever. A diet of *Kartoffelsuppe* and poor sausage, a small apartment at the end of a long waiting list, a fifteen-year wait for a Trabi, for ever for a telephone, not much choice, restricted travel, a life without surprise or good fortune, and for those who didn't like it, prison. The GDR became unloved and unlovable, *The Unloved Country* of Michael Simmons's portrait of it, published as the Wall came down, shabby and colourless and grey, a state frozen into the posture of itself, its infrastructure in ruins, polluted and police-infested. On the streets people dressed in pastels, without distinction; no one sought to draw attention. The condition here was an inner migration. Such public life as there was was subdued, hushed, fraught with irony. In the end the GDR became a redundant country, whose only contribution to history was the Wall.

On 9 November 1989 the Wall opened and the hungry millions of the East poured into West Berlin, where, bedazzled in the KaDeWe by the piles of cheeses and pastries and meats, the crustaceans flown in from France that morning, gaping on the Ku'damm at the neon-lit stores full of their dreams, at the Mercedes outlet, the banks, the electronics, the fruit and veg, the fast food, the music, the lights, those who went home again went still hungry for the West. Many joined the exodus, inundating the reception centres and the welfare services, and the job and housing markets. Rapidly thereafter in the East the shout was for unification with the Federal Republic, West Germany, the BRD, the FRG. And that meant the end of the GDR, the DDR, the dead-ear of the Republic of Workers and Farmers, the first socialist state on German soil. Forty years it lasted, this grim experiment, cushioning its citizens from the cold winds of the market, providing vast subsidies on housing, food, clothes, and a comprehensive social welfare net, but locked into itself, under the tight control of its security services. That's all over now.

Without Mikhail Gorbachov none of this would have happened. In Germany itself two things occurred in 1989 presaging the end of the post-war era. In the West the Bonn Government's refusal in March to accept the proposed new deployment of

NATO nuclear missiles was the sign of the beginning of renewed German assertiveness. In the East the turning point was the local elections in May, widely believed to be fraudulent, returning, yet again, the National Front under the tight control of the SED, the Socialist Unity Party, to power with yet another 98 per cent of the vote. Thereafter the exodus, thereafter the *Wende*, thereafter the opening of the Wall, a watershed, a moment before which and after which human time can be measured.

In the chancelleries when the Wall opened, old files were dusted off. Greater Germany is coming, and Berlin will be its capital. The 61 million Germans of the West are joining the 16.5 million of the East. And there are old whisperings and stirrings in the ashes of the Empire of the Austro-Hungarians; trade, custom, culture, ancient trackways of connection re-emerge across the borders, as the fortifications are dismantled and the border guards withdrawn. Populations are on the move West: East Germans to West Germany, Poles to both Germanies, Russians to Poland, Romanians to wherever they can get to. And East: East Germany is 60 per cent less densely populated than West, and not all of it is ruined. Some parts are preserved as they were, before fast food and theme parks. Former refugees are going back to reclaim abandoned property, and businessmen to do business, and West Germans attracted by the Polish Government's recent law allowing foreigners to buy land and property in Poland are out there seeking new *Lebensraum*.

Whatever the future, the city of Berlin will never be the same. What was a pleasant city to be in is now bursting under the influx, and groaning at its cost. Now the 2.1 million citizens of West Berlin and the 1.2 million of East Berlin are free to mingle, after twenty-eight years of separation, and the East has overrun the West. West Berlin has already lost its tax exemptions and its subsidies and its bonuses. Once it was a sequestered corner of Europe; now it is a thoroughfare, a transit camp, destined to be boom city. With all the East to develop, Berlin is set to become the business capital of Central Europe. For Berliners *de facto* unification began on 9 November. Before that, West Berlin had 87,000 unemployed and was short of 70,000 homes. Of the summer exodus from the East, West Berlin had already taken in 11,000 refugees, one-fifth of the total. Before the Wall opened, the city was expecting another 35,000 to the end of the year. But the news was good for some: as the Wall opened, West Berlin announced a DM 2.5 billion building programme. With the Wall down and the prospect of Berlin becoming the capital of a united Germany again, the population is expected to rise from its present 3.3 million to 5 or 6 million by the end of the century. At present there's uncertainty as to which federal institutions the Government will move from Bonn to Berlin, but big business, attracted by the city's new hinterland and the prospects for profit in the vast East, is building in the city centre, and land prices have risen dramatically in the six months since the opening.

If anyone can work it out, Berliners can. What other city has an Office for the Organization of Unusual Events?

What I saw first was a long wall around a vast prison, a prison wall. Inside the Wall, talking with Friedemann, who exclaimed of the books he could not read, the films he could not see, 'I feel as if I am in prison,' the light bulb came on over his head. I began to write a book about the city, both cities with the Wall between, based on the tales of those who lived there and were – or weren't – affected by it. As I sat to write the Wall came down, and now only the ghosts of the book I set out with survive in this one: Werner whom I met waiting for a train on Zoo station one midnight, Teo and Biba whom I ran into in a bar in the East on their first return visit after fleeing, Helga with her faint Manchester accent, Joachim on his sticks. With the Wall down, the book's purpose became less definable; my methods would still be a mixture of serendipity as to whom I met and what I found and what I chose to take note of, but the stories would be sharpened now by the headlong press of events into the unknown future. Before me lay months of uncharted history. This is the result, a record of the last months of the GDR on the swift countdown to unification with the West that began the moment the Wall opened, and the impact of East and West on each other, to the beginning of July and monetary union. Or rather, it's my record of what I saw, read, overheard, heard on the street, mistranslated, found, in my wanderings about the city through these months.

2

WRITING ON THE WALL

Hegel: The truth is concrete.

Lost keys, ask inside.

It is absolute, this Wall curving across the city, a solid ugliness, cold to the touch. It is not – as often depicted – made of bricks, but of grey prefabricated concrete slabs, almost seamlessly joined.

Mom, why is this wall here?

The property of the East German Government, most of it stands a metre back from the border line, leaving a strip for maintenance that is Eastern territory. Often this is the pavement of a walled-off street. Along the Wall the strip is a no man's land belonging to the other side, overgrown by bushes and tall weeds, where accessible a public walkway patrolled by the occupying Western military and overseen by the West Berlin police, who discourage activity there. Over the years it has become a thoroughfare, a route, a tourist way. And a long screen for writing on.

I am sinking.

Its graffiti proclaims a freedom not extended beyond itself, a defiance of the other side approved on this. On the other side the walls are blank white panels leaning off across the landscape. The joke is it's because spray paint's in short supply over there.

Warum habt ihr das gemacht?
(Why have you done this?)

In the early hours of Sunday 13 August 1961, East German police and soldiers and workmen blocked streets at the eighty crossing points along the demarcation line between the two halves of Berlin. 50,000 armed troops were deployed. Roads were blocked with improvised barriers and barbed wire, rail lines were cut, telephone lines chopped, public transport stopped at the sector border and the two parts of the city were sealed from each other. The number of crossing points was reduced to thirteen. On the 14th the Brandenburg Gate was 'temporarily' sealed off by armed police. For a few days West Berliner's were able to travel back and forth, but then the barriers became permanent.

Nous n'avons pas choisi d'être ici.
(We did not choose to be here.)

Then, on 17 August, starting at the Potsdamer Platz, workers began erecting a 6-foot concrete fence topped with barbed wire. At the Brandenburg Gate thousands of jeering Westerners watched troops rapidly complete the first barrier. Tear gas and water-hoses were used. Willy Brandt, then Mayor of West Berlin, came to look, and commented on 'the vacant eyes of uniformed compatriots doing their duty on the other side'. Similar barriers at other points eventually joined into a continuous wall: the Wall. On 21 August the Allied crossing point at Checkpoint Charlie opened. On 22 August a no man's land 100 metres wide behind the Wall was declared and the crossing points were reduced to six. Within a couple of weeks West Berlin became an island city in the socialist sea of the GDR, a Western exclave 110 miles behind the Iron Curtain. It was a hostile border, where the guards were instructed to shoot to kill, and to discourage the attentions of press photographers let off smoke bombs and flashed mirrors. When it came, the Wall confirmed the split already fifteen years old. From here on East and West Berlin were to be physically as well as politically separate. Nine days before, 60,000 border crossers – Easterners with jobs in the West – had been ordered to register with the authorities, and would now be redeployed. There were arrests; some Easterners were accused of being agents recruiting others to work across the border, and some were given long prison sentences. People could no longer travel back and forth; families were divided by the Wall. In an old black and white photograph a length of black graffiti from below Checkpoint Charlie, circa 1964, reads **13,000 women divided from their husbands. How much longer?** As the months passed into years, the isolation grew more severe; in 1962 telephone lines between the two Berlins were cut to 30.

Sesame öffnet die Mauer.
(Sesame opens the Wall.)

The barriers of 13 August formed the first makeshift Wall, swiftly followed in a few days by the second one, built of slabs and breezeblocks made from the compressed rubble of bombed Berlin. As this Wall went up, houses near by on the Eastern side were cleared, their Western-facing doors and windows bricked over. There are photographs from this time, of people looking out from as yet unbricked windows, of others leaping with a few grabbed possessions into the firemen's net below. Some missed, and died. Houses along the border were demolished to make way for the death strip and give a clear range of sight and fire. On Bernauer Strasse the houses on one side of the street stood in the East, the pavement in front of them in the West. The houses here were first bricked up, then demolished.

United we stand, divided we stand.

And then the final Wall, begun in 1963, known officially as 'the modern border'. This Wall consists of the long line of assertively upright dominoes dividing the city, snaking for 166 kilometres around the island of West Berlin, built of 1.20 m × 4.10 m high concrete slabs, 16 cm thick, tapering towards the top, each weighing 2.6 tons, jointed at the foot into a horizontal backing slab, the whole topped off by slit pipe, made of asbestos. The slabs are reinforced by steel rods. At intervals, hidden in the Wall, are small iron doors. In outlying districts the slabs are horizontal, the Wall more improvised, through the trees a grey-blue blur the path no longer goes to. In some parts it is sharp mesh fencing. But in the city it is formal, presenting its solid, smooth, inscrutable face to the wicked West, the 'Anti-Fascist Defence Wall'. Manufacturing costs per slab are 600–1,000 Ostmarks, depending on the quality of concrete, which comes in three forms: ordinary mix for sections on the outskirts, a harder version made of fine sand and gravel for the vertical panels through the city, and hardest of all, manufactured from a tight quartz sand, the bulge at the Brandenburg Gate that follows the semi-circle of the old tram-tracks. Ordinary concrete is graded B35 (B for *Beton*, concrete); this is the hardest, B50, harder than the mix used for flyovers and buttresses, made to withstand ramming from either side. The sections are jointed and firmly cemented to each other to form a near-continuous line stretching thirty miles across the city, seventy miles further around the perimeter. To oversee it there are 212 watchtowers, as last counted, 4,000 border dogs, 135 bunkers and over 5,000 mercury vapour lamps.

Marx, Engels, Lenin, Mao. Na und?
(Marx, Engels, Lenin, Mao. So what?)

Swiftly built, the Wall abruptly interrupted all relations between the two halves of the city, shared out in 1945 between the victorious Allies according to a formula adopted in the London Agreement. Thus the Russians occupied the eight Eastern *Bezirke* (boroughs) and the British and Americans the remaining twelve, later inviting the French to occupy two of them. The intention was that the Allies would together administer the whole of the city; in effect the Russians took their zone as booty, and contested the Allied presence in the West. It was along this fault line, along the border of the *Bezirke* of the former Russian Zone, that the Wall went up, and since the Russians had taken the historic central Mitte district, the Wall ran through what had once been the administrative and imperial centre of Berlin, cutting the West from its history. Some 150 streets were blocked. Streets with the same names run through the Wall: Kommandantenstrasse, Leuchnerdamm, Sebastianstrasse, Charlottenstrasse where a watchtower tops the Wall across the stopped road, Friedrichstrasse where Checkpoint Charlie straddles the street. Other streets are mere pavements; still others have distinctly different names on opposite sides, where Wilhelmstrasse becomes in the East Otto-Grotewohl-Strasse, and where Unter den Linden becomes on the Western side the Strasse des 17 Juni, formerly the Charlottenburg Chaussee.

Die in the West and you're half-way to heaven.

Beyond the Wall, a further wall curving parallel, its plain white-painted double, and between the two the death strip, of variable width but at least 100 metres wide, variously barbed and wired, with all its machinery of paranoia: *Grenztruppen* with Kalashnikovs, watchtowers, spotlights, ditches, tank traps, rifle pits, bunkers, trip wires, alarms, dogs, and until the latter years of the Wall, mines and automatic firing devices spraying bullets when upset. Sometimes the strip between is water, lake and canal and river. Here fast patrol boats lurk, and beneath the surface there are grilles and meshes, barbed to catch the underwater escaper. The sewers are grilled, and where rubbish collects the drains block at the border. It is all part of the Wall's hideous charm. In the death strip, where the sand is constantly raked and sprayed with insecticide, nothing grows but a thin grass on which the rabbits feed, immune to all the poison put down, along with magpies and grey hooded crows.

This is but one altar in the Church of Hate.

Out of town, north in the country around Frohnau, there's not a lot to see but distant watchtowers and empty fields fenced with barbed wire, the abandoned S-Bahn tracks rusting in the birches. Here the border is a tough wire mesh, beyond which more distant wire and watchtowers and tall lights. The death strip is a wide untilled space cleared of trees, its grass with a burned look, as if randomly doused in chemicals. Nature, loving vacuums, loves this space, and fills it with birds and animals and tall grasses. In the south, below Lichterfelde, the Wall was replaced in 1989 by wire mesh, called a 'modern fence', through which glimpses of dogs and guards, all of them bored beyond measure. The dogs lived permanently out by the wire, and ran on long leashes singing along overhead wires. They looked rugged and fierce, trained to bring down a running figure. At night they would bay in chorus. In the darkened watchtowers a match might flare, a guard on his two-stroke put-putt along the service road, and the nightingales sang everywhere. But for the change of birds and border guards, by day it was the same.

In Spandau in the north-east, and in the south-west, out in the vast Grunewald of trees and lakes that is Berlin's lung and without which the city would not have survived, the Wall snakes through woods and across water and along lake shores, back and forth idiosyncratically according to the logic of unnatural borders. In this case the logic depends not only on a line drawn by the Allies, but also on how votes were cast in outlying communities back in 1920, when the city reorganized itself and small villages on the periphery opted in or out of Greater Berlin. For those who chose Berlin there were higher taxes and better services. Those who opted out found themselves thirty years later in East Germany, newly fashioned from the Russian Zone.

So there are anomalies: neighbours in Nikolassee and Klein Machnow divided, in Glienicke parishioners separated from their church, and the tiny community of Steinstücken an exclave a kilometre beyond the border, supplied by American helicopters till the end of 1976, when after an exchange of territories a highway to the border was built. Bernhard-Beyer-Strasse, it runs its brief length, lined on either side by the Wall, closing in an onion shape around the small huddle of houses.

J'ai appris aujourd'hui que le bonheur existe.
(Today I learned happiness exists.)

There are other anomalies. The Duck's Bill salient in the north that walls off a length of the Oranienburger Chaussee, causing traffic to make a detour around its length. On Bernauer Strasse the parishioners in Wedding were cut off from their church – the Reconciliation – which stood in the death strip till it was blown up in 1985. In the north-west until recently were a couple of fields beyond the Wall, of which the owners had keys to special gates. At Potsdamer Platz a fenced-off triangle of trees, the Lenné Triangle, remained Eastern territory beyond the Wall. The British into whose sector it projected put up signs announcing (falsely) that unexploded ammunition from the war lay therein. On 1 July 1988 this section was swapped in a border-straightening operation for DM 76 million and an uninhabited section of old yards and sheds at the end of Bernauer Strasse, and there a new section of Wall still bears fresh slogans: **Das war eine Berliner Stadtrundfahrt** (That was a Berlin city tour [of the swap]). **Advertise here: call People's Ad Bureau and ask for Mr Honecker. Scheisst die Mauer zu. Adolf Honecker. DDR = KZ** (concentration camp). **Hier endet die Freiheit** (Freedom ends here). Behind it, soldiers whitewashed over the Western graffiti. Before it was swapped, the Lenné Triangle was occupied by sundry anarchists, squatters, hippies, punks, who camped out in the dense scrub in what till midnight of 30 June was Eastern territory. Outside it, the West Berlin police, not noted for gentleness with dissenters, eager to get their hands on those who defied them, waited. Come midnight, when the jurisdiction changed from East to West, ladders appeared and the squatters climbed the Wall and deserted to the other side, where they were breakfasted and welcomed, photographs were taken of this spectacular desertion from the West, and they were handed back in the glare of publicity to the chagrin of the Western police.

One day this will be only art.

There were seven crossing points in the Wall. There were Allied checkpoints at Alpha in the north, Bravo at Dreilinden in the south, Charlie in the middle of the city; the crossing for foot passengers, German and foreign, at Friedrichstrasse, 'the hall of tears'; three other crossing points exclusive to Berliners; at Heinrich-Heine-Strasse a point of entry and exit for trade between the two states. Elsewhere garbage trucks went regularly through to disposal sites in the south and around Potsdam. And once a week there was an exchange of the bodies of those who had died on the wrong side for burial on the other. At the Glienicke Bridge, built as the Bridge of Unity by the East and intended to unite the two halves – another failed attempt – there was a Russian crossing point, used by Allied officers and guarded by Russian sentries, across which Gary Powers, the U2 pilot, was released, and in 1986 Sharansky came in the snow. And there is the other bridge across which spies came in from the cold, at any rate in the movies, at Oberbaumbrücke in Kreuzberg. In the British sector, just up from the Brandenburg Gate, stands the Russian war memorial, to which the Red Army sentries come and go, guarding their monument, themselves guarded by West Berlin police. And until the death of Rudolf Hess in Spandau, there were Russian guards jointly responsible for his custody.

Satan loves East Berlin.

Otherwise solid Wall. It took two years, to the end of 1963, before West Berliners were able to get permission to visit relatives in the city's other half at Christmas. A door was opened in the Wall, and Berliners queued for twelve to fifteen hours for permits allowing them a few hours' visit with relatives in the East. Without relatives, Westerners couldn't go East, and it was only in November 1964 that GDR pensioners were allowed to travel West. Through the sixties, the Wall was a focus of tension and lamentation, and not until 1969 were attempts made at normalization, and four-power talks begun, together with meetings between the two German states; the result, after years of wrangling, was the Quadripartite Agreement of 1971, establishing in the Berlin Agreement of the following year transit arrangements and guaranteeing access to the city. Ulbricht, reluctant to come to any terms with the West, had by then resigned and been replaced by Honecker. Transport of goods across the GDR was simplified, the loads sealed, and a simplified process introduced for granting visas. West Berliners were not recognized but treated unofficially as citizens of West Germany. Telephone links, though limited, were restored. These agreements were the result of Willy Brandt's policy of Ostpolitik, and the slow seduction by the West of the East, with Deutschmarks.

Jump over and join the party.

Berliners, when they were able to travel to the East, were subject to strict controls, often to harassment or abrupt refusal of entry. Many West Berliners never leave the city; in the middle of a continent they have an island mentality. Germans do not move about a lot; if they make one move they stay there, in that city, in that district. They were isolated here, and turned more inward. To go anywhere else by land they crossed hostile Eastern territory, where the speed limits weren't posted and were never declared, along with the fine, paid on the spot in Deutschmarks. Unless they had to, many didn't bother. Some went for curiosity, finding the border hostile, and never went back. Others who went remarked that they found the East old-fashioned, calmer, quieter, more polite, the way the world used to be.

Marx wo bist Du?
(Where are you, Marx?)

'History,' said Hegel, 'is what nobody wanted.' Few wanted this. All this vast enterprise took planning, administration, bureaucrats, quarrying, manufacture, transport, fuel, energy, labour and materials diverted from useful projects, the organization of a border force, the full attention of the state on its frontiers, at what cost to its economy, for almost thirty years. Its building was personally planned and supervised by Erich Honecker, and it is with Honecker that the Wall is most closely associated. It was his baby. In 1989, only months before his and

the Wall's fall, Honecker proclaimed that the Wall would still
be standing in fifty and a hundred years. In East Berlin they
nodded into their beards: '*Ja*. The Wall might still be here. But
Honecker won't.' When he went, it went.

Lenin: Socialism without a post office is meaningless.

They came, they saw, they did a little shopping.

25 Jahre nun ist genug.
(25 years is enough.)

In the death strip immediately over the Wall, desolation defined
as empty space. At Potsdamer Platz, across what was once the
busiest city intersection in Europe, a Times Square or a Piccadilly
Circus, only the grass and the rabbits and the border guards.
They're trained to keep an eye on each other, one to
shoot the other if he makes a run for it. Here perhaps is the
most familiar imagery of the Wall: the wide emptiness of raked
sandy earth, the distant buildings and the low jumbled cityscape
of East Berlin, the malignant eye of the TV tower at Alexanderplatz winking over all, and to one side in the death strip the
mound that is all that remains of Hitler's bunker, the Wall
curving away left to the Reichstag and the Brandenburg Gate,
right to Checkpoint Charlie.

In England Walls make ice cream.

Does Gromyko live in a fridge?

In Berlin the Cold War was fought with currency, with border
controls and harassment, with winter and hunger, with passports and visas and paranoia, and finally with a concrete wall.
Wrestling West Berlin away from Allied control was for Stalin a
priority that survived his death in 1953. By then his satellite, the
GDR, was firmly set on the long march to socialism, and
locked into paranoid enmity with the West. In Berlin that had
meant in the first place a long struggle for control, of the city as
a whole, of its departments and divisions, *Bezirke*, town halls,
transport, police, money. The city became a broiler-house of
intrigue and spying.

Cut off from its hinterland and 150 kilometres from the West
German border, Berlin ought to have been easy pickings, but

having failed to besiege and starve it, having failed to blackmail or intimidate or trick it into submission, in the end the East put up a fence. Ostensibly to defend the GDR against invasion and interference from the fascist West, against 'revanchists, militarists and imperialists', the Wall's purpose was to stop the flow of population East to West that was draining the Eastern workforce and flooding the West with refugees.

Love is thicker than concrete.

After the Wall was built, each city went its own way. With the S-Bahns cut off at the ends, the S-Bahn ring system was no more. Eash system operated independently, though both were still run till the early eighties by the East. In 1945 the West had taken the U-Bahn, the East the S-Bahn. This arrangement continued, but fifteen U-Bahn stations in the East were sealed, ghostly empty stations through which the Western trains ran without stopping. Traffic developed other patterns as each side learned to live without the other. Each city developed separately around its separate centre, the East with its old Mitte district at the border, the West backing up into the Ku'damm and the flashy neon metropolis from the Zoo down to the stump of the Gedächtnis-kirche. Institutions and organizations, already in separate jurisdictions, split completely. The National Library's collections were divided in separate buildings on opposite sides of the Wall; in the West in Dahlem was the Berlin Museum's Egyptian collection, in the Pergamon in the East the ancient Middle East. Up from the Potsdamer Platz the West built the Philharmonie and the National Library, in an area projected as the new centre of Berlin after the realization of the distant dream of unification. Effectively, they blocked road access from the West to the old heart of Berlin. With the population pulled back from the border in the East, and the border area in the West neglected and unpopular, a zone of desolation settled into the city.

Take a walk on the wild side.

In a few years most Berliners had grown used to the Wall, though few accepted it, and went their ways about their separate cities, interfering little with each other. Most Berliners affected to ignore it. For West Berliners the Wall became a bore, a cliché. The Wall and the enclosure of the city became normality.

For Easterners it was barely visible, yet ever present. It was the fact of the Wall that angered people on both sides – in the East because it prevented movement to the West, in the West because it represented the frontier of a difficult and forbidden zone, felt to be still part of Germany. In the West, on the viewing platforms, tourists came to stare, politicians to pontificate, and Germans to look wistfully over into the lost country, staring at the tram-tracks cut by the Wall. On either side there was an inflexible border, and just over there the other city, within calling distance, out of reach.

Fight against bad spirits.

The Wall's jagged lines and kinks express legalistic nicety. There is something very German in all this, in the carrying out of orders, to the letter, however absurd. As a symbol, the Wall's history was at the centre of the bitter conflict between East and West, the confrontation point, the key piece in the lunatic's jigsaw. It was the site of political speeches and free world posturing, the ready propaganda symbol always to hand. Here Kennedy came in 1963 to proclaim himself a Berliner (a doughnut), Reagan in 1987 to say 'Mr Gorbachov, tear down this Wall,' and every other Western leader to have their pictures taken staring over the rim of Marxist totalitarianism. On the other side Khrushchev came to look, conceding that the Wall was an eyesore.

Working-class heroes.

Going through to the GDR, the traveller enters a thin narrow corridor, a mirror running its length showing the backs of travellers' heads. Maybe it's to make sure no one sneaks in behind. The border guard in his booth, in dim light, behind the thick glass screen, beneath which is a slit for the passport and the visa fee, DM 5. To his right a heavy navy-blue curtain. Three or four assorted small wooden file boxes for papers, looking distinctly home-made, containing various forms. A small plastic fan, not working. A video camera, its eye fixed on the glass. Behind him on a peg his cap, a blue linen bag containing his lunch. At his elbow a telephone with a call button but without a dial, a raised blank plastic disc, the same fawn colour as the instrument. He works beneath the angle of the traveller's vision, behind the darkened glass on a surface cut off from view, where he keeps his stamps and his reference books. What he does, what he's trained to do in military school, by numbers, over and over again till he gets it right, is stare at each part of the face separately. That is, he begins with the whole face, and at the end he returns to it, but on the way he looks slowly and for a long time at each separate part of the face, comparing it with the passport picture in front of him, comparing right cheek with right cheek, left with left, chin, ears, eyes, mouth with photographed mouth, quartering and dividing the face into so many fragments of itself. His own face gives nothing away, as impassive as a stone. He stares into the eyes, protected by the glass screen of his booth, by his uniform, the authority of the military and the bureaucracy of the state, the maze of information on the GDR's files, the fact that he can simply say no, and refuse entry. He takes his time, flicking through the pages, stamping the Tagesvisum, taking the visa fee, presses the buzzer that releases the door to the other side. A last glimpse: to his left his newspaper, folded over to the sports page, to a picture of a footballer kicking a ball.

Then more guards, and money to be changed, DM 25 for 25 Ostmark. Have you brought anything they can object to – a book or a newspaper that might be designated fascist literature, cassette tapes, an address book with contacts in the GDR, anything that connects you with Amnesty International or other human rights organizations, a camera? Here there's not much to photograph, except, with a deepening sense of irony, the statues of heroes and the monuments to the fallen. You're not allowed to photograph border facilities, military installations, or bridges; you're not allowed to take pictures of public buildings, and since in a socialist society most buildings are public, there's not a lot to snap. Up the road Marx and Engels, in massive bronze, face away from the Volkskammer, showing it their backs, as if it all had nothing whatsoever to do with them.

The queue stretches out through the doors at the foot of the Fernsehturm, the TV tower. Up there, all the city to see on a clear day, the East and West of it, trains, wide roads, the Dom, Volkskammer, flat humpy skyline, the country beyond. There is a guide to point out the sights. She will discourage you from looking West, and say there's nothing to see in that direction. Running through the middle of the city the Wall and a line of tall cranes along it on both sides. What you can't see from the TV tower is the TV tower itself, a dark glass and metal ball on a spike jammed into the sky, among communication pods at the top two stabs of light warning off aeroplanes. As a landmark it is useless since it presents the same shape from whichever angle, with the same two stabs of light on every side second by second, like a pulse, like a malignant eye. It can be seen from all over East and West, designed to be the focus of streets, to appear above the Wall like its dark genius, a Darth Vader, the watching eye of Big Brother. About the city it rolls across the tops of buildings, emerges from the sides of streets. Called in the East 'Ulbricht's Cathedral', what an atheist would build instead of a sepulchre, in the West it's known as 'the Pope's revenge', because on a sunny day the light on the glass panels of the great ball forms a perfect cross. The East has tried every means to get rid of the cross, to baffle its effect, to no avail. Every time the sun comes out, the cross comes out above Alexanderplatz.

At Friedrichstrasse on the other side, the door into the GDR is sheet aluminium, much bumped and dented with use. As it opens towards them the people waiting on the other side stiffen in anticipation, some in greeting. Above the door, black on white: EINGANG. Border guards stand either side of it. There is nothing particularly remarkable, save that this is *die Grenze*, the border, a frontier crossing from one world to another, across which, the stiff formalities over, travellers self-consciously step. It is where one system jars against another, the old trigger for all the weaponry in the universe, and here it is always zero hour. Many wish to cross here, for many reasons, and there are some the GDR wishes to keep out, and most of its own citizens it wishes to keep in. Many would go West if they could. So it is tense here, as befits the occasion and location. Here the guards patrol in threes. The joke is: 'That's one to read the regulations, one to witness them read, a third to keep an eye on these two dangerous intellectuals.'

Something there is that doesn't love a wall.

The Wall has been for years the screen for paint, a ready surface for slogans and figures and wit. In the early years this was paintbrush work, often done at night. There were some arrests by Eastern border guards for defacing People's property.

By the mid-eighties, with the arrival of the spray-can, the paintwork had become a permanently changing exhibition proclaiming the slogans of every struggle in Europe in primary colours: faces, figures, eyes, question marks, doors. **Can the people live on air alone? No, Mr Ceauşescu. No.** In Kreuzberg two corner slabs are elaborately painted with a picture of a fat cow, black and white, the pattern of whose hide is the divided map of Germany, with fat teats and holding a staff crowned by the Prussian Cross. Another depicts a man escaping by unzipping the Wall: *Poff*, and our hero is free.

Tear down the Wall and all the others fall.

For a wall is a wall, and invites a slogan. Some of its graffiti is passionate and witty. The bulk of it isn't. Much of it is in English, though it is largely multilingual, the work of non-Berliners. In Kreuzberg it's more native, more local. Much of it is American: **Katy Miller, your name is on the Berlin Wall; Hi Mom and Dad; Hunter from Slippery Rock Pa; Happy Birthday Lyndon La Rouche.** Much of it is run of the mill, and mostly says everywhere **I was here, Flash and his missus visit the Wall, Jo and Mo got pissed here 24/5/87.** And Kilroy's still around. Many declare their undying love, and a young lady called Sabine has inspired several heart-shaped devotions and declarations. Here it says **500 miles from Brixton**; someone asks **Wo ist Köln** (Where's Cologne?) and **Wer ist Kohl?** (Who is Kohl?). Many are content to be initials, to state their tribal affiliations and teams and beliefs, words fading under more words in a continuing commentary on the world and the Wall, overlapping, added to, obliterating each other. Most are crudely assertive, as in **Smack Dike Wizz Coke LSD Opium Pot Mushrooms and Beer is All I fucking need**; a bullseye labelled **Piss here**, another announcing **Sozialistische Peepshow, 10 Kopeken.** Some is sufficient to render the Wall almost invisible. Along what was once Prinz-Albrecht-Strasse, along where the Gestapo cellars and piles of rubble are all that remain of their trades, the Wall has been painted with trees that for a moment look real, and dissolve it. Further down Zimmerstrasse towards Checkpoint Charlie there's a section covered in broken mirror pieces that wavily reflect the Western side of the street, in which the Wall disappears completely.

Strangers in the Reich.

Durch Deutschland mit Trabant.
(Through Germany with Trabant.)

The parts of the Wall that attract the graffiti writers are central and accessible; from where the border crosses the Spree by the Reichstag, on past the Brandenburg Gate to Potsdamer Platz following the curves and corners of the Wall to Checkpoint Charlie, round the Springer building and back to the Wall at Kommandantenstrasse and beyond into Kreuzberg, **Ich liebe dich, Sabine** (I love you Sabine); **Kohl auf den Acker** (Kohl (cabbage) to the field). **Communists**, it says along Zimmerstrasse, **are only part time workers. IM + Erich Honecker. IM George Orwell. Is there anybody out there? There's a feeling I get when I look to the West, and my spirit is crying for leaving.** At Potsdamer Platz in red and black the crossed hammers of Pink Floyd's 'The Wall': **Der Kampf gegen die Mauer geht weiter** (The struggle against the Wall goes on); elsewhere **A rush and a push and the land is ours,** and this crossed out **We will march on you again, Russia.** In other sections, up around Bernauer Strasse and Chausseestrasse, a more laid-back wit: **Chris, Greg, Mike, Cal, Steve and the rest were filled with inertia. But not Simon. Oh no, not Simon.** Question marks, hallucinogenic frenzy – **Tiny purple fishes run laughing through your fingers; Daddy bought me orbiting earrings;** and simple well-meant advice: **Honi, mellow out.** By the Brandenburg Gate the graffiti is strident and dark: the Captive Nations of Lithuania, Estonia, and Latvia demand liberty. Korea demands unification. And Shelley, speaking for the world's unacknowledged legislators, the message fading out beneath the press of other urgent messages:

> **My name is Ozymandias, King of Kings.**
> **Look on my Works ye Mighty and Dismay.**

3

THE FLIGHT

The history of the GDR is the history of flight across its borders, legally or illegally. For those divided, flight became a means of reconciliation; for those who fell foul of the regime the West became the only alternative; for many who just wanted better it represented the height of their aspirations, a dream, and for some who made it, an illusion. Across the frontier the West always beckoned with the bright lights of its forbidden supermarkets. From its inception in 1949 the GDR was continually drained of its labour force by the bleeding out of its citizens, many of them skilled, many young, most of them – by definition – ambitious, inspired with a desire to get out, and the courage and initiative to do so. This bleeding out was eventually to slow the GDR down, and the demand for emigration to help bring down the Government, and the system with it. It was a state run on theories, but the original theory made no provision for the continuing drainage of its youngest and most skilled workers. In any case the regime came to use emigration as a safety valve, regulating the flow. It was content to let out pensioners and the sick to the West's welfare and medical services. It also earned Deutschmarks, and looked good to the UN – which it joined in 1973 – and to human rights organizations. Eventually, by exiling its dissidents, the regime thought to eliminate criticism. Between 1963 and 1989 some 33,000 Eastern political prisoners were brought out by the West for from DM 50,000 to DM 100,000 each, depending on their skills; at Christmas 1964 some were swapped for oranges. It was, by all measures, a cynical and silly regime, ruling by theory and fear.

Since 1949, 3 million people have moved from East to West, about a fifth of the GDR's population. Up to 1949, when anyone on either side started counting, they were moving at the rate of 2,000 a week, and through the fifties they fluctuated up and down around 4,000 a week. After the 1953 Uprising the figures rose to 6,000, and in the following year 331,000 quit. In the year after the suppression of the Hungarians in 1956, 275,000 people left. To their government they were all fugitives, traitors, and if caught they were awarded up to five years in prison. To the West, when they arrived, they were German citizens, escapees first, then refugees, then immigrants and settlers, regarded over the years with increasing resentment, but absorbed into the Federal Republic. Ideologically committed to the idea of all Germans being citizens of West Germany, the West could not refuse.

Through the summer of 1961 the numbers fleeing rose dramatically, in July to 8,000 a week. In August, until the closure of the Wall on the 13th, the figures jumped to 10,000 and then to 15,000 each week. Refugee camps were overflowing and the West was swamped; the East was in a panic and rapidly being drained of its citizens. Ulbricht's answer was the Wall, which stemmed the flow. With the Wall up in 1961, and all the borders of the GDR wired shut, the exodus diminished. Through 1962, with the frontiers more and more impermeable, some 14,000 still got out, and 54,000 emigrated legally. Thereafter the numbers fell as the GDR sealed itself in; 3,500 escaped in the next year, and as the border wire and fortifications proliferated, escapers dwindled through the sixties and seventies and eighties to a low of 160 for the whole of 1985. Still a steady stream of people left: sailors jumped ship, actors defected while in the West, people let out for a visit didn't come back, some took the hard way through Hungary and other Eastern states; some succeeded. In the eighties the numbers of those let out legally increased, as the GDR sought to relieve itself of internal pressures. Meanwhile those escaping illegally gradually rose until 1988. Inside the GDR the steam was slowly building, and it showed up at the borders.

A steady stream of escapes across the border, some successful, some ending in death or injury or imprisonment, took place throughout the Wall's history. During the first year after it was built, fifty people died attempting to flee, including border guards. Some 200 victims have been registered on the borders of East with West Germany, including, most dramatically, Berlin. Here, in the twenty-eight years of the Wall, there were seventy-nine victims, mostly in the 1960s, at least eight of these border guards. Many people were injured, and others went to prison for attempting flight, or for assisting escapees. Some 3,000 were arrested for attempting to cross the Berlin Wall. Many Westerners became involved in this activity, assisting Easterners to flee. The most reputable of these, Wolf Quesner, was never caught, but others went to prison for long periods. Some organizations were bogus, and fleeced would-be fleers; some were betrayed, tricked, agent-provacateured by the Stasi, or framed.

A few days after the first barriers went up, Conrad Schumann, a soldier in the Volksarmee, made a run for it, throwing away his weapon and leaping over the barbed wire. He was the first of many officers and men to flee over the next three decades. A year later, on 23 August 1962, Dieter Wesa, a deserting soldier, was shot dead by his comrades beneath a bridge bearing the sign GDR – THE BASTION OF PEACE IN GERMANY. Eleven days after the Wall, Gunter Litfin swam the river, just below the S-Bahn bridge at Lehrter Bahnhof, where the ship canal joins the Spree. Close to the Charité hospital in the East, it was a favoured point for attempting to cross, and consequently over the years the Charité became more and more barred and barricaded and Stasi-infested. On the Western side of the river there are discreetly placed metal ladders leading out of the water at intervals along the banks. Many died on this stretch, the first of them Gunter Litfin, who made it to the West riddled with bullets. He was twenty-four. Between the street and the riverside there is a memorial to him, the first victim of the Wall.

On 17 August 1962 Peter Fechter, a building labourer aged eighteen, attempted to cross the Wall just below Checkpoint Charlie. Shot down, he lay bleeding and crying for help for fifty minutes, without medical attention. The guards who had shot him remained in hiding. The West Berlin police attempted to throw first aid packs to him, but he died to cries of 'Murderers' from the West. On Christmas Day 1963 Paul Schultz, also eighteen, died in the spotlights in a hail of bullets.

All along the Wall are wooden crosses, with names and dates commemorating, when known, those who tried to escape and failed. They are strung out along Bernauer Strasse, with a row of them at the street's end and another row by the Reichstag at the riverside: Marienetta Jiskowski, aged eighteen, three months pregnant when she tried to cross, shot dead by eight bullets;

Heinz Scholowski, who had already served seven years as a political prisoner, *Auf der Flucht erschossen* (the German is as ever precise), shot dead 25/11/65; *Unbekannt* 22/11/86; *Unbekannt*. Others died elsewhere, in tunnels and sewers, gassed or grenaded. Some drowned. One party of escapers was deliberately trapped and the sewer through which they were escaping was flooded. The most recent of the memorial crosses by the Reichstag is for 6 February 1989: Chris Geoffroy, aged twenty, shot while escaping. In March another escaper crashed to death in a hot-air balloon in West Berlin. All those killed trying to cross the Wall are considered cases of murder by the West German authorities.

During the first year of the Wall there were fourteen breakouts with heavy vehicles, using trucks and, on one occasion (unsuccessful) a bus; full of passengers, it was sprayed with bullets and many were injured. In December 1961 a train driver hijacked a train with twenty-four of his friends and relations and drove them through the border. In January 1962 fourteen Easterners hijacked a passenger ferry across the Spree and escaped unhurt.

As time passed, and as the Wall grew stronger and the checkpoints were surrounded by more concrete and steel and wire, attempts to punch a hole were less successful, and more imaginative methods were employed. In the Haus am Checkpoint Charlie Museum many of the devices used are on display. In 1963 escapees came over four at a time inside a large cable drum; several trips were made before this method was rumbled. Others came out in disguise, or hidden in vehicles, in the boot or the engine compartment, in suitcases, in balloons, in light aircraft. Some came over hidden in the innards of a tiny three-wheel Isetta, others in a car (used twice) too low for the checkpoint boom. Thereafter iron guards were hung from the booms. One man made himself up as a Ghanaian visitor, with papers and passports for his wife and children, and walked with them through Checkpoint Charlie. Another went to great lengths to organize a fake drama group for which military uniforms were required with, for authenticity, he argued, the buttons of a US Army officer. He got his buttons and got out. Others in home-made uniforms went disguised as Russian officers, returning the salutes of the border guards.

Tunnels were dug under the Wall, the first in January 1962 when twenty-eight people escaped. On 29 June 1962 Siegfried

Nöffke began digging a tunnel to get his wife and child out, but a part of the tunnel sank, causing the Volksarmee to investigate. They dug down. Emerging from the tunnel, Nöffke was shot dead, and his two assistants given life imprisonment. In 1964 a 145-metre tunnel was dug beneath Bernauer Strasse at a depth of 12 metres, a mere 70 cm high to beat the problem of disposing of the soil. Thirty-seven West Berliners participated in its construction. After six months' work, fifty-seven people succeeded in escaping. In 1965, with his wife and child, a man went to the House of Ministers just by the Wall and hid in a toilet. At nightfall he climbed on the roof and threw a hammer with a line over the Wall, wound up a wire rope and attached a home-made hoist and pulley rig, on which all three escaped. Another man pulled a gun on a Polish airliner travelling from Gdansk to East Berlin and forced the pilot to fly to the American sector; eleven of the sixty-three passengers decided to join him. Two East Berliners used a bow and arrow to get a line across. They hid in a house close to the Wall opposite a house in the West, waited fifteen hours for the watchtower guards to look away, and shot a fishing line across to an accomplice on the opposite roof. They tied a steel cable to the line, and with that secured slid one after the other over the Wall on pulleys. A man shot his way out on the border in Kreuzberg, killing two border guards, for which the East demanded his return for murder. The West refused. In September 1986 a young East Berlin couple crashed a truck through Checkpoint Charlie. And in late 1988 a man swam the Spree at the Reichstag and made it to the Western bank, but he was grabbed by the border guards in their speedboat. There followed an argument, in which it was conceded that the man had had his hand on the Western bank of the river, and he was let go. Another, briefly imprisoned, was swapped for an imprisoned spy. In early 1989 two microlite planes were found early one morning by the Reichstag. They had been smuggled to West Berlin in pieces and assembled, flown over to pick up one man's brother and flown back, and dumped.

By 1985 over 60,000 people had been imprisoned for attempting to flee the Republic or for preparing to do so. Even thinking about it was punishable, and escapes inolving more than one person – a man and wife for instance, parents and children – amounted to conspiracy. The average sentence for attempted flight was sixteen months, for assisting others four years. In some cases of organized assistance, sentences of penal servitude for life were imposed.

Through the seventies and eighties, under Honecker's only slightly more lenient rule, the numbers allowed out legally rose. This stimulated more to apply for exit visas, most of which were refused, thus marking the applicant as a dissident. Successful applicants waited a long time, and the paperwork was deliberately complex. Each emigrant had to go from office to office removing his or her name from all lists and official registers. The determination to leave only grew. In January 1984 six people applied for asylum at the US Embassy in East Berlin, and a dozen people fled to the West German mission in East Berlin. All were allowed out.

Most refugees were under thirty-five. Many were under twenty-five, skilled and ambitious. In 1988, 22 per cent of all registered emigrants from East to West were under twenty, and only 12.5 per cent over sixty. In 1989, when Easterners began leaving in droves in the months before the Wall's opening, most of them were young families who fled via Czechoslovakia and Hungary. Many came from the south of the country. Their flight led to labour shortages: of doctors and nurses in hospitals, where departments closed down; of vets; in craft industries – woodworkers, plumbers, roofers, carpenters, joiners, tailors, machine builders. Building sites, heavy engineering plants, and car manufacturers were short-handed; public transport suffered. Distribution and supply were disrupted. The effects were similar to the exodus in 1961 that had led to the Wall being built in the first place; it was as if the exodus had merely been suspended for twenty-eight years. The effects were felt hardest in small towns and villages. The army was called in to maintain transport services, food deliveries, and hospitals. In October 1989 came reports of the GDR seeking to hire 80,000 Chinese to fill vacancies left by the emigrants to the West – this in addition to the 100,000 Asian and African workers already in the GDR. By contrast there came a report of a group of 264 unemployed Neapolitans asking to emigrate to the GDR with their families; they believed the GDR could provide them with jobs, a modest but secure home, a decent health service and an absence of crime. By the end of December Christa Luft, GDR Economics

Minister, announced that there were 150,000 unfilled jobs in the East. In 1989 the GDR lost 240,000 working people.

At the end of their journeys, refugees were described as arriving exhausted, glad to have made it, many overjoyed and not yet worried about their future. They received DM 50 on entry and DM 200 welcome money; they were entitled to full unemployment benefit, child benefit, welfare, rent rebates, tax benefits, financial aid to self-employment, sick pay and pension benefits. In addition many were granted aid by the *Länder*, and loans for setting up house and for education. All this had already become a source of grumbling in the Federal hive, where there was growing resentment at settlers from all sources, including East Germans, and at the pressures they were exerting on resources. In September, Bonn withdrew their right to unemployment pay in the West, and awarded them instead DM 1,000 per month for a year. Many were said to be gullible, falling for special offers that turned out to be low-paid jobs. The rate of departure from reception centres was slow; up to September, 25,000 Eastern refugees were out of work. Easterners accounted for about 20 per cent of the homeless. Many encountered problems getting their Eastern qualifications recognized. By contrast, rent in the GDR might cost only a tenth of earnings, food was cheap, and there was an all-encompassing health and welfare net beneath everyone. The GDR's health and welfare and social systems were not to be sniffed at, but – sniffing – the citizens went on leaving.

In 1989, *perestroika* at last penetrated the GDR; protesters shouted 'Gorbi', and wore his badge. The economy was stagnating, years and years of shortages and bottlenecks and dreariness were stacked up, and in any case the borders of the GDR's Eastern neighbours were opening as their own regimes faltered. The knock-on effect of this was to bring down the government of the GDR. Wherever an escape route opened, Easterners set out for it. In the first six months of 1989, 44,000 East Germans went West, legally or illegally. In the first seven months, 47,000 exit permits were issued. A million and a half people under retirement age were to be allowed West to visit relatives. The more the regime gave way to the demand the more the demand rose. Before the Wall's fall some 90,000 were expected to emigrate legally in 1989. In August there were estimates that up to 0.75 million people had applied to leave and that 1 million would leave immediately if they could. Over the summer, from May to September, an estimated 6,000 had crossed the border; the figures were unclear, and were at first held back by Bonn to discourage a suction effect. As more borders opened up, and more Easterners fled through them, the graph of those fleeing rose alarmingly as summer turned to autumn. In the falling dominoes of Hungary and Czechoslovakia the press of refugees at last forced open the borders.

The crucial event came on 2 May, when Hungary opened a section of its frontier with Austria. Thereafter, and increasingly through the summer, East Germans headed for Hungary, Austria, West Germany. Soon the trickle became a flood, as thousands of Easterners began to turn up in and around Budapest. The Hungarians, sympathetic to the refugees, were flooded out. But though at first they stopped border-jumpers and in the first half of 1989 sent back some 550 with a special stamp in their passports for the attention of the Stasi, who had prisons awaiting them, soon they began to turn a blind eye. The system of containment worked only so long as all the other states on the GDR's Eastern borders consented to it; once socialism, in its Stalinist variants in Eastern Europe, began to waver, the borders began to open. Many East Germans weren't about to wait and see. As their numbers increased, the Hungarians were outpaced; some they caught they turned loose, to try again. On 9 August they stopped stamping the passports of East Germans caught fleeing. Success led to more flight, encouraged by the media. Back in the GDR there was no public reaction and no comment in the media. The feeling grew that the regime was incapable of change, that nothing could change in the country. Soon the camps in Hungary were overflowing.

On 7 August 1989, Bonn closed its East Berlin mission after 130 East Germans had taken refuge there. Later, occupations forced embassies to close in Budapest, Prague and Warsaw. By mid-August, East Germans in Hungary were filling refugee camps and camping out in their Trabis, sleeping on air mattresses and on the pavements. There were 200 of them in the Budapest embassy. Food and blankets were provided by the West German consulate and the Red Cross. There were reports of some 4,000 non-returnees around Budapest. Others leaked out elsewhere. By early August there were refugees in West German embassies and missions in East Berlin, Prague and Budapest, and soon in

Warsaw. Then, on 20 August, in the guise of holding a picnic at the Austrian–Hungarian border, some 300–500 fled across it. Pamphlets publicizing the event had been distributed in Hungary, and there were many West German cars on the other side to pick them up. There were reports of West German agents paid by the skull in Prague and Budapest, actively encouraging Easterners to quit. On East German television, Western reporters were accused of being front-line war correspondents, and West German television of directing the flow to Hungary.

Then on 24 August came the first crack in the East German mask. 108 East Germans from the Budapest embassy arrived in the West, allowed out as 'an exceptional humanitarian measure that in no way constituted a precedent'. On 1 September the West German and Austrian governments announced that 20,000 East Germans would be accepted.

By 10 September some 110,000 had arrived in West Germany since January, By now the Hungarians had bowed to pressure; the West Germans were whispering of more and greater investment in their economy, and they preferred to recognize the Helsinki Final Act of 1975, expressing the right of citizens to leave their country. They opened their borders to the outflow: 12,000 left immediately, 23,000 during the rest of September. The East German Government complained bitterly at the Hungarian reversal of its treaty obligation to hand over fugitives. East Germany banned all travel to Hungary, so now they left via Czechoslovakia and Poland. In early September the embassy in Warsaw was occupied, and by the last week of the month the Prague embassy was besieged by East Germans, with hundreds climbing over the back fence into the embassy grounds. On 16 September East Germany and Poland agreed to let refugees camped out in the Warsaw embassy leave Poland. Poland and Hungary were now both open doors, provided Easterners could get across the border unseen or obtain a visa.

At the end of September came another climbdown: East Germany – again 'as a unique humanitarian gesture' – agreed to let 4,000 leave the West German embassy in Prague, providing five special trains and passage through the GDR. Others left Warsaw by the same method. Because there were more camped out who turned up for the trains without going through the West German embassies, some 15,000 left by this route. They were to be expelled from the GDR, so that they couldn't, if they ever wanted to, return. They were spoken of by the Government as 'irresponsible, anti-social, traitors and criminals'. The GDR imposed visas for visits or transits to Czechoslovakia, the only country to which East Germans had formerly been allowed to go without exit visas. But every time they agreed to let the fugitives leave, more demanded to go. By the beginning of October there were another 3,000 in the West German embassy in Prague. East Germany, furious, accused the West of breach of trust, claiming Bonn had promised to stop the flow after the East had agreed to the earlier Prague exodus. Meanwhile there were new arrivals in the embassy in Warsaw. In the first week of October 7,000 arrived in the West. On 3 October East Germany climbed down again, and agreed to a second wave of refugees leaving the Prague embassy in special trains. Like all the GDR's stopgap gestures, it backfired. The sealed trains carrying refugees which passed through the GDR at the beginning of October were besieged in Halle and Dresden by Easterners wanting to get on them. In Dresden there was a three-hour riot involving 10,000 people, with police sealing off the station and the tracks; many were arrested, and the demonstration that had begun as a demand for travel ended in demands for a change of government. All the time, massive demonstrations were building up in East German cities in response to the demand for change, set off by the growing exodus. Whatever the regime did, and it did little, blew up in its face.

Perhaps it was public relations considerations that prompted the East German Government, as it ran up to its fortieth anniversary faced with news footage of thousands of its citizens camped out in embassy grounds, to give way and let its people go, but soon the East was ceasing to function as a viable economy, as the panic spread. Throughout the summer, as more and more people left, East Germans had become more anxious and insecure. Many were described as sitting on their suitcases, afraid of being left behind, of the door closing again. Among those who stayed were many who chose to do so, but among them too there was growing insecurity as colleagues, neighbours, friends, family, lovers, took to the road and disappeared. Couples parted. There were reports, later denied, of parents abandoning their children.

As the GDR approached the celebrations on 7 October of the four decades of its existence, its citizens were streaming out through all its borders, camping out, preferring the uncertain future of refugee camps in the West to life in the GDR. By the end of September, 31,000 had left via Hungary, and by 7 October – the anniversary – 40,000. Meanwhile the leadership was preoccupied with congratulating itself. For now they seemed confident enough. Honecker appeared before a huge crowd in East Berlin to boast of the regime's achievements, with the usual bands and bunting and marches and speeches. The GDR presented itself as a stable society with a dynamic economy, with growth and improvement in all areas. Honecker blamed all protest on international reactionary forces aimed at confusing the people and sowing the seeds of doubt in socialism. He said: 'We will solve our problems ourselves, with socialist means. Proposals intended to weaken socialism will not blossom here.' The occasion turned into a humiliation. Gorbachov warned: 'He who does not change will be cast aside. If states do not react to the impulses of the time they are in danger.' He advised the leadership to discuss political and economic reform with all groups in society. As Gorbachov flew out of Schönefeld that afternoon the crowds erupted in fury on to the streets all over East Germany, especially in Berlin and Leipzig. In Berlin the demonstrations centred on the Gethsemane Church in Prenzlauer Berg, a focus for protest, and were put down with great brutality by the police and the Stasi. The country trembled on the edge of bloodshed, and for a while there was talk of a China Solution. Then the leadership faltered, confused, old, tired, gave up, turned on each other, and in ten days fell.

The migration continued unabated, the Government's collapse notwithstanding. More panic, more voting with the feet. As the Honecker Government collapsed, there was a sudden rise in the refugee rate, and nearly 4,000 left through Hungary in one day. At the same time the numbers in the Warsaw embassy rose to 1,400. It was a mass response to the vague promises of change from the leadership. Two days after Krenz's succession, 1,000 East Germans gave him a ringing vote of no confidence by crossing the Hungarian border into Austria. On 22 October the West German border police reported that 1,300 East Germans had entered West Germany via Austria in the previous twenty-four hours. By 2 November there were again thousands of East Germans in the West German embassy in Prague, and by the next day East Germany had agreed to let go 45,000 refugees camped out in the Prague embassy. As they left, more arrived. Then, on 4 November, a month after their introduction, restrictions on travel to Czechoslovakia were rescinded, and immediately 8,000 sought sanctuary in the Prague embassy. They were allowed to leave without renouncing their citizenship. Through the first week of November until the opening of the Wall, they poured out at the rate of 9,000 per day, 375 per hour. On 9 November the West opened fifty-nine new refugee camps and the Government announced a DM 8 billion building programme. The West began to wonder how much longer and how many more it could absorb. There was anxiety in Bonn over the continuing exodus, and growing resentment at the demands of the refugees. At this time estimates of how many might move to the West in the near future ranged between 1.2 and 1.4 million.

Then, on 9 November, the Wall opened. Up to that point, in 1989 alone some 1.3 million East Germans had already applied to emigrate legally to the West. One way or another 200,000 had already left for the West. The migrations through Hungary and Czechoslovakia dried up as the Easterners poured out through the newly-opened German borders.

4

THE FREEDOM OF THOSE WHO
THINK DIFFERENTLY

The opening of the Wall on 9 November surprised Berliners on both sides. So much hope had been invested and so much pressure built up, without any sign of an end to the historical impasse. Pundits were sure the East Berlin regime was secure, and that while the dominoes might fall in Poland and Hungary, and while the leadership must surely change, if only by dying off, for the time being it seemed confident enough to carry on without *glasnost* as the caretaker of a Stalinist museum. After years of institutionalized repression and persistent opposition, the end came rapidly. The Government resigned, the Politburo and the Party structure disintegrated, and within three weeks the Wall opened. Only *Bild*, with good contacts in the East, predicted the Wall's opening.

If the history of the GDR is the history of flight, it is also the history of struggle and opposition. The GDR, set up on the Soviet model of command socialism, centrally directed, Stalinist style, despite Stalin's remarks to the contrary, created opposition to itself from the beginning. In 1945, as the gunfire died and the Russians drove into ruined Berlin, ten German Communist exiles returned from Moscow, where they had spent the war in preparation for the setting up of a German Marxist government. There were others, including Germans fighting with the Red Army, but the leaders were Karl Maron, who became Interior Minister, Otto Winzer, who became Foreign Minister, and Walter Ulbricht, head of state. Between them and men like Erich Honecker, who had spent ten years in a Nazi prison in Brandenburg, there was friction, but it was the Moscow group that was to stamp the Stalinist model on the East. Under Russian occupation, opposition was ruthlessly suppressed. Though initially thought to be weak, the Communists rapidly consolidated power, and, infiltrating the Social Democrats under Otto Grotewohl, in 1946 persuaded them to merge into the Socialist Unity Party, the SED. The prisons began to fill, no longer with ex-Nazis but with opponents of the regime, many of them Party members. Nazi prison camps such as Sachsenhausen and Bautzen that had been used by the Russians were now used by the regime to imprison its opponents; these included a Minister of Justice, a Foreign Minister and a Minister of Supply. Ulbricht's secretary was executed. The conservative CDU and the liberal LDP were allowed for the moment to survive, but between 1947 and 1950 most of their leaders fled West, and, replaced by tame placemen of the SED, the parties merged into the National Front. Grotewohl became Prime Minister. But Ulbricht, deputy chairman of the SED and in 1950 its secretary general, had won the power struggle.

In September 1948 came the definitive split in the city when the administration, located in the Eastern sector, divided. Communist demonstrators, abetted by the SED-controlled police in the Eastern sector, took over the city hall building, the Rote Rathaus, in East Berlin, and non-Communist deputies moved out and set up shop in the West. 300,000 protested in front of the Reichstag. On 30 November the SED appointed a municipal council of its own choosing in the East. The city was administratively divided. In the East businesses were either taken over by the state, went bankrupt, or set up in the West. Many organizations split. There were arrests of anyone opposing the Party line. Some students were arrested, and, following the relegation of three students from Humboldt University, they and some faculty went over to the West to found the Freie. There were two currencies, two economies, two police forces, two administrations, two systems.

In the West, on 7 September 1949 in Bonn, the Bundestag constituted itself and the FRG was founded, with Konrad Adenauer as Chancellor. In the East the People's Council constituted itself as the Volkskammer on 7 October 1949, and the GDR came into existence, unrecognized by West Germany. In West Berlin a new constitution set up the city's government in October 1950, with Ernst Reuter as mayor. Meanwhile, in the city, freedom of movement through the crossing points continued, where the lopsided economies of the two states undermined each other. For the East the problem was the constant flow of population to the West in search of better opportunities. The socialist experiment could not work with its front door always open, and the GDR moved into more and more isolation. The wonder was that, given the rate of flow of refugees across the open border, it took another twelve years for the East to wall itself in.

Anyone not sharing the reigning ideology was regarded as opposition, and therefore enemy, and so from the beginning many who had opposed the Party line – or who were swept up innocently – went to prison or to the West, some to the latter via the former. Anyone who made a complaint of any kind was liable to imprisonment; the Stasi – set up in 1950 – grew more efficient and less discriminating over the years. Even when the Kremlin began to soften a little, the GDR continued its hard line towards both the West and its own people. In 1971 Ulbricht, rather than give in to Soviet demands that he respond to the West's Ostpolitik, resigned. By the eighties, with *glasnost* lapping at the Eastern regimes, the East Berlin leadership had dug itself in, ossified, distant, unapproachable.

Opposition to the regime's policies, or opposition to the regime itself, continued throughout the forty years of the GDR's existence. The isolationism of the regime encouraged it. The GDR had declared its zonal border with West Germany a national frontier in 1952, following the signing in the West of the European Defence Treaty. Telephone and road links in Berlin were cut off, and West Berliners were forbidden to enter the GDR. At the same time internal repression intensified; farmers, students, businessmen, priests, were arrested and imprisoned as spies, saboteurs and disruptive elements; young people joining the *Junge Gemeinde* (Young Christian Association) were expelled from schools and universities. The children of 'class enemies' were refused education; anyone refusing to join the Pioneers or the FDJ, or refusing to accept compulsory military instruction in schools, was suspect. Opposition grew out of frustration, out of police harassment, out of being refused a visa or permission to do something perhaps quite banal. Between would-be emigrants and civil rights protesters there was not always amity; while the latter were bravely seeking to change their society, the former were intent on leaving it.

In the early fifties the regime began its programme of building socialism, introducing new quota systems throughout its industrial organizations. In 1953 what had begun as peaceful protests in East Berlin by building workers against the new quotas which they interpreted as a 10 per cent wage cut, broke into open revolt. Building workers on Lot 40 on the Stalinallee, now Frankfurter Allee, marched into town to the House of Ministers, and demanded to speak to Ulbricht or Grotewohl. Some 5,000 workers joined them on the way. The leadership declined to appear. The next day large sections of the workforce downed tools in a general strike and came out to protest the quotas, the shortages, the whole system. Prisons were broken into and prisoners set free, sector signs between the two Berlins were torn down. In the afternoon of that day, 17 June 1953, the Russians declared a state of siege, tanks were on the streets, and troops opened fire. Many were killed: twenty-five, said the East, 200–400, said the West. At least twenty-one people were tried by Soviet military tribunals and shot, and eighteen soldiers for 'moral capitulation'. Some 1,500 were imprisoned, many for life. The leadership blamed Western provocateurs and fascist elements, and claimed the workers had been seduced, but abandoned the new quotas. Socialism would take a little longer. But the first Marxist–Leninist state on German soil now had blood on its hands. The revolution was to be carried out by force, if necessary. Brecht suggested, in a poem for the occasion, that whereas formerly the people had dissolved their governments when they no longer served their interests, now perhaps the government should dissolve the people. Thirty-six years later a similar suggestion was monitored by Christa Wolf in the autumn of 1989: that at the next May Day parades the leadership should walk in front of the people.

The repression intensified, its beneficiaries the secret police, the army, and the leadership, which began to withdraw into seclusion, moving, after the Hungarian uprising in 1956, to the compound at Wandlitz. Over the years opposition grew among peace groups and church groups, some of whose members refused conscription. It boiled down to demands for freedom of speech and assembly, veiled in requests for dialogue, and many went to prison, or had their careers closed down, or never got started. In imprisoning and alienating so many, the regime guaranteed itself a continuing opposition, seeking to intimidate it, to keep groups small and isolated from each other. In the end, in its own windy socialist spaces, the people came together to defy them.

From the start the leadership of the GDR had inherited the suspicious mind of its protestant forebears: stern, prudish, Prussian – and proletarian. For them there was always the enemy, the ever-present devil, the fascists biding their time, who would take advantage of free discussion to introduce poison and subvert the workers. By extension, anyone who called for open discussion became an agent of the imperialists, of the West, perceived as fascist, the eternal threat. The security system grew tighter and more efficient. Through the fifties the leadership suffered from paranoia of class enemies, spies and agents from the West (some of whom were flesh and blood), internal dissidents and traitors, and, after Stalin's split with Tito, in an imitational rash of trials on the model of the Slansky tribunals in Moscow, an obsessional persecution of anyone connected with Yugoslavia.

Discussion was out from the start, and in this way criticism was eliminated from the system. Nothing was to stand in the way of the all-out march to socialism, which must struggle to build itself from the ruins it inherited while being constantly vigilant of the enemy, the capitalist West, which in Berlin was the next street. Every organization and every citizen was to be enlisted in the struggle – or eliminated from it – and since ideology required it, everyone must believe in the rightness and certainty of its success. Marxism–Leninism was the mode in which all this was thought out, but it required, as the years went by and experiment faltered, a medieval blind faith to go on hoping. Education was to be the motor of this march; the young were to be moulded in socialism; at six they were to join the Young Pioneers, a nationwide cheerleader squad, and at thirteen the FDJ, the youth movement. In these ways they were to be channelled and directed into citizenship, and into the Party. Failure or refusal to follow this, the only route to a career, diverted those who refused from further education. Branches of the church objected to the indoctrination that membership of the FDJ brought with it, and refused membership, and some refused military service. There were, therefore, always outsiders, and the church became a ground of opposition, though on the whole it preferred to help the peace groups rather than would-be emigrants. In the early years, ideally, the churches were to be eliminated gradually from the socialist paradise, as one faith replaced another; unable to achieve this, the regime struck compromises, restored some rights, allowed the cross to return to the dome of the Dom in East Berlin.

Particular congregations and pastors and churches of the Bund of Evangelical Churches, with about 4 million members, were active in opposition. The Bund, a union of eight regional Protestant churches, retained a strong tradition of democratic self-organization; its press, though censored, was freer than most in a country where most of the newspapers and three-quarters of the publishing houses were owned by the state, and – as it turned out – many of them directly by the Party. The authorities saw this as a safety valve, and kept many eyes trained on its members, but nevertheless the church became a main area of protest.

Because of the dangers of contamination by foreign ideas, travel to the West was discouraged, even in later years when permits were easier to obtain. In any case, the shortage of hard currency and the pitifully low rate of permitted exchange – 15 marks in the West, 30 marks in the Eastern bloc – made travel virtually impossible. Travel agencies in the East offered vacations in the approved countries of Hungary, Czechoslovakia, Romania, Bulgaria, Poland, Yugoslavia, and the Soviet Union. For all except Czechoslovakia an exit visa was required. Though the costs were prohibitive, Cuba, North Korea, Vietnam, Mongolia were also permitted. Given school holidays, people applied up to a year ahead, and didn't always get what they applied for. To visit the West they had to have close relations there, and produce proof in wedding or birth certificates, and then there had to be a special occasion – an anniversary, a silver wedding, a confirmation, a significant birthday, a funeral – and even then they might be turned down. As some safeguard of their return, spouses of those allowed to travel to the West had to stay behind.

The Western press was out; Western publications were forbidden and seized in the post or at the border. A West Berliner told how he had gone through the border without thinking. In his car was a British newspaper (the *Guardian*) and several cassette tapes. They didn't like the music, and they designated the *Guardian* 'fascist literature'.

Censorship was firm as to what was allowed in print or on stage or screen. Some writers and film-makers left for the West; others were expelled. Others, such as Stefan Heym, were fined for publishing in the West works already turned down by the censorship in the East. Many books were forbidden. Censorship was in any case operated through the publishing houses, many of which belonged directly to the Party, and through control of the paper shortage. Many books published were for export only to the West; a print run of 80,000 of a book by Christa Wolf went immediately to the border, though another 20,000 passed into circulation via employees of the publishing house. None were available in bookshops. Ideas got about in surreptitious circulation. The role of the writer, as Brecht discovered in the fifties, was to convince the workers of the rightness of the theory. In time, this became understood as the rightness of the regime, the correct Party line.

The correct Party line insisted on the Soviet model, Stalinist version: all power to be concentrated at the centre, where all the decisions were made, to be carried out by the lower echelons without question, at whatever human or material cost. All the energies and resources of the state were to be bent to one purpose: the creation of the socialist commonwealth of the future, as perceived and defined by the leadership. Since nationalism would fade away, what did a model more suited to German conditions matter? In the name of the future the present must be totally reorganized, the past reinterpreted.

By the mid-sixties the frost had fastened hard, and in this period, with the Cold War at its fiercest and the GDR firmly walled in, the internal world shrank further. Artists and writers were subject to the attentions of the Stasi. Some left, some were exiled. For those who remained, life was circumscribed. Others who attained a certain eminence, who through the hard-currency earnings of their publications in the West contributed to the economy, or who merely threw their weight around and exercised some clout in the Writers' Union, were allowed to come and go to the West. In this, when the time came, they were already undermined. When towards the end of the year a group of prominent writers put out a declaration calling on East Germans to stay in their country and make it a better place to live, they were quickly shouted down. The writers could come and go at will, and therefore they could not speak for anyone else. 'Christa Wolf,' said the legendary man in a bar, 'what does she know? She could leave anytime. I couldn't.'

Thought control was well developed: the Stasi opened mail,

they listened on the telephone, they listened in bars and restaurants and queues and museums and on the street. Smoking a
Western cigarette or drinking a Western drink could be prosecut-
able offences. To be overheard saying, if only as a joke (so no
one joked), that Honecker was a buffoon might lead to charges
of public vilification. People were sent to prison for 'wasting
state time' by filling out a visa application, or for 'anti-social
behaviour' for refusing to accept demotion at work. Political
crimes were many and varied, and if they didn't catch you for
one they caught you for another. There were charges for contact-
ing foreigners ('Making illegal contacts'), for hindering state or
social activity, for incitement to hostility towards the state, for
passing on any sort of information. A man convicted of attempted flight was given a stiffer sentence when his job –
driving a garbage truck – was taken into consideration; as the
driver of a garbage truck he was the possessor of non-classified
information, but for this he could be considered an agent. A
retired doctor wishing to go to the West was refused a visa on
the grounds that, as the head of emergency services in his
district, in which was a factory with an emergency evacuation
plan in case of accident, he was party to the plan, and the plan
was classified. Offences included Article 99 (Treasonous com-
merce: supplying non-classified information to foreigners); Article 100 (Treasonous espionage: contacts with enemies of the
GDR); Article 106 (Malicious propaganda: criticizing socialism
and social conditions); Article 220 (Public disparagement);
articles covering illegal assembly and meetings, illegal organizations, *und so weiter*. To be sent to prison, or merely to be on
file with the Stasi, meant the end of any prospects in the GDR,
and many who went West thereafter went in despair. Political
offenders had their passports withdrawn and replaced by a
PM12 (*Polizeiliche Meldebescheinigung*), indicating that they
were politically unreliable.

It was a paranoid world of dire possibilities proceeding from
casual beginnings, and its effect was to repress and inhibit the
whole of society. No one criticized openly. No one made
suggestions. Spontaneity was discouraged.

Lucky's story will illustrate this. Lucky is in her mid-twenties,
bright, vivacious, serious. She works in publishing, she has her
life and her career in the city she defines as Berlin East. The
GDR is her country. She doesn't want to go elsewhere; this is

her home. She would like to go to distant places and return. She has a boyfriend in West Berlin. Before the Wall came down, he could visit her on a day visa, out by midnight. Otherwise they took holidays together in foreign capitals where she was allowed to go. In Budapest in the summer of 1989, when the Hungarians opened the frontier, she grew weary of explaining to Budapesters eager to drive them to the border that she wasn't going anywhere. She was on holiday. She was going back. Her life is much like anyone's anywhere; in East Berlin it was circumscribed by caution, the ever-present need to watch what one says. So she moves in a small circle of friends, people of around her own age, people with careers not dissimilar to hers. She is an intelligent young woman. Her parents are journalists, good Party members. She grew up in a Communist household, went through school and the Pioneers and the FDJ, passing exams and making all the right noises and on to journalism college. Like her parents, she would be a journalist. In another department of the college was a course for typesetters. Lucky liked the typesetters; they had more fun, they had better parties. With her journalism colleagues she stood around all evening with a drink in her hand, making useless conversation. So she went to the typesetters' knees-ups, for which she was carpeted. The Party Secretary called her in: didn't she realize she was letting down her cadre by not participating in their social gatherings? She must associate only with her cadre, and not to do so was betrayal. It was that or leave the course, so Lucky left the course and enrolled as a typesetter, graduated, and eventually got a job typesetting for the Party newspaper, *Neues Deutschland*, in East Berlin. One night, setting type, they realized that the mirror image of the news they were printing read that the CIA had mined the harbours off Nicaragua. Incensed, Lucky and her comrades organized raffles, bring and buy sales, raising a small symbolic sum of money to be sent in solidarity to the Nicaraguans. She was called in again: 'Who authorized this jumble sale? Who gave it permission? These things must be planned in advance. They must be properly organized.' Lucky got the message then: spontaneity not allowed.

In the seventies, under Bonn's Ostpolitik policy towards the East, the West began to provide subsidies to the East of DM 4 billion per year; part of the deal was freer travel to the West. Those who went out and returned brought back tales of wonder.

The inevitable result was dissatisfaction with their lot. Whatever the Party did in the deepening crisis rebounded on itself. Towards the end, the GDR grew only tighter, drawing in more and more to itself. The Russian *Sputnik* magazine, and many Russian books and films, were banned after an article compared Stalin with Hitler. This ban alone caused many to question the tightening system. The leadership had set its face against *glasnost*, and only gradually did the Gorbachov message seep through the information sieves of the GDR. What they couldn't prevent was the airwaves, and electronics has a leading role in the *Wende*. There wasn't anything they could do about television and radio, via which messages from the West – the West's message of itself – came constantly. In Leipzig, in an effort to appease the population, Western television was brought in by cable. From West Berlin RIAS radio spread music and news and messages down its wavelength; every week there was a different box number to write to with requests, because they figured it took the Stasi a week to catch up. Television sent its seductive images of Western abundance. It also carried news, and drama, and documentaries that showed the scabby sides of Western life, and in the East few were fooled. In an attempt to counter its effect, GDR TV ran *Der Schwarze Kanal*, a heavily edited version of the horrors of the West. Up around Dresden, in the 'valley of the innocents', where conditions block the signals from the West, there was a larger ignorance and therefore greater curiosity about the West, and it was from there that many emigrants came. In the East they call ARD TV from the West *Ausser Raum Dresden*: except area Dresden.

In the end, as events demonstrated, the leadership cut itself off from the rest of the world and its own people, developing a system in which all criticism was opposition and therefore of interest to the Stasi. Initiative was stifled, spontaneity frowned on. 'Without contraries is no progression,' saith Blake. Without discussion, argument, life gets dull, and without stimulation the brain goes to sleep. Daily life outside the circle of trusted acquaintances was hazardous. No one talked to anyone, especially not to strangers; no one made eye contact. Ideas stagnated, and so, therefore, did society. The economy stagnated, its targets for the last five-year plan ending in 1990 falling ever further behind, and failing to keep pace with inflation. Growth in industrial and high technology was offset by shortfalls in other areas; there were shortages of shoes and clothes, and demand was satisfied only at higher prices in the Exquisit and Delikat shops. With growth and inflation at about the same rate, living standards stayed low. The only growth area was protest and emigration. And the Stasi. Some younger academic economists in the Party modestly suggested the introduction of moderate market forces, but the Party was unable to contemplate the consequences. Back in 1985 Honecker had initiated a programme of discussions with every Party member; all 2.5 million were interviewed. It was found that many Party cells lacked motivation, and concluded that not enough was done for the public, but the report itself was never published. In the meantime the system ticked itself out, the leadership a closed system, without feedback, without dialectic, in the end without growth.

All these pressures served to distort daily life. Without criticism, there were no voices raised at the rising tide of pollution, the wrecking of communities and landscapes in the name of brown lignite and electricity. Mistakes were ignored or glossed over; there was a shortage of everything in the GDR but whitewash. Two habits became characteristic: *Doppelzüngigkeit* – doublespeak, or ambiguity, thinking one thing and saying another, and the habit of looking over one's shoulder, as the pressure to conform with Party thinking intensified. Citizens and employees were expected to cheer the leadership, attend the parades and the meetings, and vote as they were told. Where families were divided by the Wall, life was further distorted. From the East, contact was discouraged; visits by relatives from the West were difficult and fraught, and the contrast in aspirations and living standards worked to the discomfort of both. In such contacts Easterners felt patronized, looked down on by their Western relatives. At home, comparing themselves with their Western cousins, they felt cheated of forty 'lost years', and the feeling grew that while both halves of Germany had equally lost the war, they were the part severly punished by the Russians. Why? At home their mail was checked, their phone conversations listened to and taped, hidden microphones were planted on suspects and in their homes and offices, and they were followed everywhere, their contacts monitored and recorded. People with contacts or relatives in the West were not trusted, not promoted; they were watched, the subjects of files at Stasi-

Zentrale. Stasi operatives, members of the armed forces (through conscription, most males) and Party officials were required to sign an undertaking that they would turn their backs on their Western relatives and regard them as the enemy. The GDR turned itself into a distorting mirror.

By the beginning of the 1980s peace movements were active, and many of their members were expelled. Demonstrations and vigils were treated as cases of *Rowdytum*, rowdiness, or as 'riotous assembly' or 'impeding public and social activity'. Under a decree of 1980, permission to assemble had to be applied for to the Office for the Organization of Events, and in anticipation of its not being granted, most protesters assembled without permission and were automatically arrested. Through the eighties environmental groups were also becoming active, as the extent of damage to the environment became noticeable even in the GDR, where matters affecting the environment or industrial emissions were treated as state secrets. Peace groups and environmentalists were therefore set on a collision course with the authorities.

In July 1987 an amnesty had cleared the jails of political prisoners, but within three months they were filled again. At the beginning of 1989 there were 10,000 political prisoners. These included those convicted of attempts to flee the country and conspiracy to do so, and those convicted of more genuine political offences. Though differently motivated and differently manifested, all were treated as political offenders. Many trials were in camera, and documents were not made public, the proceedings not reported in the press, and details difficult to come by. Amnesty International's report on the GDR provides what little information there is, and it is from that publication that the following example is borrowed. The case will serve as an example of what had become by then routine methods of stamping out opposition. In January 1988 a number of people were arrested in East Berlin for attempting to join an official demonstration commemorating the murders of Karl Liebknecht and Rosa Luxemburg, founders of the KPD. Though icons, neither was popular with the leadership. Some people, activists, frustrated emigrants, carried banners proclaiming Rosa Luxemburg's 'Freedom is the freedom of those who think differently', the *Andersdenkenden*. Some protestors had been warned to stay away, but went on the grounds that citizens were encouraged to join the demonstration.

The trial of three of them was exemplary. Their defending lawyer was Wolfgang Schnur, of whom more will be heard in the future. Though theoretically open to the public, the court was packed with security officers, and others stood outside the court preventing friends of the accused entering. Only a few close family members got in. The prosecution provided a conspiracy scenario involving members of the Zion Church, the Initiative for Peace and Human Rights, the *Staatsbürgerschaftsgruppe* – a working group giving legal advice to would-be emigrants – and the Environmental Library. A statement from a witness who was not present was read out to the effect that there had been prior agreement between the groups on attending and carrying banners, and the wording of the slogan. It was said that the legal advice group had agreed not to carry them, so as not to be provocative, whereas the Initiative members would do so. The accused were said to have known about these arrangements, though all affirmed that they had heard only individually about the demonstration. Because none had made statements when first interrogated, but had agreed separately later on details, the court accused them of agreeing things in advance. Questioned about the quotation on the banner, all three amplified their views that society could not progress without public discussion, but that dialogue could not take place between people who were not free. The prosecutor made his speech: the wording on the banners coincided with the wording agreed earlier, and therefore bespoke planning and conspiracy; their intention was to disrupt the demonstration for egotistical ends. They were sentenced to six months' imprisonment, but released on probation a few weeks later.

Petty harassment, petty offences, often petty punishments.

After the May 1989 local elections there was widespread protest at alleged ballot-rigging and gerrymandering, and through the year this added to the dissatisfaction. The system of voting in any case guaranteed compliance with the chosen candidates; the voter inserted in the ballot box a pre-printed list of approved National Front candidates; any changes to the list required a visit to the voting booth, and that was noted. In May about 100 people were arrested in Leipzig protesting alleged local election rigging. There were many such protests, most of them unreported in the Press. In Berlin in mid-August fifty young East Germans went to the West German mission, from where they were driven off by police. They then went to the Brandenburg Gate demanding to be let out. There the police took their names and addresses, and prevented them throwing roses over the Wall. Some were detained. A few days later a young woman sat on a carpet in front of the Gate holding a placard that said FLYING CARPET. A petrol bomb was thrown at the Wall.

In mid-July Honecker was reported ill with gall-bladder problems, and nominated Mittag his deputy. Before he went off to the surgeon's knife, he proclaimed unification 'as unlikely as uniting fire and water', and announced: 'Socialism is the only society in which a person can be a person, in which work and initiative are not exploited.' No doubt many would have disagreed with him. As protest became more and more open, thousands were heading for the Hungarian border. While Honecker spoke, East Germans were occupying West German embassies in East Berlin, Prague, and Budapest, and the borders were leaking on every side.

In September 1989 protest became mass protest, much of it centred on Leipzig though spread through all East German cities. At this time Valentin Falin, the Kremlin's expert on German affairs, predicted mass demonstrations in the GDR by 'next spring'. It came much earlier than that. In Leipzig, where during the previous two years the Nicholas Church had become a magnet for protest and a focus for human rights and peace groups, Monday night services were now turning into huge demonstrations. On 4 September, demands for the right to leave were supplemented by demands for a new government. On the following Monday, the 11th, the demonstrators were back, and several were arrested. On the next Monday, 18 September, more than 100 were arrested. On the 25th, 8,000 demonstrated, calling for *Freiheit*, human rights, *perestroika*, and against the ban on New Forum. The police were said to be restrained. Some demonstrators were taken away. New Forum, founded in Leipzig at the beginning of September and promptly banned, had applied for legal recognition on the 19th, and was rejected by the Interior Ministry as 'a criminal organization'. It was a collection of groups working for change, formed to press for reform independently of the church, and calling for dialogue and the improvement of socialism rather than its abolition; in the words of one of its founders, Bärbel Bohley, there was to be 'no reunification, no return to capitalism'. The following Monday, 2 October, the numbers in Leipzig grew. It was the largest protest in the GDR since 1953. Workers' militias were brought in to cordon off streets.

At the beginning of October there was a three-hour riot in Dresden involving an estimated 10,000 protesters. They wanted to draw attention to the special trains leaving Prague with thousands of East Germans fleeing West: yet another example of how the regime's decisions blew up in its face. Many tried to board them. Police used water-cannon and batons to drive back crowds trying to reach the special trains, and sealed off sections of track. The crowds who had come to demand exit began to demand change.

In October, with its fortieth anniversary coming up on the 7th, the leadership faltered, giving way on the exodus from Prague and Warsaw, and later backing down before determined protesters. Perhaps they were moved by public relations considerations; perhaps, at the end, they didn't have the stomach for a bloodbath. The anniversary turned out to be an own goal. The celebrations turned into mass protests in East Berlin and other cities. Despite the exodus, despite the ferment throughout the country, the flags were out, the parades went past, the leadership acknowledged the cheers and salutes, and went off with its distinguished foreign guests to dinner. As usual the Party faithful and the workers delegated to be there were there. But the mood was expectant, and terminal, and when Honecker spoke it may have crossed his mind, then, that the days were numbered. On film, that sudden fear and recognition appears two months later on the face of Ceauşescu when his enforced audience finally turned against him, and later still in 1990 on the face of Gorbachov himself in the May Day demonstrations in Moscow. Such sudden confrontations with the people in whose name the oligarchs of the East ruled, recorded live, render history into drama. What's also clear, here, is the irony of the leadership's provision, through compulsory attendance at its rallies and parades, and the vast urban spaces in which they took place, the spaces and the crowds that eventually toppled them.

Then, however, Gorbachov was the man of the hour, the icon of hope, and everyone was waiting to see how he would respond in this situation. Only a few months before, in June, his attendance at China's anniversary had added fuel to the fires of

protest, culminating in the massacre of demonstrators in Tiananmen Square on the 4th. Honecker stood up and said all was
well, and that socialism was unbeatable. Any protest was the
result of Western provocation, the proletariat of the GDR still
apparently susceptible to the lure of capitalism; as in 1953 and
1961, so again in 1989. Gorbachov warned: 'He who is late will
be punished by life itself.' In the streets the crowds, frustrated,
turned earnest and determined, and refused to go home. In East
Berlin it began in Alexanderplatz, that vast parade ground
around the S-Bahn station, where the police began putting up
barriers and beating demonstrators. Soon it spread down the
wide spaces of Karl-Liebknecht-Strasse into Unter den Linden,
from which some 10,000 people marched to the Gethsemane
Church in Prenzlauer Berg. The Gethsemane had become the
focus of protest in East Berlin, a forum for speeches and
discussions and, as a result of the police beatings, of hunger
strikers. Through the weekend of 7 October the protests continued. 2,000 sat down in the Schönhauser Allee. Police attacked
demonstrators outside the church, and there were many arrests
and violent beatings. An estimated 1,000 were in jail in East
Berlin after the weekend's protests. Almost all foreign journalists
were ordered out, and the checkpoints to the West were closed
for four days and only opened again after Allied protests.
Ominously, Honecker compared the unrest with events earlier
in the year in China. It was remembered that only East Germany,
Czechoslovakia and Bulgaria had condoned Peking's abrupt
solution to protest. Honi went on to say that attempts by
the imperialists of the West to undermine socialism in the GDR
would fail, and compared their efforts to Don Quixote tilting at
windmills. There was widespread fear of a crackdown.

This was scheduled for the following Monday, 9 October, in
Leipzig, but it didn't take place. After the widespread and
violent protests following the anniversary, up to 70,000 protested
outside the Nicholas Church in Leipzig. Their demands were
now more radical: for democracy, and an amnesty for those
arrested. Troops were ordered in. Again, police and the militia
were deployed, and live ammunition was issued. This date, as it
later turned out, was the crucial turning point. Honecker gave
orders to suppress the demonstrations in Leipzig; local officials
persuaded the military to hold back. Confronted by a hostile
crowd, the authorities wavered. Conscript soldiers began openly

to sympathize with the protesters, and had to be withdrawn. Later there were reports of blood plasma, body bags and dressings being stockpiled in anticipation, of an emergency medical station being set up in the hall used for the city's biannual trade fair, and of local hospitals being ordered to clear 10 per cent of their beds. The authorities were readying themselves for confrontation, but the expected Chinese solution didn't take place. In all reports the militia were willing, but somewhere the order to open fire was never given. Who intercepted the orders remains unclear. The local leadership broadcast messages calling for dialogue, and eventually the crowds dispersed, their leaders having exacted a promise from the city's Party leadership of a meeting the next day. But the next day the leadership were too busy to talk, and the crisis had spread to the whole of the GDR. In due course the meeting took place, and set the model for round table talks all over East Germany, defusing a potentially bloody situation. Meanwhile there was talk of guerrilla conflict, as young men remembered that their military training had taught them how to sabotage and disarm tanks.

Having come to the brink, events thereafter moved rapidly towards the eclipse of the Honecker leadership. The old East SPD, which had been obliged in 1946 to merge itself into the SED, where it had remained ever since, declared itself independent. The focus of opposition was now moving to New Forum and the SPD. There were stirrings of independence in the other satellite parties, the Liberals and Christian Democrats. The media were becoming responsive to the demand for change. And SED membership and recruitment were falling.

In East Berlin the stream of visitors to the Gethsemane Church was continuous. Outside and inside were candles guttering on great banks of wax, and hunger strikers lying down in sleeping-bags. People from all over Berlin pressed into the church, reading the declarations and statements, looking at the photographs of police brutality. There were speeches, discussions, and Stasi. There were photographs of a demonstration in Cracow in support, a Polish drawing of the GDR surrounded by wire and watchtowers, a concentration camp. In the windows of apartments in the dark streets, people lit candles. Young people, bearing the marks of vicious beatings, were released from prison, no doubt to discourage the others, but their cuts and bruises had the opposite effect, and fuelled popular anger. Then, miraculously, the Stasi were withdrawn.

Elsewhere, with reforms in Poland and Hungary, the writing on the wall was becoming clearer. In Budapest the Communist Party had voted to change its name to the Hungarian Socialist Party, and to hold free elections, junking socialism. In East Germany the protests and the exodus continued. Meanwhile there was open speculation on the search for a new leader, someone in the Gorbachov image, who could bring the Party and the state into some process of renewal. Candidates were few and far between, and included the names of Markus Wolf, the former Eastern spymaster, the writer Stefan Heym, and Kurt Masur, conductor of the Leipzig Orchestra. Whether they would or no, the search was on for an honest broker in a society where most public figures had been corrupted by the regime. Hans Modrow's name was first suggested at this time; he was said to be a reformer, though without any evidence to show for it, but the record said he had been moved to Dresden to get him out of Berlin. In Dresden itself there were talks between the local leadership and twenty members of the church and New Forum opposition groups, and it was agreed that those arrested in the previous twenty-four hours were to be freed unless charged with violence. Seventy members of New Forum had been detained. Five hundred of those arrested were released.

On 11 October it was reported that police had baton-charged 3,000 silent marchers through Halle. On the same day, a long statement was read out on East German television from the Politburo: they were 'not indifferent' to the exodus, then in full flood, and they promised to discuss economic performance, democracy, better goods, a better environment, better travel opportunities. But they rejected any idea of reforming the system, and were 'against suggestions and demonstrations aiming to lead people astray and change the constitutional basis of our state'. The Party already had the necessary channels for debate. 'Socialism on German soil is not in question. The people of the GDR have opted for socialism forever.'

In Berlin, on the 13th, most of the demonstrators arrested over the previous weekend had been released. Over that weekend New Forum held a nationwide gathering of 120 delegates from all of East Germany's fourteen districts to discuss stategy. On the Monday, the 16th, 120,000 demonstrated peacefully in Leipzig. There were resignations, by the mayor of Leipzig and five Politburo members. All that week mass protests continued throughout the GDR.

On 18 October Honecker resigned, allegedly at his own request, on health grounds, after eighteen years in power. Also sacked were Mittag (economics) and Hermann (media). Egon Krenz, chief of external and internal security, who took over from him, was widely regarded as a stopgap, as the Crown Prince, soon to be the Clown Prince, a gear in the Party machine. Later he described this period as one when 'at just the time clever decisive and united action was urgent, there was mute indecision at the head of the Party'. In discussion with a number of other comrades Krenz had seized the initiative, facing strong opposition from Honecker. In the Politburo a fierce two-day discussion ensued, 'but the former General Secretary failed to draw the relevant conclusions'. Apparently it was Stoph, Prime Minister for twenty-two years, who proposed the resignations. Later it was revealed that Honecker had been toppled because he had ordered the Leipzig crackdown on the ninth, by a concert party consisting of Krenz, Schabowski (Berlin Party chief), Lorenz (Karl-Marx-Stadt Party chief), and Modrow (then Dresden Party chief). As head of security, Krenz would have seen the build-up of protest recorded in the Stasi files. Schabowski secured Moscow's support, and they brought down Honecker. Suddenly the leadership was visible as a group of enfeebled old men, too long in power and surrounded by nodding donkeys: Honecker, seventy-seven and ailing; Mittag, sixty-two, a firm opponent of market forces who had run the economy since the mid-seventies, a diabetic who had already lost one leg and was said to be soon to lose the other; Mielke, who at eighty-one still presided, spider-like, over the Ministry of State Security; and Stoph himself, who was seventy-five. Three weeks later it would be Stoph's turn.

Erich Honecker was born in 1912, the son of a miner in Neuenkirchen in the Saar, in the West. A roofer by trade, he so described himself to the end. An old Communist, he had joined the Communist Youth Federation at fourteen and the KPD at seventeen. Later he went to Party school in Moscow, coming back as a local youth leader before going underground in 1933. Two years later the Gestapo arrested him. He was interrogated violently for eighteen months, and jailed for ten years for 'preparation for high treason'. He was freed from Brandenburg prison by the Russians in 1945, returned to Berlin to set up the FDJ, and was a top official by the time the GDR was founded in 1949. He was promoted to the Politburo in charge of security in 1958, and in 1961 he was responsible for the building of the Wall. In May 1971 he succeeded Ulbricht as Party Secretary, after Ulbricht stepped down, tired of resisting Moscow pressure for *détente* with West Germany in response to Ostpolitik. He was a simple man, a lifelong and hardline Marxist. He had the reputation of being a womanizer. His wife, from whom he was said to have become estranged, became Minister of Education, and the upbringing of the young became the Honecker family business. When he came to power he promised relaxation of the rules of censorship in art and literature, but it was not to be. But Honecker – Honi – was responsible for some small amelioration of the rules, and in recent years more and more people were allowed out of the GDR, if only as a safety valve. This led only to demands for more to be allowed to leave.

In the end, an old man steeped in his ideology and cut off from the real world, unable to listen, Honecker seemed unable to grasp what had happened. His attitude proved too simplistic: that it was enough to share out the wealth more or less equally, and that the state's provision of housing, education, food and jobs, none of which had been free in his youth, was sufficient. All the rest was planning, and suppression of opposition. When the first failed, the second came into play.

Egon Krenz, who succeeded Honecker, inspired no one. The great toothy smile was too clearly false, the jovial air too unnatural and too recently acquired, the act too transparent, the hair just a little too shiny, and the voice too much speak-your-weight. He was seen as a sinister joke, his name something said swiftly in a diner, and regarded from the start with suspicion. *Er geht ooch noch*, they said in Berlin dialect, spelling out his name: he goes next. For a long time Honecker's protégé, he had come up the youth route. In the twenty-three member Honecker-dominated Politburo since 1983, he was its youngest member, and was generally regarded as arrogant and a hard-liner by his colleagues. Opposition groups pointed to his record: as security chief he controlled the Stasi, and enjoyed a huge power base in the security apparatus, in the FDJ, in the Party and in the armed forces. He, it was pointed out, had been responsible for the police crackdown in the run-up to the fortieth anniversary. Soon it was recalled that on 1 October, China's birthday, East Berlin had sent two emissaries bearing support and congratulations for the Chinese way with dissenters; one of these was Egon Krenz. Slippery, he made a distinction between his mission as a member of the Government and his personal sentiments, which were, of course, different. It was put about that it was he who had diverted violence in Leipzig on 9 October. He was said to be diabetic, and an alcoholic. On appointment, he criticized the Party's past insensitivity in not reacting fast enough to widespread discontent, sympathized with families divided by emigration, and made vague promises of improvement. But he felt the country already had enough channels for dialogue, meaning the Party. New Forum, it was pointed out, was 'not a party', and was dismissed by Party members from the debate. His speech on appointment was pages of gobbledegook, about the need to preserve and defend and renew socialism, calling for 'patience and work, work, work'. It was a 'blood, sweat and tears' speech. It was not what the refugees camped out in Embassy compounds wanted to hear, nor those who remained, and the debate was in any case moving elsewhere. New Forum had 26,000 signatures by now.

The exodus continued, the protests continued. At this stage the sticking point was the opposition demand for the freeing of travel restrictions. On 20 October, 5,000 marched in silent demonstration in Dresden. On the 23rd, at the Monday night protests in Leipzig, thousands turned out, calling for free elections, freedom to travel and a leading role for the people. Placards proclaimed EGON, WHO ASKED US? 10,000 marched in Halle. There were more protests in East Berlin. The new administration seemed no more resolute than the old, and Krenz waffled. He lifted the year-old ban on the Russian magazine *Sputnik*. On 20 October, Party leaders appeared in a phone-in programme on television. Such events were unprecedented, but the system was beginning to break up under its own inertia. On the 23rd, workers at the Wilhelm Pieck engineering plant on the outskirts of Berlin announced that they were leaving their official union to form their own. At the same time the Volkskammer began to stir from its forty-year slumber, and on the 24th, 10 per cent of its members – the bloc parties – refused to

endorse Krenz's appointment. These represented the newly re-
surgent Liberal Democrats and Christian Democrats, till now
tied to the SED in the National Front. The LDP called for
reform and free speech, and their leader, Manfred Gerlach,
questioned for the first time the leading role of the Party. The
CDU spoke out for the separation of Party and state, and free
elections. The other two parties, the National Democrats and
the Democratic Farmers, still kept a low profile, but were under
pressure from their membership. Now that the SED boat was
clearly sinking, everyone wanted to get off. Krenz promised a
more active role for the Volkskammer, and said travel was
under urgent discussion. Here there emerged the 'economic
question' of travel: if GDR citizens were allowed to travel freely
and took with them only 500 marks, half the country's hard
currency reserves would rapidly be exhausted. On 25 October,
20,000 marched through Neubrandenburg.

The first official meetings between the Government and New
Forum, still not legalized – the first of the Round Table talks
established on the Polish model – took place on 26 October in
Rostock, Dresden and other towns. In the coming months the
absence of an effective government and the movement for
reform were channelled through these round table meetings.
They were to continue until a week before the elections in
March 1990. New Forum now had 100,000 signatures to a
declaration calling for democracy. The Democracy Now group
demanded a re-run of the local elections back in May. On the
27th the Government declared an amnesty for everyone convicted of escaping or trying to escape. By the 28th, ten days
after the resignations, the economic and media portfolios were
still vacant. The cracks widened. On the 30th, Schnitzler's
thirty-year-old programme on East German television, *Der
Schwarze Kanal*, which had regularly attacked the West and
West Germany, went off the air for ever after five minutes,
without explanation. Two more *Betonköpfe*, concrete-heads,
resigned from the Politburo: Harry Tisch, leader of the TU
movement, under pressure and accused of failing to defend
workers' rights, and Margot Honecker, Education Minister
since 1963. Alexander Schalck-Golodkowski, a state secretary
and Foreign Trade Minister, was appointed to succeed Mittag,
though not for long. At the beginning of November Krenz was
in Moscow, consulting with Gorbachov. In the subsequent

photo opportunity shots he beams beside his mentor, positively pleased, a squirrel with a bushy tail. In Moscow he said that the removal of the Wall was 'out of the question' and unification 'not on the agenda'. He expressed interest in *perestroika*, and claimed that East Germany was embarked on its own process of renewal. He pledged loyalty to East Germany, to Communism, and to the Warsaw Pact. But apart from an unspecific promise of free travel, he remained vague and gave no hint at the shape of further reforms.

On 1 November, 20,000 marched again through Neubrandenburg. On the 2nd there were mass demonstrations throughout East Germany – in Erfurt, Gera, Guben, Halle, Potsdam, Karl-Marx-Stadt, Dessau, Magdeburg, Rostock, Altenburg, Arnstadt . . . the roll continues. On the 4th, half a million turned out on to the streets of East Berlin. On the 5th, new travel laws were announced, allowing all citizens to have passports to travel for up to thirty days a year. The law still required an exit visa for permission to go, at thirty days' notice, and could still be refused on grounds of national security, health, morals or public order. No arrangements were proposed for currency exchange. Through the next days there were huge demonstrations (60,000 in Halle, 50,000 in Karl-Marx-Stadt, 25,000 in Schwerin) rejecting the new travel rules as inadequate and demanding free elections. On the 6th came the biggest march yet in Leipzig, estimated at half a million, calling for free elections and an end to the Communist monopoly of power. Clearly the population were unimpressed by the new travel laws. It was too little too late. What had begun as a demand for travel was turning rapidly into demands for freedom.

On 6 November the Council of Ministers resigned *en masse*, and on the 7th so did the Prime Minister, Stoph, with all forty-four members of his cabinet. No explanations were given. The announcement was made by a Government spokesman at the first-ever press conference, at which no questions were answered. The Central Committee, consisting of 163 members, mostly Party leaders but also scientists, trade unionists, industrial managers, artists, and fifty non-voting candidate members, began an intensive three-day meeting to elect new members to the Politburo. Meanwhile 5,000 Party members demonstrated outside SED headquarters. In the following week a new cabinet was to be elected by the Volkskammer. The same day its constitutional and legal committee threw out the new travel laws, objecting to the thirty-day limit and the exclusions, and demanded abolition of the exit visa. New Forum was legalized. On the 8th, Hans Modrow was appointed Prime Minister, subject, again, to the Volkskammer's approval. Krenz resigned and was reappointed later the same afternoon. When announced, the new Politburo contained about half hardliners, mostly from the previous Politburo, and some 'liberals'. Membership was cut to eleven, plus five non-voting members. Among those dropped were twelve old Stalinists, including Mielke, Hager, and Stoph.

And on the 9th the Wall opened. Freedom to travel was announced as a decision already made by the previous regime, and the decision was slipped through without anyone, apparently, making a decision. Krenz had been on the phone to Moscow. It was from there the suggestion to open the Wall had come. Free to spill into the West, the pressure eased. Almost everyone welcomed it. The Soviet Foreign Ministry spokesman, Gennady Gerassimov, remarked: 'These changes are for the better, that's for sure.' In any case Czechoslovakia, under the constant influx of Eastern refugees, had threatened to close its borders.

The Central Committee continued its crisis meeting. New travel regulations were brought out, now that the horse was bolting, allowing people to come and go as they wished. As the system crumbled, Party bosses in Bautzen and Köthen and other towns committed suicide, there were many resignations, and the membership of the Party began to bail out in large numbers. On 11 November, Schabowski, now Party spokesman, announced that the Central Committee would propose a new election law allowing all political forces to participate. 'The SED will accept the challenge,' he said. The Central Committee's programme for renewal now included free elections, a democratic coalition government, an independent judiciary, economic reform and a free press, autonomous trade unions, scrutiny of the secret police, parliamentary investigations into malpractices and abuse of power, and a control commission to investigate misconduct by Mittag and Hermann and other members of the old hierarchy. There was no mention of an end to the Party's monopoly of power. It began to be revealed that top Party members had taken advantage of their positions to enrich themselves and had 'squandered national wealth'. The luxury of their lifestyles began to be reported. Krenz repeated that unification was not up for discussion; in the West Kohl remarked that they were still a long way from their goal. Four members of the new Politburo were sacked.

The Central Committee announced a special Party conference for 15–17 December. Modrow addressed the Central Committee, criticizing its past record and presenting his ideas for economic reform, including decentralization and more incentives for the workers. But the debate was shifting rapidly away from the Party. By the end of November New Forum had 2,000 members, and other groups had emerged, such as Democratic Awakening, the Greens, and the SPD. To date there had been little that was concrete; the Wall was breached and the borders open, restrictions on travel had been lifted, and there were to be passports for all; the Stasi was to shed 8,000 of its 33,000 Berlin members, and further Round Table talks were promised. On 20 November Modrow had announced an amnesty for political prisoners and all those convicted of seeking to flee. Wolfgang Schnur, who had campaigned on behalf of political prisoners, was confident that the only political prisoners left in prison were military, plus between fifty and a hundred whose cases had criminal complications. Then, at the end of November, came the announcement spelling the end of power for the SED, as the Volkskammer abolished the leading role of the Party.

These were the events known in the East as the *Wende*, the turning, the change. The *Durchbruch* is a Western image, seen from a Western perspective, the prisoners breaking out of the jail. But for the East the struggle culminating in the end of the Honecker regime constitutes the focus of history, and thereafter for many who had suffered and struggled under the regime the *Durchbruch* was the safety valve diverting pressure and attention from the issue: renewal of the GDR. Thereafter the masses of the East lost interest in reform, bedazzled by the West and lured by the sudden prospects of unification, and the swift political and economic intrusion of the West into the East.

Wende zu Ende.

5

SO MANY I HAD NOT THOUGHT

'And I looked and saw a whirling banner running so fast it seemed it could never make a stand, and behind it came so long a train of people, so many I had not thought death had undone so many.'

Dante, lines 52–7, Canto 3, *The Inferno*

When the Wall opened to let the dazed inhabitants of the East through to the West at last, 3 million Easterners were said to have travelled through the Wall and back again in the first three days. Like all such figures, it depends who's counting, and in the first confused hours of the outflow no one was. However, in the first two days visas were issued to 2.7 million people. More than a million exit visas were issued in five hours. By Friday, the next day, the guards were insisting on stamps, and were issuing visas for between three days and six months and efficiently stamping the cards of the queuing Easterners. Soon they accepted ID cards in lieu of passports. They themselves were magically transformed from sullen border guards, encouraged to be hostile to everyone and answerable to no one, into fellow citizens and public servants. They smiled, gave directions, answered questions, wished travellers a good day. They might, after all, soon find themselves redundant.

Initially it was chaos, a scrum for the border. Towards eight in the evening, Easterners began arriving at the crossing points saying they'd heard they were free to travel to the West. All anyone knew was that at 6.55 that Thursday evening the television news had carried a statement that said all GDR citizens were free to travel abroad, and here they were. But nothing was written down. The border guards had no instructions. No one had told them anything. No doubt urgent telephone calls were made to headquarters and the offices of the new coalition government, itself not yet confirmed by the Volkskammer, which was beginning to act independently of the Government and the Party. By 10 p.m. the pressure was heavy on both sides of the checkpoints. The press focused on Checkpoint Charlie, and there the traffic and the foot passengers were backed up into Friedrichstrasse, the crowd hungry at the border and demanding to be let out.

Then the guards, overwhelmed, let everyone through. West German television reported a first couple through the Bornholmer Checkpoint at 9.15 p.m. Soon Easterners were emerging at the crossing points into the flash of cameras and the popping of champagne corks, all the world and his wife cheering and crowding to the barriers at Checkpoint Charlie, gawping at the first rush through the door, the Easterners gawping back. People hugged each other, wept, shrieked with excitement, Westerners offered money, drinks, invitations to dinner, to stay. No one really believed it. Everyone thought it a temporary aberration on the part of the East, and that the gates would surely close again. It was only two days since the fall of the Government, three weeks since the fall of Honecker. The Prime Minister designate, Hans Modrow, was said to be a liberal but was a new and unknown quantity. With the exodus and the continuing mass protests throughout the country, events had been happening fast, and those at the checkpoints had decided they could wait no longer. *Carpe diem.* It was a great day for Kodak.

No one knew what to do. Used to taking orders, the border guards were stumped: uniformed German officials without direction. They knew only what anyone else knew: that Eastern and Western television had shown a press conference – only the second such event in the GDR – at which the Government's spokesman, Gunter Schabowski, in answer to a reporter's question about freedom to travel, had announced that henceforth all GDR citizens would be free to go where they pleased. It was assumed there would still be some sort of visa. This was announced as an interim solution, adopted by the outgoing government, pending deliberation by the Volkskammer, which was to reconvene the following Monday. In the meantime it was Thursday, and the country was between governments, and the incoming administration could lay the decision to the outgoing, and in the dreamtime between the worlds the Wall opened. **Sesame öffnet die Mauer.** Within the hour, taking Schabowski at his word, Easterners were presenting themselves at the checkpoints demanding to be let out, and no one knew what to do.

The crowds were not best pleased to be held back while the buck passed upwards. While they waited and the guards worried, Krenz was on the telephone to Gorbachov. Suddenly the Wall ceased to be a wall.

To supplement the existing checkpoints, new ones were quickly opened. On the Friday night work began at the end of Eberswalder Strasse, which opens into a corner in the West on the old front line at Bernauer Strasse. Volksarmee drove up in trucks, the mechanical grab that had been clearing up what had recently been swapped with the West for the Lenné Triangle began working at the Wall's coping, and the lights came on. They worked all night. Having taken off the coping, it was the turn of the welders with their arc lamps to cut the joining rods along the top, and then the drills came out. In each slab were two holes plugged with cement and, these having been drilled out, rods were inserted on a chain from the grab, which now lifted up the great slabs one by one, to the cheers of the onlookers in Bernauer Strasse, and set them aside. On the Western side the row of crosses commemorating those who died on this old killing-ground were moved aside. By 8 o'clock in the morning the crossing was in business, the guards ready with their stamps and the Easterners, still unbelieving, pressing through. All that day the crowds moved through the new crossing, while pioneers struggled to lay a road under their feet.

Meanwhile the army moved on, and by Saturday evening the grabs were busy at Potsdamer Platz. By now the West Berliners had caught on, and through the night thousands gathered to watch, cheering at each stage of the proceedings, rhythmically handclapping, shouting 'Take it down, take it down.' The excitement was infectious, and as the slabs came up in the glare of camera lights and headlights, there was more applause. By the morning, Sunday, the crossing was open, and the Easterners crowded across what had once been vast empty space and long before that the crossroads of the city. West Berlin police and Eastern border guards linked arms to hold the crowds till the moment arrived, and then they surged through. East met West. The Easterners emerged into the arms of West German yuppies, leaning on their BMWs and spraying champagne to welcome them, yelling, boastful: 'Our system has beaten your system.' That morning the new crossing was to be the meeting point of West Berlin's mayor Walter Momper with his opposite number from the East, Erhard Krack. They shook hands, and Momper spoke of the prospect of good neighbourly relations between the two cities, recognizing their difference, their separateness. Later at a press conference he went on to attack Kohl for raising the unification issue at the moment the GDR was trying to re-create itself. Later still in the day Richard von Weizsäcker, President of the Bundesrepublik, came to Potsdamer Platz.

Soon there were new visas, but in the first days and hours many crossed without. In those first days to do so was still a daring adventure, the fulfilment of a long-forbidden dream. Later, as more breaches were made in the Wall, the flood began in earnest, and it was a great day then for Sony and Mitsubishi. Within twenty-four hours there were five new openings; soon there were to be eighteen, then twenty-two. To cope with the influx, cross-city bus services linking East and West were started, and on the Saturday the first of the old U-Bahn stations to be closed down in 1961, Jannowitzbrücke, was opened. At the same time, because of the crush, other stations in the West were temporarily closed. Some parts of the system broke down under the strain, and some stations became lethal, the crowds pushing over the platforms.

From the crossing points the Easterners fanned out over the city, an invading proletarian army in faded blue denim, staring at the lights, envying the goodies of the West. First they queued, as was their habit, in long lines at banks and post offices for their *Begrüssungsgeld*, their DM 100 greetings money. But where they had been a trickle, now they were a horde. Banks and post offices stayed open all weekend to cope with the rush. Some ran out of money. The first weekend invasion by the East cost Bonn DM 150 million.

They were made welcome, the Ossis, long-lost relatives suddenly returned. Those first encounters were full of goodwill. There were free tickets for Easterners for that Saturday's soccer game at the Olympic stadium, there were free tickets to a concert at the Philharmonia. There was beer and sparkling Sekt everywhere, and bartenders accepted the Ostmark one to one and gave away drinks. People handed each other sweets and flowers, roses and geraniums. Everywhere loudspeakers played music. The place was packed, and no one could move. In the streets swift merchants were selling cans of beer from the backs of cars. At the beginning there was nothing but goodwill, toasts and free drinks and hundreds dancing on the Wall at the Brandenburg Gate. East and West sides of the city were stunned by the event, and for weeks and months afterwards they struggled to understand the speed of the changes. History was outrunning its protagonists' ability to keep up, and turning into apocrypha: an Easterner was said to have returned two library books to the West, borrowed in 1961, and was pleased to have the DM 5,000 fine waived, while another tale concerns the man who came over, bought a lottery ticket, and won DM 1.2 million. On the first day a man came into the British Council Library from Potsdam, and borrowed a copy of *1984*.

In that first week East Berlin invaded West Berlin, and over the next months the invasion ebbed only little, till the end of January. At the beginning in the East the streets were deserted. In the West the Ossis overloaded the transport system, their Trabis jammed the traffic, they thronged the stores and blocked the paths of West Berliners, who soon began to grumble. 'Guests and fish are alike; after three days both stink.' They welcomed them, but there were suddenly too many all at once. On the Saturday the West Berlin authorities halted bus traffic through the city centre and closed some stations. At the West German border at some points, traffic was backed up for twenty miles.

Soon the lines were endless, stretching back from the border from dawn till past midnight at the new, hurriedly opened crossing points and the suddenly expanded old ones. All day they flowed through the checkpoints, men and women and their children, young and old, families and friends. At the In-validenstrasse crossing, across which in the old days only the occasional foot passengers had gone, men in pairs with brief-cases on grim negotiations between the two cities, long lines of people queued patiently, waiting to show their identification cards for the *Stempel* – orderly Germans, and Easterners to boot, schooled and disciplined for two generations to stand in line. As the days passed the border guards relaxed into their new role, becoming more and more user-friendly. Yet all this still had a strong air of unreality about it. No one had expected it. No one could really believe it was happening.

More crossing points were announced. As the days passed, two parallel lines strung out in both directions at the crossings, one going out, one returning. By 12 November the East German

Ministry of the Interior announced that 4.5 million visitors' visas had been issued, to more than a quarter of the population. By the 15th, 8.8 million had been issued. Up close it looked like the Escher engraving of two parallel lines of figures walking endlessly up and down a stairway that has neither up nor down but both; they seemed to be travellers on a Möbius strip, returning again and again on opposite sides. People crossed several times, just to convince themselves. People were crossing, walking around the block and going back, then coming out again, bolder, going further, staring at everything, queuing for their gift money, spending it, going back with Western rarities. Coming back they brought cassette recorders and radios, plastic bags marked Woolworth and Aldi. West Berlin is East Berlin's KaDeWe. Some carried groceries, some fluffy toys, sweets, disposable nappies, paper tissues, things different and unobtainable in their own country; a man with planks of new wood over his shoulder, another with a set of tools, another with a small computer, another with a new crash helmet, burly men carrying cases of Berliner Kindl beer. And oranges. And bananas.

And more bananas. Everywhere banana skins, Ossis carrying plastic bags of them, boxes and bunches of them. It almost seemed as if this whole massive upheaval was about bananas, to which the Easterners were strangers. Soon the joke was bananas, the Ossis perceived as simple folk easily satisfied. Cartoons appeared, depicting the first people through the Wall slipping on the skins. A West Berlin car went by with a sticker saying D for Deutschland surmounted by a banana and underwritten DEUTSCHE BANANA REPUBLIC, meaning Berlin. In a procession in the East a demonstrator appeared wearing a big cardboard banana on his head and spoons in his ears. It was all one with the old cabaret of Berlin. This was no longer split city, but banana split city, and the Easterners suddenly the butt end of the joke.

There is a history to bananas – or lack of them – in the GDR. Since they represented hard currency they were not imported, except, as it later emerged, for the leadership to enjoy. Many people had never seen one. Oranges were a Christmas luxury. Bananas were a mythical fruit, numbered in the tales of old men. Four weeks before the opening, when there were fierce riots and savage police beatings in East Berlin and other cities, suddenly bananas appeared. On fruit stalls and in shops, especially around the Prenzlauer Berg district where the demonstrations centred, there were abundant piles of bananas and oranges. Vast quantities of both had been shipped in hurriedly in the hope of calming down the population. In English prisons, when a riot threatens, the practice is for the Governor to distribute Mars bars and ten cigarettes to each man. How low the regime valued the aspirations of its citizens, and, since it claimed to have moulded them, how little it valued its own education! Here, as with everything else the regime tried, the ploy backfired. Thousands of tons of bananas were rushed in to the railheads, and an army of trucks assembled to ship the fruit to Berlin. But then truckers from Leipzig and Dresden, hearing where they were taking their loads, rebelled, and insisted on taking them to their own cities. Yet more bananas had to be imported for Berlin.

At Bernauer Strasse the same queues, people coming through with an air of expectation, young men butting each other in fun, families out on an adventure. For the most part they are quiet, calm, visibly nervous, reserved, hesitant, lighting up cigarettes, not yet comprehending that they are free to come and go, like anyone. 'Noch mal,' says one man to another, 'here we go again,' as they wander off to inspect the graffiti on the Western side. Along the street a viewing platform looking into the East gives a view of apartment houses and parked cars across the Wall, and needle-straight in the distance the television tower at Alexanderplatz. Easterners climb the steps to look back into their own country. A little girl runs up the steps, calling down to her mother, still labouring up: 'Mutti,' she says, pointing excitedly across the death strip to the street beyond the Wall, 'that's where we live, that's our apartment.'

Later, at Eberswalder Strasse on the Eastern side of the Bernauer Street crossing, by the Klub der Volkssolidarität, the same faces come back. They carry the same plastic bags of groceries and cardboard boxes of electronics. And oranges and bananas, and fluffy toys and kitsch. Coming through they relax; some giggle, checking the contents of their packages, home again from the great adventure.

Once there was a Bizone, merging those parts of Germany under British and American administration, including Berlin. Then the French Zone joined in to form the Trizone, which eventually became the Federal Republic, distinct from that other

Germany, the German Democratic Republic, forged by Stalin's engineers out of the Russian Zone. Then came division and hostility, then forty years of cold and twenty-eight years of a Wall. When the Wall between the two Berlins was breached, the Trabis poured through, put-putting like lawnmowers, cluttering the streets, parking everywhere about the city. It had become the Trabizone.

Trabis are neat as Prussian gardens, with seat-covers knitted or made of artificial fur, blankets and rugs and crocheted cushions, toys on the back seat, thermos flasks and sandwiches. Though they fall far below Western emission standards, burning a pollutive mix of cheap fuel laced with oil, the West German Government has made exceptions to its stringent rules for Trabant and Wartburg cars. Motoring and insurance organizations were helpful; emergency services were out from the first days repairing broken-down vehicles. Already there were enterprising mechanics cannibalizing broken-down Trabis for parts and repairs, handing out leaflets at the crossing points. Trabi petrol went on sale in the West.

Unreality. Everyone behaves as if drunk, without having to drink. Not everyone is happy. In the West some have mixed feelings, remembering the years of bitter division, and the heartbreak that went with them. There are those in the East whose world has come to an end, who are disoriented by the changes, and who fear for the future. Some are believers, whose ideals have been shattered by the failure and corruption of the leadership. Some are careerists, those whose status and jobs depend on the favour of the Party. Many are loyalists to the GDR in and out of the Party: the unofficial opposition of the church, peace groups, New Forum. By opening the Wall, the East pulled the plug on the revolution, and the future is uncertain. Some already foresee their state running out at its borders, destined to be taken over by the West.

A week into the *Durchbruch* and they are pouring through the checkpoints still, on foot and in Trabis. Fortunately most of them are pouring back again. There are two rates to watch: first the exchange rate, running currently at the exchange booth at Zoo station between 1/8 and 1/12; outside in the street it is roughly the same, though in a few days it has run to 1/20. Many Easterners, responding to the rumour that their currency was about to be devalued, bring their savings over and change them at whatever they can get. Already money is being run through the border. The second rate to watch is the flow of emigrants West. With the Wall open and anyone free to go and return – or not return – 13,600 had decided to stay by the 14th. At Zoo station they wait for trains to the West, with their suitcases and packages. There are many more of them at Bahnhof Friedrichstrasse, waiting for the long-distance trains to Hannover and Hamburg and Cologne. Not all of them are young. Some have children. Some are middle-aged couples. They fill the platform and the stairs, sitting on their bags and parcels and cases, expressionless, waiting, some sleeping.

From the checkpoint at Friedrichstrasse the Western S-Bahn fills with Ossis. The packed trains pour in and out all day, every few minutes. From here it is four stops down to the Zoo, six to Charlottenburg, where there are markets, cheap clothes and shoe outlets, electronics shops, C & A, fast food, bars, sex shows, and an import-export agency, where the Poles gather. Around Charlottenburg seems much to Ossi taste, and is clearly destined as a growth area selling cheap goods. As the train pulls out of Friedrichstrasse they begin looking for the West, which is not yet, staring out at cleared spaces behind wire and Wall and watchtowers, the river and its coal barges. West Berlin begins at Lehrter Bahnhof. On the train they are excited, happy, consulting their maps, the stamps in their passes, looking out at Reichstag and Tiergarten and Zoo. For them it is a great adventure, older folk identifying buildings from the past, marvelling at the changes, the young – anyone under twenty-eight – seeing for the first time the other half of their city.

About the streets they are paler, thinner, from a Westerner's point of view without style. Bright colours are reserved for children, who in the winter are dressed like Christmas trees. Cold in their thin clothes, they have the look of people just released from prison. They keep to themselves, and seem shy. Recognizable in their blue jeans washed and faded with use, they have an old-fashioned look about them. They're not smart. They're not street-smart, not arch, they have no edge and no act, they're just who they are, coming over to take a look. To the West the Ossis are poorer and naïver than anyone thought, and West Berliners are shocked by their taste and their poverty. They see the West as a city of bright lights and windows, full of goods they can't afford, and they clutter the pavements, staring.

They're hesitant, sticking together in groups and couples and families, holding hands, children suddenly in Wonderland, where they can only look. They are recognizable not merely for their pallor and their stonewashed pants and jackets, but also for their hesitance, their reserve. They are not sure they can go, yet, they are not sure in any case if any of this is for them. Since they can't afford much of it, most of it isn't. To begin with, at any rate, they act like strangers abroad. They are reserved, as are most Germans, but more as Germans used to be, before the war, before the west became the West; they are also waking suddenly from the long straitjacket of the GDR, where contact with foreigners, foreign travel, spontaneity and curiosity were forbidden or firmly discouraged. For many of them, these are the habits of a lifetime, and *this* is their style.

They are out on an expedition to the glittering supermarket across the Wall. With their home-perms and home-knits, their make-do-and-mend look, their old-fashionedness challenges Western modes: how have we changed in the meantime, behind our Wall? Old-fashioned or not, Westerners find them ill-mannered and pushy. At the end of the first week the welcome is wearing out. TEST THE WEST, says the ad for West cigarettes. COME TOGETHER, says Stuyvesant, AND LEARN TO LIVE AS FRIENDS.

And in the West is the irritation of dense traffic, disrupted transport, excessive demands on distribution and supply in a city supplied from West Germany, crowded pavements and stores, so many strangers bumping along. The impact of two different and incompatible economic systems with their inconsistent currencies leads rapidly to disruption, and there are opportunities for speculating in the currency, in cigarettes or antiques. In West Berlin some people put on blue jeans and pretend to be Ossis for a free ride and free drinks; others borrow ID cards to get Ossi concessions and free tickets. The event is a boost for the black economy, and for the cheap end of the retail trade. Cut-rate jobs for cash are already being arranged, undermining workers in the West. With the influx of nurses from the East, the nurses of West Berlin, who had negotiated long and hard for a pay rise, suddenly didn't get it. The Ossis begin moonlighting, working off the books, and undercutting the Western labour market. Shoplifting is on the rise. The net result of seeing all this glitter that they can't afford is resentment.

In West Berlin it turns out to be no big deal, though there's plenty of feeling on the matter. West Berliners take most things in their stride; they are cool, cosmopolitan, unfazed. Everyone was so used to the Wall that no one thought it would ever come down, and so when it happened there was, at first, a gasp of disbelief all over the city. They were surprised, stunned, and then for the most part got on with their business. Berliners are used to most things. They had the Nazis, the war, defeat, much to be ashamed of and ponder on, ashes and rubble and economic miracle, and meanwhile forty years of isolation; they have an island mentality with an international outlook. Through the last forty years they have been at the eye of the storm, but they worked out how to conduct difficult and complex negotiations with a sworn enemy whose existence, for most of that time, they did not even recognize. They are skilled at diplomacy, here. If anyone can solve a complex and volatile problem, eyeball to eyeball and gun muzzle to gun muzzle for a very long time, Berliners can. It is the sudden peace that is difficult to cope with. Already as the old scenarios for just this event are dusted off, the future is turning into question marks. What will happen now, to Germany, to both Germanies, both Berlins? It has already occurred to many in the West that the days of showcase Berlin are over; for all the years of the Cold War, Berlin was the West's window in the East, and DM 20 billion per annum in subsidies from the Federal Republic made sure it was decently turned out. Similarly, East Berlin was the GDR's showcase, to East Germans much as West Berlin was to citizens of the Federal Republic: the capital, a little freer, a little better fed and watered, to which labour and materials had long been diverted at the expense of other cities in the GDR. Resentment for this in other Eastern cities, Leipzig especially, accounts in part for the greater determination of protesters there. The *Wende*, that country-wide mass refusal that finally brought down the old regime, was in part the revenge of the provinces on the capital, the Saxons cocking a snook at the Prussians. On the other side, in the West, Berlin may not be needed any more; it may sink into the heartland of the East, and, while at this stage the question of unification had only just been mooted, either way Berlin could lose out. Though it was honourable, it didn't help that the West Berlin mayor, Momper, publicly disputed with Kohl when he came to speak to thousands of

Berliners assembled at the Schöneberg Rathaus the day after the opening. The Berliners were not so crazy for Kohl, who proclaimed, 'We are and will remain one nation,' and with that gesture pushed off the bandwagon. From that moment, unification, or reunification, depending on historical viewpoint and emphasis, was on the agenda. Momper demurred from Kohl's fulsome call. Kohl's supporters were quick to point to the subsidy, the carrot on the stick.

All the same, most people were happy all that first week through, some over the moon, some borne along on a wave of sudden new-found nationalism, the long-denied atavistic urge to embrace their Eastern brothers. Nationalism is a feeling Germans have not been able to have for half a century, after the Nazi nightmare, and all this was a sudden tipsy release into how people normally feel about their countrymen. Suddenly it was all right to be German again. That first weekend, crowds gathered at the Brandenburg Gate, dancing on top of the Wall with glee, and began to attack it with pickaxes and sledgehammers. The border guards turned water-hoses on them, the West Berlin police pulled people back and put up cordons. Soon the Gate became a regular gathering place, like a carnival at a prison wall, with fire-eaters and jugglers and pamphleteers. By Sunday the hammers and chisels of the Wall-peckers had opened cracks along the seams of the slabs, peep-holes to the other side. Everyone wanted a souvenir. In vain the West Berlin police appealed to people to leave the Wall alone. In vain the Eastern guards pointed out it was their Wall. One way or another, it was coming down. The Brandenburg Gate maintained its symbolism as the old heart of Berlin, through which the armies of Napoleon and the Prussians and Hitler had marched, and which the Russians took with the Reichstag as the formal conclusion of hostilities. Around here, the battered statues among the Tiergarten trees still bear the evidence of machine-gun bullets. In the first days after the opening, Schönhuber, ex-SS, leader of the Republicans, began a march with his supporters on the Gate. Crowds shouting 'Nazis raus' forced them to turn back. After 14 November the Gate became a media circus with the arrival on the Eastern side of Volksarmee trucks, which led to speculation that it would open soon. The East stalled and said they were thinking about it, and the crowds built up in expectation, among satellite dishes and cameras and TV trucks, *Wiener* stands and *Glühwein*. But right then Kohl was stalling Krenz on the promise of aid, withholding support, pushing him to go further towards the ultimate goal of free elections. And *Vereinigung*, unification. Krenz's only bargaining chip, at this moment, was the opening of the Gate.

Most West Berliners who went through the Wall to the East did so symbolically, to go there and back again, to reclaim the territory. Most were relaxed about it, and took their time. Others went to buy cheap groceries in the Eastern supermarkets, emptying the shelves and disrupting supply lines in the East. In the West many had their own particular crossing point in mind or in reserve, some bit of the city that had once been part of their lives. Many were waiting for the opening of the Brandenburg Gate, the symbolic hub of the imperial city.

But the shine was wearing off the shilling. The crowds milled back and forth across the old barrier of the Wall, the Trabis and the Wartburgs bumbled through the streets, and the long lines struggled back home to the East like ants with their plunder of boxed ghetto blasters and giant television sets. The *Grenze* was now both an international border and an open frontier, and the spirit of free enterprise part of the traffic. Sellers of biscuits and little foam-rubber toys posted themselves at the crossing points. There were free copies of newspapers and magazines. Some Easterners rapidly learned a dodge or two: mother took the kids through on her pass, claiming DM 100 for each of them, then Dad went through with the kids on his card and claimed again. Some 'lost' their card and reclaimed. Some, seeing their opportunity, turned their Deutschmarks into easy transportables to sell: cheap jewellery – *Schmuck* – pin-up magazines, porn movies. With the proceeds they had working capital to go back again and buy more stock. No doubt there will be millionaires of the future who got their start at the *Durchbruch*. Some will be East German, some will be West German, and some will be Polish.

Westerners found themselves appalled at the materialism of many Easterners: 'All they can talk about is their DM 100 and what they will do with it.' All the same, in the West it was a bonanza for stores selling cheap clothing, electronics, self-serve supermarkets, takeaways, *Sex-Kinos*. In effect the West Germans, giving money to the Easterners to spend, were stimulating their own economy in a set-piece of Keynesian economics.

The big stores didn't do so well, their prices out of reach. KaDeWe was packed, but they didn't come to buy. Through the Mercedes showroom windows on the Ku'damm, Ossis stared at the cars they could only dream of. One couple went to the Bristol Kempinski, the swellest hotel in town, and blew their money on coffee and cakes.

The second weekend, ten days after the opening, Ossis were coming through as if they'd always come, every weekend, to the West. For those coming a second time there was no greetings money, and most of them were skint in anyone's currency. At Friedrichstrasse young men with sleeping-bags and rolled blankets sang football songs, cans of beer in their pockets: 'Here we go, here we go, here we go.' They had learned this mode from the manners of the football crowd. 'We are the people,' they had proclaimed at the demonstrations, suddenly realizing their power to dethrone the powerful, the ultimate refusal of Vaclav Havel's powerless. Mostly they were good-humoured, out for a night on the town on what little money they had, content to curl up in a corner of the Europa Centre and sleep till the morning, waking to stare at the water-clock measuring out its coloured hours, whatever the time. In town they swirled about the busy noisy spaces, inspecting everything and each other, somehow strangely oblivious of Westerners. They seemed to resist queuing, and at the bus-stops stood all over the pavements, blocking the passage; free at last from their own rigid and straitlaced country, where they queued all the time for everything, and life was reduced to the business of waiting a long time for not much. Perhaps this was how they demonstrated their freedom.

All weekend it went on, the traffic a long slur, movement impossible, the howl of ambulances cutting through all. Too much excitement. Too many people. Too many heart attacks waiting for the train at Zoo. After three days, guests and bad fish. Westerners who had ecstatically welcomed once-lost relatives from the East were cooler the second time around; their guests were poor, and dependent on their hosts. 'Socialist paupers.' The realization began to sink in: the Ossis were broke and their greetings money didn't go far, as they themselves soon discovered, and they were fervent materialists. At night they were still wandering the promised land, staring into shop windows, even those in darkness, into bookstores and jewellers and showrooms, inspecting videos and stereos and cinema posters and motorcycles and cars on the street and the neon display lights. Saturday night in the dream city, broke. Emboldened, drinkless, some wandered in and out of the Irish pub, listening to the music, where the band played 'I'm a believer', 'Ain't gonna study war no more', and 'When the saints'.

Down in the south-west corner of the city the long-deserted Glienicke Bridge had been open for a week now, and was continually packed with cars and foot travellers. When it opened there was a five-mile tailback to Potsdam. Once Easterners and Westerners were confined here to their own sides of the water, and the Russian and East German flags fluttered in the wind, and the Russian sentry in his glass booth stared at nothing. All that had changed. Potsdam, the old imperial parkland of summer palaces and private royal residences, of gardens and vineyards and orchards, was suddenly accessible again to West Berliners, and to Potsdam and people living west of West Berlin, suddenly the city was open. From the bridge's opening that first weekend there began a pincer movement as the city was invaded from both sides. Via the S-Bahn from Wannsee to Friedrichstrasse it was a short cut for Easterners from one side to the other. All Sunday the crowds flowed over the bridge in both directions, the cars of East and West, and buses from both sides crossing the bridge to turn round.

Elsewhere, the exodus through the other borders ceased; through Czechoslovakia it slowed to a trickle, through Hungary it stopped completely. Here, it just went on, the poor saints marching in.

6

HISTORY ON FAST FORWARD

At Potsdamer Platz, people pour through both ways and the lines of cars in both directions move slowly. The souvenir kiosks and single-storey shops near by that are all that remain of what was once metropolis haven't put up the prices of their T-shirts and toy bears, and they are supplemented now by people with a few chips from the Wall laid out on a plastic bag or a jacket on the ground. The British, in whose sector this is, have set up a canteen.

At the Brandenburg Gate, British Military Police in their Incident Control van, showing the flag, sergeant, corporal, officer, padre. They don't know anything either. The media circus is still growing, with daily rumours of the Gate's imminent opening. The world's press are waiting, cameras in high jibs and tall scaffolding, bored cameramen staring into the East, where nothing happens, an Eastern television crew staring back, and the guards looking confused. The satellite dishes are being fine-tuned for the historic moment that doesn't come. The crowds are constant, along by the Reichstag and down to the river, all day every day flashbulbs pop and there's yet more champagne. Coaches in the Reichstag car park are from Holland, France, Denmark, disgorging their passengers to join the carnival.

As the news from Berlin rippled outward, dousing everyone in instant history, tourists began pouring in, from the rest of Germany and from Europe and America and Japan, just to see, pick up a souvenir, take pictures, live briefly in a moment of significance. 1989 was a boom year for Berlin tourism, and in the first week after the opening British Airways carried 30 per cent more passengers to Berlin than at the same time a year before. By the Wall there was a fair amount of strutting by those who felt their system vindicated. The spirit of free enterprise was soon in evidence with *Wiener* stands, beer, *Glühwein*, Coca-Cola. Souvenir-sellers sold bits of Wall, and everywhere the Wall-peckers were busy with hammers and chisels, hacking the Wall to bits, and the cracks between the slabs widened. The West Berlin police at first chased off the peckers, and sometimes confiscated their tools. The Eastern guards objected, pointing out that it was still an international frontier and the property of the GDR. Over the weeks to the year's end they relaxed, and the persistent Wall-peckers returned.

Die Mauerspechte: the Wall-peckers. There's a stall selling badges of a woodpecker hammering on the Wall. The woodpecker just happens to be the official West German bird of the year. In the East there are other woodpeckers, the *Wendehälse*, the neck-turners, so called because they are like the birds that can turn their necks instantly at 180 degrees to face in the opposite direction. In Bulgaria, where after thirty-five years of power Zhivkov fell on 10 November, just as the Wall opened, such people are called *sunflowers*. They are the former functionaries and apparatchiks who are bailing out of the Party, suddenly finding a conscience. At a huge demonstration in Alexanderplatz just after the opening, Christa Wolf spoke of them as 'the greatest obstacles to trust in the new policies', so smoothly were they turning on their heels to support the demand for democracy and dialogue, and profit from the *Wende*, Krenz's phrases to describe the change of direction promised by the new government. 'We are dreaming with our reason wide awake,' she declared, describing the new fervour of discussion that had broken out everywhere in the East. Bars were suddenly meeting places, the habit of silence suddenly broken. What the thinkers wanted was a reformed GDR, socialist and democratic, the other Germany, following a 'third way' between capitalism and communism. Meanwhile what the workers wanted, sauntering down the glittering Ku'damm while the lights flashed *Schmuck*, *Sex*, *Disco*, *Mercedes-Benz*, were electronics, oranges, Western fruits.

Modrow's proposed reforms, the 'change of direction', were a loosening of rigid central planning, some limited private enterprise with joint ventures with the West, an independent judiciary, limits on the Stasi, commissions of inquiry into abuses, freedom of association and assembly. It was not yet a promise of free elections, or an end to the Party's monopoly of power, but in retrospect it was the thin edge of the wedge. Nevertheless, in those heady days East Berlin was suddenly busy and talkative, some calling for retribution, some for concrete reforms. Round table discussions between opposition groups and the Government were gaining momentum, and there was everywhere the certainty of change, the confidence that the old system was dead. But most of the voices being heard were not yet calling for one Germany.

November became December, and the crowds went on pouring through the border with no let-up, adding to the Christmas crush. In the first two weeks of the opening there were 5 million visitors. Eleven million travel visas had been issued. The exodus West continued, no doubt encouraged by Christmas. So far, 300,000 had left the country. The wonder was that it was a mild winter; had the winter been severe, how many more thousands would have fled to the West, if only in the hope of keeping warm? Between the two Germanies there was still much goodwill, extended at any rate until the end of the year. But in West Berlin the honeymoon was quickly over; it lasted perhaps a week, as the realization sank in that this invasion was to run and run. Easterners took temporary and part-time work, commuting back and forth across the border. They were willing to take on anything for cash. In the East the addresses of illegal employment agencies in West Berlin were for sale. Ossis were cheap and compliant, with no tradition of industrial action and in no position to complain, and as Germans they didn't need a work permit. They placed ads in *Volksblatt Berlin* and *Zweite Hand* offering themselves as bricklayers, painters, tilers, cleaners. Some called in sick on their jobs in East Berlin and went West for the day. Since in West Berlin everyone is allowed to earn DM 470 a month tax-free and free of social insurance contributions, their wages, translated into Ostmarks on the black market, represented a mighty sum. Even the prostitutes in West Berlin were complaining that Eastern whores did it for half the price and because they didn't know much yet about Aids, without a condom. But for now there was a feeling that nothing would happen till the year's end, and that the period between the opening and the solstice was an interregnum. West Berliners were holding their breath until the New Year, when they were promised the party of the century at the Brandenburg Gate.

But this was no limbo, and events followed each other in rapid succession. In the East mass demonstrations continued. On 18 November, 30,000 protested in Dresden, 50,000 in Leipzig. There were banners calling for Krenz's resignation, for the resignation of the Party leadership, and for free elections. In Berlin protesters demanded an end to the Party's leading role, and called for the trials of corrupt officials. The GDR tottered on under its new government, formed of a coalition of the SED and the former block parties, each of them acting with degrees of growing independence. There were meetings throughout East German cities to discuss the problems of ecology, the Stasi, how to establish democracy. In these, officials were often reviled for their lifestyles and mistakes. Within a few weeks the GDR had witnessed the emergence of the beginnings of a national identity founded in struggle and success. But this was quickly dissipated by the opening of the Wall and the lure of the West. Within a few weeks more, the cry that had shifted from demands for travel to demands for a new government was to change again into demands for unification.

Meanwhile the economy was decrepit, and the exodus continued to drain the workforce. Productivity was running at 40 per cent of West German levels. And with the new Government committed to cutting subsidies, prices would surely rise. The condition of the economy, and the precarious position of the Government, and the increasing shakiness of the GDR itself, fostered insecurity. Those who now took advantage of the open border to resettle in the West came through in the first days at an average of 1,500 per day, but as insecurity increased in the East this began to rise towards 2,000. In a year that could be a million. On 6 November, concern had already been expressed in Bonn about the continuing tide of refugees. Before the Wall opened West Germany was already severely short of housing, and had 1.9 million unemployed. Among the Ossis unemployment rose; many had the same problems as their predecessors getting their Eastern qualifications recognized. It turned out to be not so easy in the West, in the elbow society. Easterners complained of the coldness, and after the opening some, though few, went back. Many were gullible. At a demonstration in Kreuzberg there were slogans like THE FREEDOM YOU HAVE IN MIND IS THE FREEDOM OF THE BUNDESBANK.

In the West the camps were full, and all over West Germany

schools, colleges, offices, warehouses, factories, barracks, bunkers, transport containers, barges and ships were being hurriedly converted into emergency camps. The pressure on services, and the diversion of resources from other sectors, strained social and welfare services beyond their limits. Now, with the influx, they were swamped. The refugees were too many to absorb and, it turned out, had different habits and attitudes to work. Most Westerners regarded Easterners as lazy. Their society had never rewarded initiative; they were unmotivated and fatalistic. Most came with a high expectation of quickly finding work and a flat; most were disappointed. They missed the East, for all its desolation; life was calmer and slower there, with a camaraderie they did not find in the West.

In Berlin Westerners and Easterners grew used to each other. Some normality began to settle into the proceedings. Trabis, at first a novelty, became a nuisance and a hazard, for their pollutive smoke, distinctly not *bleifrei* in a lead-free West, for their parking habits (all over the pavement), their numbers, their slowness on the autobahns, and for the often abrupt habits of their drivers, used to rough and empty roads in the East and given to sudden stops and U-turns. There were reports of Trabis burned out by angry Westerners. In the months after the opening there was a sharp rise in road accidents. At the same time in the West the cult of the Trabi grew; 90,000 went West in 1989, and the Western price rose from DM 300 to DM 1,000. On a twelve-year waiting list in the East, they were immediately available for hard currency.

Made of fibreglass, when disposed of in the incinerator Trabis explode into noxious gases. Available in three shades, pale grey, blue, and beige, they have a two-cylinder 595 c.c. engine and three-brake horsepower. Some are multicoloured, where panels and wings have been replaced. On the level, without passengers, they hold a steady 60 km per hour. Even the latest model, the 601, is noisy and uncomfortable. On the other hand they are relatively cheap, fairly reliable and easy to maintain. The other East German car, the Wartburg, a two-stroke three-cylinder model, was intended as a family car. Both are environmentally disastrous. **Durch Deutschland mit Trabant.** But on the other hand they do say the Trabi is the quietest car on the road; because it's so small you drive with your ears between your knees, so you're not troubled by the engine at all.

In the week after the opening, the East German press for the first time published Western television listings, and maps of West Berlin. Formerly, maps of the West had been whited out, the territory of dragons. The Eastern media was growing bolder, after years fulfilling its uncritical function of praising the leadership and the country's achievements. By 20 December there were twenty-two crossing points, and the traffic seemed to increase with each new opening. West Berlin imported buses and crews from other cities, and buses from Kassel and Kiel were soon plying the streets. West Berlin became a crossroads for Easterners who had formerly had to go all round the city to reach the other side. West Berliners complained of being locked in to Berlin by the traffic on the transit routes. For the West, the East began to open up: newspapers carried articles about holidays in the GDR, on the theme of 'our beautiful country'. With DM Westerners were rich in the East, and the Easterners were soon complaining of their displacement. In the imagination at any rate, Westerners began to reclaim the East. In the East a shortage of doctors, caused by their exodus to the West, would be solved by many of the qualified doctors in West Berlin, who couldn't get jobs (no doubt because of the Easterners), working internships in East Berlin. There were fast-developing communications at all levels within the city, between the police forces, between emergency services, between the transport and postal authorities and the offices of the two mayors. From the beginning the practical Berliners took a positive attitude by hastening to cope with crisis.

Meanwhile, at the border, currency-runners were busy. Refusing to devalue the Ostmark from its official – and ludicrous – 1/1 exchange rate, it was open season for speculators. Germans, Poles and Turks were running money back and forth across the border, exchanging Ostmarks for between 10 and 20 to 1 on the black market. It was their activities that forced the rate up, so that in one week the Ostmark was devalued by 50 per cent. Hearing rumours of a currency devaluation, Easterners were bringing their savings over to change for Deutschmarks and smuggling the proceeds back into the East. Some were caught, and the cash seized; in the first two weeks after the opening there were reports of as much as 100,000 Ostmarks confiscated. Rumour was busy. In the East there were queues at banks to withdraw savings and exchange the DM 15 every Easterner was allowed to change per year. There were more queues outside antique shops, jewellers and domestic equipment stores, as Easterners turned their money into durables, buying washing machines and television sets, anything that would hold a value. On the border there were seizures of cigarettes and other goods. Some changed their welcome money into Ostmarks at 1/20 and took them back, Ostmark-rich. All these devalued marks re-entering the GDR began wrecking the currency, and there was fear of consequent inflation and of the flight of East German savings into Western goods. There were at this time an estimated 150 billion Ostmarks in banks or tin boxes. Billions were believed to be going illegally over the border. Some smuggled subsidized Eastern goods to the West, and the electronics traffic worked both ways. Antiques were favourite. Porn and pin-up mags went over in bales. The Poles, well established before the opening in cross-border trading of goods bought cheaply in the East and sold in the West, were now emulated by East Germans. On 24 November New Forum appealed to East Germans not to join in the selling out of the GDR through speculation and smuggling and taking jobs in West Berlin. By that date, in the space of two weeks, almost 3 billion marks had left the country, and there was every opportunity for a flourishing black labour market as Easterners took part-time jobs in the West. Westerners regularly shopped in the East, at huge discounts: to buy shoes, to get a suit made, to go to the beauty parlour, many Westerners now took a ride East. The result of all this activity in a centralized economy played havoc with the distribution system, never efficient in the first place. The Deutschmark was becoming a parallel currency, much preferred to the small proletarian notes of the GDR, and the Christmas-tree coinage they referred to as *shrapnel*.

By the end of November, measures were introduced to control the illicit traffic. The sale of subsidized goods was to be restricted to East Germans on production of an identity card. Customs controls were to be stepped up, and about this time the blue customs uniforms became more noticeable than the green of the guards on the crossing points. At the same time restrictions were placed on Polish travellers, who in future were not allowed to leave transit routes or break their train journeys across the GDR. At the same time in the West, Poles were being singled out at customs posts, and some turned back.

Already freed of travel restrictions, the Poles had taken to travelling central Europe, exchanging tyres for watches and watches for shirts and shirts for tinned peaches, exchanging currency for currency and living out of suitcases and station lockers and the backs of battered cars. There were other nationalities, notably the Hungarians, but the Poles were the rough riders of the long-distance entrepreneurial trade. They say a Hungarian last into a revolving door will be first out, but of the Poles they say stop one and he'll have at least a dozen pairs of shoes on him. They took a lot of hassle, but they kept on coming. And they were hungry, in Poland. In the West they took jobs, any jobs. Up to 10,000 Poles crossed through East Germany every day, most of them trading in something, back and forth in their long peregrinations through the currencies. In West Berlin they had established the Polenmarkt, originally by the Potsdamer Platz, its stalls plastic sheets on the ground or the bonnets of cars. They sold anything: butter, sausage, salami, shoes, sugar, sweets, flour, cheap clothes, dodgy digitals, domestic articles, cigarettes, booze, sometimes an ornament that looked as if it had just come off the mantelpiece. Later, because food sales broke EC regulations, they were barred. Eventually they were moved off by the police and the space was fenced. For a while then they were everywhere else, all over West Berlin, Poles in their cars looking for a place to stop and set up shop, women signalling between the trees in the Tiergarten. Eventually they re-established the market behind the state library and, following complaints about the use of the library's toilets, were given a couple of Portakabins. In such tiny ways, recognition was established.

Opened at last, the GDR began to reveal its dirty secrets. Tales began to surface of the corruption of the Eastern leadership, of the working methods of the Stasi, and the extent of pollution in the East. After 1956 and the Hungarian uprising, the leadership had removed itself from Berlin to villas in splendid isolation near the village of Wandlitz, half an hour north of Berlin. A wall, painted green to blend with the forest, patrolled by armed Stasi and surveyed by video cameras, concealed the lifestyle of government members, more country gentleman than Marxist–Leninist. There the shops were stocked with Western goods, and there was access to Inter shops accepting only Western money. They enjoyed personal servants, many of them

Stasi employees, chauffeur-driven limos, Western movies (and porn, some said), Western electronic gadgetry and satellite dishes, and a high standard of living compared with what the rest of the population queued for. Fresh fruit was said to have been flown in every day, and presumably the Honeckers were no strangers to the banana.

A couple of weeks after the Wall opened, it was announced that the former inhabitants were to be moved out in February, and that the place was to become an area for retired people. Krenz was reported to have moved out of his Wandlitz villa to a modest home in Pankow, and appeared on TV *en famille*, living just like everyone else. No one was impressed. Elsewhere around the country there were hunting lodges and private dachas provided by the government for itself, there were luxury holidays abroad, and expensive surgery in Switzerland. On 15 November Honecker's hunting grounds in the forest, posted 'for military manoeuvres', were abolished. In the Baltic he had a private island, Vilm, 'reserved for scientific research'. He was said to have spent 2 million marks repairing the harbour, and to have shipped in sand for a private beach. His house there had underfloor heating, marble bathrooms, tennis courts, a sauna, a satellite dish, and he travelled there by helicopter. What galled the Easterners were the years of privation and shortages while they were being preached the virtues of austerity and struggle and socialist morality by a leadership sealed into its own, luxurious lifestyle. They were, it was said, 'a cheated angry generation'. The leadership had regarded the state's resources as its own.

On 24 November, investigations were opened into the activities of Honecker, Mittag, and others. Mittag had been expelled from the Party after losing his seat in the Politburo on 18 October. Honecker was said to be too ill to make a statement. On 28 November the trade union leadership resigned, under accusations of fraud. They had set up and enjoyed a DM 40 million 'sanatorium' equipped with bars, saunas, and barbecues. At the end of the month Honecker was stripped of immunity from prosecution and criminal investigations were begun into his abuse of power. New Forum activists filed suit on charges of breach of public trust. On 1 December the Volkskammer heard details of the corruption of the former leadership, from state-funded hunting lodges to Swiss bank accounts containing an estimated 100 billion marks. It was reported that a large part of the housing budget had been used for providing luxury accommodation for relatives and children of high-ranking Politburo members; in some cases the houses were sold to third parties. In 1988 the upkeep of private hunting grounds used up 10 per cent of the forestry and land protection budget.

Then came the defection of Alexander Schalck-Golodkowski, previously state secretary in the Economics Ministry, where he had been in charge of procuring hard currency for the GDR. Crowds had begun raiding the hunting lodges and private preserves of the former leadership, and Stasi complexes. In Rostock they discovered an arms factory, IMEs, which they claimed exported arms to the Middle East, South Africa, and Latin America. Responsible for it was Schalck-Golodkowski, who was alleged to have salted away profits in Switzerland and Austria. His position gave him control of foreign currency reserves, and he had formed shell companies and fronts to carry out arms deals and siphon off profits, put at 5–12 billion marks. Called upon by the Volkskammer to account for the Swiss bank accounts, he was in Bonn negotiating the formation of a currency fund with the West, and didn't come back. He was stripped of his posts, and a warrant for his arrest was issued. He was said to have fled the country, and rumoured to be in Israel, the Bahamas, or Colombia. He was in fact in West Berlin, where he gave himself up to the police on 6 December, claiming to have returned DM 60 million to the GDR. The West Berlin police held him in jail for a week but, finding nothing with which to charge him, let him go. It was unclear whether he still had access to the foreign accounts.

On 7 December the deputy director of the Communist Party's foreign exchange agency, a subordinate of Schalck-Golodkowski, was detained on suspicion of diverting, with his boss, DM 200 million abroad. Together they had procured DM 1.4–1.7 billion, but were alleged to have made up to DM 10 billion through a network of cover firms and deals in the West, and to have channelled these back to East Berlin, to the Party, to the West German Communist Party, to the secret police and to individual politicians. It was also their task to procure luxury Western foodstuffs and consumer goods for the leadership. Schalck-Golodkowski was said to have sold items from East German museums to the West, and even to have had cobblestones taken up from streets and sold for hard currency.

On 4 December Mittag and Tisch were arrested, with others, and charged with 'misuse of power and abuse of what rightfully belongs to the people'. They and Honecker were expelled from the Party. On the 6th Honecker was put under house arrest. The chief public prosecutor resigned. There were a number of arrests, including Wolfgang Vogel, the civil rights lawyer who had freed many from the GDR, under suspicion of criminal blackmail. Mielke, already under investigation, had left only empty safes in his office. It was said that he had rigged the results of football matches in favour of his favourite team, Dynamo. There were even rumours of the leadership dealing in cocaine. Mielke's two former deputies resigned and seventeen top Stasi officers were dismissed. On the 9th criminal proceedings were announced against Honecker, Stoph, Mielke and three others; their homes were searched and they were arrested, charged with inflicting grave damage on the economy and enriching themselves through abuse of office. Honecker, still too ill to be questioned, was put under house arrest in Wandlitz.

As these revelations came out, Party membership fell further. Almost the last act of the Party had been to open the Wall and announce moderate reforms, and thereafter it became less and less of a force. The rank and file were confused and angry, and felt betrayed by the leadership. Some stayed on, determined to be part of the reform process. Others left. According to the Party daily, *Neues Deutschland*, 200,000 quit in the two months following the *Wende*. The 2-million-strong FDJ was also losing members, and announced that it would break away and form its own party. The initiative was now being taken up by the Party rank and file, furious at the revelations of corruption. The Party was waiting for its congress in mid-December, but to most East Germans the antics of the Party were increasingly irrelevant. The new government had its hands tied, and could do little. Kohl still refused to deal with Krenz, and dangled the possibilities of cash injections against the promise of free elections. There were resignations of top officials, suicides, accusations of corruption and ballot-rigging on all sides. On 15 December the editor of *Neues Deutschland* was sacked. There were resignations by, among others, some church leaders: the bishop of Greifswald, who was a friend of Honecker's, resigned. The GDR was undergoing a thorough house-cleaning.

Mittag, formerly in charge of the economy, was held responsible for its wreck. The figures having been fiddled for years, no one now knew what the real figures were. In charge while Honecker was ill in hospital, Mittag had done nothing about the mounting crisis. At their sacking on 8 November, Stoph had blamed Honecker and Mittag. The knives were out. The search for scapegoats and the desire for revenge was evident; the people of the East were hungry for their lost years.

But no one trusted the Modrow Government, though he himself earned a great deal of respect. He too named Mittag as responsible. But his cabinet included eight members of the former regime, and all were members of the former block parties who had submitted to the Communists for forty years. There were few who were clean enough for the role of honest broker. The civil service, the judiciary, and the ministries that served the old regime were still in place. As were the Stasi.

Meanwhile the Stasi were brushing up their image. They were downgraded from a ministry to a department, and it was announced that their numbers would be cut. They would be known in future as the Office for National Security. They would concentrate on fighting terrorism, Nazism, and drug-running. As a gesture they would make available film of the Dresden riots on 4 October, when the refugee trains to the West were besieged. The commission set up to investigate allegations of corruption and misuse of office and other charges against the former leadership targeted Mielke, boss of the Stasi for thirty-two years, as a prime suspect. Mielke's speech to the Volkskammer before he was deposed, in which he described the Stasi as 'sons and daughters of the working class', concluded 'Ich liebe doch alle' (I love you all), illustrating how out of touch with the world he was. And as the media loosened up, news came through of Stasi methods. On 25 November officials admitted that torture was used, but as *ad hoc* police excess and not as an organized system. Their methods included sleep deprivation, prolonged interrogation, and isolation. However, tales of ill-treatment and torture began to surface. Former political prisoners from Leipzig claimed they had been beaten and forced to handle chemical waste without protective clothing. Women from a village near Karl-Marx-Stadt told how the Stasi had locked them into their factory during a strike only a month before, and then stripped them naked. Stasi regularly threw people out of their homes and took them over for their own use. There were reports of ill-treatment in prison, of filth, rats, and cockroaches. From Halle it was reported that troublesome prisoners and those who failed to fulfil their quotas were sent into solitary confinement, where some were chained to the wall on tiptoe for three days at a stretch, one hour on, one hour off. In the violent demonstrations of the weekend of 7 October, when many were beaten in the streets, 3,500 people had been arrested; in Stasi prisons and barracks many of them were beaten, young women were stripped, and many were made to stand facing the wall with their hands above their heads for hours. Many Easterners had good reasons to fear and loathe the Stasi, and now the move was on to get rid of them. But they were persistent. Not till the middle of January was it announced that telephone tapping and mail censorship had ceased. But by then the crowd had taken matters into their own hands, and invaded Stasi-Zentrale. For now they were calling for the Stasi to be put to work in factories, to replace the workers who had fled.

On 20 November the Monday night demonstration in Leipzig numbered 100,000, demanding reform, free elections, the resignation of Krenz and the rest, and in support of New Forum which, since applying for legal status on 8 November, had collected 200,000 signatures. All of East Germany was now a huge round table, with animated debate on all sides. Krenz appeared on television to defend himself. The sticking point now lay in the number of the old guard retained in the Politburo and the Central Committee, and clearly no decisions would be taken till the Party congress in mid-December. Kohl continued stalling, pushing Krenz to commit himself to free elections and a market economy; Krenz, fearing that to give way on either would spell the end of the GDR, prevaricated. Kohl was hoping Krenz would be booted out at the Party congress, and clearly had no desire to subsidize Eastern socialism, or be contaminated by association with Krenz. The demonstrations continued. The exodus continued. The demand for fundamental change continued. The Government made vague promises of elections in a year's time, in autumn 1990 or the spring of 1991. Neither the embattled SED nor the newly independent block parties nor the new parties just forming were ready for elections. On 22 November the Party proposed round table talks between government and opposition groups to discuss the implementation of reform and free elections. In the months that followed, the round table meetings throughout East Germany were an important conduit of ideas between Government and people, though as time went by they became irrelevant to the proceedings, a talking shop discussing change in a country that was fast disappearing. Kohl kept up the pressure, postponing a visit to East Berlin until January, after the Party congress. While Western banks and businesses were still hesitant, waiting for the East to make up its mind about the introduction of market forces, shares in West German construction firms were soaring within two weeks of the Wall's opening. Clearly someone foresaw a building bonanza in the East. In the West the crowds and the media were still concentrated on the Brandenburg Gate. What for the East was a matter of the life and death of the state was for the West largely a media event.

But the Party was losing the struggle, deprived of its power bases and deserted by its members. Krenz was continually under pressure, suspected for his background and his congratulation of the Chinese leadership. On 24 November he conceded to opposition demands that the Party renounce its leading role. An East German opinion poll, the first in the GDR, found most support for Modrow, derisory support for Krenz, but showed that 83 per cent of those polled wanted the GDR to remain a socialist state. At this stage the demand for unification was muted; the target was the Party, and the main demand free elections. On the 27th the Greens and Free Democrats set up as political parties, bringing the number of opposition groups to nine, with New Forum the largest. Independent groups were urging the Government to bring forward the round table talks, which first took place on 7 December. On 30 November, 20,000 Party members demonstrated in Leipzig and Erfurt against corruption in the Party. Wolfgang Berghofer, the reformist mayor of Dresden, revealed that in early October, in the Dresden riots, tanks had already rolled up as demonstrators battled with police outside the railway station. He and Modrow had mediated to avoid bloodshed. Once again, a Tiananmen solution had been close.

In the first week of December the workers' militias were disbanded, and their weapons handed in. The army was to be reduced, and in mid-December Manfred Gerlach, Prime Minister in succession to Krenz and leader of the Liberals, proposed that the GDR take leave of Prussian military traditions and abandon the goose step, modelled on the Russian rather than the Nazi style, a difference clear only to a connoisseur of military marching. Everywhere Citizens' Committees, Vigilance Groups, and Citizens' Initiatives were forming to investigate the past and discuss the future. And all through the GDR the Stasi were under pressure, as demonstrators identified Stasi buildings and attacked them. It was said they were getting rid of their files. On 4 December in Leipzig demonstrators occupied the Stasi headquarters to prevent files being destroyed. On the same day in Erfurt a crowd surrounded the Stasi building and tried to force its way inside. When representatives of opposition groups got in they found that all the files had been removed. They locked up the staff while a search was made. There were rumours that attempts had been made to fly the documents to Romania, still at that time Ceauşescu's fief, but ground crews had refused to fuel the plane. In Dresden there were claims that staff had been injured and threatened, their homes surrounded and windows broken. In Suhl tear gas was fired at demonstrators trying to break into the Stasi building; they were later allowed in. Near Gera citizens forced their way into a bunker where they discovered a communications centre belonging to the Stasi; truck-loads of files had been taken out of the bunker on previous days, and apparently burned.

On 6 December the army warned of chaos and anarchy, claiming that crowds were attacking armouries and military installations, and called on troops to protect bases. But there were no reports of such attacks, nor of attacks on Russian troops. The warning caused fear of a coup; out there was the army, under the direct control of the Soviet army, who outnumbered them three to one. There were the police and Alert units, 12,000 strong. Movements of particular regiments, the Feliks Dzierzynski Brigade in particular, named for the founder of the Soviet *Cheka*, forerunner of the KGB, were watched with interest. Back on 17 November, when the Stasi were demoted from a ministry to the Office for National Security, 1,200 Stasi troops had been sent south to work in the open-cast lignite mines. Among them were 300 men from the Feliks Dzierzynski Brigade transferred from Berlin to near Leipzig. But there were those who saw this as a blind, pointing out that the men were new recruits, conscripts volunteering for better pay on a three-year contract. 30,000 conscripts were released from military service to work in understaffed factories. Everywhere, it was observed, the Communists were still in control of the administration and the economy; many officials had left the Party but not their jobs. It was said the newly emergent SPD was becoming a home for SED members. There was fear of a comeback.

At the beginning of December, prisoners demonstrated with strikes and hunger strikes against prison conditions, and the Government granted amnesty for all prisoners with sentences of less than three years. Some 8,000 were released before Christmas and as many again after. About 1,000 prisoners not affected by the amnesty were given a general pardon, most of them political but among them hardened criminals, and of those released many went immediately West. In the East 135 were quickly back in custody. All who had been convicted of flight were released. Wolfgang Schnur, who had defended many political prisoners, said at the time: 'My life's work has been fulfilled.' He was reported to have lost his marriage, survived threats to debar him and suffered discrimination against himself and his family: he described it as 'a very lonely struggle, but we did it'. But with Schnur, the truth, when it emerged, suggested otherwise.

At the end of November a group of thirty artists and intellectuals including Stefan Heym, Wolfgang Berghofer and Christa Wolf issued an appeal 'For our country', endorsing demands for freedom and justice and warning of absorption by the West, foreseeing that the West would attach such conditions to aid 'that a sale of our material and moral values will begin, and sooner or later the GDR will be taken in by the Federal Republic'. Sooner, as it happened. They urged the continuation of the struggle for a democratic socialist GDR.

The media turned investigative, and the population scented victory. On 2 December East German television showed Krenz being booed off stage as he tried to explain to a crowd his new role as a reformer. The next day thousands of Party members hooted him outside SED headquarters in Berlin and called for him to resign. On that day, a Sunday, thousands formed a human chain across the country. There were reports of strikes in support of the demands for democracy.

On 4 December Krenz was stripped of Party power. Party reformers convened a special session forcing the resignation of the Politburo and the Central Committee, disbanding the Party leadership. A steering committee was set up to manage the affairs of the Party till the congress: it was stacked with reformers, none of them former Politburo members, most of them from Dresden, and included Markus Wolf, the former spymaster, and Wolfgang Berghofer. Two days later, on the 6th, Krenz stood down as head of state and chairman of the Defence Council after the five coalition parties withdrew support. He was replaced by the Liberal Democrat leader, Manfred Gerlach.

But the demand was switching to unification with the West. On 6 December, workers in Plauen staged a two-hour strike and threatened an all-out stoppage on the 15th unless the Government organized a nationwide referendum on unification. On the 12th the Leipzig demonstration was huge, estimated at 150,000, with widespread demands for unification. There were hundreds of red, black and gold West German flags, the same flag as that of the East but without the hammer and compass motif. The crowd sang *'Deutschland Deutschland über alles'*, and banners proclaimed DEUTSCHLAND EINIG VATERLAND, and REUNIFICATION = PROSPERITY. At the front of the procession were between 300 and 400 neo-Nazis, some of whom had travelled from the West, and there were clashes between factions. Schönhuber's Republicans were active. West German gun sales were increasing. With an open border, contacts between rightists were being established. The thirst for revenge continued. In Dresden there were reports of a man dragged from his car to cries of 'Communist swine', and a tow rope put round his neck. They would have hanged him but for someone in the crowd who persuaded them to stop.

By now an estimated half a million had resigned from the Party. There were more resignations, including the abdication of the district council of Rostock. On 7 December the first round table talks began, and voted for elections on 6 May and the disbanding of the Stasi. On the 12th the Stasi were abolished. It had at first been proposed to replace them with an Office of National Security, an organization whose acronym spelt Nasi; this idea was dropped, and now the security services were to be disbanded. This, it turned out, took some time. Among the Stasi hierarchy there were suicides. Officers were attacked, and in many places agents were described as living in fear of reprisal.

The Party congress was brought forward to 8 December. It

convened with 2,700 delegates, and elected Gregor Gysi Chairman of the Party, abolishing the post of General Secretary. The Politburo was abolished, and the Party planned to change its name. In SED headquarters staff were told to take a holiday till they knew whether they still had jobs. The offices of senior figures were sealed to ensure no documents were removed. A week later, at the reconvened congress, the Party renamed itself the SED (PDS), later PDS (SED), then PDS, the Party of Democratic Socialism.

Gysi, a forty-one-year-old lawyer with a clean record of defending dissidents, had helped legalize New Forum and had personally accompanied back into the country some of its members who had formerly been expelled. A reformer, born in East Berlin, he had studied law at the Humboldt. He said he looked forward to a socialist and independent GDR, neither Stalinist nor monopoly capitalist, and, opposing reunification, said it was playing with fire and would bring with it a wave of nationalism. But the unification bandwagon was gathering speed, and with it the visible presence of the right at demonstrations around the country. Stefan Heym, a signatory to the appeal 'For our country', was reported to be chastened by events; the cry of '*Vaterland*' reminded him of the cries he had fled when he had quit Germany under the Nazis. So far there had been no deaths, and the bloodless revolution rolled on. But it was revealed that back on 7 November, the Politburo had rejected by one vote a proposal to put the army on the streets. In a state of near revolt, high-ranking officers loyal to the hardliners had put troops and tanks on alert, and issued ammunition. For the third time in a month, bloodshed had been close.

Honecker was reported unwilling to admit mistakes. In a statement to the control commission investigating his conduct, he said, 'I've somewhat deceived myself and was often misled' – but he denied any wrongdoing. The country was tearing itself apart. On 13 December it was reported that East German social services were stretched to breaking point; 1,500 doctors and dentists and 4,000 specialized technical staff had left the country. Military and civil defence forces were called in to staff some hospitals and West German doctors were asked to help. The mood of the country was 'no more experiments'. The population no longer wanted democratic reform of the GDR, but wanted unification with the West.

By the end of the year unification had become the rallying cry. Till now it had been an abandoned issue, in the East after 1955 when Ulbricht dropped it, in the West after the building of the Wall. Long before, after a series of abortive four-power meetings of Foreign Ministers, the last one in Geneva in 1959, the problem had been shelved by the Occupying Powers until the long-promised peace treaty formally ending World War II came about. For Germans, following the Treaties of 1971 and 1972, whose effect was to formalize and institutionalize the division into two separate states, the matter was one of lip service. On 8 November, the day before the Wall came down, Kohl spoke of the possibility of unification in his State of the Nation address and offered to bail out the East in return for free elections and an end to the Communist monopoly of power. At the same time he failed to define the eastern border with Poland. This was to prove a contentious issue, certainly for the Poles, whom history has not taught to trust the Germans. On a state visit to Poland when the Wall opened Kohl again failed to assure the Poles. The issue was not helped when the Chairman of the Federal Constitutional Court declared that the German Reich still existed in its 1937 borders, which would take in half of Poland and a bit of Russia. At bottom lay the lack of a peace treaty formally ending World War II. At Potsdam in 1945 the frontier had been drawn on the Oder/Neisse line, pending 'final delimitation of the Western border of Poland'. The excuse was still the missing treaty.

When the Wall opened, Kohl had hurried back from Poland to give his one-nation speech in West Berlin. Thereafter the issue rose to the top of many agendas. Both Bush and Gorbachov said early on that it was not on the cards, Thatcher and Mitterand likewise. But in street demonstrations banners began calling for unification, for UNITY AND LAW AND FREEDOM, for DEUTSCHLAND OUR FATHERLAND. The sudden self-discovery of 'We are a people' and 'We are the people' became 'We are one people'. Kohl, fond of the phrase 'Vaterland', proceeded to seduce the East with Western promise. A week after the opening he proclaimed in Bonn that Berlin was the capital of the German nation. In mid-December the opposition SPD, more cautious, called for unification, while at the same time a public opinion poll in the East showed 71 per cent in favour of two German states. In East Berlin, for now, they still wore Gorbi's badge in their caps and lapels, but the appeal was heard more and more from the West.

Kohl held out, still omitting to confirm the Polish border at the Oder/Neisse line. The condition of aid was the Party's surrendering of its leading role, which Krenz conceded on 24 November. On the 29th Kohl produced his plan for unification: first East Germany was to introduce free elections, then confederative structures – joint commissions and committees – would be set up, leading to a new federal order, and all this within the context of the EC and NATO. Krenz had said that unification was not on the agenda. Modrow, on the 30th, said likewise. The Kremlin accused Kohl of planning the future of both German states, and Shevardnadze rejected the idea of one Germany.

But not for long. The fact was that Berlin was moving out of step with the rest of the GDR and, especially in Leipzig, the call grew stronger. In the East the SPD were beginning to fall into line, and the concept of confederation lost ground to complete unification with the West. On 15 November Democracy Now had become the first to call for full unification. Till now the CDU (motto '*Wir sind das Volk*') had wanted confederation. The difference was that now people had been to the West, and seen its variety and abundance, they had less and less patience with reforming the GDR. They'd seen the lights on the Christmas trees. They wanted goods, not talk.

In early December, for the first time in eighteen years, ambassadors of the Four Powers met in Berlin to discuss links between the divided city. They proposed to give up control of air traffic. Allied control over the air corridors into Berlin created a huge gap in air travel across central Europe. Flights from Dresden to Hamburg had to fly up the East German air corridor and north over Denmark; from Frankfurt to Leipzig planes flew south over Czechoslovakia. The monopoly of flights into Berlin by British Airways, PanAm and Air France was to end. Lufthansa would again fly to Berlin. The East German Government was to apply for membership of the Civil Aviation Commission, and Interflug to join the International Airline Association.

While Western firms had been at first reluctant to get involved in the East, the removal of Krenz and the promise of free elections encouraged them, and the great takeover now began. First it was a matter of putting in drains and telephones. On 13

December East–West talks were held on road, rail and air links. Priority was announced for a high-speed rail link between Hannover and Berlin, the line to run parallel to a proposed new motorway. Costs were not stated, nor the division of them. The groundwork was laid for reciprocal insurance agreements. Eastern and Western postal services agreed to cut bureaucracy and speed up postal services and improve telephone communications. The GDR, with only 1.6 million telephones, one for every ten people, and a twelve-year waiting list of over a million, lacked infrastructure, fibre optics, digital exchanges. Now they would have them. In the East everything was unmaintained, old, and rotting away. On 14 December the Economics Minsters of both states agreed to set up a joint commission to promote economic co-operation; the West's programme of start-up assistance for small firms was to be extended to the East. Plans were announced to co-operate in such areas as automation, medical technology, and metal-working. At the same time the East German Government was to introduce an investment protection bill by the end of the year to encourage Western investment: West German firms would be able to buy into Eastern companies and transfer profits out of the country. Bonanza time. Just as the opposition had feared, the East was perceived as a source of cheap labour and materials, and a market. It was against this that the Wall had originally been built. This was textbook colonialism, in one country. At the same time the environment, in dire straits, required urgent attention; pollution isn't interested in whether there are two German states or one. The two Environment Ministers met and agreed to reduce West German exports of waste to the East. By the end of the year seventeen joint projects were in progress or under negotiation to monitor and reduce air and water pollution. Joint efforts were to be made to clean up the atmosphere. Agreements were reached on smog warnings, and Bonn announced that it was to put DM 1 billion into environmental co-operation. There were to be joint projects on the infrastructure. There were to be twinning projects, and autobahns would be rejoined where they had been severed in 1961 and new ones developed. Railway connections, most of them separated for decades, were to be re-established; the Western DB (*Deutsche Bundesbahn*) established an information office in East Berlin, and DR (*Deutsche Reichsbahn*) opened a mission in Frankfurt. For Christmas and the New Year there were to be 1,359 extra trains.

Electricity lines were to be reconnected, and the two big gas companies met to discuss linking up the systems again. Interflug and Lufthansa announced plans to link the two Berlin civil airports, Tegel and Schönefeld. A joint committee was set up to deal with practical problems in the Berlin area. Later in the month West Berlin promised the East emergency medical aid. Both countries were to contribute to a DM 3 billion currency fund to help stabilize the Ostmark. There was an exchange of spies and prisoners between East and West Germany. And from 1 January, visa-free travel across the border in both directions was to be introduced. From that date, Germans of both states would be able to travel freely, and the obligatory exchange of DM 25 at 1/1 would cease.

And there were growing political connections. Wary at first of its Eastern CDU counterpart, which had been a puppet party for forty years, the Western CDU held back at first, approaching Democratic Awakening which formed itself into a political party on 15 December. East and West SPD parties began to form links and the Western SPD produced a plan for unity that differed mainly from Kohl's in being slower. The message was no longer *if* but *when*.

Elsewhere, throughout Germany, where there were now 105 crossing points, co-operation broke out. There were state links – Hessen with Thuringia, Baden-Württemberg with Dresden – with plans for the provision of infrastructure, telephone exchanges, business loans, information offices, and restoration. IG Metall, the same-named metal workers' unions East and West, signed a co-operation agreement twinning branches, exchanging experts, sharing training schemes.

In West Berlin the crowds and the media at the Brandenburg Gate were rewarded on 23 December by the opening of crossing points there. Many who had waited in the West now streamed through. Above them, the Goddess of Victory on top of the Gate was to get a facelift. Installed in 1793, the Quadriga had been looted by Napoleon (the 'horse thief of Berlin') and taken to Paris in 1807, and returned in 1814 after his defeat. On 4 December it had been announced that the Quadriga was to be taken down and cleaned up, and her Prussian cross and eagle were to be restored. When in 1958 a new cast of the figure had been presented by the West to replace the original, damaged by Allied bombing, the East had removed both as symbols of Prussian militarism and placed the figure on top of the Tor facing east. Now cross and eagle would be restored.

In the West, down by Checkpoint Charlie, Rostropovich plays Bach before the Wall. On the other side in the dark city the streets are quiet as ever, strings of people straggling home from the checkpoints with their Christmas packages. Behind Friedrichstrasse station two middle-aged couples are struggling to get a 51-inch television set into a Trabi. It won't go. They take it out of its box and throw away the cardboard. It still won't go. As usual, by ten most places are closed. There are lights on late in the House of Ministers, but the SED headquarters is in darkness, abandoned. The ministers are up late, because history is in a hurry. Christmas is coming, and the stores are doing their best to put on a show. Across the great squares Christmas lights are strung out. Normality, which isn't normal here, is doing its best to keep up appearances. It's still the same cold, uninviting place, where the prevailing wind is from the west; for this reason the rich and powerful built their villas and castles at Potsdam and Wannsee, where the air is cleaner. Here, by the time the wind arrives it has travelled the city, and it is grey and full of smoke. Otherwise the greyness applies to everything, as if all colour had been leached out, the clothes pale blues, browns, nothing to attract attention, the shops full of perpetual autumn pastels, the buildings darkened by smoke, many still war-damaged, pockmarked and holed by Allied bombing and invading Russians. The streets, swept and wide, retain the greyness, as if the sweeping merely turned over the dust. In bars and restaurants empty tables still carry *Reserviert* signs, and the waiters are as sullen and indifferent as they were before. But the customers are different. It's as if there were a whole set of new people here, or as if they had, in a variant of Brecht's phrase, elected themselves a new people. They talk. They make eye contact, stranger with stranger, excited now that they are free to talk. 'We are free now,' a man says. *Free. Free. Now.* If anything they are too free, over-excited, vulnerable, like children let out of school. Or prisoners from the jail.

7

TEO, BIBA

She had just got in from work when she heard it: the Wall was
open. She had poured herself a cup of coffee and taken her
shoes off, and sat down in front of the TV to watch the evening
news on ARD from West Berlin. The news was that GDR
citizens would be allowed to travel, without visas, across the
border. The rest was vague, as to when, from when, with what
paperwork. It was enough for her. She packed her bags. She ran
to see her father, who lived in the same block, to tell him,
breathlessly, that she was going and that she was sorry if this
meant goodbye. She took one last look around her apartment,
crammed some last photographs into her bag, and slammed the
door. She drove her Trabi straight to Friedrichstrasse, dumped
the car in the street, hoisted her bag on her shoulder, and joined
the crowd demanding to be let through at Zimmerstrasse,
known to the West as Checkpoint Charlie.

She'd been here before, several times, just to look down the
street between the concrete overhang and the red and white
barriers and the border guards, to where she could see the rest
of Friedrichstrasse, and Kochstrasse crossing it with its traffic
and its lights. Her man – Teo – had left over a month before
her, travelling via Hungary and the open border, and then on
one of the trains that recrossed the East, and then immediately
to West Berlin to wait for her. They had agreed he should take
his chance and she would follow when she could. They had no
idea how long it would take. And there beyond the barrier and
the Wall somewhere beyond the U-Bahn station he'd be, Teo.
They did not know or expect the gates to open so abruptly.

She describes it, though she noticed little, intent as she was
on getting out. All this was probably a mistake, and at any
moment the doors would close and the guards would drive

them back, and there were so many like her pushing to the gates demanding to be let through. She remembers it was quiet, for so many; no one shouted, no one wept, not yet. Everyone held their breath and pushed forward. The guards were nervous, without instructions. She only knew she wanted to get out. Then she *was* out, the guards not so much waving them through as holding up their hands in despair, and with the crowd she was stepping into the camera lights and flashbulbs on the Western side. People embraced, kissed, whistled, cheered. What she was thinking of was a telephone, to call Teo and tell him she was out.

She shrugs now, drinks her wine, relapses into silence. Its Teo's turn to talk. Yes, they lived together in the East. No, they are not married, not to each other. In the East he had been a salesman, of traffic lights, bollards, street furniture. A salesman in a non-competitive system. He is out of work now, and has been since he came here. He is vague about the details. It is all a blur of trains for him: to Budapest, the embassy garden churned to mud, then more trains. Since coming to West Berlin he has been looking for work, but seems without much hope of it. He's not equipped for it. He seems wary, as if exhausted with all the effort of flight. He hunches forward, as if the wire that kept him upright had been broken.

Both of them are forty, he says, 'the same age as the GDR'. Biba breaks in: 'But I will always be GDR. Even when I am here. Even when GDR *ist zu Ende*.' She explains, in her schoolgirl English, that her impassioned loyalty is not to the government nor to the regime nor to the system, but to the people of her country, their struggles and their suffering. The people there, she says, will always be different, they will always be GDR, even when they are absorbed into Deutschland, which she passionately hopes for. In the West she has two sisters, who have lived here for many years. Sometimes they came to see her father, sometimes they would talk on the phone. She felt they condescended to her, patronized her, their poor Eastern sister. They do not know or want to know her feelings, she complains. They are distant, far away in miles and sympathies. 'It is my problem,' she says, excluding Teo from it. 'Here I must work, there I must work. Everywhere. There people get too little for their labours. Here perhaps too much.'

Her voice is thickening, her tongue failing around the words. Biba is getting drunk on white wine, on her day off from the hospital. She is a nursing sister, highly skilled, working in a hospital treating leukaemia and bone marrow patients. She is impressed by the technology available, in sharp contrast to the East. She is inspired by the possibilities of saving lives, beating sickness, defeating cancer. 'We are close,' she says. 'We are close.' Part of her work is to teach recent arrivals from the East the technology involved. Some of them were in prison, she says, for political offences. Unlike her, they do not want unity, and feel their struggles and the protests for which they went to prison were in vain. It ends in a Western takeover. *'Legende,'* she says. *'Zu Ende.'* And then 'Cancer,' she says. *'Krebs. Zu Ende.'* And she stubs out Teo's cigarette. He protests and lights another. 'Why why why why?' she croons, singing the word over, singing a song she learned in her English class: 'My bonnie lies over the ocean.' It is an old-fashioned English, as viewed from the GDR, and with each glass of wine she's less steady in it. She still has the book from which she learned English, a curious fifties version of Britain published in 1987 with pictures of morris dancers and Aldermaston marchers and East End pubs, badly written texts taken from the *Daily Worker*, curious sentences such as 'The loss of the airport was a great inconvenience,' and stilted conversations greeting trade-union delegations at railway stations. A delegate from the NUT compliments his hosts on their hospitality and the progress of their country before going to telephone his wife in England to tell her how well he's being treated. Chance of a telephone would be a fine thing. Another goes into a bookshop to ask for a book on women's progress in the GDR, and is quickly assured all is well, though there is always room for improvement. 'The more languages you speak,' Biba quotes, 'the more lives you live.' 'Lenin,' she says.

For now, they are happy to be in the West, and think West Berlin the finest place on earth. They have a flat in the nurses' quarters, she has a good job and is quite oblivious to the fact that when she and all the other nurses who fled West took work, they displaced Western nursing staff, just on the brink of a pay rise. What they both want is unification, quickly. Why not? Within Europe. It's all very simple, for these two. As for many Easterners, the West has answers to all problems, and all these problems can be solved. It is a touching faith. Meanwhile they are discovering that the West is *unpersönlich* (impersonal), cold and distant, running out of sympathy with their case: the elbow society. For the rest Biba would like to claim back her flat in the East, or at any rate the contents. After she left, the flat was sealed. The contents would normally have been taken by the Stasi, but the Stasi didn't get round to it. The people got to them first. Her brother there is looking into it.

'Why why why why?' She withdraws again, sitting back with her wine. He gets a word in. He has no regrets, nothing to go back for. His mother has lived in the West for many years. Indeed, it was the occasion of her sixtieth birthday, three years ago, that disaffected him finally. He had applied for a visa to go to the family reunion in Hamburg, and was refused, as ever without explanation or appeal. From that point, he wanted to get out, simply because they would not let him out. Till then, he had had no trouble. He'd kept his head down. He elaborates: in the GDR relationships are very close. Families are closer, partly in response to the monolithic state that encouraged family life, and housed it in close quarters, in part because that is how it always was; it is we in the West who have loosed the bonds of family. Otherwise in the East people move within a very small, very tight circle of friends whom they have learned to trust. Within that circle, warmth, loyalty, trust. Outside it, hostility and danger, the world and the state and the Stasi with their agents and informers forever sniffing about. Within such a circle he had maintained himself. Then when he began to apply for exit visas: strangers on the corner watching him come and go, trouble at work, edgy interviews in anonymous offices. Why did he want an exit visa? Because he wanted to leave the GDR. And why did he want to do that? Because, he explained carefully, having applied for such a visa he was a marked man, continually in trouble, and he was finished there.

'Why why why why?' She cries a little. It is the drink. 'Why why why why? My bonnie lies over the ocean. *Zu Ende.*'

8

PETER: WORK ON WHAT HAS BEEN SPOILED

Peter lives beside the Wall on Zimmerstrasse, near Checkpoint Charlie, close to the old flashpoint. What's left of the street on the Western side is the metre of Eastern territory that is the pavement, so the way by the Wall here is a dark alley between the Wall and the short bomb-remaindered row of tall crumbling houses, in one of which Peter lives. His front door is in the West, but the path in front of it is in the East. He is a sculptor, working mostly in wood, sometimes in plaster, leather, stone, bone. There's a hollowed bone in which he's placed East and West marks, a pun on *die Mark*, money, and *das Mark*, marrow, on the artificial separation of East and West, and of their currencies. It's wood he loves – its grain and flow, its texture, colour, smell. And working it, chisel and file, silence, patience. Hard by the Wall he has a gallery, a white room, where he works at the back by a wood stove on which the teapot stands, surrounded by his sculptures and his tools, making. By the door there is a tall carved figure with a revolving head on a string that spins and spins against the background of the window and the Wall. Around, there are photographs, of installations on the Wall, of events along the passageway outside, of armed Americans in troop carriers parked along the pavement. He's indifferent to the sale of his work; having made it, it's part of him. Once it was quiet here along the narrow alley, but the tourists are suddenly too many, and too many of them with chisels pecking at the Wall, by day breaking into his quiet and at night into his sleep. Despite them, he is re-creating the forest, here by the Wall. He sees that what he does is an organic response to the dead presence of the Wall, with all its armament and suspicion. In his years beside it he has registered some of the effects of paranoia.

He wishes he could devise a pulley system to take the Wall up and down. There are times when a little shade and a little privacy would be welcome, and times when the sun is falling into the Western sky just beyond the House of Ministers when he would welcome sunlight. A young reporter from the *New York Times* comes in, all Burberry and leather bags and microphone: How does he feel about this Wall in front of his window? 'I wish they'd take it down as soon as possible.' End of quote. But he fears that with the Wall down, the street and the traffic will come back. And the Wall-peckers are driving him crazy: day and night, for months now, the chipping has gone on. Tourists gloat over the redundant Wall, and take a piece for a souvenir, a photograph of them taking it. What Peter's lost with the *Durchbruch* is silence. What was a quiet corner up against the Wall, where no one much wanted to live, with a grim view over into the other side, is now a thoroughfare, soon perhaps to be a street again. Now it's full of tourists gaping at the Wall, just then a Japanese woman taking out her chopsticks and pecking it, giggling into her boyfriend's camera. The peckers knock on his door at three in the morning to ask him to lend them a hammer and chisel. His neighbour has got into several fights, and he has several times gone out, seized the tools and flung them over the Wall.

'In 1971 when I first came to Berlin, in the first few weeks I wanted to go over to the East. I remember I was very curious. But I had a passport with lots of stamps from everywhere. I had been travelling for years, many of them in African countries, so my passport was full of stamps. I went to Friedrichstrasse, and they took away my passport and made me wait over an hour, and I think they photocopied it. It was a lot of harassment, so that I didn't much enjoy the visit. So I gave up very early and then it took another two years and I went over with a friend of mine from West Berlin. It didn't interest me much, for West Berlin was at that time very new to me and much more interesting. In those days I was attracted here, to this side.

'And then after fifteen years West Berlin didn't attract me so much. I grew interested in what lay on the other side of the Wall, in East Berlin. About the same time I moved to this house by the Wall, in 1986. From the beginning there was conflict, and there were attempts to control me from very early on, from all sides, from East and from West. Most of it was in 1987. It began with my first work here, which was called, from the *I Ching*, hexagram 18, *Ku: Work on what has been spoiled*. What the Wall spoiled, I would work on, and so you see here a photograph, a large square of cloth and plaster, about 3.5 by 2 metres, and through the folds of the plaster faces peering, as if pressing through the Wall. This was the *Arbeit*, the work. It hung there for about eight days. A lot of people came to photograph it. I guess there were some soldiers, some Stasi possibly, also photographing it. I have another picture here of a painting by someone else on the Wall, and here are four officers making a video of it. I can't imagine what they made of it.

'One night a few days after I had put up the *Arbeit* some soldiers came over and smashed it, but before they smashed it up they measured it. So they took photographs and measurements and then they smashed it, and threw it in front of my door. Then later that evening, after the demolition of the *Arbeit*, West Berliners came here and to Checkpoint Charlie, shouting "Berlin Berlin." And then from the other side a great shout came back: "Berlin Berlin." Then we knew it was not for ever.

'In the *Arbeit* there was a little mask which I reproduced on the Wall. They came again, and smashed that. Then later I froze the Wall. It was January, very cold, and I kept throwing water on it, and the water froze on the Wall into ice sculpture. It was very beautiful. It's a pity but I have no pictures of the frozen Wall. Only in the last couple of years have I been taking photographs of this place. It's too bad because it looked brilliant, like a fairy tale, ice, cold Wall, fairy tale, frozen Wall. Possibly somewhere in this world is a good photograph of it, by a tourist who saw it. Maybe in Japan. So then they came and knocked at my door and they said, "Now you show your politics, with the ice you are celebrating the Cold War." I said, "Oh come in, let's drink tea, let's talk about this," but they stayed on their side.

'Then they came again and said, "OK, OK, if you don't stop doing these things on the Wall we will nail you in, we will board you up." They could do this to the front here, because it all belongs to them, not the front door but up to it.

'And I wrote a letter then, asking about putting work on the

Wall, asking properly if I might do it. But I didn't know where to go with it, who to send it to. So I went over to Checkpoint Charlie, and asked if they could help me: "I need your help, please, I need the address, I have written a letter to you." The first soldier shook his head, he didn't know what to say, and sent me to the next soldier. Same question. Same answer. Next soldier. He said to go into the transit area, but I'm a Berliner, and not allowed to go through Checkpoint Charlie, which is an Allied crossing. He said it's OK, no problem, so in I went. "Where do you come from?" Just around here, I said, Zimmerstrasse. And the same question: I wrote a letter to your superior and I need the address to send it to. "Oh, that's interesting, have you got your passport?" Possibly he phoned, he phoned somebody he wanted to ask to say I was there, I wanted to ask some questions, was he allowed to do this. "Can you give me your passport?" I had to wait outside wondering what was going on. I said I just have this question of your address, why can't you just give me your address? "No," they said, "somebody is coming for you, somebody is coming." So I waited and after an hour somebody came, a young man, very friendly, very polite, very seriously interested in what I was doing. I've never been taken so seriously, by an official, by any administrator. Then he said, "Forget the letter, you will never get an answer. With things like that, we don't write letters." And then he said to just come over say, next week, and we could meet somewhere sometime. And I could get informed. And I was curious, so we arranged it, and I went over.

'This time there were two of them. They invited me into their car, a little Lada, and we drove off. "We'll just drive around," they said. "We'll take a little tour." OK, I said, I don't mind. And we drove through the town and suddenly we were on the border of the city, and I said stop, stop, I'm not allowed to go further, I have a permit only for East Berlin. They said, "Don't worry, don't worry, with us you can go anywhere." I thought: interesting. I said who are you, are you Mr God? "No, no, what do you think we are?" I said I think you're Stasi. They said just "Ummmm." I knew their names, but I have forgotten them. So we drove outside Berlin and took a little walk in the forest and they said to me, "With what you're doing, it's impossible, we can't help you." I said why couldn't you tell me that before? They said, "You think you're fighting for peace, we're fighting for peace too. So let's fight together." On the way we had some very interesting conversation, and they had a lot of questions: where did I live, how did I live, what work did I do, what did I work for, how well or how badly did I live from my work? And why did I do these crazy things on the Wall? What good was it? I took these questions very seriously, I answered very seriously.

'The young man I had met first at Checkpoint Charlie, he was dedicated, interested, intelligent and quick, but very narrow, thinking between the lines. He looked about eighteen years old, like an arrested high-school Prima, though he was the father of two children. We met another time, and went to a restaurant, and then no more. Should we meet again, he asked, at a certain time? But there was no reason for it. He couldn't answer my question, therefore I couldn't ask it, so there was no purpose. He couldn't help me and I couldn't help him. Then funnily enough in the restaurant, which was full, there was just one half-empty table and we sat down, and there were two other men sitting opposite. And then for me the tale turned a little strange, because I recognized one of them as H., an East Berlin painter, a man whose work I knew but whom I had never met. It turned out, H. said, that it was his birthday, and he was having coffee with a friend. We made conversation, and of course I found him much more interesting then the Stasi man. His friend left then, and we continued talking. Then the conflict; maybe H. was Stasi too? Perhaps they had arranged an artist for me to meet. Perhaps they had tricked him into working for them in some way, and this was a ploy to involve me. Berlin is a village, but this was a big coincidence. But after that I went over several times, and met with H., and he showed me East Berlin. He has since come over to the West, and we are friends now, and our first meeting really was by accident, but at the time I was suspicious. *Stasi war Staat im Staat.* Secrecy was the strongest thing the Stasi had. They made everyone suspicious of each other, paranoid. This was their success, and their failure. You could not see them. Their trick was to vanish. Over there it was difficult to talk with people; you never knew who anyone was.

'Then after the meeting with the Stasi the West Berlin police came to see me to tell me that the East had made a complaint to them. They had met at Checkpoint Charlie with a man who came from the East and stood behind the demarcation line and said, "We will take away everything you put on the Wall." The police tape recorded what he said, and they came to tell me. I didn't know what to say. Then – there is a cop who is in charge of the area around here, I have seen his face before – one night he stood outside with a camera taking photographs. I went outside, I said, "Hello, aren't you from the police?" He said, "I'm from the police but today I'm off duty." I laughed. And then again the police, always. One night there was a phone call; tomorrow, they told me, the cleaning trucks are coming and the old cars standing outside will be towed away. The cars belong to my neighbour, who uses the parts, and I told him that tomorrow they would be cleared. He said how did I know; I said I didn't want to tell the whole story, but I knew. He didn't believe me. Next morning they came and cleared everything. They didn't touch the things I had on the Wall and I asked why they didn't touch them. "Oh no, we don't touch the Wall," they said. "That's for them. That's theirs." But my neighbour's cars, they just took them away, and then he didn't trust me for weeks because he thought I belonged to the police because I knew.

'Then some guys came along, they had a very French accent and said they were from Canadian television. They wanted to make a film of me working, they came again and again and we went out together for drinks, they wanted me to invite all my friends and have a party, and we did so, and they filmed that. For three days, for six hours, they were here. Then they went away, promising to send me a copy of the film. It never came. They disappeared. After half a year, a year, I wrote a card asking what was going on, but I didn't get an answer. I wrote again a few months ago. And I think it was the secret service, maybe the CIA, at any rate a Western secret service, just checking me out. And they couldn't have done it better. This is how you get watched. There will always be a secret service, I think for ever and ever. I don't have anything to hide, but this is the thing, it's a game. One person's watching you and then another person notices them watching so they watch too. Soon everyone is looking at you. This is what it was like then, living just here.

'This was about the time I started to go over to East Berlin. Before that, in fifteen years I went over only three times. Since I have lived here by the Wall I have been often. I have made friends there, in these last three years. Recently I was in the GDR staying in a little town, Hoyerswerda near Cottbus. There were three roads that had the names of three soldiers who were shot guarding the Wall, shot from the West, they told me. As far as I know in East Berlin there are two or three streets with the names of such dead soldiers, and in the whole of the GDR about sixty, said to have been killed here on the Wall from the West in the sixties and seventies. Sixty dead soldiers. Here some border guards we know were shot, by their comrades, to escape or while escaping, and one or two by escapers. But these they say were shot from the West out of a high window, perhaps at night, with a telescopic rifle, an assassin. He could pick his target, shoot, and be gone with no one knowing a thing. For years there was no communication from East to West. So we never heard about it.

'The Wall changes every day, with the light, with the season, with the people beside it. Beginning from the early eighties the Wall became a tourist attraction. And it was easier to write on it, with less trouble from the other side. There were books of photographs, very colourful, and competitions for artists and projects to transform the Wall. The graffiti began early, and most of the early things from the sixties and seventies were political, directly about the Wall, about the situation here. Black paint, written quickly, because in the early days they chased people off, though mostly they didn't see them, on the other side. For years and years they fought against graffiti, they discouraged it, the West police discouraged it, there was so much uncertainty about what the other side might do, could do. In some places such as at Potsdamer Platz which were very sensitive points, they tried to keep it white, continually white-washing. When Jimmy Carter came to West Berlin the West whited out anti-American slogans there. But eventually they gave it up and slowly the Wall writing came together into a compact continuous whole, in the mid-eighties as I recall. Mostly it was tourists, outsiders, Americans, West Germans, sometimes Berliners. But it's hundreds and hundreds of square metres, the work, which first they fought against. And along came the spray-can, and then along came more tourists. There were some very beautiful spots which changed, continuously, right up to now, and some other places untouched from the first moment, which means you can find graffiti as old as the Wall itself. Together with what was done yesterday all this forms a long line like an endless message, a long sentence.

'But if you put a drill to the Wall, or tried to fix anything on it, they came down very quickly. They seemed to know where you were immediately, and a ladder would appear on the other side and they would lean over and shout *"Verlassen Sie das Territorium der DDR."* They never allowed things to be attached to the Wall because they were afraid of dynamite. For me this was just a place by the road, on the street, forget the Wall, forget Berlin. But the Wall brings people, and brings out confrontation. It brings out aggression. Most people here are travellers, between one point and the next, and I think that nowhere else are people so true as when they are on the road, travelling, when they are preoccupied with their journey. The real aggressive power against the Wall belongs to the sixties and early seventies, when it was a background for politicians to make speeches against, very much the Cold War image, especially here at Checkpoint Charlie.

'Now suddenly we start loving it, and now everyone wants a little piece of it, and will pay for it. For years Berliners were themselves indifferent to the Wall. It was strange to be in such a place in the presence of such an emotional object and yet get used to it, live with it, not react to it. Up to 9 November it was very very seldom they came to the Wall, I think none of them, the professional middle class Berliners who have lived here a long time, and who are closely related to this town. And there were many voices that said let's get rid of the Wall and then all the millions of tourists. It was perhaps more of international significance. People attacked the Wall, and set fires against it, and tried to blow it up. There were several attacks with dynamite. I remember, it must have been in 1983, right here by Checkpoint Charlie, some people blew a square metre hole in the Wall on the West side, and caused horrible damage with glass. Which is why you can see it's made of very strong concrete, in solid pieces, to withstand explosions and also ramming by lorries. It's very strong.

'For me here the opening began with an American television crew with cameras and microphones, coming along fast here by the window, and after a while I said what's going on, and went outside. "Oh we're going to Checkpoint Charlie to film the first GDR people coming over." This is how I first heard, and I thought they must be crazy, the Americans, just like the Americans. But after ten minutes I couldn't hold myself back and I went to see what was going on at Checkpoint Charlie. And there were camera teams and journalists and a few people, twenty, fifty people. I went back and forth that night, I'd say twenty times. I couldn't believe it, but also I couldn't stand it, waiting, because it was hours and hours until they opened the Wall. Seeing all these faces, it wasn't what went through television: the big funny festival, the carnival. It was not a carnival. It seemed so in the newspapers and on the media, but there were a lot of tears. There were the faces, pushing through; it was like my *Arbeit*. Mainly they looked as if they knew but after so many years they still didn't believe it was true. Was it really true? Of course on the Western side there were thousands of people after ten o'clock. They poured champagne over them, over the Trabis, gave them bottles of champagne, invited them for drinks, invited them home. In a way it was of course a festival, but it wasn't just this; there was a sense of unreality, as if this were not really happening, and so in a way it wasn't.

'I have a friend, he is Italian and lives in Berlin, he's in his eighties, he speaks fluent German and has been here for years; he feels like a Berliner, and in November when all the people came over, and the Wall opened and hundreds of thousands of strangers came into town, he said he felt very strange, and wondered what they felt being here. He felt stranger than the strangers. For example, there is a sex shop, he never knew about it, it had no interest for him, but suddenly there were long lines of Eastern men in front of the sex shop, and he wondered how they knew about it, when he didn't know. How do they find out such things?

'To have the shit in front of my door every day, day to day, and now just to get rid of it, it's so exciting, especially at night. But I get tired of it too. Now with the Wall open it gets bigger and bigger, there are days when 10,000 people come marching through. There was a time two years ago when it was the 750th anniversary of Berlin, and the tourists came, and there must have been thousands of photographs taken out there, and films, and video, and flashlights. They weren't interested in the 750 years, but in right now, in this Wall here.

'Last night I was in Kreuzberg, where they have taken away part of the Wall and put up a fence, and there were about twenty West Berlin police and thirty East Berlin police, and soldiers. And they spoke to each other sometimes, but then they were very stiff. They smiled at each other, and they ordered hamburgers, and some for the Eastern soldiers too. It's good. But still they don't have orders, their system is falling down, and there are still two systems, there is a gap between jurisdictions. There is a difference in the language between East and West. There they say *Plaste* for "plastic". There is a difference in tone, in intonation, in the type of words used. I have just a few hundred English words, enough to say fragments of what I want to say, yet with the English we are much more related in democratic thinking, in our experience of 1968, of movements in the seventies and what went on in the Western world. It's a different thinking. Politically with the East it's not a shared culture. Theirs is a different history. Especially for my age. I'm forty-two, and very distinctly a man of my age.

'A few weeks ago some young soldiers came over from the other side, privately, for the first time. They were excited to find out what's going on here, having been sitting in the watchtower with a Kalashnikov before that, looking over, looking in. So they came in and we drank red wine and they described how it was sitting in the watchtower. Very boring. Sometimes they found a note saying to look at this or that window between eight and nine o'clock because there'd be a woman taking off her clothes. That was much more interesting than watching out for someone setting dynamite against the Wall, watching for the enemy.

'Now the Wall is coming down, and soon I will be able to see out of my window to the other wall on the other side. Maybe we should keep a few parts of it here and there, or maybe we should get rid of it totally. We don't need it, but what we need is not to forget it, which means take the area and do something special with it, not the usual thing. I have tried to find someone somewhere who feels responsible for it. But nobody. It belongs to the GDR, it's their property and if you have a question about it you must go over to East Berlin, but – again – where to, to what address? They don't know what to do until they have the election. In any case it's just the way it goes and soon it will be too late. Soon people will drive their cars along Zimmerstrasse here and park, and they will forget about the Wall because it was a horrible thing. We have the right to forget, and yet we must not forget it. And it wasn't so horrible, it was just a piece of concrete. We made it. So part of it perhaps should be incorporated into a memorial, something special could be made out of it. I want it taken down, but what I want to know is what parts do we begin thinking about, what parts do we separate, and what can we do with the area where the Wall was?

'We don't know what's coming. Great changes in the East, and at any rate it's better there, at any rate without the Stasi, though they are still there. There are great forest areas, military reserves, where they could disappear. Many of them are looking for work. Some of the cruellest they pressed into horrible jobs. Some of my friends over there say, "Now we've got a Stasi at work. Nobody helps him. He packs things, carries things in the back yard." There are several hundred doing jobs like this.

'What I did was I provoked a little, like a little insect, working in stitches. I am interested in the political, the social power of art. An artist is a surrealist, an artist is a dadaist, an artist is a hero and an existentialist and also an anarchist. Most people just get bored without noticing, without taking notice of how bored they are. For some people there is an adventure to going through the Brandenburg Gate, but I don't want to go there. I don't want this feeling I'm supposed to get. I don't even know if I get some strange feeling there. I don't want this German feeling. It's such a prime symbol. The point is we have to build people to ask questions, the right questions, because we can't speak to people who don't have questions.

'And now they're going to sell the Wall. It's a funny object to buy, but if it helps renew the health system of the GDR by selling it, why not? That's turning something bad into something good, into art, into health. I call that work on what has been spoiled.'

9

SOPHIE: THE BORDER IN THE HEART

'I was born on a very interesting date, 20 April, Adolf Hitler's birthday. I was born in the year he took power, 1933, and if my father had called me Adolfine, the female version of his name, I would have been presented with a bank book. I had the names of my mother and my grandmother but I remember that my father said if we had called you Adolfine, you would have got a bank book from Adolf Hitler. On his birthday everybody had to hang the flag outside, and so on my birthday there was always the flag hanging in the garden. We had a very nice girl helping my mother with the housework, and once there was a garland of flowers over the swastika flag and people thought, "Oh, these are the real Nazis," but it was just my birthday, and she did it to please me.

'We lived at Bellevue, near the station. You cross the Spree, and there is a bridge where you go to Lehrter Bahnhof. In that house my father had his bachelorhood, and when he married my mother she moved into his apartment. My father foresaw the war, the coming war, and he said the first bombs will fall here, because Lehrter Bahnhof, the next station after Bellevue, was the big terminal for western traffic stretching between the two stations, and that will be bombed because that's the line that brings the goods for the army and the supplies. And right he was, because the house where I was born was destroyed in the first bombing of Berlin. But we had moved here to this house in 1936.

'My father worked in the District of Tiergarten. He was an engineer. He studied at the Technical University of Berlin, and had a doctorate in engineering. He built sluices, streets and bridges. He was an architect, not for high buildings but for low. He was the director of the department of rivers, streets and bridges in the Tiergarten district. The street that is now called Strasse des 17 Juni that runs to the Brandenburg Gate, when Hitler had this street widened for his troops to march upon, my father was the architect who enlarged it. So he worked for the City of Berlin, but Berlin was not historically one city, there were a lot of cities. Charlottenburg was a city, Zehlendorf was a city, but in 1920 there was a unification to make Greater Berlin, though the districts kept a certain authority for themselves, with some independence. It is still so that we have a mayor of Zehlendorf, a mayor of Tiergarten. So my father worked for the administration of Tiergarten but he was promoted to the administration of Greater Berlin, into the Rote Rathaus, now in the East. Later he was sent back to Tiergarten because a Nazi got his post, and after the war he applied to have this revised, and he got his title back and a little bit more money. But it was justice my father was looking for, not money.

'At the beginning of the war my father expected to go into the army, though he had been in the First War and did not want to go again. But his eyes were not good, and so he was not called up and remained with us in Berlin through the war. I knew, though he did not talk of it, it was not wise to talk, that he did not like the Nazis. He was deeply offended by them, he was disgusted. His sister-in-law, my aunt, was Jewish, and was sent to work in an ammunition factory, though she was a skilled milliner. Because she was married to a non-Jewish man she was not sent to a camp. But he was sent to a camp for the husbands of Jewish women, and had to work in the swamps, digging trenches for drainage. It was very hard work, done by semi-prisoners, and it ruined his health so that he died early.

'In my class at school one of the other girls was Helga Goebbels, the daughter of Hitler's Propaganda Minister, and I remember everyone wanted to be friends with her. When she had a birthday party she invited the whole class, but I told her I would not go because my father did not like what her father did. My mother worried about that. In those days anything could get you in trouble. I remember asking why we had no picture in our house of Adolf Hitler. Some of the other houses I had been to had one, but not in our house. My mother said: "We love God but we have no picture of him either."

'I remember the bombing, and at Grunewald the S-Bahn trains burning, and the drivers taking the burning trains out to save the buildings. In 1943 schools were closed down because of the bombing, and I was brought to my cousin's parents. They lived in Salzwedel. Salzwedel is on a railway line and there was not much industry. It was just a little town, among meadows, and so they never feared being bombed, but the aeroplanes passed over on the way to Berlin. I had lived with this bombing in Berlin, I was very anxious, I was ten years old then. They had a red brick house, an old house, and the sleeping rooms were under the roof and their room was in the back and my room, the guest room, was just on the staircase. And my mother had promised to think of me, to direct her thoughts towards me. At 8.30 I had to go to bed and I was thinking of my mother and she was thinking of me. If somebody tells me I'll think of you on a certain day, I'm sure he does, and I always think of my children when they have something important to do and if they get into a panic they know their mother is thinking of them. So I was thinking of my mother in the evenings and I lay awake, listening to the bombers on the way to Berlin. Often by ten o'clock they would be over Berlin, maybe at eleven, often twice, three times a night. And when the first came I was still awake and then I heard this *mmmmmmmm* and then the planes in big herds overhead, hundreds of them passing over this little town. And I thought we should get up and go down to the cellar, it could just happen that a bomb falls but my uncle and my aunt slept and I sat alone on the staircase. It took twenty minutes, half an hour, as they passed over and I was listening to the noise the aeroplanes made and I knew they were going to Berlin. They were terrible nights. It was like being lost in a wood with wild beasts. Normally a child should fear the bogeyman or the wolf in the fairy tale, but this was reality. Of course I should have told my aunt and gone into her bed. I would have felt her warmth, she would have stroked me, comforted me. It would have been better. But the fact is I didn't. I was trying to be alone. There were so many terrors coming, to all of us, even to the children.

'When I was in Berlin at Christmas 1944, my father didn't send me back to my uncle. I had caught a cold and it was January, and then he decided not to let me go because they could already hear the Russians shooting beyond Frankfurt an der Oder. I think they sent something written by a doctor that I was ill. And I had three marvellous months without school and I was thankful to be here with my parents when the Russians came. That morning my father had gone to the baker, it was said he had bread to sell, and he got bread and heard that the Russians were coming from Klein Machnow. We lived in the cellar and we had water in our tub and water in pots because water would be short, and for a time we had no water. And it was me who cried "There is a tank outside in the garden," and father, who always said, "Sophie has a blooming fantasy," didn't believe it. I hear this now; there stood our table and there my father and it was no fantasy. There was a tank standing at the side of the house and the trees were mown down like matches. It had come in behind the houses through the gardens. We hadn't even heard the cracking of the trees.

'When the war ended and the Russians came, I was twelve. A short time before they came my father talked to my mother and then he decided to tell me what could happen if the Russians came and raped my mother. It must have been terrible for him to tell me, and though I understood, of course I didn't understand at that age. You knew a part and the other part you didn't know. I have a friend who stood in the room when her mother was raped by Russian soldiers and I think she has a lot of difficulties resulting from this event. She has a very good husband, and she lives a normal life, she often comes and I give her advice. She could do this for herself, but she hasn't got the nerve to find the solution to her problem and I think underneath these events are stirring her up. She has difficulties I think she could handle, but there is a closed door to this terrible time.

'My father had opened all the doors because he foresaw that the Russian soldiers would open them with their guns, and then the doors would be broken. And then the tanks returned and the Russians came in. We were in the cellar and a young soldier, he must have been an officer, came down and they were looking for gold and watches and furs. The family jewellery was buried under the coal with the gold watch and the watch of my father's grandfather. My father had just his steel watch, and the young Russian asked, "What time? *Wieviel Uhr?*" He spoke a broken German. My father took out his watch and said it is quarter past seven. *"Na. Wieviel Uhr?"* "Ah," my father said, "of course you have Russian time." And then he calculated and told the young man what time it was in Russian time, in Moscow. But of course he didn't want to know the time, he wanted the watch, but because my father was old he didn't dare take it. Later they sat here in this room, and looking into the bookcase there was a book on construction my father had written, and they asked him what he was. One was playing the piano, others were eating the pears my mother had bottled. There was no alcohol in the house. And then my mother had a very bad feeling. I had long pigtails, and a young soldier came up to me and seized one of these pigtails. My mother said, "Oh god what will happen now?" and put her face down into her hands. But all he said was he had a sister of my age, and that I reminded him of her. He was only sentimental.

'And then we lived for some time in the cellar. There was not much plundering in our house because it looked so terrible, and that first tank by doing so much damage had spared us. They thought we had already been plundered. There were some days when they were drunk and you could hear the drunken soldiers, driving their cars, and going into the houses, where they shot people, and they shot people on the streets. There were a lot of people who were Nazis and others who were not Nazis. If somebody pointed and said, "This is a Nazi," away you went. It wasn't necessarily true. A rivalry, an enmity. Or just for malice. I can't tell these things precisely because I mostly lived in the cellar and heard only what my parents told me. I remember it was a lovely feeling to go upstairs after a few days and wash myself in the bathroom. The water was icy cold. I had always disliked cold water because I always had to wash myself with it, but this cold water was delicious.

'At the end of the war we were hungry for a long time. There was nothing to eat, and every day I would help my mother to find food, bartering what she had, and gathering herbs and nettles from the roadside for soup. We ate potato peelings, anything. She it was who must struggle to keep the family together, and to stave off the victors. And in the winter without heat it was bitterly cold. I remember once spilling water on the stairs, where it lay as ice for days after. I have no souvenirs from childhood, no toys, because everything had to be exchanged for food. Once I remember my mother had got a bag of peas, and with these she made soup, and I noticed that in the soup were little black specks, which were the beetles in the peas, and I had to eat the soup without protest. And once she got a bag of flour that had been swept from the floor and mixed with sand and husks, and she sieved it, but the sieve let the sand through with the flour, so whatever she made of it the sand gritted in your teeth, and gathered at the bottom of the bowl.

'And Berlin was ruins. My father worked in an office at the Tiergarten then, and of course he was needed to get the city working again. There were no trains, nothing. From here he would walk to the Tiergarten along the S-Bahn tracks on a Monday morning, about twenty kilometres, taking his food for the week and sleeping on the floor of his office, and walking home again at the weekend. Then, because it was a hot summer, his food was tainted, but there was no other so he ate it, and he was ill. He passed out, and smashed the side of his face as he fell. They brought him home, and then my mother had a sick husband to nurse, though later this saved our house being requisitioned by the Americans. They still used it, or part of it, as a dispensary, open twenty-four hours a day, so there wasn't much rest for anyone.

'Everything was in short supply. Clothes and shoes, everything was rationed. At the end of the war my mother was lucky to get shoes for me, good brown leather shoes. I was twelve years old then and the war ended and there were no ration cards. There were no shoes, no clothes, and I wore these shoes. And my feet grew but the shoes didn't grow. And so the first part was cut out so that my toe looked out of the shoe, like sandals, yes. I had three pairs of shoes. These, and one pair a friend of my mother gave me, too long and too high-heeled for a young girl. I couldn't walk in them very well. And then a pair of shoes made of corded paper, paper made into a cord and then rolled and they were hard, hard, hard. Normally I wore these with the front cut out and my toes out and I wore them in winter and in summer, and we had a very cold winter from 1946 to 1947. And then in springtime there was a lot of melting snow, and a lot of water rushing in the gutter. I came back from school with my precious shoes on, now two years old, and I still growing, and the sole of my shoe opened its mouth and I decided: "Now I do what I want." It was March and it was cold. I stepped from the sideway down to the street and went home against the running waters. Now I soaked the shoes deliberately. It was just like killing an enemy. They were already gone but I wanted to destroy those shoes. I had had to take so much care, you know. I hated taking so much care with everything. But it was a good training. I *am* strong. I hear it from others, and I'm used to making decisions for myself.

'In the summer of 1945, because there was so much confusion and nobody dared to go out of the town, we couldn't go to the country, to Werder, out beyond Potsdam, to pick fruit. There are orchards there, and in happier times in the springtime a favourite expedition for Berliners was to go to Werder to see the blossom. Now it was all grey, and famine, and times of no hope. In 1945 after two months we were under American administration. Our sector was the American sector, but Werder was in the Russian Zone. So it was in 1946 we went, I with my mother to pick fruit at Werder. Many people went, and bartered bracelets, rings, earrings, porcelain, textiles, for fruit. We paid for ours, because we had old friends there. The train from Potsdam was overcrowded, with people riding on the outside of the train, standing on the steps, holding the grip of the door with both hands so as not to fall off. Inside no one could move a limb, eight people were standing in the toilet. Finally we reached Werder and our long walk through the town began. We picked fruit for the people we knew there, and we ate all the fruit we could, and then began our way home. The police stood at the station, taking away what people had brought, so we avoided returning by train from Werder to Potsdam but walked all the way, a very long way. Werder is a street that never ends, we thought. This day we got a boat to cross the Havel. It was dangerous because the Russians often shot at people, and that day they shot at us as we crossed the water. We reached the other side of the lake and got to Potsdam, but the last S-Bahn had gone. Nobody was allowed to stay on the streets after ten o'clock. Russian soldiers controlled everything. My mother and I slept in a house which belonged to a church, an asylum. We lay with others on the bare floor, glad not to be out in the streets. That day we had been picking plums, and I had eaten so many I had the belly-ache and couldn't sleep. Nor could the man next to me, who suddenly reared up in the dark holding a knife. At my request he cut the belt of my blouse to release the pressure. And so I slept. In the morning the first S-Bahn brought us home with some tomatoes and some plums that helped us against our permanent hunger.

'When I tell my story, I know there are gaps in it. For instance, something I didn't know, my parents didn't tell me, here on the little green before our house there were Stalin Organs, the special machine-guns. This my neighbour told me, and that there was a tank standing at her house, at No. 5, you can still see the holes of the bullets on that house. She told me there was a young woman soldier driving the tank, and she was hurt and brought into the house at No. 5. And the woman had lost her fingers. And then the soldiers went out looking for the fingers and brought in a finger with a ring. You know of course that a lot of men and women were killed in the war, but when you see a finger without a hand, a finger with a ring, it's quite different to reading it in the newspaper. Another neighbour, their daughter was my friend Christa, committed suicide, the mother killed the whole family of four with poison out of fear of what was coming, everyone except the grandmother, who was left alone and desperate. The mother was from the Baltic, and had seen what the Russian soldiers had done conquering the Baltic States. The children and the father all knew that they would die. My friend shouted to her grandmother who was standing at the locked door, "Goodbye Doda" – that was her name for her grandmother – "We are going to die." When my friend was buried with her family they were just wrapped up in blankets, not even in wooden chests you'd bury people in normally. We stood there with the old grandmother who could swim and so couldn't drown herself in the Schlachtensee, and I remember she had been a Baltic baroness and spoke Russian. Some Russian girls passed and then there was talk between them and scolding, and the vicar, anxious, coming and just saying a prayer and then running again. It was terrible. My mother dug the grave with a neighbour. The old lady couldn't do it and so the neighbours buried the family.

'As to going into the Eastern Zone, I can't tell very much because nobody travelled for pleasure, nobody went there just to see how it was, what it looked like, you were so busy getting your food and what you needed, you only went for these purposes. My mother had a friend near the Elbe at Tangerhütte, and she was a widow and her farm was let, but she kept the house and she had a pig and hens and a garden and she gave my mother potatoes and pears from her garden. I once went with my mother to visit this aunt, my mother left me there for a fortnight, so I got better food than at home. She was a nice lady, Tante Toni. I only remember that I couldn't go for a walk to the village because it was dangerous to walk in the woods. There were the Russians. They would just shoot you, or rape you.

'Things were hard for a long time. And even when they were better there were still the Russians in the GDR, and the division, just a kilometre away, and we were isolated and trapped in Berlin, and there was no certainty we would not be swallowed up in the East. It was not easy, living behind the Wall. I think my adolescence was foreshortened by the war. I think this is so with all my generation. There are some feelings that aren't developed. Of course there was some joy, and there were sometimes dances, and in 1948 I recall my mother taking the old swastika flag to someone to make into a dress for me to go to a dance. Another time I went to the other side of Spandau instead of going to a ball. There I was not dancing but picking rhubarb. My mother was ill, but she had an appointment with her brother. Since nobody had a telephone I had to go with my uncle for the rhubarb. They were years of few kisses and many letters that should have been the other way around. Swallow your tears and bite your teeth, my mother used to say, and of course, I swallowed my tears. In my daydreams I went off with a pony and cart, but I always took with me salt and flour. And I remember my rabbit. When my mother brought it home in 1947 it should have been eaten, but we couldn't kill it. It was quite domesticated and came into the house, and when I used to play the piano its ears would move up and down with the high and low notes. I could play my rabbit.

'I have lived here all my life, but for my time away at university. I would have liked to have got away from Berlin for a few years, so that I could have seen it from elsewhere, and come back with an outsider's vision of the city, but I didn't. I have always felt hemmed in by the Wall, but here we live in what was my father's house, and here I married and had my children.

'Most of my friends and schoolmates are now dead. At the war's end many of the boys were taken to fight in the last days, and died. I lost nearly all the friends of my youth, some moved away and some were killed and died, those that survived the war dead before their time, in their 40s and 50s and early 60s, of heart attacks, cancer, stress. This division is part of it, this

Wall, this border dividing my country, and it is all so stupid. You have to feel it to understand it, and it can't be argued about. It is a border through the heart.

'The Wall went up in August 1961. My son was born on 19 March 1961, and he was my first child and you are always very occupied with your first child. When my third child was born I asked myself how I had managed with the first one and still had time for three of them. So when the Wall went up I was very busy with him because he was not yet five months. We could not go there, and most of my relatives living there had died. My Uncle Erich and Aunt Jenny the Jewish aunt had lived in Lichtenberg in Ost Berlin. My uncle died in 1958, very early because he had brought home from the camp a sick heart. My aunt died in March 1961, so I had no close relations in East Berlin. Wolfgang, my cousin, lived beyond Berlin. Of course after 13 August there were a few days when the Wall wasn't really closed. But when you are a young mother and have a child of five months, you have other things to do than just go over the Wall and look how it looks from behind. The first I remember that there was an opening, a possibility to go over, we got passes just for the day. Wolfgang is twenty years older than I am, he's seventy-six now, he was a young man, he was a young doctor when I went to school. And of course I was very proud to see my handsome cousin, but he didn't care for me back then, nor did I care really for him. After the war of course both of us did, when we were older, but you know here we are more reserved and though he adored my mother and liked me, he never took me on a sled, or in his arms or kissed me very much. But when we met the first time after the Wall we left our car and went by foot, and we just went through the hole and there he stood. He took me in his arms, and my mother took his mother, who was like a sister for her, and everybody was crying to see each other again. I can't remember which year this was. Robert was a small boy and Dorothea wasn't born, so it must have been, could have been 1963. We went to a café and my aunt had brought wooden toys, and I still see my son with a little railway, three pieces, crawling on the floor. And that was just for one day, just an afternoon. This would be the first opening of the Wall in 1963 at Christmas, there were masses on the street, not only our family waiting, you know, it was like the Queen arrives in Reading. And then again we couldn't meet for several years.

'Wolfgang and his mother lived in Salzwedel. It was her eightieth birthday, but where to meet? My mother and my husband and I lived here in West Berlin. One sister of Wolfgang's mother lived in Magdeburg in the East, not far from Salzwedel; another sister lived in Marburg, in West Germany near Frankfurt am Main. We couldn't go to Salzwedel, they couldn't come to West Berlin or West Germany. There was nowhere the parts of the family could meet. Normally everyone would have gone to Salzwedel and Wolfgang would have ordered a nice dinner, there would have been cake and family toasts in a good hotel. Instead we met in Prague, the whole family, to celebrate an eightieth birthday, and the old mother too. And on the way back, a stone came up from the road and shattered the windscreen, and we had to go on through the GDR without. When we went through the border the Volkspolizist didn't say a word. He didn't ask what happened or I wish you a good voyage home. No. Nothing. He didn't take notice because taking notice would have meant discussion. For half an hour we were picking glass out of the car, and I took glass out of my legs, and my mother and my husband. They were tiny little needles. I was like a hedgehog. There was no blood or just a little bit, I wasn't hurt, but with all these little pins in your legs you can't go on. And while we were discussing what to do, we came to the conclusion that it was impossible to get a replacement windscreen there, so we had to go on.

'It wasn't to see Prague, though of course we saw Prague, but that wasn't the reason. The year before, it was in spring, we had another family meeting in Czechoslovakia, before this birthday. Wolfgang came with his mother to Spindlermühle, that's in the Riesengebirge, the mountains between Czechoslovakia and Poland, a beautiful landscape. Wolfgang came with his mother and I was with my mother, I and my son, and then there was the grandson of Wolfgang's mother's sister, the son of his cousin. I'm his only cousin from the father's side and from his mother's side he also has a cousin, and her son came. He was a young man of twenty-five, a student, I was then thirty-three, Wolfgang fifty-three, a little boy of six and two old mothers. And we were in a hotel and later we talked to the other people and the first thing they said was: Oh, how are you connected? The one was too young to be my husband and the other too old to be my husband, though of course he was like an old husband, he was my cousin. They were thinking how are these people connected, two mothers could be mother and mother-in-law, but two men, one ten years younger, one twenty years older? And it was all only to be together with the family. For me it was to see my aunt. Her picture and my uncle Robert's are hanging on the wall here, because I loved them deeply. There was no other way to meet. West Berliners were not allowed a West German passport, and as West Berliners we were not allowed to the East, and so it was difficult to get out. Later, in 1971 when we had obtained West German passports when we were visiting my husband's mother, who lived by Lake Constance, and because we had relatives there, we could travel to the East, so we went to see Wolfgang in Salzwedel with our West German passports.

'We could only go via the transit routes, we couldn't say let's go by Leipzig or stop in Dresden, though we did, once, illegally, on our way to Prague. Another time when we were lost we asked a Volkspolizist for directions, but he would not speak to us, he would not make contact, for fear of betraying some state secret. Travelling, you felt you would be trapped. And you could be trapped. Today I wouldn't have this fear any longer, but then you had to have this fear. I did not like it there much. Once we had been to see Wolfgang in Berlin East and he came to Friedrichstrasse to see us off, and when the border guard looked so intently into my face I couldn't help saying "It has been a long time since a young man looked me so closely in the eye." He said nothing. I found that people there treated us either over attentively with a mixture of flattery and subservience, or they resented us. To them we were rich Westerners. We were not rich, but to them we were. In 1987 when we were visiting Wolfgang in his country place – his dacha, they call it there, from the Russian – I stopped to talk with a museum guide about his garden. You know we were all wearing old clothes, and there it was a holiday and the Easterners were all wearing their best clothes, so I wondered how did they know we were Westerners. They told me: it was our whole way of being, of acting and talking, asking questions, being inquisitive, an individual. There the individual is part of society, not encouraged to ask questions.

'There were always these little restrictions the Volkspolizei gave you. We were driving through the border once, there was a stop sign and he was sitting in his booth. Normally they looked at you or made a sign, and this time we misunderstood his look and thought we could go on, and we went slowly, slowly, the next ten metres with our car. Then the policeman said, "I didn't give you a sign. The next time you come out you will have to fly, you will have to go by plane." He reprimanded us for nothing. You felt like a four-year-old child, not knowing why your parents were angry with you. And you couldn't answer. So you were always nervous. You knew there was no reason, but nevertheless you knew there were reasons to be nervous. We were always glad to have left the GDR, even though we knew nothing would happen. If we drove too fast we would have to pay the fine, but nothing else could happen. But there's so much irrationality in our feelings for the GDR, and the GDR for us, it's hard to explain. Always this tension. Then last year after 1 August, if you had a pass it was possible to decide in the morning and to go to the East the same day. And we are glad now that we did it last year under the old GDR, to see it before it changes. But it was always a stress. Always something a little unusual happened. If I tell this to my grandsons and granddaughters in twenty years time, no one will understand why we were so upset. That this is gone now is quite unbelievable. That we can now live on normal terms, as we live with our Italian friends, with our English friends, with relatives. We no longer live in a hostile country, in the middle of the GDR, cut off, isolated and shut up. What for everyone else is normality is something beyond normality for us. The tricks people played were complex. There they were very thorough, but not imaginative. They were what we call *kleinkariert*, thinking in little squares, so sometimes you could outwit them. You know you cannot send money to the GDR, but I found a way to do it. First you sent a letter to whoever is to receive it, saying to expect bad news in the post. Then you sent a black-bordered envelope, as if announcing a death. In that you could put the money. They did not open that.

'The other day I was writing to a friend and I wrote that I had just come back from Potsdam, and now we are leaving Berlin again and it's more than going to Ceylon, it's more than going to China. We would never have thought it would be possible in our lives. I was sure our children would live in a united Europe and that we would live to be together again.

For me it's coming back to my youth, more probably than for my husband, who was away, who was older, who was in the war.

'Despite all this there has always been close contact in the family. Wolfgang is a very dear uncle to my children, and with my husband he is like a brother. Now we can visit often, though we managed before just as I have said, and the children always go and visit him. Since he moved to East Berlin they went to see him even when they had to pay DM 25, and he would invite the girls for their birthdays to a restaurant and afterwards to the opera. So the children were always informed and since we talk a lot of politics, they knew what was behind the Wall, but in reality only East Berlin was what they saw. In the last years various of us would go to Dresden to see an aunt with our passports, and later we were allowed to go with our *Passierscheine*.

'And now the Wall is open, and we can go through when we want. I did not think it would happen in my lifetime. Especially we like to go to Potsdam, across the Glienicke Bridge, which the Easterners called the Bridge of Unity, though for years no one crossed there, only the exchange of spies. Before, every time we went to the Philharmonie, going along by the Siegessäule towards the Brandenburg Gate, always, really always, I would say I want to go on and see Wolfgang, he lives just on the other side, behind the station near Alexanderplatz. I was always saying this, repeating myself, and I had decided when the Wall opened that I would go through when the Brandenburg Gate opened, because there is where I have felt this division most. My daughter said she would come with me, and we made a contingency plan, if she heard it in the University she would telephone me, and we would meet at Bellevue. But the Brandenburg Gate opened on 22 December and it was a day when my son was coming from Frankfurt, his mother-in-law from Paris, and I had to be at home to receive my guests. But I went with a friend of mine, not with my daughter, we just went in the evening, and I can't describe my feelings. In this moment you don't look clear into yourself. We went very slowly to enjoy, to really take hold of this moment. All the people had gone, it was not so busy as in the afternoon. In the afternoon I saw it on the television, and we were looking at how they went to and fro. And you know here in Germany, people don't call each other very often by their Christian names. I do it with old friends, but

I have other friends who are friends just with their family name. It would be funny now to change to Christian names after twenty years. So I went with a friend and we call ourselves by our family name, but when we were around behind the Brandenburg Gate she just looked at me and then we embraced each other and we kissed each other. We never did this before, but it was just a moment when you couldn't talk. We were talking before, "Oh look, and here are these," and "Oh," just talking facts. But in the moment when we stood on the other side, our talking stopped. You couldn't talk any longer. You just felt. And my friend had brought a little bottle of champagne and a plastic glass and we divided the champagne and we toasted, and then we went arm and arm down Unter den Linden and came back to the floodlit Brandenburg Gate, and we thought, "Is this real?" I was thinking all the time, we didn't realize on 9 November what this opening of the Wall really meant. We sat at the television, and Schabowski – it was on *Aktuelle Kamera* – he said, "Oh, I just got a little note: from now on everybody in our country can travel." Don't think that we clapped our hands and said hurrah; nothing. We just sat there staring and hearing what the journalists asked. One said, one of the journalists said, "Does it really mean they can travel?" "Yes yes, from now on." But of course we thought, there will be a law and they will say how they intend this to be. There will be visas, passes. They didn't intend to open the Wall on the 9th, but at 10 p.m. people stood there, and we saw later on television an officer of the Volkspolizei saying they had no directives, no orders, they knew nothing. And when they telephoned they were told yes, yes, let them pass, and they were overwhelmed. And next morning a friend telephoned and said – it was 8 o'clock – "We are sitting at the television, have you seen?" And we too had heard it in the morning, the Wall was now open. My son phoned from the United States; he had seen it in the evening, it was evening there. And he said, "I was born in the year the Wall was built, and my son was born in the year of the destruction of the Wall." And then I realized that half of my life, exactly half of my life, twenty-eight years, I have lived behind the Wall. Half my life, imagine.

'This opening brings many changes, and not a little trouble. With the traffic on the exit routes, it is even more difficult to leave Berlin, and the streets and transport are crowded with people from the East, mostly sightseeing. And there is crime too, shoplifting, because these people from the East, they see what we have and they want it too, but they have not the money and their DM 100 are soon spent. A neighbour here has hired a cleaning woman from the East, for DM 8 an hour instead of the usual DM 12, and now there will be more of this undercutting. When I talked on the telephone to my oldest daughter on the evening of 10 November – she lives in Lübeck – she said there were a lot of people coming from the north of the GDR. Lübeck was overcrowded. She was irritated by this, lots of people. We educated our children to be tolerant, and to think politically. It doesn't matter to me whether they vote Green or Communist. But for my daughter this was too much. For me it was coming back to former times. But not for her. She was irritated by the situation, by the people, by the crowds, and above all by the consumers' minds of the people of the GDR.

'But these things don't matter really. That there is freedom now in the other part of Germany, that the people there can now do what they want just as we do, that they can talk as free people, that's really important. As for the elections, what matters is that there should be a clear majority, it doesn't matter which majority it is, but that there is a majority so that then there won't be quarrels about how to go on. You know there aren't many ways to democracy. There's really only one way. Here is a clear decision of the people, and so there shouldn't be arguments for weeks or months on what to do next. Because if they want the freedom we have, that means they have to take over our constitution, and our economic system. Of course this with reservations for the present state, but there is no third way. I think that we have lived quite well for forty years with our constitution. Of course little things could be altered, and nothing is perfect because nobody is perfect, but why not for a new beginning use this constitution? It was conceived to avoid the faults of the Weimar Republic. And it has worked. I think it would be better to join with Article 23 than to have a new constitution, because this negotiation about a new constitution would take too long. But whatever comes now, it will be change, and Berlin will never be the same.'

IO

JOACHIM: LUCKY MAN

'I was born here in Berlin, in Pankow, now in the East. My father ran a small transport firm. Due to the difficulties of the war – the First War – to shortages, deficiencies, my parents had to struggle. But they kept me well, they fed me very well, and they educated me, and they helped me to become a boy who did not have to suffer from the war, and from the difficulties and troubles after the war. They had a large house in which we had an apartment on the first floor, and they had a large, large garden where I spent my play time. I was so fond of playing that when school time began – I wasn't a good student during school time – I was so full of ideas and invention, playing with other children. School in the Nazi time was for me a duty, while playing and studying for myself was life. And perhaps because of this love for a beloved child I learned only late that it is important to study and to be very assiduous in school time.

'But then here in Germany school, after the Nazi period began in 1933, had a lot of deficiencies. I recognized that school didn't give me enough instruction for life. Not knowing what direction to take nor what profession to choose, I decided that there should be in my life – in anyone's life – one thing you knew thoroughly. I decided I would try to learn one thing. And I decided, after years of hard Latin in school, perhaps it might be the Italian language. I thought it possible I might learn it thoroughly. So I began to learn Italian, in private lessons outside school. My parents both spoke it a little, my mother because she had studied music, and my father because he had been sent as an apprentice to a transport firm in Genoa, so both knew Italian to some extent. They could talk in the language, but theirs wasn't a full knowledge. They met in the first place because one heard the other speaking Italian during a concert, and then speaking together – "Oh I know some Italian" – they spoke Italian, and they went on to learn the language together, and they got married.

'So I set out to learn one thing as completely as possible. I think I managed it because I had the great luck, later, when I was in the Army, to become an interpreter. I became a soldier in 1940, when I was still a youth, and then I was an instructor from 1941 to 1942. In 1942 I became a sergeant. From April 1942 I was in German Occupied France for half a year. I was sent to the Channel, stationed on the Atlantic Wall. I was employed as an instructor in an anti-aircraft unit stationed at Lille, between the coast and Lille. During this time I learned some French and continued learning Italian. Then my unit was ordered to the Russian front. Everything was on the train, all our equipment, my baggage, and just then I got the order to go to Rome to take my examinations in Italian. So I was sent to Rome, when otherwise I would have gone with my unit to the Russian front, where most of them died. So I was saved because I had decided to do one thing well, and that one thing was to learn Italian.

'In Italy I first had to translate the German regulations and instruction books on anti-aircraft guns into Italian. At that time Italy did not have anti-aircraft units, only ordinary artillery. So I had to retrain Italian artillery officers to take over German anti-aircraft guns. This helped me to learn a great deal of the language, but I would say at that time I was perfect only on the technical side, but not in all the other aspects of the language. Later I learned them. After the war I took a second examination here at the Freie Universität to qualify in Italian language of the courts, but my first examination was with the military. I took the highest marks – *ausgezeichnet* – and got the desired yellow certificate. This qualified me to serve only as an Italian interpreter, and this protected me from being sent directly to the front. With the yellow certificate I could always say I was an Italian interpreter, and they could only employ me as one. I served at the staff headquarters in Rome, and then I was at a place south of Rome, Anzio Nettuno, where there was an anti-aircraft school for officers, and there I was an instructor for a year. After the revolution of Badoglio, when Italy left the Axis and went over to the Allies, I was sent to Serbia, to supervise thousands of Italian prisoners. Then I was sent to accompany a group of Italians, a special unit of experts in aircraft production, twenty-five of them, to Poland, where I was for half a year, from October 1944 to January 1945, near Warsaw, close to the Eastern front. And it was my good luck that when the Russians advanced west I was sent back with these Italian aircraft production experts, provided with permits issued by Goering's Air Ministry, from Poland to Berlin. It was a real escape. I was lucky enough to find a track-laying vehicle, and with my twenty-five Italians I set out leading them back to Berlin. But by this time we were near Danzig and had been outflanked, and so we must go through the Russian lines. I told the soldiers with me to keep going, and in that track-laying vehicle we drove through the Russian front in a snowstorm. The Russians were close by and saw us, but we were fleeing from the front, we were withdrawing. They let us go and we had no fighting with the Russians. So I got through the Russian front, over the river Vistula, and then a long journey by train to Berlin. Again, I was lucky, and reached Berlin in the last days of January 1945.

'Then I was sent to repatriate another Italian unit of experts to Italy. They were miners, tunnellers, and they had been employed building anti-aircraft shelters and bunkers for Hitler and Goering at Berchtesgaden. On 25 April, when it was thought the war was over, it was conceded that these Italians were to be repatriated and I was ordered to conduct them home. On this journey we were caught in the uprising of the Italian partisans near Udine. We threw away our German uniforms, and the Italians helped me to pass through the controls. It was a very funny situation. Then one day we were captured by Italian partisans, myself now dressed as an Italian peasant. We had thrown away anything that identified us with the German army, and all the others, the Italians, were able to show something that said they were Italians trying to go home. I of course spoke Italian, but with a northern accent, and so my story was I was from Trieste. All I had with me was a letter from an Italian girlfriend. She had written to me by my familiar name – "My dear Achim" – and in her handwriting it made my name look like *Achille* to the man who was questioning me. "You are Achille Osvaldi," he said, and so that became my name, instantly. And so once more I passed through.

'At the end I was not captured, though I was a prisoner for half a year. At first I succeeded in reaching Milan, and I stayed there for a week in the hope of getting back to Germany. But it wasn't possible. I lacked documents, as I had thrown away all my German papers, and I was trying to pass as an Italian. But as an Italian I could not return to Germany. So I went to the American headquarters and they treated me very well, except for food. We starved away to nothing on a few pieces of bread, and spoon rations of milk powder, raisins, cornflakes, corned beef, tea. I got a new German uniform, and I was a prisoner-of-war for six months, at Rimini. There, in what was called the Camp University, there was a chance to study law, and in that time I decided law was better than economics. Before, I had intended to study economics, which would have better suited me to take over my father's company. But now I decided to study law. Afterwards I studied law at Munich. When I was released as a prisoner-of-war I told them that my parents lived in Bavaria, not in Berlin, because I had heard that prisoners who were released and went back to Berlin might be recaptured by the Russians. My mother and sister had been evacuated to Bavaria for the last months of the war, and so I said my mother lived near Munich, and as one with a domicile in Bavaria I was released earlier than the others.

'I was released in October 1945, and had the chance to work in the state attorney's office at Landshut, which is about sixty kilometres north of Munich, a very nice place. I worked there for a year because it was impossible to go to Munich to begin study. The university was still closed, it was under reconstruction, and only Bavarians could attend at that time. Then in 1946 I was admitted, I finished my job as a clerk at the state prosecution office, and went to the University of Munich. I studied there till August 1948, but when my studies were almost finished they were interrupted by polio.

'The polio broke out while I was staying in Milan. I had taken a four-week course in Rome, where I was a representative of the University of Munich for an international exchange between Italian and German students. So I was in Milan, where I was very well treated for three years in Italian hospitals. At first I was paralysed all over my body, I had no breath for ten days. I was in an iron lung, breathing artificially, when the nurses called a Catholic priest to give me the last rites. With the little breath I had I said "I am ... not ... going ... to ... die." At that moment the priest packed up his patent altar, extinguished the candles, and left without another word. But they treated me so well that they saved my life. After the first year I was able to move my hands, after the second my legs, and after the third year I could walk with sticks, as you see me now. After three years' treatment in Italy I was able to come back to Berlin, by myself with the sticks, first to Munich to collect my belongings. I decided to come back to Berlin because I realized I could not continue my studies without the help of my parents. And again I had been lucky, because if I had been struck down in Germany – or elsewhere – I wouldn't have survived because there were no medical means available to treat my illness. And during this time of course I learned more Italian.

'So I came home at last from the war. I had come back to Berlin for the first time in the winter of 1946–7, after my release from the prison camp, but I feared recapture by the Russians, and so I returned to Landshut. At that time, in 1946, my impression of Berlin was disastrous. It was in ruins, everyone hungry, cold, grey. I knew that little bit of life which had developed in Munich, but coming here to Berlin and seeing the terrible life and the Russian weight, I knew I could never live under Russian power. I couldn't live here. There is hardly any air to breathe, to live, to work, where Russians have control.

'Here is one experience I had during the war. In 1945, when I was in the Balkans, in Serbia, there were Russian prisoners-of-war. They had to help German soldiers, German units, in their military duties. Several of these Russians fled. The Germans decided that as many as fled had to be shot, and as there were three or four fled, three or four more were to be shot. I did all I could so as not to take part in this. But I heard all about it, and this really was the first time I knew that Germans did things which were illegal. Until that time I had always had the impression that what German officials did, even Nazi officials, wasn't illegal. I did not know then about the fate of the Jews, it was all kept secret. Jewish people disappeared, and we were told they were sent to forced labour camps in the East, but as a soldier I had no way of knowing, realizing, that they were gassed or that they were shot. All this I learned only during the time I was a prisoner-of-war. But the first occasion I realized – recognized – that Germans were capable of illegal acts was with that shooting of those poor devils of three or four Russians, shot only because their comrades had fled. And I said if that is possible, then anything illegal is possible in Germany. From that time I knew Hitler was a delinquent, a criminal. Only from that time. Until then I was a young boy, a youth, then a soldier, taught to believe the Nazi media that claimed that everything they did was legal. My mother, who stayed at home much of the time, listened secretly to foreign radio broadcasts, and so she knew more about what was happening in Germany. She told me: "Jews are gassed, Jews are shot, Russians are shot." I could hardly believe it. I said to my mother, "Is that possible? No. That's only foreign propaganda, anti-Nazi propaganda." I couldn't grasp that it might be the truth. And so a large part of our people didn't know the truth, and unfortunately – let me say it in these poor words – the Allies didn't do enough to let the German people know what their Nazi government, what their Nazi officials, really did. We were in the dark. We lived in the dark. We were cut off. If we had better information, we would have known earlier about the illegal things they did.

'The other experience I had with the Russians was in January 1945 when they let us pass through their front line in the snowstorm. We saw them, they stayed at a distance of about fifty metres; we waved, they waved, we passed, and they did nothing. I was astonished that the Russians could do that, for the first time in my life I realized that the Russians were men and not the evil-thinking people we were told.

'During the time I was in Munich my sister came to stay with my mother in her exile in Landshut, after they were bombed out in Berlin. After the war my sister met an American officer, and became his girlfriend. She hoped they might get married, and things were going very well, but when the officer was sent back to America in 1946 he cut the relationship and my sister didn't hear anything further from him, and of course she was very disappointed. I am afraid she was angry with me for her loss; I had reproached her for her relationship while I starved in a prison camp. The American must have heard or sensed my reproach. But she never said anything about it, and then by the time I returned to Berlin in 1951 we had become politically separated, and we remained so. She spoke good Italian through my mother and through myself, and so she learned Italian and English too on the basis of her relationship with the American officer. She took her A-level in 1947 and afterwards when they returned to Berlin, to Pankow, she applied for a job with RIAS, Radio In the American Sector. And she was given a job, but after a week they told her that because she lived in the Russian sector they were unable to employ her. She told them she would leave the Russian sector and move to West Berlin, but no, they said, you come from the East, we can't employ you. The Cold War was just beginning to affect daily life. So she decided she'd never have anything to do with the Americans again; her boyfriend had left her, RIAS had refused her. So she decided, as she wanted to be a journalist, to go to ADN, the official Communist press agency for the media in the East. And there she met this man who later became her husband. He was in the Party, a Communist, a man whose career depended on the Party, so everything he had was because of the Party. She married him, and so I lost my sister. Thereafter if we spoke on the telephone she was brief, without warmth. She knew of course that they were listening, and I that their system required her to turn her back on me. Once when we visited them there, he drank beer and watched the football game the whole time, and invited in his neighbour. He ignored us. So she became a Communist, 100 per cent, with all the deficiencies of a Communist, but in my opinion it was the disappointments she had experienced that caused her to settle her life another way. "With the West I can't deal, I'll try the East then," I think she said. And so it happened that she became detached, that she became a Communist. I myself couldn't talk to him, because he was so full of ideology that everything he said to me I disagreed with, and there was no subject we could discuss. He was always trying to convince me that their ideology was superior to ours, that their economic system was superior. He was very good at economics, very good at figures, but he was always looking at their general line, at their directives, asking himself "What am I to do?" and answering "I have to do what they say and not what I think." Meanwhile I had my own idea of freedom, of a natural life, not a life ordered and imposed on me by some higher authority. We were totally different, and I regretted from the very first day that my sister had become acquainted with that man. I could no longer be on normal terms with my sister. From the first time we met I had the impression I had lost my sister for political reasons. And so it was, and the gap between my sister and myself grew further and further, and the family was split. For political reasons. First by ideology, then by politics, then by the Wall, and then by the distance they were able to put between families living in the West and in the East. From the beginning of this separation, my sister refused contact with us, either by phone or by letter. She was controlled. But there were other means to remain in contact, by letters posted in the West, or by someone coming over who could bring news to us. But no, she was told she had to refrain – herself and her family – from contact with Westerners and with her whole family. And as they told her, so she followed, and she avoided any contact with us. When we phoned her she always spoke in a low voice. She never gave me a real answer, she answered only with "Yes" and "No", she asked no questions. I got no information from her, she stood at the other end holding the telephone saying hardly anything, never any personal information. And no other information, whatever it might be. It was an imposed silence. Even while we were speaking there was all this silence. Frozen. All our relationship for a long time before the war and after, was frozen. By real political means.

'In the East they have a term, *abgrenzen*: *ab* – from, *grenzen* – to border, to stay back from the border, to put up a barrier between yourself and all your kin on the other side. And she followed that rule meticulously as only Germans can. And it is my impression that unfortunately Germans are able to disregard their personal feelings, to forget them completely, and instead to follow official orders, imposed rule. We like orders too much, we Germans. So many things here are *verboten*, and the language of public signs is so bossy. Unfortunately that's possible here in Germany.

'In 1951 my parents lived in East Berlin. When I came back from Milan, I lived in the Western part of Berlin, in Charlottenburg, and recommenced my studies, and studied a further two years, to 1953. In 1951 I had succeeded in convincing my parents there was no life for any of us in the East, not for me, not for them. I felt the East like a prison. Later, when the Wall was built, East Germany became a real prison, a huge concentration camp. I persuaded them to do all they could to leave Berlin East. My father agreed with me, he had the chance to start a new firm in the West. In August 1951 we left Berlin Pankow. Because I was handicapped I was able to get all the papers to leave East Berlin legally, because they said the old parents and their crippled son, they are worth nothing to us, and so they let us go. It was an exception, but we could go, and again I was very lucky to get out. For my mother it was hard, she had her life there. She had a large estate, large grounds, two houses, one that was destroyed during an air raid by firebombs on 18 March 1945, and another we lived in, a large house which legally perhaps we still own, I don't know. We had a third house at Charlottenburg. When we left East Berlin in 1951, because my parents were owners of this property in Pankow with its grounds, they entered in the land register a note saying "This estate is put under state administration." It meant we couldn't legally dispose of this property any more, with the consequence that we were expropriated and lost all our property, not according to our legal system here but according to their system there. So my parents came to live here in Nikolassee, near the station in a small flat, and here I met my future wife, and had the chance to begin a new life together with her, in this house with this garden. This was for me really the great chance for my life to begin again. Then in 1959 my parents sold the house at Charlottenburg, bought a new house on the Bodensee on the border between Switzerland and Austria and West Germany, and had five years there to live in freedom, because later after the Wall was built in 1961 all of us in Berlin didn't feel free any more. We knew we were free, but always we had the feeling we weren't. My parents wanted to be free, with space, freedom to move and to go where they wanted without controls and crossing points and all these interceptions and difficulties. In the East, before the Communists built the Wall, if tomorrow you wanted to go to West Berlin you never knew whether you could go. There was always uncertainty about everything: jobs, housing, studies, food, neighbours. You either whispered behind your hand or said nothing. There was no smiling, hardly any greeting, no look from eye to eye.

'In 1953 I took my examination, and began working in the Berlin courts as a legal trainee. Then I took my second examination on 20 December 1956, and became a prosecutor on 2 January 1957, interrupted by some periods as a judge. I returned to prosecution from 1959 until I retired. From 1965 I was a prosecutor in the High Court, and during my time as a prosecutor there were some periods I had to work on political matters. The first political subject I had to deal with was when the Wall was built. To protest against the Wall, some people put explosive against it, and blew a hole in it. It was quite a large hole, of some square metres, in that section between the

Potsdamer Platz and Checkpoint Charlie. Of course, they did more damage on this side with broken windows. One of the perpetrators was a man I had trained during his time as a judicial trainee, and so you could say I had trained him whereas he had learned only to blow up the Wall, but I felt responsible for the young man. They were arrested, and I was the prosecutor in their case. I had to charge them for blowing up the Wall. They had to be prosecuted, but I had to ask myself what was the right way to do it. My personal opinion was that they couldn't be prosecuted for blowing up the Wall; the Wall itself belonged to no one. Nobody was the owner of the Wall. The Eastern state was not acknowledged by the West of Germany, and so we could say that the Wall was put up by a non-existent government. We call this *res nullius*, something which is owned by nobody. Basically, if an object is damaged which is in no one's ownership, the accused can't be prosecuted for damage to property. And therefore I reasoned that for the damage to the Wall they couldn't be prosecuted. On the other hand, they had handled explosives, and just by the possession of explosives they had broken the law. Here again, there was a way out. Fortunately they had not used a high explosive. Several experts examined the chemical mixture and found only what is called black powder. In our statutes there is a special article which says for handling or possessing black powder there is only a minimum fine, and not the normal conviction of at least five years and more for a more powerful explosive. So they got a fine and that was all, and for some few hundred marks they went free. Later on the statutes on high explosives were amended, and the minimum penalty reduced to two years.

'After the Wall was built our whole future was uncertain. The day it happened I looked at my firstborn, my son, and thought what future would there be for him. The day it was begun was Sunday 13 August, soon after midnight, a date I will never forget. We got up in the morning and heard about it with the first news on the radio. The whole day we couldn't help but cry about the uncertain future. Life entered a new phase, though with my parents having left Berlin we hoped we could go there and recover. But still I feared Berlin would be closed up, as it was from 1948–9 when we had the Blockade and the air bridge, which saved Berlin. I feared we might be occupied by the Russians. It was their expressed will to get West Berlin, because after Berlin would follow the whole of Europe. Berlin was the key. Stalin said it: "Who occupies Berlin controls Germany, and who has Germany has Europe, and who has Europe owns the whole world."

'The first Wall wasn't built of concrete, but of bricks made of crushed rubble from the bombed houses of Berlin, mixed with concrete. They had a faint reddish colour. It's an irony of destiny. A little part of this old red Wall you can see, opposite the Brandenburger Tor at the crossing of the 17 Juni Strasse with the road from north to south. There is a five-metre section of the Wall built in the shape of the old red Wall.

'When I look at this monstrous Wall through our city, I feel a stitch in my heart. For us, travelling from Berlin to the East was always a journey with many difficulties. Every time we left Berlin, we felt free only when we passed the Western borders. We felt as if a stone was taken away from our hearts. Right up until the last year, we would say now the holiday begins when we leave the GDR. That's not just our feeling but the feeling of all our friends. We knew nothing would happen, but nevertheless, we felt free only when we entered West Germany.

'As a prosecutor I travelled into the East, and to Poland. Beginning in 1965, from 1965 to 1971, for six years I had to investigate Nazi criminals. At first after the war the Allies prosecuted many Nazis, but later it was undertaken by the West German authorities. In 1951 the Allies decided they had done enough to prosecute Nazi criminals. Everybody thought everything had been done on the subject, but the Allies prosecuted only the main criminals, ministers, and some Nazi leaders and then the lower ranks, but what we call *Schreibtischtäter* (desk-criminals, desk-perpetrators), the criminals who did their crimes at a desk, they weren't prosecuted and nobody cared. The Germans weren't allowed to prosecute them until the treaties, the *Deutschland Verträge* in 1955, which restored almost full sovereignty to West Germany and West Berlin. At that time everybody thought that with respect to Nazi crimes, everything had been done. Only in the early sixties did they discover the *Schreibtischtäter*, who had never been prosecuted. So we began to do the work the Allies had not finished at Nuremberg, and here in Berlin the Prosecutor's Office was instructed to handle the inquiries into the *Reichssicherheitshauptamt*, the RSHA, the former Nazi security headquarters. It was from there that criminal acts were ordered or approved. It was such a huge task to perform that we couldn't undertake all our inquiries at the same time. All the rest of the investigations into Nazi crimes not connected to the RSHA were conducted in West Germany. All the 5,000 former civil servants at the security headquarters itself were checked by the Berlin West prosecutors' office, who found about 500 still living to be prosecuted. My main task was to prosecute those civil servants who had dealt with Russian prisoners. Russian prisoners, if they were Jewish, or if they were so-called *politruks*, or commissars, were to be shot immediately. The German army refused to carry out this order, and so the SS and the German police were ordered by Hitler to check all the Russian camps for *politruks*, Jews and Russian prisoners connected to them. The checking squads reported their names to the RSHA in Berlin, where specialized high-ranking SS members – the desk-criminals – wrote the orders to execute them in specially prepared barracks or rifle ranges to hide their criminal acts from other staff or prisoners.

'I went to Warsaw to look at the archives, as I did in the whole of Germany, to find the files concerning the official servants of the Reich office. I found a lot, I found a lot in Warsaw, in Nuremberg, and at Arolsen near Kassel, the so-called Archives of Death. At Arolsen are archived all the files of the concentration camps, and there you can look up the files and apprise the death of every inmate in a German concentration camp. If an inmate was shot, there the order is signed saying why he was shot, by what order and by whose authority, and there would be the registration number and from that number I worked out by long investigation who was the man responsible who gave the order to shoot that man. And there were many who were prosecuted as a result of these investigations, though the prosecutions based on them were in West Germany and not here in Berlin, for reasons of competence. Another time for three weeks I went to Freiberg to examine the army archives there, conducting further investigations, and there were many other places over there I had to go to. I did not enjoy my visits.

'As a prosecutor I was limited by the Wall, I was circumscribed by it, and could mostly only work here in West Berlin. I could not work in the areas around Berlin. For a prosecutor in Munich it would be normal to work in Nuremberg, in

Regensburg, and so forth. Without the Wall, and the division, I might have worked in Brandenburg, in Oranienburg, in Cottbus, in Potsdam. I was involved in meetings and negotiations with the East from time to time, over disputes and legal matters. These meetings were always unofficial, and they always denied everything after they had our official claims or our agreement. They always came over in twos, and they could make no decisions, but must always refer back. They were always very well briefed on the questions under discussion, but if we raised another point with them they would have to adjourn the meeting. That is, they had no authority of their own. They had to have ministerial permission to come over, and more often they came to us. They were keen to come to West Berlin, where they were allowed DM 5 a day to spend, and could see and taste and smell the free world.

'From 1975 to 1979 my work was to cancel the convictions of Easterners who had come to the West. Their convictions were for *Republikflucht* – escaping from the East, for illegal possession of West marks, or for slandering the state, or for *Asoziales Verhalten* (unsocial behaviour), for *Staatsfeindliches Verhalten* ("rebel rousing attack"), for *Staatsverleumdung*, saying something bad about the state. If you said Honecker was a liar, you would have been convicted, but that's a nonsense. And all these sentences, all these convictions, I had to cancel when refugees applied for it, and every time I had the file of such a subject and I was confident of the final decision, I was happy to discharge it and to relieve the convicted person from the sentence.

'In the East after the *Wende*, after the turning, there have been many changes in the administration, but scarcely of state prosecutors and judges. They were only begun to be removed after the storming of Stasi-Zentrale in January, but there are still too many of them that remain. Retired lawyers from the West are being called to go over there to train lawyers in our law, in preparation for unification. And unofficially there are lawyers from the West negotiating with lawyers in the East, sitting in on their meetings with Western interests. Eastern law, GDR law, is not compatible with Western law, and when the unification comes there will be many adjustments to be made. Many companies – Mercedes, BMW, Siemens, Schering, banks, petrol companies – most of them with headquarters formerly in Berlin before the war, are planning to return, and negotiations have begun with the East. Many partnerships between Eastern and Western companies are being formed, as yet unofficially, but they are drawing up the ground rules for future arbitration of disputes. All this will come with the new government in the East.

'Also there will be many claims and suits over property and land in the East confiscated, like my parents' house in Pankow, by the state. Many West Berliners, many West Germans, have been over to see their former properties; some have told the present occupants to leave, it is their property and they want it back. It is a great problem. Recently I heard that where the TV tower stands in Alexanderplatz is land claimed by a Western insurance company, and they would like it returned, or a proper rent. Also I heard that the Volkskammer, the Palace of the Republic, the building is full of asbestos, and will probably have to be demolished. There is more irony. On this question of property in the East, I am not without interest. Lately, since the Wall came down, I have been back to the house where I was born in Pankow, and where I spent my childhood. I saw the places I used to play, and the windows of our apartment in the house, and the garden. In the garden now, shared between this garden and the next, there is an old people's home.

'Now, when my father died he would have left that property to me and to my brother and sister, and we would have inherited it. But my parents, who left East Berlin in 1951, lost that house under GDR law, but under our law I would have had a one third share. So now what happens? Perhaps we are now the owners of an old people's home? This is a problem that will have to be sorted out by the government and the law. Many Easterners may find themselves losing their homes because of this, and this will only make conditions worse in the East. Many more of them will come here, and they are still coming, though with the elections over the refugee movement has slowed down considerably.

'Now the East has had its elections, the result is clear. I'm glad that the elections went quietly and without upheaval and that it was a clear election for democracy. Who won isn't so important, what is more important is that democracy won the election. If it had gone more in favour of the PDS, it would have been an indicator against democracy. Even 16 per cent for the PDS is too high. But this is only a provisional election, and only the next election will show what sense of democracy the people of the East have preserved or regained. The next one.

'In politics I am a liberal, though I have voted for other parties from time to time. Once I voted SPD, it was about the year 1970, 1971, when I had the feeling that only the socialists were able to make the treaties with the East. I thought them more likely than the CDU to get clear with the East. That was to do with the particular Berlin situation. We are normally liberal voters. We aren't fixed voters. We will always vote against somebody. I am always interested that no one gains too much power. For foreign policy and for politics the most important and skilful personality we have at the moment is Genscher. He is the most able. Why don't the Liberal Party get more votes, as Mr Genscher is a Liberal? Because the Liberals are in coalition with the CDU, and therefore everybody confounds Genscher with official policies.

'You know I am a lucky man. My wife compares me to "Lucky Poodle", after a sketch by the painter Wilhelm Busch. He was a cartoonist who knew the weak side of mankind. The cartoon is about two dogs, one a clever poodle who could open the door and escape when he was caught, the other a fat dog who knew nothing and who was slaughtered and eaten and later his skin sold to his former mistress. So I am the lucky poodle who always escapes. You know *clever* in Germany has a bad meaning: a clever man, that's someone that's a little too clever. I had the good fortune to have decided, early, to learn one thing thoroughly, and to have chosen the right thing, and then the opportunities to acquire the language. By what I learned as a young man I survived the war; if I hadn't learned Italian and become an interpreter, if I had been just an ordinary soldier, I wouldn't have survived. I would have gone to the Russian front, where most of my comrades perished. Of my class of more than twenty, all of them died but for three. That was the rate of killing. Not even 20 per cent survived. Later, I was lucky to pass through the Russian lines, and later again when I was Achille I was lucky to pass the partisans. Even when I was struck down by polio I was lucky to be in Italy, and to recover. I am lucky to have travelled. You know, wherever I am, when I know where the north is, I know where I am. I am lucky in my wife and my children and my career, in my home and now in this coming down of the Wall, in this end to our isolation. I was afraid I would not live long enough to see it coming down, but I was always absolutely sure it would come down one day.'

11

WERNER: FLIGHT FROM THE REPUBLIC

'In 1961 when the Wall went up I was in the Volksarmee, on military service, serving in a unit on the Wall opposite Kreuzberg, here in Berlin. I was the clerk to the Colonel of my regiment, and I remember all that busy activity. There was a lot of concrete, a lot of bricks. He was a good man, the Colonel. Six months after my release from the army I heard on RIAS that the Colonel had defected to the West; they said he was commander of the regiment guarding the Kreuzberg/Mitte sector. The same man. A year after that I heard that the Stasi had kidnapped him back from the West. They had come to his hotel room, drugged him at gunpoint, rolled him up in a carpet and shipped him back over the border in a furniture van. He was a good man, and he would go to prison for a long time. After my arrest and while I was awaiting trial I met another high-ranking officer who had defected and been brought back. "Your crime," he said, "it's nothing. I'm going away for years and years. I did the same as you, but me they trusted."

'I was never in the Party, but in my early days, ten, twelve years before I decided to leave the GDR, I had identified with Communism. What I wanted was to make socialism better but by the time I planned to go to the West all my interest in Communism was gone, finished, collapsed.

'There came a turning point, over the years. This was because in my career in the GDR I saw more than most people saw. I saw the fine life of the functionaries, for all of them. The way they live, it's not at all how ordinary people live. I've seen the hard structures in it all. I heard a lot of things about *Staatssicherheit*, state security. Such things I've seen, and I've heard stories from good friends with other and better connections than mine. One Christmastime I was in Cottbus, staying as a guest at my girlfriend's parents. There was also her grandfather, who had a flat below in the same house. My girlfriend's father was his son. He was an old man, and he was the director of the biggest factory in Cottbus. He had been an old SPD man before the war, and then in 1946 when the SPD and the KPD were put together to form the SED, he was therefore automatically in the SED. He was an SED man then, from that date. In Cottbus that time at Christmas we were having a meal, drinking a little wine, and I told the old man small stories – true stories – about officials in high positions in Berlin, about the life they lived, how they ate and had people to do everything for them, and the things they had. He wouldn't believe me. He wouldn't hear me. He said, "It can't be, it can't be. I cannot hear this." I was forbidden to speak of it. "Not in my house," he said.

'My work was in computers, in operations research. My field was economic mathematics. My first training was as a mechanical engineer, so this was my second education. I have two diplomas. I was not a programmer, but more I dealt with problems with systems, sorting out the mathematics, troubleshooting, brainstorming. Through my work I had to go from time to time into Ministries and the offices of high officials, and there I could see how they lived. So I was able to see what normally people could not see. This changed my thinking about socialism. I worked at the Ministry of Construction, and before that in the Ministry of Health. In the Ministry of Health there was a special institute for the further education of professors and health managers, and I had to teach my subject. Another time I worked in East German TV, which isn't a ministry but is in the same position as a ministry, with the same identification cards and so on. The committee for radio and television was a government department with the status of a ministry. And once I was in Wandlitz, the luxury concentration camp for chiefs, in the house of a high Politburo member, Hermann Axen, who was at the time responsible for Foreign Affairs. That day, that afternoon, his daughter was going to visit a friend in her flat. I saw the car that came to take her, a Western car, a Mercedes, with a young woman driver, only to visit a friend.

'This was my offence: I tried to go from Hungary to Austria to get to West Germany, and the Hungarian border guards saw

me. Hands up. I was charged with *Republikflucht*, flight from
the Republic, under Paragraph 213 of the East German law
code.

'In 1979 I decided I was going to leave. It was May, and I
made my attempt in July the same year. I heard that from the
first of August there were to be new laws, a tough new code for
political offences. I had heard it was in preparation. So I had to
go before the end of July, and it was now or never. So I went to
Budapest, a city I know where I had been before for work and
on private visits. Budapest has the same position as Paris in
France. It's central, and all the railway lines radiate outwards in
all directions. So I would set out from there, but I had to find
out how to cross the border. I realized Hungarian state security
would have agents in Budapest. One night I was in a restaurant,
in this place, and I was trying to work out my plan. I must go to
the border, to Austria. That was clear. In the restaurant I had
been watching a Hungarian man who had been a worker, a
Gastarbeiter, in the GDR. He was speaking in German. He was
not a good man. He asked me for money. But in the restaurant I had heard him say he was a soldier in the border
guard half a year before, on the Austrian border. Before that
he was in the GDR, and after that too, but I worked out he
was Hungarian and so he must have been a border guard in
Hungary. I heard him say all this. I gave him money, and
invited him for a beer. And slowly as we talked I learned more
and more about the border, about the best points to cross, the
rhythm and frequency of the control. Gently. To this day he
will not know what it was I asked him. He was too foolish. But
I heard everything.

'This was on the Saturday. On the Tuesday I would set out
to the border. I said to myself, "Werner, be hard now, be
strong." So I worked out my plan. I cannot speak the language,
and to the ticket seller on the station I would obviously be East
German, and so I decided to be dumb. I was a mute. On a piece
of paper I wrote out the time of my train and destination and
bought a second-class ticket, pointing to my mouth to say I
couldn't speak. So I got my ticket without using my voice and
without giving away the fact that I was German. On the train I
saw a lot of soldiers going off on service, on duty, and also
guards. I was hungry, and I realized I must use the same method
to get something to eat. There was an old woman who was

selling things to eat, and I pointed and mumbled and it worked. I knew that on the train the border controls come in before the border, because it was easier to catch refugees before they reached the border. All this was OK with me. Before they got on I got off the train at a station. I waited a while for evening, and had a meal in the restaurant in a train station. It was absolutely empty; there was one table for two people and the other table was the first class. I can read a little Hungarian, the dishes and so on, and I showed him what I wanted to eat, and made the same dumb play with the waiter. So far everything was OK. Then there came two policemen, just normal cops, as I could see from their uniforms. They checked the restaurant, and talked to the waiter over in the other corner. I saw him nod in my direction, and he said a word, perhaps "dumb". "It's OK, he's a Hungarian." Then in front of the train station was another type of uniform, border guards. It was a tricky moment. It was a dangerous situation, being there close to the border. I left, I went to another place, and I changed my clothes, and took off my cravat, so that I would look more Hungarian with just a shirt and collar, the style I have seen in small towns in Hungary. I was ready to go. As I had learned, my best crossing point was twenty kilometres away through the woods. Then at evening I set out for the border and the wire.

'Everything went well, and I reached the border through the woods. I got through most of the wire, very carefully. But one thing I did not know was the wire in the ground. It was electric, an alarm wire. I heard the alarms go off. The border station was two kilometres away, but thirty seconds later there was a jeep, and an armed border guard. Five minutes later there was a bigger car, with eight men, armed too, lights, and dogs. I'd already heard the dogs. I realized, oh shit, they've found me. "*Hände hoch.*" I was interviewed by the Hungarian secret service, and transported to Budapest where I was held for a month. Then I was handed over to the *Staatssicherheit* in Budapest, and they brought me in an aeroplane to East Berlin. It was Erich Honecker's aeroplane. He didn't always need it, so the Stasi used it. The pilot was Stasi, the stewardess was Stasi. In the aeroplane I had to wear handcuffs. Where could I go, I was in an aeroplane? There were other prisoners, people like me from the GDR, and for each prisoner there was a special Stasi. At the airport we waited in the car for an hour before take-off, and we had to sit absolutely still. I tried to look sideways at the other prisoners, but my guard ordered me to look straight ahead. I could not look sideways at all. It was ridiculous. Then we got on the plane and it was the same: guard, prisoner, prisoner, guard. And so they brought us back to East Berlin. But before I left I had a good talk with the Lieutenant Colonel from the Hungarian secret service, the liaison officer with the GDR. He spoke fluent German, and he said to me "We are ashamed of this practice. What's the matter in the GDR? It's all so good there. You can buy more in East Berlin, you have special shops. And you have more money there. For you there aren't the political reasons there are for a lot of us." I hope to meet him again. Perhaps he's a general now, or better he's unemployed and he doesn't have a job at all.

'So then they brought me back. For about half a year I was in the Stasi prison in East Berlin for investigation. I was taken first to Stasi Berlin district headquarters. In each district of East Germany – in every *Bezirk* – there was a Stasi department, with a prison inclusive. As I was a Berliner it was the right place for a Berliner, and so there I was. But there were other matters, complications, because in my career I had worked in three Ministries, and so there was a question of security. So my case was transferred to Stasi-Zentrale – in Normannenstrasse – and I was moved there. What they did at Zentrale had to do with central problems to do with the whole country, with the security of the GDR, and with foreigners too, of course. I heard one when they brought me out of the cell for twenty minutes. We had a place to walk between concrete walls, so, so big, maybe three metres by twenty, for some fresh air, some exercise. And above us was a gunpost, a guard with a gun, observing us. *Wachregiment Feliks Dzierzynski.*

'My interrogations were on a regular basis. Twice a week, for two hours, I would meet my interrogator. They were very thorough, and interviewed my mother, my brother, friends, people I had worked with. That was the only person I saw. He was very polite, very civil, taking notes, trying to find out what I might know that might be a secret. They were very thorough. He told me they would get what they wanted in the end, and I thought in that case I would take my time. They did not use violence or threaten me with any. I was not beaten, but I could hear beatings around me in other cells. I am not the kind of man they can do that to. There was the regularity, the solitude, and then he would break the rhythm to throw me. In the corner of his office was the pennant for Dynamo, their soccer team. He tried to get me talking about football, about fishing, he would try anything. When we first met I was newly locked up, I had no money, no cigarettes, and I am a heavy smoker. This was the Thursday, he offered me a cigarette, left me the pack, and said he would come back with more the next day. He didn't come, not for many days. I'd ask the guard, but he knew nothing. No cigarettes. It's not so much, but how they wore us down.

'Then after six months it was over and I was tried. I was sent to the Stasi district prison in Frankfurt an der Oder to await the decision of the court. They gave me two years, for fleeing the Republic. I was sent to Cottbus, where I was a year and a half, so it was two years in all. Cottbus was another situation. In East Germany there were two places for political prisoners, Cottbus and Bautzen, both for men, only for men. Cottbus was called a "normal" prison, a "normally political" prison, containing mostly political prisoners, but some criminals just to add to the entertainment. And there in my cell I read in *Neues Deutschland* that Erich Honecker had said to Robert Maxwell there were no political prisoners in the GDR. All my comrades laughed. At the moment he spoke there were 6,000 political prisoners. In the GDR the Stasi, *Staatssicherheit*, was only for investigation. It was under a separate Ministry, but the guards in the political prison came from the Ministry of the Interior, from a special department for prisons. The normal policeman on the street wears green. Our guards wore dark blue, with grey epaulets. And they were separate from the Stasi, but all the important things, all decisions, came from the Stasi. We had two so-called VO, *Verbindungsoffiziere*, contacts between the Stasi and the prison. They gathered information. There was a VO in all the big factories in the GDR with an official sign on his office: VO. For his self-confidence. So he's the man who reports to the Stasi. Our officers, the normal guards, were small people, not well-educated and not in high ranks, but the hierarchy in prison was educated. We were divided into sections, called EB, *Erziehungsbereiche*, education areas, with around 400 people on one floor. On the floor were the cells, and at the end of the floor was a metal door. The chief of each department was an officer who was called an *Erzieher*, an educator, a political educator. These people were in blue uniforms like the other guards, officially with the Ministry of the Interior, but their second profession was *Staatssicherheit*, without the uniform.

'I was in two cells, with nine in my first cell. We had beds for three, triple bunks. It was not so big. There was a toilet in the cell, but that was only since 1977. Before that a bucket. Then in 1977 the GDR was trying to gain international respect, and United Nations commissions were in the GDR, and they said they must have toilets in the cells. It was built in the corner, with a door. In front of the cell windows there were sheets of metal. They let in air but not light, and you couldn't see out. The commissions said they must go, but in my time they had put up new metal sheets. In our factory the windows were all metal, on the outside. And at all points cameras, automatic cameras. There was a central control in front of the prison wall, where officers observed everything.

'Half-way through my time I had to go to another department, because with other people, my comrades, I destroyed a gang of criminal prisoners in my department. The policy of the chief of that department was to control it through the eight or nine strong criminals within it. The criminals were privileged. I was the leader of the resistance to this gang and so I was moved to another department. In the next cell, in the other department, we were twelve. Same conditions. Food was sufficient, not good, but enough. And we must work. And we must not work. But I'm a heavy smoker and without work I cannot have money. In my situation I could not get money from outside, from friends. Nothing was allowed in. We had two factories in our prison. One was for plastics, plastic parts. The other where I worked made camera cases from aluminium. Praktica cameras, Dresden. Most of my time I was on a special machine, automatic, hydraulic, pneumatic, pressing out cases, all I had to do was push buttons, but very fast. I am a mechanical engineer, in the first place. I could work exactly to tolerance, with maximum precision and quality. I calculated with my watch, and checked the machine, and regulated it a little bit. The norm was 100 pressings per day, and between 100 and 200 pressings my money was progressive. I was able to make my 200 pressings for the day by midday, and then I could read books. But other people, my comrades, could not make so much money, sometimes only

POFF!

Love is thicker than concrete

Peter's *Arbeit*: work on what has been spoiled

The Death Strip

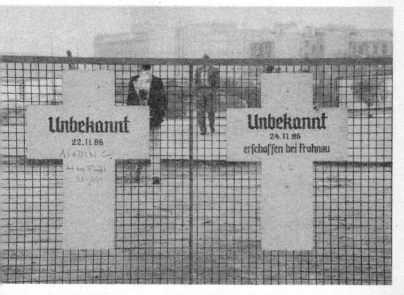

Unbekannt: unknown, killed on the Wall

Kreuzberg! Cow, cross, divided Germany

Piss here

Checkpoint Charlie: Charlie's retired

Brandenburg Gate: border guards loosened up

Wall-pecker with power saw

Wall, hole, border guard

The Wall of the Dictators, November 1989

The Wall of the Dictators deconstructed, January 1990

5 marks a month, for cigarettes, for sausage in our shop, for fish, for chocolates. I had 300, 400 a month. I was a millionaire there. I was rich, one of the richest men. I could help my friends. That all came from the machine. It was faster than normal.

'Our factory was only an affiliate, a sub-factory. We had civilian foremen from the main factory in Dresden. They were mostly from Dresden, they got more money for working in prison of course, but they were not qualified for the work. As an engineer I told them a lot of nonsense. We had doctors and others, technical doctors, medical doctors, writers, all good people, among the prisoners. There was a great relationship among us in the factory. For me life in the cell was hardest. I was an old man of thirty-nine and I was qualified. Most of them were between eighteen and twenty-three, twenty-five, and uneducated. You had to listen to the nonsense, hour by hour, day by day. We did eight hours work a day, officially in normal conditions like in Dresden in the main factory. We worked in three shifts – early morning, afternoon, night – and the next week changed. Sunday was free, Saturday till two. Eight hours, day by day, and the rest of the time we were locked up in the cell. One hour walking. And in this time, exercise time, we had a little shop, where you could buy things if you had money. The cellar of the shop was crammed with things the shop leader had stolen. He was a thief on the outside, a thief on the inside. We had books. And we made wine from bread, bread wine, illegally of course. We kept it in a bucket in the machines in the factory, where it was warm for the wine to ferment. Also we had TV, not in the cell but in a room. There was only one TV, with only one GDR programme. They have two but there was no switch, which was separate. There was not much space in the room, perhaps for 200, when we were around 800 or 900 in the whole prison. On Sunday we got a list for the next week, for the whole week, and we wrote in our names for TV. From each cell only one or two men were allowed to watch. It was a point of hard discussion in the cell. And then the officer would come round and he would say, "This man no, he didn't do good work last week, he didn't answer the officer properly." So the TV was a reward. And I said, I will never go to TV. I don't want to be educated by the officer. I went only twice. Once because I had heard there was a film made by my brother, who is a camera operator. Also it was a good place to meet, in the

TV room, with friends from other departments, on other shifts. You don't see people from the night shift. I had friends from my old department, but we were separated now. One day it was someone's birthday there, and he signalled me through the window to come over, to try it. I spotted a good guard, and he took me over to the other department and I could sit with my friend. We had cake, from someone else. A birthday party.

'We had one visit a month, for one hour. These were held at a long table, with eight, six prisoners along one side, six, eight visitors along the other, the officers sitting at the short sides. Talk talk talk talk talk. The officers were listening to our words, watching for anything we passed, papers. For my first visit I sat in a corner without an officer, and then the next month it was different, and after that I was always positioned near an officer. I couldn't say a word against the order, which was: nothing about prison; family business only. Our method was to cover each other. For instance, one day next to me was a comrade from my cell, and he had a visit from his pretty wife. Sitting next to me he said suddenly, "I have a lot to say to her today," and I just had my mother there, it wasn't so important what we said, so I talked louder and louder to cover him.

'There was mail, but what you needed was connections. When you had connections, connections outside, then you got mail, letters and also parcels. And visitors. But visits were only possible from family of the first grade, *ersten Grades* – wife, brother, close relatives. In the prison law under paragraph one it talks about the first grade of visitors, but that's all they tell you. They don't mention the next paragraph, where it describes second grade, and that includes people you knew before prison, friends, work-mates. Now, I had a mother, old. And I have an uninterested brother. He was afraid of the whole situation. But from before prison I had two good friends, one in the court, an elected official. The other was a doctor. I knew they would visit me, but in prison they will not let you see the book, they won't let you see the rules. However, in Frankfurt I had been fortunate to meet an experienced young criminal in my cell, and he told me to request to see the book, the prison law, that I could ask to see it. So: paper, please; written request. "Yes." They took me to an empty cell, gave me the book. I was not allowed paper, nothing, nothing, no notes. But here it said people of the second grade, friends, can also visit a convicted prisoner, and I memor-

ized it. "Thanks for everything." Later in Cottbus I asked my
officer the law. He told me Paragraph 1. I said I want to hear
Paragraph 2. "Hmhm." Nothing. OK, I said, I'll write a letter,
tomorrow, to the Stasi. I can do it. Below our building where
we went for exercise was a post box, for the VO, for denuncia-
tions, confidences. I wrote the letter. The situation with medicine
in the GDR was critical at that time, and I knew about it, and
that it would get harder with more doctors going to the West,
and I said *Staatssicherheit* I knew about it, but it's not my
problem, it's your problem. And I asked that friends be allowed
to come visit me. I said to all my comrades in the cell that
tomorrow when we went to work I would put this letter in the
post box, and I read it out so that all could see what I was
putting in the box. One month later I had the first visit from
one of my friends. I was the only man in Cottbus at that time
with a friend outside. And from then I had parcels from both
friends, and letters from both, and visits. Connections.

'We were allowed one parcel every two months. In special
cases you were not allowed to have a parcel, if your work was
bad. We were allowed three letters a month. Three in, three
out. And one visit from one person a month. I have seen the
conditions in Honecker's memoir of Brandenburg prison. It
wasn't a concentration camp, it was an official prison. But he
had more visits, for longer periods of time, and that was in war
time, under the Nazis.

'I did two years, altogether. Half a year with the Stasi plus
one and a half in Cottbus. I still wanted to go to the West, more
than ever now. In fact I was bought out. I am one of the people
the West Germans bought out from prison in the East. I don't
know much about how it happened, and they wouldn't tell me
my price, though I asked for it. I think it was DM 110,000. I
looked quickly in the file and saw that sum. So that's my price.
This is what happened. In prison on my third or fourth interview
I had asked for a lawyer. Yes I could have a lawyer. Why not
Dr Vogel? I was allowed to write a letter to him. His assistant
came to interview me, with Vogel. Vogel asked for my crime,
and if it were only *Republikflucht*, and nothing criminal
involved. I told him no. He wrote the details down on a
Western form. That's how they came to have my name on the
lists. But for me the price of my freedom was two years in
prison.

'I was released from Karl-Marx-Stadt prison. A week before I was to be released I was told I would go to the West. In my prison account I had 800 marks. I must get rid of it. I asked could it be sent to my mother: "No." I bought three packs of Camels, not my brand. I couldn't go in jeans, and bought a jacket, and other clothes. On my last day – Friday – I had to go to the cellar, thinking what now? They said here are your papers, your driver's licence, identity card, etcetera. Then we went through a white door, where they took a Polaroid shot for my release paper. Back to the cell. At twelve o'clock, key in the lock. They brought me to the front of the building, where was a green Lada, with a Colonel and his driver. I tried to ask the Colonel questions but his manner was rough: forget it. It was a spring day, the end of March 1981. Karl-Marx-Stadt prison stands on a hill in the centre of the town. He told me to get in the car. We drove off. At the end of the corridor out of the prison was a huge iron door, maybe five or six metres high. It opened electronically and then we were in the town, on the autobahn. I saw a young woman on the street in blue jeans, the first I had seen in two years. Shops, trees, people, where before were guards, comrades, walls, dogs, grey. On the autobahn my eyes couldn't adapt. It was 1 o'clock, I calculated. We would be in the West by three. The Colonel had his wife with him. She drove at 200 kilometres an hour, both of them wanting to get back home. I recalled that it was Friday, for them it was the weekend. The car was relatively quiet. "What do you want to hear on the stereo?" The Colonel was a James Bond type, like Sean Connery, wearing an original English jacket – a Daks, an expensive watch, good pants. At ten to three we were there, picked up by a Westerner in a three-litre Opel. The police and the Colonel were friendly, on familiar terms. The Westerner came out and shook hands with the Colonel; they were colleagues about their regular business, making family talk, inquiring about each other's wives. The Westerner was chief of the bureau of inter-German relations in Giessen. He was a man in leisure clothes, also dressed for the weekend. The Colonel moved to the other car, his driver moved over my baggage. We went over to the Western side. The first Western border guard saluted us. Then the next step, we went to an office on the Western side with the Colonel. I was asked for my papers from prison, though I had no ID. But I was on the list. Then, twenty minutes later, we were in a restaurant on the autobahn, and the man from the West was asking what do you want to eat, perhaps a beer? At the Giessen camp I was given DM 150 and a key for my room. To have a key again, a door I could go through when I wanted, and to be in the West where I wanted to be. My life began again, and I have learned a lot from my experience, I am the stronger for having been in prison. But I know the price of freedom. A half an hour later I was in the town, phoning my friends in the East, with tears in my eyes. I sent a telegram to my mother. Then the next Tuesday we were given clothes by the churches, and there were officials and papers, my first impact with Western bureaucracy. My wish was to go to Berlin. I had my ticket. At Tegel I met a comrade from prison, with his wife. That same evening we were in the Irish pub.'

12

HELGA: SAME BLOODY STORY

'I was born in 1922, in Leipzig. In 1938, when I was sixteen, to get me away from the Nazis my parents sent me to England, so I was there during the war and for a few years after. They themselves perished. I was in England for ten years, and worked there, and though I never earned very much money I recently found I was entitled to a pension. It's tiny, about £14 a week, but it's better than nothing. For a year I worked at a company in Manchester, in Hulme, making drawing instruments for the navy. And for some time I worked as a waitress. And I did dress-making.

'In 1948 I went to the United States to stay with relatives. You see, my father had given my uncle money to emigrate to the United States, and I went there to try to retrieve some of it. When I got there, I realized he was too poor to pay me anything, so he gave me two fur coats. And with these on my back I came to East Germany a year later. In the United States I was in Chicago, where I had relatives, still have. They called me about three or four months ago after the Wall's opening and for thirty minutes we talked on the telephone. They paid the bill so to me it didn't matter. We're still very close, our family. Back in 1948 I didn't like my relatives very much, but I liked the children. They are grandfathers and grandmothers now. I worked in Saks Fifth Avenue. I liked the girls I worked with, in the jewellery department, and I had quite a few friends there. I stayed with relatives – not the relatives my father had paid for the journey to America, these were born in America. They were stinking rich and I was the poor relation and treated as such, which I was. It made me feel awful. I had permission to stay for a year, and I stayed to the day, 365 days, from 12 January 1948 until 12 January 1949. Then I came back on the *Queen Mary*. I flew to the United States and I returned on the *Queen Mary*, in the cheapest class. A year before when I left for the United States my friends in England had taken me out for dinner in London, in Dean Street. But the restaurant wouldn't let us in, though it said open till twelve midnight and this was not yet eleven o'clock. The waiters were on strike. So I said, how can you do such a thing to nice people like us? We support you, we are trade unionists, we support you. And so they let us in and gave us a meal. And when I returned after 365 days the same friends that had given the dinner a year before picked me up in Southampton and we went to the same restaurant. The waiter came and he said, I know you, you are the one with the union.

'When I came back from the United States in 1949 I was supposed to go back there, but I used Britain as a jump-off point to return illegally to East Germany, with false papers. I came to follow the man I had met in England, also a German refugee, who had returned here in 1946, and who became my husband. I already had a passport in my own name, but to get to what was then the Soviet Zone was difficult, so I had to buy false papers in Frankfurt, and with these I returned to what was then the Russian Zone. And as soon as I got here I went to the police and explained, and all was all right then. They accepted me.

'One of these days I intend writing the history of my family, using the family tree and my own biography. For my grandson. I remember saying to myself and to Thomas, my son, the things I write I have to write about, though they will never be printed in this country. Now perhaps, but not before. I've had my ups and downs in this country of course. Does the name Noel Field mean anything? It's a political context, from the Stalin era, 1952, 1953. He was a Western agent. At that time anyone who had been abroad or who was a foreigner was suspected of being a spy, and this of course included me, though I was no such bloody thing. By then I was permanently established, and I was more or less unbothered by them, they left me in peace. But they didn't leave my husband in peace. My husband was born in Bremen but he was a graduate of Manchester University. In economics. He left Bremen overnight in 1933, because somebody had warned him, and went to Britain. George Cadbury, one of the Cadbury chocolate people's sons, had studied with him in Hamburg, and the Cadburys paid for his university course in Manchester. From there my husband went to Spain and joined the International Brigades. He was a German, a resident of Britain, but he was put in the Lincoln Brigade with the Americans. He was wounded, he returned to Britain, and completed his studies, and worked through the war. He joined the Communist Party in 1943.

'Then in 1946 he returned to this country, with the help of a friend in Yugoslavia whom he'd met in Spain, and this was his downfall. Later on, in the early fifties, though this actually started in 1944, 1945, Stalin began to be at loggerheads with Tito. At that time in this country where anyone who'd been outside was suspect, anyone with anything to do with Yugoslavia was particularly under suspicion. Obviously they were looking for people, for Western spies and anyone who had anything to do directly or indirectly with Yugoslavia. They were trying to copy what was happening in the Soviet Union. And because they found out that my husband had returned to the then Russian Zone via Yugoslavia, he was suspected. By then he was the managing director of a big Kombinat, a string of seventy factories. He was arrested on false charges. He got two and a half years for economic crimes, so-called. False pretences. Stalinism. It was a political act because they said he was a spy for the Englishman Noel Field, though they charged him falsely with economic crimes. So they took this political thing and turned it into a criminal matter. It was almost like the trials in 1937 in Moscow, ending not with death but with prison. It was then the beginning of the Cold War and everything had this touch, of the criminal. All Eastern European countries were like this then, Czechoslovakia, Bulgaria, and also the GDR. Everyone who came back from Western exile was suspect.

'So my husband went to prison. I only know that money is the root of all evil, though in those days there was none. Everyone, all the neighbours, were very poor. Because my husband was in prison people kept their distance. There was no hate, but distance. During this time he was in prison, I could not get work, and I worked on the trams. My son Thomas was two years old, and I couldn't find a place for him. Terrible. And nothing to eat. Oh God, nothing to eat. I don't want to dwell on this, but those times were very hard. This was Stalinism in action.

'In my efforts to rehabilitate my husband since the *Wende* I made a short write-up of what they did to him, the trumped-up charges. They wanted to get rid of him, because he had dared to criticize the minister. This was in Karl-Marx-Stadt, and the judge who sentenced him, and also the attorney-general there at the time, had worked for the judiciary under the Nazis, and the Communists also used them. I wrote a letter to the new attorney-general, a page and half, very short, very precise, all the facts, including that there had been a search of my house when my husband was already in jail, and they had taken away my papers certifying my stay in England. They were never returned. I wrote that I had been under suspicion as well, having returned from abroad. I asked for financial restitution, and told them the records I have are at their disposal. There are two witnesses surviving from those years. We went to visit one in Karl-Marx-Stadt. He told us a few things, but they're not terribly important. He advised us to go and see the attorney-general of Karl-Marx-Stadt district. So I took this page and half with me and he read it very carefully and said this is most interesting, and most important. And he said he would try to find the records although it was thirty-seven years later, and would I please have a little patience? Normally the records are destroyed after fifteen years, but because this is from a certain era they kept them. I have had a letter from him telling me that they are searching for the records now. And they said they had sent it on to the Ministry of Justice so that its contents could be included in the new rehabilitation law, which is being worked out. But I want my husband rehabilitated by name and not with a whole lot of others. So now I wait. So it may well happen. Anyway, I'm not leaving them in peace.

'I have a boyfriend now, but I have been a widow on my own for the past thirteen and a half years. I met men occasionally, they were all terrible. I remember meeting one man and his eyes started shining when he talked about his experiences in the war. And that was the end of the evening. My boyfriend is Jewish, as I am. We are both from the Jewish community here in Berlin. We met at the Jewish Community Centre about two years ago. I had known him before, and his wife, who died a year and a half before. And he knew I was a widow and of course I sent condolences when his wife died. She was quite a famous scientist. He was very sad, and I had been all through this and it took me two years to get over my husband's death. And so we met again at the Jewish Community Centre and he was very depressed. And he said to me, how am I going to get out of this depression? I feel terrible. And I said, you know what you have to do is talk talk talk, and cry, you have got to cry, it's got to come up. And when I said that he began to cry. And I said to him look here, I'm the one to talk to. We went to his car, it was cold, it was winter, it was snowing outside. We sat in the car and it was freezing and he talked for about an hour and everything came out. So it started from there and then he rang me up and when I came back from Israel about seven months ago I discovered he'd been waiting for me to come back. We meet maybe once a week during the week, and we usually spend the weekends together. We are not married. He proposed marriage and I said no, it wouldn't work out. So on this basis we get together on Friday evenings. On Saturday he goes to see his father-in-law, who is very weak, and does the shopping and a few things for him, and they eat together. He returns here Saturday evening and he leaves me Sunday night. And that's that. It works well. It works out well on this basis. I wouldn't like to share my flat constantly with another person. I like my freedom and a new person would be to me like a Berliner Mauer.

'I was in Israel for the first time last year, never been before, to visit my relatives. There I met old classmates of mine from the Jewish school in Leipzig. We got together again after fifty years. They thought I had died in the Holocaust, so you can imagine the reunion. I went to the Wailing Wall and I found someone to say kaddish for my parents. I found a young rabbi, because only a man is allowed to say kaddish, and I told him in Yiddish my parents had died in the Holocaust, and he said kaddish for them. Myself, I'm not convinced, I'm not convinced at all, but this was a promise I had made. And then I went to the Church of the Holy Sepulchre, where Christ was supposed to have been buried. Very clever people say he was actually buried one mile further down the road. I went to see it. It was incredible. Before you enter you're checked for weapons by the police. I gave them my handbag and said help yourselves. I would go back there tomorrow.

'I'm going to vote for Gregor Gysi's party which is also my party, the PDS. Despite everything I am still a Communist. I joined the Party in 1969, and I'm not going to leave it now,

although I'm somewhat disillusioned. I think, now, that socialism as we understood it, in it's pure form, is impractical. It just
cannot be translated into reality. But here we've started to make
a new beginning, and with the little I have, I can do, I will try to
help. What we have had to uncover about the past, about
people who were caught up in it, it's shocking, it will take a
long time to get over. A long time. We talk about nothing else
almost, me and my boyfriend, me and my friends, but what's
the use of talking, we've got to do things, and we can't really do
much until the elections. After the election we can make a new
beginning. I suppose there will be a bit of chaos for the first
couple of days, some people will be crazy with joy, and others
will be very sad. A new start has been made for this country
and it's going to take us to one united Germany. Eighty million
Germans. It's frightening. They've already started to demand
back the old borders. The West is coming. I don't like this
swallowing up business at all. The GDR is going to be a low-
cost country. I think those who shouted at the top of their
voices for unification will awake in a short time. It will be a bad
awakening for them. In a few years they will be very disappointed. The way they see the West is an illusion, they don't
know how hard it is to survive under capitalism. It's hard
because of this rivalry which has to be and which we didn't
have here, and that's why we never got off the ground.

'You know, I haven't been to West Berlin since the Wall
opened. I was there once, years ago. So I feel I've seen it, and
I'm not interested in DM 100. I've seen the West. I live here, in
East Berlin, and the Wall never bothered me because I had no
desire to go through it. I went to England. I went to Israel and
Iraq. Occasionally I go to Britain, and whenever I go there I feel
at home. You have to pass through immigration, and every time
it's the same bloody story. The immigration officer says to me
do you speak English and I say yes I do and then I begin to cry.
And he says why are you crying? and I always say it's tears of
joy. I feel at home there, part of my heart is in England. And
then he asks me questions and I tell him I realize it's awful
being in the secret service. He seems to understand me and he
shakes my hand and wishes me all the best. There's a feeling
you're talking to a human being, which is very clever of the
British. This is the way I feel: England saved my life. Otherwise
I would have gone down the drain with my parents; I lost

twenty-seven members of my family in the Holocaust, in Poland and in Germany. Nazism as a form of fascism could only have happened in this country, with these people, with these people. They are still racists, and you know there was anti-semitism in the GDR under Ulbricht and under Honecker. I have a sentimental attachment to the Russians because the Red Army liberated my grandmother from Theresienstadt concentration camp, which doesn't mean every Russian is wonderful. It's England I feel at home in. But I don't live in the past. What's the use of that?'

13

ROUGH BEAST

New Year's Day: another year sent to go stand in the corner. It's the first day of the century's last ten. Last night was the party of the decade, from the Reichstag along the Wall to Potsdamer Platz and Charlie, and in the East up into Unter den Linden, but especially at the Brandenburg Gate. Thousands from East and West climbed the Wall, traded drinks, jokes, news, embraced, sang, waved flags, danced, got drunk together. Today the Pariser Platz and up into Unter den Linden is lethal with broken glass. Last night, when about 200 people were injured, most slightly, the ambulances couldn't get through for the crowds and the smashed glass. Beside the Brandenburg Gate GDR TV had put up scaffolding and on it a huge screen whereon they showed the crowd themselves, the film they were filming. '*Wir sind das Volk.*' Via the scaffolding, people climbed up on to the Gate. There they painted VIVE L'ANARCHIE in bold white letters on the ancient symbol of Prussian order, and attacked the Quadriga, chipping souvenir bits out of it. They hauled down the GDR flag and the red flag and hoisted first the blue Euro flag with its circle of stars, then a Canadian flag, then a white flag that might have been someone's underpants. One young man, a West Berliner, was later found dead some way down Unter den Linden. He had died of multiple injuries, some internal, including a severed aorta, injuries consistent with having fallen off the scaffolding on to broken glass, but how he had staggered, bleeding, unseen in all that crowd to where he was found dead remains a mystery, one that no one seems interested in solving. Later it was reported he fell out of a tree. But the trees on Unter den Linden are too small to fall out of.

Ich verstehe nicht. Nichts. Ich verstehe Bahnhof.

It's another unsolved mystery no one seems pressed to unravel.

Here everyone's only coming to their senses and beginning to grasp the pace of change, and if everyone has a hangover this morning no one's surprised. In the last two months the impossible has been happening all around, as the old regimes in central Europe have fallen one by one, abandoned by their Soviet mentors and no longer policed by the Red Army. The old dinosaurs ran out of ideas, their systems perished of inertia, and only in Romania was the change violent and bloody. In the East those who were in prison for demanding freedom are now free, and coming into power themselves. The pace of change, where in just a few months structures and institutions that were thought to be permanent and unassailable have collapsed, has left everyone breathless. Here in Berlin, where everything that happens in Europe eventually ripples in, they're still gasping, on both sides of the Wall, barely able to take it all in. Populations are on the move again, and all the old certainties suddenly in question. Last night's party was to affirm one certainty: the Germans will be united. History, from the point of view of all her neighbours, is about to throw up another critical German mass at the centre of Europe, and no one but the Germans is excited about it. Everywhere here they run out the same argument: a united Germany constrained by the European community, within NATO. What can go wrong? You do not trust us? they ask. It is a German opportunity. Gorbachov is far too busy, and Bush is playing golf, the French and the Poles are disturbed, and the British Prime Minister blusters, but in Bonn Herr Kohl has seen his chance. By January unification is the name of the game, and by its end even Gorbachov has yielded to its inevitability.

Whatever happened out in the vast East, whatever leaf falling in the forest or eddy stirred by a butterfly's wing, the eventual avalanche is evident all around here. Though it was Gorbachov's initiative, in part the accretion of years of pressure and resistance, in part the eventual failure of the centralized economy and the slow collapse of systems without access, the sudden changes had many slow beginnings and false starts: in frustration, in isolation, in despair. In those tight-meshed and suspicious societies beyond the Wall, whose regimes knew best and governed in the people's name, mankind was proclaimed on its way to peace and freedom and equality, as close to perfection as it was possible to be. History unrolled slowly and in good order along the lines of the next five-year plan. In reality the individual was reduced to the status of an ant in society's anthill, the secret police and constant surveillance of the captive populations the negation of personal freedom. In the GDR freedom from hunger, illiteracy and homelessness; but in the end it was all too boring.

Down Friedrichstrasse to Charlie, turning aside down Leipziger Strasse past more grey and bullet-pocked buildings to the House of Ministers, originally Goering's Air Ministry, built by Speer in high Nazi style. Goosestep architecture. From the Western side across the Wall it is a gaunt ghost of a building, and from here it is no less so. It is dour and sour on five and six storeys, blocked out in slabbed windows and pillars, its grubby windows backed by cotton curtains and beyond them, here and there, a few pale neon strips. Along the side, behind tightly shut iron gates, the grand entrance of Goering in his medals and pink suit, with at each side four rusting spotlamps, and space for pomp and ceremony. By the public entrance at the front, behind the line of dark slabbed pillars, a long frieze made of baked tile, dated 1952, depicts the imaginary life of the GDR. Here everyone is smiling as they work, driving tractors, building, pouring hot metals, inspecting plans, constructing the state. To one side happy workers, some in overalls, some in white coats, one in a suit with a briefcase, advance under the banners of socialism; ahead of them, blue-shirted maidens of the FDJ, the Communist youth movement, young folks with instruments, singing, one a blond-haired blue-eyed youth, a *Wandervogel* in *Lederhosen* who could be just back from a Hitler Youth rally. In the centre, a woman with a sheaf of corn, a workman shaking hands with a grey bespectacled gentleman in a brown suit: the leadership congratulating itself. At the far end the object of it all: a young family, the infant on her father's shoulder clutching a blue flag with a white dove of peace, walking out in their best clothes and their sensible shoes to the celebrations in the stadium, where distant crowds waving red banners are to be seen. And in the background of the frieze's length the factories, their chimneys and smokestacks. Everyone here is smiling, happy, healthy, enthusiastically busy, in stark contrast to the pinched and sallow reality about the streets, where everyone is old before their time.

*

Ich verstehe Bahnhof, nur Bahnhof. I am the man on the train who understands only the names of the stations, and of them it is only the one I get off at and the one before that I recognize. *Mein Name ist Hase, ich weiss nichts:* my name is Hare, I don't know anything. At New Year's at Potsdamer Platz graffiti appeared on the Eastern side of the inner wall. Quickly rubbed off, it depicted a line of hares – or rabbits – heading for the exit. It was quickly overpainted. *Angsthase:* worried hare, scaredy cat, chicken.

An old man with his maps. He pores over old maps of the city, pointing out the roads that are changed, the roads that are blocked, the roads that were built to go round the blockages. Down here, in the south-west corner at Checkpoint Bravo that he calls Dreilinden, is the crossing point for the long-distance traffic south to Nuremberg, Stuttgart, Munich and Frankfurt, with all its outworks of customs and checkpoints, allied control points, police, and all the flags fluttering in the wind. Just south of it, as the traffic enters the transit route into the GDR, there's visible in the distance a plinthed Russian tank, World War II vintage, there to remind everyone who was really in charge here. He opens an old map of the S-Bahn, from the fifties, folded carefully away like a forbidden manuscript, and points to the ring system all the way around Berlin, an inner and an outer, with crossing points at Westkreuz (West) and Ostkreuz (East), a network connecting at every point all around the city and its suburbs and far out into the countryside. It looks like a rose. All over Berlin there are derelict stations, dead lines, tracks running off into the trees. Next to this map, the maps of Eastern and Western systems reveal where the rings were broken, the routes stopped, though trains run up and down the lines on either side, their passengers oblivious of each other. He points at the cut-off arms of the system: at Wannsee, Spandau, Heiligensee, Frohnau, in the city centre at Friedrichstrasse and Schlesisches Tor and Anhalter Bahnhof, in the south more broken arms at Lichtenrade and Lichterfelde Süd, and traces the missing sweep of the north and south S-Bahn rings, abruptly interrupted by history at Gesundbrunnen and Sonnenallee. But for the Wall it would all work. And now with the Wall gone, it will work again. He folds his maps.

*

At Friedrichstrasse, along the S-Bahn platform and down the stairs to the checkpoint, the border crossers are a slow river. In the lobby of the *Ausgang*, the tide divides. Most of it, East German, loaded with packages, boxes and plastic bags, exhausted and excited, streams off to the right, to their own border crossing. To the left the line for the *Andere Staaten* – foreigners – which here includes West Germans and West Berliners, moves quickly, where once it would have dawdled, each traveller subject to thorough scrutiny. Now the Grepos are merely immigration officers, who still turn some away. More and more it is the blue-uniformed customs officers who come to the fore. In East and West, newly faced with an open border, they are reported short of customs officers.

But they cannot hope to control the amount of smuggling on this border, in and out. Much of it is in subsidized goods bought cheap in the East and sold in the West, by the Poles, and now by Ossis. In January GDR customs investigated some 9,000 cases. Among items being smuggled out are children's clothes, underwear, shoes, sausage, meat, herbs, baking materials, antiques, carpets, amber, icons, booze, furs, caviar. And drugs: the East has quickly become a staging post on the junkie supply route. In January 137 weapons were seized, thousands of cartons of cigarettes, and one individual was stopped with 184 cans of caviar. And currency speculation continues, heating up as the month wears on and discussions develop as to monetary union and currency reform, and uncertainty increases as to the eventual exchange rate. Black market speculation, as Easterners rapidly convert their savings into goods or Deutschmarks, is still undermining the Ostmark. At the Rudower Chaussee border crossing an Easterner was stopped with 45,000 Ostmarks that he planned to convert into Deutschmarks. In January on the borders of West Germany and West Berlin customs confiscated over 2 million Ostmarks.

With a legal exchange rate of 1/3, not much more realistic than the 1/1 rate insisted on by the GDR till 1 January, the Easterners, forbidden to exchange East for West, are pushed on to the black market. This flourishes openly around Zoo station and more furtively in the East, and its rate fluctuates wildly: 1/5, 1/6. Around the New Year it was 1/10, up to 1/20. In the first week of January at the Wechsel by the Zoo it was at 1/8, outside on the street at 1/5. Through January the market turned down, in anticipation of a buy-out of the Ostmark by the West. Even at such rates, the Ossis are still turning their savings into Deutschmarks. Westerners, who may buy what they like, are not allowed to take Ostmarks in, unless they can show a receipt for the 1/3 exchange in the East. Money in, money out. The black marketeers don't make much; they're trading on the edge, speculating.

At the New Year the welcome gave out. The West withdrew it, and Ossis were no longer entitled to DM 100. Through the month the pressure on the border eased little, as the last of the *Begrüssungsgeld* was picked up. Now GDR citizens were allowed to buy DM 200 per annum in the East, at 1/3. This slowed them down a little, and clearly the welcome mat was being withdrawn. From 1 January resettlers from the GDR who used to get earnings related benefit, depending on professional qualifications, now get about DM 1,000 per month, for twelve months at the most. Then they are on their own.

But the question of currency reform keeps many East Germans awake at night. 155 billion marks in savings are endangered. In an economy where there wasn't much to buy, most people put their money into the local Sparkasse. Depending on the rate the bankers and the politicians in Bonn finally agree, savings could be at parity, or halved or further fractioned. Rumour has it that only the first 5,000 marks of any account will be changed 1 for 1, so people are opening accounts for their children and splitting up their funds. Some branches of the Sparkasse were said to have run out of savings books. In January Easterners opened 104,000 Deutschmark accounts at the GDR state bank. In the same month they drew out 1.7 billion marks. People are spending their money on consumer goods, domestic equipment, washing machines and televisions and electronic goods, bought East or West. Much of the money goes over on the black market to Zoo station.

Just as it always was, the Wall is still a symbol: photographed, chiselled at, bits taken away as souvenirs; it can be climbed on, danced on, and now that the Wall-peckers have widened the gaps they've opened between the slabs, it can be squeezed through. People begin to venture on to the forbidden death strip, marvelling that two months before they might have been shot there, which adds to the frisson. Vaclav Havel, the new

President of Czechoslovakia, comes to Berlin and is taken to the Wall. He expresses surprise that it's still standing, and offers the help of Czech demolition teams. The event, the opening, begins to recede, a moment of *kairos* that altered the chronology and meaning of before and after, ravelled up the past and realigned the future, and Berliners East and West are beginning to reassess the changes brought by it. Not all of them are welcome.

Grego has little faith in the East. In the East, he says, are all those who didn't have the gumption to flee: the dumb, the stupid, the Party faithful, the ones who will take any order and carry it out. The East, he says, carried on the military and bossy traditions of the Prussians, inheriting the abrupt manners of the Nazis. Those who grew up there endured forty years of dictatorship. He doesn't think much of the prospects. Party membership has fallen to 2 million; out of a voting population of 8 million, this will give them about 25 per cent of the vote, not enough to form a government, and no one will join them in a coalition. Unless they pull a putsch, they're out. The GDR will then reorganize itself into a democratic regime with a mixed economy. He thinks it will remain independent. Why not two Germanies? There is already another German state, in Austria, and parts of Switzerland and Italy are German speaking. But the Stasi and the Communists must go. Then, he foresees, in ten or twenty years there'll be no difference. Then, if that's what people wish, there can be some form of federation. But he is not hopeful.

Hüber is off duty, drinking with his mate Christoff. Hüber is a waiter, Christoff is training to be a chef. Hüber sings over and over in a deep bass Paul Robeson voice, 'Nobody knows the trouble I've seen/Nobody knows my sorrow.' Christoff is drunk. He wants another drink. He wants a girl. He wants a stereo. He wants a 50 inch TV set. He says that when he finishes his training he's going West straight away. Hüber objects: this society educated and trained him, enabled him to make a living, and now he'll just go West for the money. Doesn't he feel he owes his fellow citizens some loyalty, some gratitude? Has he no better desire in life than money? I'm going, says Christoff. No one will stop me. It is an old argument, and they know every step of it. Hüber's anger is mock anger, but he means it none the less. It's his responsibility to dissuade his comrade from deserting. Hüber's a Party member. In his work he's in charge of a section, a cell of workers, of which Christoff is a member. For Hüber it's a long fight, and he's not yet out of patience. It goes back a long way, to 1848 and beyond, in the long struggle for what he calls, affirmatively, social justice. 'Society we have, the other not. I will stay here to fight for it.' Christoff will have none of it; he sees the lights glittering beyond the border. He gets up to leave. He will go now. Hüber decides to go with him. He sings, 'Nobody knows the trouble I've seen, Nobody knows the trouble I've seen.'

This man, he was a painter and decorator, in the East. Some years ago he got out through Czechoslovakia, and came West. A young man, he'd been cooped up all his life; he travelled the world – America, Europe, Australia – working his way with his trade, painting, paperhanging. Then he'd had enough. He wanted to go home. He came to West Berlin, he bought false papers and went back East with his new identity. He went to work, painting and hanging paper, as usual. He discovered that in the East there was a shortage of wallpaper, and it came in only one pattern, say chrysanthemums. What everyone wanted was plain heavy paper, lumpy like porridge, dog's breakfast. Then they could paint over it whatever colour they wanted, or could get. So our man came over to West Berlin on his West German identity card, bought up all the dog's breakfast he could carry, and went back on his East German card. He was doing well. His painters' and decorators' brigade was in high demand, and there was a good price on the paper. They did so well the brigade was distinguished by the authorities, and given a medal. Then he was caught. It wasn't serious. He was admonished and told not to do it again. The fact was, they told him, the dog's breakfast paper was made in the GDR and exported to the West. It wasn't for sale in the GDR. He'd been reimporting it.

Since the opening of the Wall, Easterners have poured through to stay at the rate of 2,000 a day, and the tide shows no sign of turning. It flows at the same rate through January. In 1989, 343,000 moved to the West. In West Berlin at the beginning of

January, about 200 a day were reporting to the Marienfelde refugee camp. Bonn expects over half a million this year, a figure that could rise if economic conditions and uncertainty worsen in the East, and this figure is additional to another half a million of German origin expected to arrive from other parts of Eastern Europe, the *Aussiedler*, descendants of German emigrants from Poland, Russia, Romania. From the latter, following the fall of Ceauşescu, the numbers are increasing. For years the flow of immigrants of German descent has been steady, satisfying the image West Germany projected of itself as the homeland. But now the case is dramatically altered; the policy of accepting German immigrants as fellow Germans evolved as a response to division, the Cold War and the Iron Curtain, and was affordable so long as that was in place. Reception schemes were geared for it; now they are inundated.

The Federal Republic has been ensnared in its own propaganda. Policies and agreements that worked so long as the border crossers were few are now hopelessly overrun. In the health service, a reciprocal treaty agreement between the FRG and the GDR in 1974 provided mutual health care for each others' citizens while they were on the other side of the border – hospitalization, medicine, the services of doctors, dentists, opticians, hearing. But in recent weeks demands on health insurance have been so heavy that the health authority is about to run out of money. Once they arrived in the West many GDR resettlers went sick; some were, but others had heard that sick paid more than unemployed earnings-related. In 1989 over half the resettlers arriving in Berlin obtained a doctor's certificate saying they had 'problems adapting' or 'resettler's syndrome'; the numbers of compliant doctors are put up in phone boxes at the Marienfelde refugee centre. Subsequently, sick pay has been cut to the same level as unemployment benefit. As to pensions, in 1960 the FRG granted GDR resettlers the same pensions as West Germans. This too was based on a political situation no longer true: people who escaped through the borders often risked their lives, leaving everything behind, and were regarded as the victims of political circumstance. By a further treaty, made at a time when the Polish government didn't allow its citizens to travel abroad, this applied to Poles too, provided they had been granted political asylum. All this grates on

Westerners, who cannot see why they should pay for people who have contributed nothing to their social funds. And in all these areas anticipation of a change might provoke an increased exodus. There is the devil on the one hand, the deep blue sea on the other.

The acceptance of anyone with a German ancestor into full state benefits is beginning to produce a growing chorus of resentment among the natives. Many settlers are culturally foreign and many cannot speak German. It all adds to the drain on resources and the growing tension among Germans who regard the newcomers as outsiders, throwing themselves on to the West German state. And among the incomers there are tensions and pecking orders: between GDR resettlers and Germans of Polish origin, whom they call *Polacken* in contempt; GDR settlers who came over before 9 November resent those who came over after. It is all turning into an orgy of small-mindedness. GDR people feel they should be looked after first, as 'proper Germans'. Cramped into tight quarters and frustrated in their efforts to find work, there are fights, drunkenness, drugs. The West turns out to be hard: hard to find work, hard to find somewhere to live. In 1989 the job centres found work for only 2,600 immigrants, with the Romanian Germans bottom of the heap; on the other hand GDR settlers find it easier to find work. Chances are good for nurses, construction workers, air traffic controllers. The rest go on struggling in the refugee centres, where it currently takes a year to resettle most of them, but the inrush continues.

In Berlin the problems sharpen each day, and it's harder and harder for anyone to find accommodation. In West Germany there's a shortage of 1.2 million homes, and in West Berlin 250,000 people looking for a place to live must now compete with resettlers, increasing social tensions. At the end of January Bonn set aside DM 550 million for temporary housing, and the Berlin Senate decided to build 28,000 new flats in West Berlin, but the question is where? On the job market trained and qualified refugees find work at the expense of Westerners; there is fear that employers, given a ready supply from the East, will not invest in training. In the city, where this problem is particularly pressing, Easterners commute to part-time work off the books. What they are doing is illegal in the East, disapproved of in the West. So they keep their mouths shut and work for low pay. For Westerners, bitten both ways, it is becoming apparent who must pay for all of this.

Resettlers, no doubt weary after flight and nervous of the next event, do not want to leave their emergency accommodation, even for a better flat. Up at a site in north Berlin, refugees had been housed in transport containers; they had done them up, put up little curtains, made them into homes. Then came the news: they were to be rehoused in flats. But they would not go. They wanted to know what would happen to their little homes, and on being told that Turks would be moved in, refused adamantly to move. They weren't making way for *Kanaken*, for the *Abschaum*, the scum, as they defined them.

In West Berlin emergency accommodation is designed for people seeking political asylum, of whom, in January, there are some 2,500. Of these, 1,268 are Vietnamese and 348 are Poles. There are Kurds, Iranians, Iraqis. West Berlin, in its public relations role of bastion of freedom, has long been an arrival point for refugees: from Eastern Europe, from the Far East, from the Middle East, from Iran and Iraq. Those who achieve refugee status add to the rich mix of Berlin life, but while they wait their plight is unenviable, uncertain, and indefinite. They must stay in hostels, they are not allowed to work, and they are afforded a pitiable sum in pocket money.

And the *Gastarbeiter*, of whom the Turks form a large minority of West Berlin's population, some 180,000, concentrated in Kreuzberg, are under threat. In the West they do the dirty work, often under conditions no European would tolerate. But now with so much cheap labour from the East, they have become dispensable. Already they are finding it more difficult to obtain citizenship or extensions to their stay. Programmes that directly affect non-German immigrants, such as language teaching, are beginning to dry up, as resources are diverted to the resettlers.

In the East they have their counterparts, though fewer, in the foreigners living there – students, who may stay only for the duration of their studies, and 100,000 contract workers from Vietnam, Mozambique, Angola, Cuba and Korea, brought in to fill the gaps opened by emigration. The contract workers work and live in bad conditions, often in cramped hostels, as in the West doing work no German would do. They are despised by the insular East Germans, many of whom as they emerge from their totalitarian cocoon turn out to be virulently racist. For the foreigners there is a language problem, no provisions or concessions are made to their cultures, and most of them are scared of being sent home if they complain. The 60,000 Vietnamese are watched constantly by their embassy, which retains their passports, and are not allowed to travel to the West. They can be seen working on construction sites and work gangs on the railways. Most of them live in poor conditions, shivering even in a mild winter. Those who are assigned proper flats are the focus of resentment. Vietnamese women are forbidden by their contracts to have children; if they become pregnant they must have an abortion or go home. The events of the *Wende* largely passed the foreign workers by; the Wall did not open for them, and they are not allowed to travel to and fro, and their own governments, emphatically Castro's, forbade them to take an interest, on pain of immediate return home. The Korean government ordered their students home. But at New Year, in the mêlée of the celebrations at the Gate, where the border was wide open and the guards no doubt distracted, hundreds of Vietnamese decamped to West Berlin and asked for political asylum. To the end of January some 2,000 Vietnamese had escaped West since the opening, and there were threats to send them all back home, though a Government spokesman declared they would not be sent back till their contracts ran out. And there was a story, officially denied, that the West Berlin police were sending back Vietnamese.

The future begins to look awesome. Everywhere in the East there are strikes, go-slows, street protests, the continuing exodus, disintegrating local government. The GDR foreign debt, put currently at DM 16 billion, has been pegged by slashing imports of capital equipment, technology and Western expertise. Hostility towards foreigners is increasing, and right-wing groups are emerging. Part of their target is the Russian presence, and at the Soviet War Memorial in Treptower Park someone with a red can of paint has been busy, repeating all over the stone friezes of heroic warfare depicting the Russian liberation from the darkness of Nazism, *Besatzer raus* (occupiers out). There is a lot of *raus* about. There are attacks on foreigners, and anti-semitism. It's said that some former members of the SED, the party of proletarian brotherhood, are particularly racist. Racism is on the rise, East and West, stimulated by the exodus, the change, and the opening. Ossis come across the Oberbaumbrücke into Kreuzberg, where the Turks live, and mutter that they'd better move: 'We're going to gas you,' they say to their new neighbours over the river, and they have been known to spit in the prams of black babies.

There's something depressingly familiar about it all, and as yet no one can say what rough beast has shambled through the opened frontier to be born. Or reborn. In West Berlin it's all beginning to rub wrong, and, after the initial enthusiasm, the difference is beginning to show and resentments to form. If things were tight before, they are tighter now, on the job market, in the search for somewhere to live; clearly health and pensions contributions, and no doubt taxes, despite what the politicians say, will rise to pay for all these guests, and the economy will heat up, and inflation will nibble at the Deutschmark. It's said that after 9 November a lot of GDR resettlers were dropouts, some of whom came directly from prison after the pre-Christmas amnesty. Others abandoned their families. Most were attracted by the wealth of the West when they came to visit; others were responding to the increasing insecurity of the East. In the weeks before Christmas many fled, fearing West Germany would soon close its borders.

Since then more qualified people have been coming over, many of them seeking work in the West though planning to go on living in the East and take the best of both worlds. But the West is beginning to groan, and pressure of numbers is closing the doors of emergency reception centres. In January 74,000 settled in the West. In West Berlin between 200 and 250 are still arriving every day at Marienfelde, and of these some 40 per cent are allowed to stay because they have close relatives living here. The rest are shipped on to the Bundesrepublik. 26,000 are living in temporary accommodation, 1,200 in emergency camps.

As ever the peckers are busy along the Wall, hammering and chipping, outlining a painted eye, a letter, half a word, a slap of colour, chipping it out. Wherever the Wall is accessible, and painted, there are the peckers, hammering out a death knell, slowly demolishing it. To reaching height it is chipped away, and they are beginning to expose the steel rods within the slabs, and here and there a small iron door, previously invisible in the

Wall's white-skimmed face. Stripped of their painted surfaces, the reinforcing rods exposed, the irregular shapes look like loaves of bread. Chipping at their edges, the peckers have opened gaps through which the other side can be seen, sometimes a couple of border guards leaning out, shy, curious. Most of the best graffiti has already gone. The peckers climb on stumps, boxes, ladders, each others' shoulders, to reach the higher paintwork. People who live along the Wall go crazy with the hammering, day and night, sometimes at three in the morning. They hang home-made signs bearing a black hammer barred red. Many of the peckers are tourists, getting their souvenirs. Some bring champagne to drink, in celebration. Many are American, given to making impromptu speeches about freedom. Some are Allied servicemen with their buddies and wives, chipping out a genuine chunk of Communist tyranny, 'Yes, Sir.' Some are Ossis come to look at what contained them, come to make a little Western money selling chippings. They sell cheaper than Wessis, a further source of complaint. Some are Russians. Others are entrepreneurs, native Berliners Ossis and Wessis, Poles, Turks – '*Wir sind alle Berliner*' – at it for the money, as a job, chipping hard in the cold afternoon. They spread their wares on the ground, various-sized lumps of painted Wall: DM 3, 5, 10, 20 and up, what the market will stand and the tourists pay for. By Checkpoint Charlie the trade is busiest; someone has a camera and for DM 10 will take a picture of you chipping the Wall, to authenticate your lump. Someone else is hiring out hammers and chisels, DM 5 for 15 minutes. Just by Charlie a Breton sculptor has cut out a piece of Wall from which to make a sculpture, in early response to the GDR's offer of wall space to artists.

In East Berlin Friedemann is glum; for him the important event was not the opening of the Wall but the overthrow of Honecker, the *Wende*, and the possibility of renewing the Party and the country. It is a possibility that is retreating, visibly, every day. The Party is kaput, though it is fighting a vigorous rearguard action. When the elections come, they'll be voted out of power. If not, an even vaster exodus will rapidly develop. It's possible the Party may be banned. Friedemann himself will not leave the Party, not yet in any case. Perhaps when the election's over. He'll not jump like a rat off the ship now. He has been with it all these years, and feels responsible for it, that he didn't speak out and didn't see what was happening. He's angry with himself. He's angry with the leadership, with their privilege in a world of privation, and wants them tried. And with their inefficiency: the GDR produced 27 million pairs of shoes last year, and there are only 3 million pairs of children's feet to fit them, yet they are in short supply, so where are all the missing shoes? He feels betrayed. A hundred and fifty years of struggle, some of it violent, many of whose participants were killed brutally and imprisoned, and all of it down the drain now.

But his son is not unhappy. Schools are abandoning compulsory Russian, and his son is pleased about that. The teaching of English is rapidly being expanded as its replacement, but books and teachers are in short supply. His son's teacher, whose husband was Stasi, miscarried due to the pressure on them from neighbours and colleagues. Her husband is now driving a tram. Friedemann reports that in his housing block a neighbour told him he'd been an informer for years, on him, on anyone and everyone; his main complaint was his loss of income. Friedemann thinks it is finished here; the struggle will go on, he says, in the Third World, and the GDR will be a historical example of how not to run socialism, but he says this with great resignation. Mainly he is ashamed of it all, though he himself had no privileges or benefits, living in his tower block flat with his wife and two children, before that all four of them for eight years in two tiny rooms, living his life, working with his Party. A lifelong believer, he sees the growing likelihood of the GDR being dismantled and taken over by the West, and is determined to fight it. This is their state, they have worked hard for it.

In the last week Friedemann has been to West Berlin, with his son. He grins. So much he does not want there, and his son soon noticed, looking in the shops, how little DM 100 would buy. He thinks that with the Deutschmarks he has saved up he will buy a television set. Recently he was in the FRG, in Hamburg, and stood outside a building in which a party was taking place for the demise of the Western KPD. He laughs. He couldn't afford a ticket to go in, to the party for the end of the Party. As to the Wall, he shrugs, much will now come through from the West that the East has managed so far without: drugs, Aids, crime, violence. And there will come the vicissitudes of capitalism, the draughty market-place he must now learn to compete in. Now the border is down the frontier is everywhere. 'Over there your walls are internal, psychological,' he says. Here too, I reply, sitting in a bar drinking beer and Korn. All around the conversation buzzes. This is not the way things used to be in the East. Friedemann agrees it's better. It's more interesting, if nothing else.

He's busy, tied up with the Party in his local branch, and in the Union, struggling to save what he believes in: socialism, the Party, the GDR. He's part of the great ferment going on all over the country. Despite all odds, he goes on believing. Marxism is his faith, and no amount of *Wende* and *Durchbruch* or *Vereinigung* is going to change that. He seems wonderfully naïve, with a faith I've not encountered except among students since the days I was one. For him the choices are black and white, in contrast to the other side, my side, where the choice is bland and white. And he can't just switch, as everyone around him is doing, to believing suddenly in the glories of the free market and the joys of liberal democracy. So Communism has failed, here, and capitalism is gloating over its triumph. And capitalism: how successful is that, in Africa, Latin America, the Third World? For Friedemann there is no alternative but an alternative socialism; he is of the party of socialism with a human face, of the party of the seekers of the third way.

What do I think?

Bahnhof, I think. I think the whole shambles is kaput, comrade. I think it all demonstrates that a system without a mechanism for criticism and dialogue is doomed to ossify and putrefy, more and more reliant on its police. It's a system without feedback. In time it will implode. Therefore, the Stalinist donkey being dead, socialism must ride the democratic pony, down a road it will grow thinner on, its leaders bought off and its policies watered down. But then I'm Western, sceptical and cynical. The rich win this one, as they win them all, comrade. So we may as well have *noch zwei Bier, noch zwei Korn, bitte*, and I'll go back to the West, up the *Ausreise* steps littered with dog-ends, among the fag-ends of frustration, so to say.

On this side the track by the Reichstag is ploughed into mud by the sightseers. The crosses to victims killed on the Wall have been added to, new facts supplied about the dead. Written in black fibre-tip, they record that Chris Geoffroy, the Wall's last

victim, was an *Opfer der Honecker Diktatur*, twenty years old:
a victim of the Honecker dictatorship. *Wir sassen im Gefängnis*
(We sat in prison). *Dein Leben gegeben* (You gave your life).
Wir werden Dich nie vergessen (We'll never forget you). For
Marienetta Jiskowski, 18, +22/11/86: *Wir kämpfen für Dich
weiter* (We struggle for you still), *Auntie & Jenny*. Heinz
Scholowski, killed in 1965, was a *Politischer Gefangener nach 7
Jahre* (A political prisoner for seven years). *Auf der Flucht
erschossen* (Shot dead in flight). And *Unbekannt* (Unknown) +
22/11/86, turns out to be still pseudonymous, *Aladin G. Auf der
Flucht erlegt* (Killed in flight). The dead rise, with names and
brief stories, from their anonymity. *Unbekannt* +24/4/73 turns
out to be Manfred Gertzki, from Karl-Marx-Stadt, born 17 May
1942 in Danzig. Winfried Freudenberg, *Ballonflucht* (Balloon
flight), who crashed in Zehlendorf in March 1989, had drawn
Denkt an dieses Jahr! (Think of this year!) *Ein Opfer und Täter*
(A victim and a culprit).

Peter tells a tale he heard recently, about the East. It seems there
were five young men, aged about fifteen, boys, teenagers who
some years ago were arrested spray-painting Nazi symbols on
Jewish graves, so what they were doing was nasty, and from the
GDR's point of view very nasty indeed. They may have been
awful little shits, but they were political, the class enemy. They
were each sentenced to five years in prison. They've spent most
of their sentences in isolation. When the Modrow Government
declared an amnesty at the year's end for prisoners with less
than five years to serve, the court that had sentenced these five
revised their sentences, and put it up to six, so they were
excused the December amnesty. So when they do come out they
will be Nazis, if they weren't before, and prison-hardened,
isolation-tuned, probably crazy. They'll be heroes and martyrs.
Very stupid, Peter says. Just boys.

At Friedrichstrasse the crowds. In out, up and down the stairs,
in and out the border, on and off the trains. Those who choose
to spend their days all day here are drunks, spilling around
the benches, occasionally squabbling and slanging each other,
begging cigarettes, occasionally asleep, occasionally breaking
into snatches of song, occasionally moved on by border
guards nervous in crowds. They come here to buy booze at the

Intershop on the platform, though the Deutschmark prices are no cheaper than anywhere else in West Berlin. Western derelicts in Western cast-offs, some with bruises and bandages, scruffy, they are the West's window in the East, in Friedrichstrasse. Some, when they are allowed, go through the border where the booze is cheap. Most of them kick around here all day, drinking exotica, eggnog and plum brandy.

At Zoo station the usual scramble on and off trains. Trains in, trains out. The Ossis with their packages, the crowds as ever. The young man wants to talk. His name is Ingo. He has come through to buy a calculator, for his work. He is a toolmaker, apprentice-trained, and works in a factory. He likes his work, his life, and feels no desire to move West. He lives with his family, and doesn't come through much, except for instance now, for the calculator. He is enthusiastic about the changes, and values the freedom he now has – 'to think, to speak, to write', he says – and he doesn't think the GDR can survive, though he thinks they should retain its social welfare system. He repeats the standard argument for German unification within the context of the Common Market. The West must help. They have many problems, the chief of which is the pollution of the planet, and in principle of the GDR. 'No more experiments. *Scheisse Scheisse Scheisse*. The economy is *Scheisse*, Communism is *Scheisse*, but the whole GDR is not *Scheisse*. The social system is not *Scheisse*. There is nature, and we cannot kill nature. Nature is not *Scheisse*.' Otherwise he spends his spare time sailing, on the Müggelsee, where he has a sailboat. He likes the air, the water, nature, but he fears that in the spring, with the way wide open, Westerners will bring their boats to the Müggelsee and there'll be no more peace there. He gets off at Savignyplatz, to hunt for his calculator.

The Ossis thin here as many get out, then others pile on going home via Wannsee, with all their packages. Ossis carry in their pockets little print cotton bags with a drawstring; it's force of habit, for they never knew when they might find something they needed, and there was always a shortage of plastic bags in the East. There was no machinery to manufacture them. They settle on to the train, fussy and old-fashioned. They are family-oriented, looking through the windows at the other city, some with babies, others in family groups, many with young children

whom they cuddle, talk to, read to from newly purchased
Western picture books and comics. They carry the usual crop of
oranges. At Charlottenburg a group of dark-skinned men and
women get on, Turks or gypsies, their skins leathery and
weathered. They are five, two dark men and three dark
whippet-skinny women, each with long straight hair and an array
of bad teeth, alert and vivacious, talking, laughing. They have
been shopping, and have bought oranges and T-shirts. The train
drives south, through Westkreuz where no one boards or dis-
mounts, and then through the long woods to Grunewald and
Wannsee. At Wannsee, the gypsies take the 67 Ringlinie to
Heckershorn.

At Wannsee the long-distance trains come and go, some stopping, some easing through to the West, carrying Ossis with their
bags and packages, emigrating with all they can take. Other
trains come in from having crossed the East, passengers at the
windows ready to get off at Zoo. The engines purr, and over a
loudspeaker there's a woman calling out the destinations in an
indecipherable distant German echo, in a *Bahnhof* sort of voice,
between the wind and the traffic. The S-Bahns from Friedrichstrasse and Anhalter Bahnhof terminate here in a long squeal of
brakes, unload, go up the line for a sweep and a break and a
cup of coffee and a clear out of the empties, and return on
another journey through the city for another load of Ossis.
From the new crossing point at Potsdamer Platz and the old
Friedrichstrasse crossing is a short cut by the S-Bahn across the
city, where formerly they had to go all the way around on the
Eastern S-Bahn ring, three hours where this is one. They climb
up the stairs out of the station, and cross the road, and clutter
the pavement around the 99 bus stop. The 99, newly inaugurated
as the first cross-border bus to Potsdam from Wannsee via
Dreilinden, takes them home, with their bags and their tales of
what they've seen. Every few minutes a bus comes in from
Potsdam, disgorging its load of Ossis, who head for the station.
Some stand about looking at the shops, eating *Wieners* and
Bratwurst, ice-cream, drinking Coca-Cola. They look cold in
their thin clothes, still reserved and hesitant. They walk around,
inspecting everything, a little mystified perhaps, vaguely suspicious, shy, withdrawn, keeping to their own company. It goes
on like this all through January, all day from early in the

morning to late at night, and when on the 22nd in *quid pro quo* for the bus the East gets to run a train from Potsdam to Wannsee, the traffic is even heavier. And on and off the roads it's still Trabi Trabi Trabi.

Days and weeks, all day. Two months after the *Durchbruch* they are still coming through, carrying back string bags of oranges and bananas, plastic carriers of groceries, biscuits and *Schokolade* and mandarins and Western sweet things. At Wannsee many of these visitors seem as if here for the first time, lost, nervous, abroad in a strange land, country folk unused to the city. Some of them have come from further afield in the East. They carry back fewer electronics than at other crossing points in the city; here, the *Grenzgänger* seem older, more worn out. Their clothes are the same – washed denim and faded jackets, older people in clothes they have worn for many years. The young seem thin and hungry-looking, huddled into their thin clothes in the January cold, in plastic anoraks, plastic shoes and thin socks, some in a treasured plastic jacket. They look like the welfare poor of the West, underfed, badly clothed. Most are sallow, many with spots, walking evidence of the GDR's bad diet. The new green Sputnik double-decker train from Potsdam to Wannsee has only increased the traffic, making it possible for people further out to come to West Berlin. Every hour it shuttles yet more travellers across the border and back. Till late at night they stream out of the station and gather at the bus stop, patient, impatient, in clutches over the whole pavement, forcing pedestrians out into the traffic. Perhaps, at last outside their own regimented country where they must queue for everything, they refuse to stand in line any more.

From 1838 until 1961, when the Wall cut the service, Wannsee and Potsdam were linked by rail, and now it's back, nineteen minutes' journey time, every hour on the hour through the day. Wessis pay DM 2.70, Ossis 20 Pfennig. Three engines, one up, one down, one reserve, they were Honecker's engines, which drew his special train around his fiefdom. Now they are assigned more popular duties. In the subway under the station one of the Eastern drivers, between journeys, is studying the map of West Berlin in its glass case, looking at something he hasn't seen before. Joachim talks about the trains here – how when the Russians came reparations were an extension of plundering, and here they took up one side of the track through to Potsdam.

That was how it was in the East anyway, he says, often a single track, and that is what we Germans did to them so they were merely reducing us to their level, and carting off the track for scrap. So only an up train or a down train could use the track. Then for years while the S-Bahn was run by the East – till the eighties, it was falling to bits from lack of maintenance. The signal cables rotted away, and there was a baton system: the driver of the up train would hand it to the driver of the down train, and neither could move without the baton.

Later we fail to make the journey to Potsdam together, Joachim and I. I am not a German of either state and so cannot pass through the checkpoint at Griebnitzsee, though I have a resident's visa for the East. The train pulls into the long alley of the station, between parallel enclosing walls, watchtowers, fences and wire, all the old paraphernalia of the border. Across the Wall, the old film studios of Hitler's film-makers. The guards come on the train, throw us off politely, directing me back to Friedrichstrasse, and we cross the line and wait for the up train. When it comes Joachim wants to sit in the guard's van, which is easier for him with his sticks. As we sit there, and as the guard checks the platform, he peels off two Eastern tickets from the guard's supply, and puts them in my pocket. A souvenir. And him a judge.

Border incident. Along the Reichstag the Wall's full of gaping holes, with the reinforcing rods showing. At one point, two slabs have been so eroded and the rods bent back as to form an opening, a new door to the other side. At the same moment the West Berlin police drive up, and the guards on the other side drive up, and each on their opposite sides station themselves around the gap so no one can sneak through into the GDR. There's a checkpoint for Germans only yards away, but appearances must be kept up. The West Berlin police put up cordon fences, with red and white plastic tape fluttering in the breeze, and push the crowd back. All this, like everything that happens hereabouts, is recorded on film, and will be available in the archives of family albums the world over. Between the two forces there's no contact, except between the two officers in charge, and they work as if oblivious of each other. The Eastern officer comes out through the hole, shakes hands with his opposite number, they discuss the situation, conclude it is in hand, and chat politely while their men do what little there is to be done. In the police van several officers sit about, reading the paper, smoking, all in the same zippered brown sweaters they wear to look identically unobtrusive. The crowd mills about, bored that nothing's happening, and a bunch of young men start barracking the Grepo officer: '*Wir sind ein Volk*,' shouted in mockery, with a collective laugh. '*Wir sind alle Jugend. Egon Krenz kommt.*' (We are one people. We are all youth. Egon Krenz is coming.)

'It will be a country of the old,' he says. 'No one will be left. The West will have to rebuild the Wall to stop them. This country is dying, everywhere you look. It has all gone wrong, and it is now such a mess that we must come to the West and say, "Please, *meine Herren*, will you help us, you must help us." Our machinery, our factories, our equipment is old and leaking, we cannot get parts to repair them, and we have wrecked the country's land and rivers and the air. Here in Berlin, even this was better than elsewhere in the country. Supplies, food, building materials, were diverted here at the expense of other towns and cities. Berlin: showcase East, showcase West, showing each other. Out there beyond the capital things became so bad the people could not stand it any more. Many left from the southern part of the country, from Dresden and Leipzig and Erfurt, many young people but also many with children. They were closer to the border with Czechoslovakia, and if they could get there and through the border, or through Hungary, they would be in Austria, and then they would be in West Germany. Then perhaps, they would be in West Berlin, still somehow inside the GDR. So it was out there they finally said no more, in Leipzig and Dresden and Halle and the rest of the country, where they were perhaps more isolated, more without hope. They set the pace. So you see East Berlin no more leads the rest of the country than West Berlin does. That is because it was once but no longer is the capital of the whole of Germany, so it is like an anti-capital, a powerless absence where the whole centre of the power was. The Wall for us was only the edge of it.'

At the Gate on a Saturday afternoon a brass band on the Eastern side, in black and white uniforms, is playing 'Amazing Grace', how they were lost and blind and could not see, but

now are found. Down the road the Russians are still guarding
their war memorial, standing to attention in the drizzle, the
West Berlin police still guarding them. History is happening
again, where it has happened before, marching along through
the Tiergarten and the Gate, Napoleon, the Emperors and
Kaisers, and little Adolf, who appealed to the inverse snobbery
of a people riddled with self-doubt and paraded them through
here prior to smashing up Europe.

At the Oberbaumbrücke crossing, which on the other side
across the Spree is Warschauer Strasse, it's getting dark. It's
Friday. Across the bridge the people come and go, a traffic of
returning shoppers with their purchases one way, in the other
the blue-jeaned young, for an evening in the West, going out on
a spree across the Spree. Over two months have passed since all
the excitement, and this is now normality, but the traffic is
thinning by not much. Here it's busy because another weekend
has begun. By the exit, a couple talking, she about to go back
across the bridge, another young woman waiting for her date to
come through. Globus and Penny Markt, Woolworth, Aldi,
boxes marked Siemens, Sony, the same spoils going East. Between the bridge and the end of Linie 1 at Schlesisches Tor the
two files pass each other, and here and there are pitchers selling
cookies, chocolates, sweets, little dolls, *drei Mark, drei Mark*.
  Normal and not normal. There's still a sense this may not
last, as if it all might be a dream to wake from, a loop in time
before the world snaps back and the border is as before: shut
tight. Coming through, the Ossis have an air of suppressed
excitement; this is still a lark, a brief adventure outside time.
The West is still very strange to them, a dangerous and vicious
place they have been told, and they're not all that wrong. This
corner in Kreuzberg has its own air of unreality in any case, and
its own ghosts. Now in the Turkish quarter, where the sector
signs on the bank of the river are printed additionally in
Turkish, it was a district that saw vicious street battles in the
times of the Nazis. The huge brick superstructure of the bridge
carries the severed link of Berlin's first U-Bahn, and it was this
bridge across which Richard Burton came in from the cold. To
one side of it, overlooking it and the river and the other side, is
an observation post of double planks between which is a foot
thickness of sand to absorb bullets, and with three slit-holes

from which to observe your man coming over. It looks incongruous, as if it might be sculpture, an artist's comment on the other side, but it is real, built to withstand bullets. Around it are real sculptures, in stone, metal, resin, so the whole area looks like a little sculpture park beside the ramparts lifting the track on to the bridge. The two-way crocodile of Ossis threads its way through the sculptures, going home, going out on the town.

Along the Wall the border guards are transformed. Instead of stern Grepos with Kalashnikovs, here are young lads from Rostock and Halle, grinning, trying to look responsible, without much success. They peer through the widening gaps, smile shyly, pose for photographs, accept cigarettes and sweets, eye the girls. They look uncertain, and from their faces it's possible to speculate that their officers are uncertain, their orders to keep the crowds back from the Western side of the Wall, as best they can, politely. Along by the Gate on the thick concrete bulge, a team of army engineers is on top of the wide flat Wall's top, fixing falling slabs so heavily chipped that great caves have opened in the structure, revealing dark interiors packed with horizontal slabs of more concrete. The outer slabs have been mined out, and have taken organic shapes, dark recesses glimpsed through the trunks of old trees, stalactites. On the other side there are more uprights, keeping the whole bulk together, where the graffiti is new and scrappy, wishing the world a happy new year from united Berlin, demanding *Nazis raus* (Nazis out) and *Nie wieder* (Never again) and *Nie zwei Deutschland* (Never two Germanys), and awarding the byline for it all to Gorbachov. On the Wall the work-team is welding and fixing, where the top slabs have slipped and become dangerous. They smoke, joke, mess about, one cuts through metal rods with his arc flame, another takes pictures of them all at the Gate, for the people back home, for the albums. They too are aware they are present and accounted for in history, in this long moment of the Wall's fall, conscripts whose hour has come round at last.

It's still coming down, in flakes and lumps, the peckers absorbed in their chipping. They're still there by night, where there's a bit of light, or they face their cars to the Wall and work in the headlamps, or search with torches for a likely spot, and one or two, like all night fishermen, camp out with a gaslamp. By day they work, tapping, hammering, the hammer and chisel chorus, their wares at their feet, their lunch, Thermos flask, beer. There's an old guy with a pile of loose paintless chippings laid out on his jacket, but he's got no chance. There's a man in an industrial mask working hard with a pneumatic drill, *1 Stein = 1 Mark*, collecting money for a *Polyklinik* in Leipzig. Many are here for the duration, for as long as the market lasts, and are assured by what they hear from elsewhere: that bits of the Wall are being marketed in London and New York and Tokyo, that everybody wants a piece. President Bush has a piece on his desk in the Oval Office, presented to him by Foreign Secretary Hans-Dietrich Genscher. It's full of chrysotile asbestos, says the University of Oklahoma. On the night of the opening at Potsdamer Platz in November an enterprising American paid some daring young men something in the region of DM 500 for a piece of Wall, and shipped it to America, where he plans to break it up and sell it for souvenirs. But the fact of the matter is it takes a mechanical grab to lift a slab, and industrial equipment to break off a piece and a truck to move it to the airport, and a slab is too heavy to shift quickly and surreptitiously from under the noses of the guards. So my money says what he has is a length of coping from the Wall's top, taken from the Gate section and later replaced by a piece from the opened section at Potsdamer Platz, identifiable because it has part of a John Runnings poster on it. The coping, slit sewer pipe, is said to be riddled with asbestos. Beware the coping.

And then the selling of the Wall begins in earnest. A Dick Dale from Missouri is reported to have bought seventy-five tons of Wall – that's about thirty slabs – and transported them to Chicago, to break up and sell as souvenirs. On 20 January *die Mauervermarktung* (Wall-marketing) began, with the appointment of the East German company Limex-Bau Export-Import offering initially forty sections so far taken out for crossing points, at prices between DM 100,000 and 700,000, to private buyers, museums and galleries, firms, hotels. Some firms are expected to use parts of the Wall for publicity purposes, and the Getty Museum in California and Disneyland are said to be interested. The proceeds are to go for health care in the GDR, and the renovation of buildings and monuments. It is estimated that from the sale of 99.8 kilometres of Wall the GDR could make about DM 800 million. The State Secretary for Inter-German Affairs in Bonn found the sale macabre and cynical, and said proceeds should go to the victims of the Wall.

When the chipping began it was a novelty, now it's a nuisance. Eight weeks ago, the Eastern guards were hosing people with pickaxes off the Wall, and the West Berlin police moving people on, sometimes confiscating their tools. Now no one cares. It's coming down anyway, and it seems the world has come to see it; it is the same procession along the main section from the Spree to the Springer building, with cameras, and through the two openings either side of the bulge at the Gate. The early January snow gives way to drizzle and mud. In the East they're allowed to walk now on the Pariser Platz where they were not before, where there were only guards and Stasi in white metal frame chairs, watching all. In the inner wall is a section of metal gate built and painted to look like the cement blocks of the castellated wall it opens in. People crowd down from Unter den Linden through the old ghosts and the forgotten memories of the vanished Adlon into the Pariser Platz and down beneath the vast oblong arches of the Gate, and out to the other side in the other world. Nowadays they look used to it, but they still come out looking a little abashed, working out their bearings. On their own side, they were in the Mitte, in the heart of their city, at its edge. On this, they're down at the far end of the Tiergarten, among the trees, a bus ride to the Zoo.

Tourists stoop among the roots of the trampled bushes, picking missed chippings flown off the chisel, the painted bits gleaming in the muck. Along the Wall there's a line of cement dust and gribbles too small to bother with, but here and there a flash of blue or red, shining like a pebble in water. In little bits the Wall is being distributed around the world, as if to spread the ugliness of it thinly over the planet, so that it can never be reassembled. And no doubt already there's a trade in fakes, though who'd need it when there's so much of it; one day perhaps it will be like the True Cross, and there'll be enough to build a dozen Berlin Walls.

Other peckers are industrialized. Some work in pairs, some bring stone saws and hammer drills, and some are respraying sections already stripped, producing instant counterfeits. Some bits sold at Potsdamer Platz have been chipped off at Bernauer Strasse. Others bring hacksaws to saw away at the steel rods.

Along by Charlie a couple of American preppies walk earnestly along, one with a crowbar, one with a sledgehammer, both with determined looks on their faces. 'Gonna get me some serious piece of this wall here.' There's a team with a truck backed up to the Wall, running a stone-cutter from a portable generator and ripping the chunks off and straight into the back of the van, two of them at either side catching the flying bits in cardboard boxes. Down towards the Heinrich-Heine-Strasse checkpoint, where a kink in the Wall makes an L-shape out of Stallschreiber-strasse, someone has been with a core-cutter and taken thick round cakes of Wall, through the holes of which can be seen the other side, snowy and deserted. And further down along Wal-demarstrasse there was a slab painted red, the cover of a book, *Die Deklaration der revolutionären Internationalistischen Bewegung* (The Declaration of the International Revolutionary Movement), and above it a frieze of Engels, Marx, Lenin, Mao, Castro. With an industrial drill someone has dug out the frieze of revolutionary profiles.

Such vandalism is approved of, and the other side seems indifferent, though attempts have been made at shoring up the wreck; at opened gaps they've laid slabs of concrete, lengths of mesh, metal plates. But the chipping goes on. Some mount their chips as badges, brooches, earrings, sculpture, assemblages of wire and glazed surface. Others are set in PVC resin. Others are authenticated by various sorts of certificate (as if these couldn't be faked as well), including one that claims the provenance of the British Army. There are first-day covers and stamps, photographs, paintings, leaflets, and the first epaulets and badges of the border guards beginning to work their way into the trade. The carnival continues. Across the Wall are deserted watch-towers, many with their windows broken by stones and bottles thrown from the West, in the sand tyre tracks, bootprints, crows' feet, rabbit tracks. Along the path from the Reichstag to Potsdamer Platz along the edge of the Tiergarten there are grilles, and beneath them thin electric light, the faint sound of a radio, a drill, work in progress and distant voices, and then the sound and wind of a train, distantly. Down there is the old Potsdamer Platz S-Bahn station, abandoned since 1961, and men at work. From the grille rusty iron steps go down, thick with thirty autumns of dead leaves.

*

Beneath the East U-Bahn Linie 8 goes up to Voltastrasse, running through the grid of overlapping lines of the other separate system of the other, separate, city. It stops now at Jannowitzbrücke and Rosenthaler Platz, hastily opened and renovated, where it had not stopped for many a year. It still slows through the other closed stations. At Bernauer Strasse, deserted and palely lit as ever, a blast of music from a tape player. More workmen working. More stations opening. Eventually these two systems will become one. The wooden S-Bahn clatters along, red and yellow, like a line of garden sheds on wheels, up from the West to Friedrichstrasse, then back to the West on the S2 north to Frohnau, running for miles along the Wall that's mostly distant and inaccessible behind tracks and waterways. So much of the Wall is just a wall. In the East, grubbier and greyer, the stations are dilapidated, scabby with decay, but the trains still run. From Ostkreuz down to Schönefeld, and along the long south of the outer ring through woods and farmland, fruit trees and vineyards, all the way to Potsdam Hof, two hours. Then north through well-tended farmland on the Sputnik train to Hohenneuendorf in the north, and south on the S-Bahn to the Frankfurter Allee and the darkening city, total journey time: five hours, all the way around the tale of two cities.

It's all over, the suspicion, the paranoia, the tales each side made up of the other, half of them true. Maybe. Or it's just a new twist in the old game. They say the GDR's spies, estimated now at 5,000, are still at work in the West, they say the Stasi is still at work in the East. The crowds are out on the streets calling for one Germany, *Wieder Vereinigung*. Is it unification or reunification? It depends what you start with. On the streets, more so in the East, everyone talks about it, and Rumour's front stage, and no one knows what's really happening. The GDR is coming apart, its people deserting, the Party being pushed out of power and fighting on all fronts, and the West has won the pattacake. History grinds on with its remorseless chronology of facts significant and obscure. To avoid calling the little winged figure on the Christmas tree an angel, it was sold as a *Jahresendflügelpuppe* (a year's end winged doll). GDR TV shows old peoples' homes squalid, the diet unhealthy. It's reported that when they travelled, Honecker and the others took bottles of pure drinking water, so when they visited parts of the country they alone knew were dangerously polluted, they'd not be inconvenienced. He and Mielke are to be charged with conspiracy and high treason. Local governments put in place in rigged elections in May face fraud charges.

On 15 January thousands of young Berliners invaded Stasi-Zentrale in Normannenstrasse, scattering files and smashing furniture. 'The head is cut off but the body still lives.' Modrow and New Forum hastened to condemn it, but it highlighted the continued existence of the secret police, not yet disbanded as promised. A week later there were more rumours that the Stasi were preparing a putsch; *Bild* carried a report by an ex-Stasi officer to this effect, and there were sightings of the movements of a Panzer regiment of élite troops, said to be *SED-treu*. Resignations from the Party continued; at the end of the month Wolfgang Berghofer and forty other top officials resigned, Berghofer declaring that the Party had destroyed the country 'politically, economically, and morally'.

In the East sudden freedom proves heady, and as ever in revolutionary times the pendulum swings rapidly from euphoria to paranoia, and doesn't swing back. East Germans, strangers to freedom, react as if drunk with it; they have no training in responsibility, other than socialist responsibility, and to hell with that, they say these days. There are wildcat strikes, demands for huge pay rises, which if awarded would bankrupt what's left of the state. Meanwhile the news everywhere in the East is bad: the East is falling apart, with a shambling infrastructure and environmental disasters all round and a demoralized population. Jens Reich of New Forum puts it this way: the overthrow of the old regime exposes many unsolved problems, and makes them visible. He adds: 'Ours has been the history of sleeping people.' Now they are waking, but to what? Chaos seems close, and the desire for revenge prominent.

The fever goes on, the huge demonstrations and attacks on Stasi buildings and personnel. Due to the resignation of many town councils and officials, and the desertion of specialists, whole areas of the GDR are no longer functioning. Nevertheless, despite wholesale desertion, the Party apparatus is still in being, their control over the media, though no longer absolute, still formidable, the Stasi still in existence. The police are without instructions, and the army disoriented. And the question is who, if not the members of the Party, is to run things, since few others are qualified, and anyone with any responsibility is tainted by association with the former regime?

Hans Modrow is a case in point; his brief record since his appointment on 8 November is a fair one. He was for sixteen years Party chief in Dresden. By the public, and particularly in his dealings in the Round Table discussions, he is perceived to be struggling not to save his Party, the motive of the despised Herr Krenz, but to keep the GDR together, at any rate until the elections, when it will, presumably, no longer be his responsibility. Expectations of the turnout for the SED run from 15 to 30 per cent. So Modrow will not be in power long, though he's respected. But his Party is despised; a good man in the wrong company, they say of him.

Party membership – on 1 January 2.26 million, one-eighth of the population – keeps falling. By the 18th it is down to 2 million, by the end of the month 1.5. And it's eyes down to the election. In the infighting beforehand the Communists failed to write into the new electoral law a clause banning foreign financial aid for the opposition parties. Aid comes in, from the SPD and the CDU in the West to their reborn counterparts in the East: computers, word processors, programs, systems, printing facilities, advisers, funds, pour across the border. The East complains of interference from a foreign state; the West, which doesn't regard itself as foreign, goes on helping, arguing that the Party still controls most of the media and resources in the East. After the middle of the month Modrow seems to have committed himself to an orderly rout. But after forty years of lies, everyone remains suspicious, and as the majority of the government until the end of January, the Party still retains control. It commands vast funds; the opposition groups, starting from scratch, have neither funds nor expertise nor resources. Meanwhile the Republicans, the NDPD, the neo-Nazis, are about, their posters on the streets, their presence increasingly noticeable at Monday night demonstrations in Leipzig and elsewhere. They now have an official representative in the East, a Leipzig pork butcher. On the one hand there's the Party's fear of the fascists; on the other the public's fear that the Party is planning a comeback. The Stasi is still lurking. And so are the Nazis.

On 16 January the West German government, torn between contrary desires to stabilize its neighbour and yet not be seen to prop up a discredited regime, said there'd be no treaty with the East, and no aid, till after the elections, and it was a long way, three and a half months, till May. At the same time, in mid-January, Christa Luft, Economics Minister, announcing that there were 250,000 unfilled job vacancies due to the exodus, called for the introduction of a free market economy. It was a signal to Western big business. She announced that equity limits on foreign ownership of GDR companies in some cases would be expanded to beyond 49 per cent, one of the sticking points till now holding back the inrush of Western business. The GDR would encourage the development of small and medium enterprises, but clearly the big companies like Siemens and Daimler-Benz and Volkswagen were hunting the lion's share of the spoils, and they will be the beneficiaries of the collapse of the East German economy. The Eastern markets, long targeted by the West, whose own markets are saturated, are to be the new bonanza. There was to be no third way between capitalism and Communism, and talk of it was abandoned at this point. From here the sellout of the GDR began, and the West moved in in earnest. In the absence of instructions, the directors of Eastern enterprises began to act as if they were the owners, and complete deals with Western firms. The takeover began to assume the shape of a textbook exercise in colonialism.

No doubt because of the upheaval throughout the country, as January wore on and the creaking ship of state fell to bits, by the end of the month Modrow had moved the elections from May to 18 March, six weeks away. From here he would head a coalition government, drawn from all parties, including New Forum and participants in the Round Table. End of Communist control. It was a shrewd move, an attempt to give the population something to focus on, and keep them in the country, and working. But Modrow, for all his honest efforts, became increasingly sidelined. At the beginning of February he put forward a ten-point plan for unification; Kohl ignored it. People in the East were sick of it all, and furious at being cheated by the leadership, sick of privation, declaring 'no more experiments', unwilling to stick around to see if things improved. The intellectuals bemoaned the collapse of their revolution and of their state, and the Round Table became more and more a talking shop. The decisions were being made elsewhere now, in Bonn.

The party of the hour became the Social Democrats, born

again from the ribs of the SED, to which many former SED members were now defecting. This made the SPD suspect, the haven for *Wendehälse*, but as the old party of the democratic left it was expected to attract votes and was emerging as a strong bidder to win the elections. They ruled out a coalition with the SED. In mid-January they linked up with the SPD in the West, and called for unity. '*Wir sind ein Volk.*' The Monday night demonstrations in Leipzig were still massive, and on the 22nd 100,000 marched beneath a sea of West German flags, calling for unification, and there were clashes between them and smaller groups of GDR supporters carrying their flags and singing patriotic songs. And the Republicans were there, performing for the cameras. The future darkens.

On the evening of the 22nd, Volksarmee engineers began to demolish a section of the Wall 350 metres long running down one side of Sebastianstrasse in Kreuzberg. As they worked the West Berlin police cordoned off the area. Reserved fraternal relations were established between both sides, with coffee, cigarettes, *Wieners*. The Wall section was replaced by wire mesh fence – the 'modern fence' they had installed elsewhere around remoter districts. Rumour had it that the whole section had been bought by Disney, for re-installation in Disneyland. And I remember saying, once, a year or so ago, that if they knocked it down Disney would rebuild it. Along this section, in the lee and shelter of the Wall, lived squatters in old buses and little wooden workmen's caravans, with their dogs and kids, scrapping, dealing in cars, gathering firewood. Living by the Wall, they had not chipped into it, and their presence had preserved this section almost intact. For a thank-you, they were now encouraged to move on by the cold wind blowing from the East through the mesh. An example of East/West Berlin co-operation.

At Wannsee, with the trains crying through and the lights glittering and the rain dripping from the trees in a mild winter, it's late in the evening, and the Ossis are thinning out. They come up from the S-Bahn and cross the busy Kronprinzessinnenweg, and mill about the buses, looking for the 99 stop. The empty buses turn here, swinging from one carriageway to another around the median strip, and wait in a long line for their schedule times, the drivers smoking, drinking from flasks. Here between two of them is a flat-bed truck, parked out in the traffic lane with emergency lights flashing. Two workmen are busy on the street's side, where they have spread a fine white sand, and they are carefully sweeping and shovelling it back into a sack. The sand is thickly stained with blood.

I4

SWORD AND SHIELD

Up the Frankfurter Allee, a wide straight boulevard bordered by huge blocks of Stalinist wedding-cake flats, beyond the S-Bahn bridge to the Magdalenenstrasse U-Bahn stop: Stasi-Zentrale, the central HQ of the GDR's security service, the Stasi. This is the hub of the vast network that watched everyone, to greater or lesser degree, and kept files on a third of the country's population. Housed in a city block of tall buildings of varied heights, all of it is tight as the tomb, guarded and still lethal.

This is the real wall, the dark centre of the story. In the future, students of total control will study the procedures of the Stasi – thorough, patient, complete, inquisitional, in the end self-defeating, a system that closed on itself. Are they plural or singular? Orwell might have imagined it, them. Or Machiavelli. And what tense are they in? Are they past or still in the present or waiting in the future?

Stasi-Zentrale is a massive city block, a complex of thirty-eight buildings 350 metres by 250 metres, a locked-in fortress on four sides around an inner unseen courtyard, barred and bolted on the ground floor all the way round, and every steel entrance watched by video cameras. Other cameras watch the traffic on the streets around, and no doubt there are other unseen eyes. Aerials bristle on the roofs, among whorls and spires of wire, and at every corner there are green-uniformed policemen, three and four at a time in a scramble of stars and shoulder flashes. The streets that contain the complex – Frankfurter Allee, Russische Strasse, Magdalenenstrasse and Normannenstrasse – are patrolled by Volkspolizei in cars.

Attacked two nights ago on 15 January by thousands of angry citizens – 7,000, the press generally agrees on – most of them young, too many for the police to control or the Stasi to repel, they stormed the complex and broke in. The attack was part of a pattern of attacks on Stasi buildings throughout the country. Impatient, the citizens had had it with the Government's promises to disband them, and in this manner the Stasi were exposed and routed, and afterwards came the citizens' committees to oversee their dismantling and investigate their activities. Around the area are a few broken windows, a damaged supermarket, but this was no random riot; the violence was concentrated on the buildings and their contents.

Here and there over its sides are scrawled crude hurried graffiti, still fresh, across the invaded territory of the hunt. Along Russische Strasse, the front of the building, a ditch and wall arrangement to repel assault has been included in the overall design, part of the brief of some architectural team, back in the early seventies when all this was begun. At the corner, a crescent of flagpoles, flagless. Half-way up the street another smaller arc of flagpoles, also flagless, by the official entrance, closed, guarded, sticky with more graffiti: *Securitate ade* (Goodbye Securitate), *Wie viele Menschen habt Ihr zerstört?* (How many people have you destroyed?) Then *Stasi-Gestapo-KGB-Securitate Blutsauger alle* (bloodsuckers all), *Stasi Schweine vors Gericht*/Stasi pigs to justice. A few cars are parked along the side, and young tough-looking men in shiney blousons come and go through the door that bears the only sign on the whole complex, announcing itself to the world as *The Oscar Ziethen Krankenhaus Polyklinik*. This was the cover name used on its letter-headings by the Stasi, their home address. By the door two plain clothes men hang about smoking, looking everyone up and down with an air of confident arrogance, young and tough. One has a boxer's nose. Whatever these two are, they are not paramedics.

Inside, 3,000 offices, now unoccupied, where 33,000 people worked. On the ground plan of the complex, later published in *Spiegel*, are the Databank, *Wachregiment*, munitions bunker, barracks, canteen, the aforesaid polyclinic, operations, departments subdividing the management of total information, and at the centre of it all the Office of the Minister, Erich Mielke, currently in prison awaiting charges of high treason, the cancer in the heart.

Along the Normannenstrasse side, a tall red-slabbed building whose windows are gold non-see-through glass. Across

Normannenstrasse and up into the next block, more Stasi buildings. In East Berlin some fifty further buildings were used by
Zentrale alone, and others were used at local district level. All
over East Berlin, all over the Republic, offices and bunkers,
flats, district headquarters, prisons, communications centres,
observation posts, are being uncovered. Around the country,
some 2,000 buildings. So far.

Das Haus der 1,000 Augen, it was the centre of the sticky web
of information and fear and blackmail that was the motor of
the sluggish German Democratic Republic of Workers and
Farmers, that haven of peace and orderly progress, where history
had effectively stopped. Its function, to be 'the sword and shield
of the revolution', was to maintain the orderly progress of the
economic plan in the slow inexorable march to Utopia, and to
uphold the leadership in its secret life of luxury, cutting off all
criticism and complaint. By their activities they maintained a
constant level of paranoia that damped everyone down. What
they established was what Wolfgang Templin, a member of the
Initiative for Peace and Human Rights, himself exiled to the
FRG and now returned to Berlin, has called 'the habit of being
watched'. They ensured a continuing supply of enemies within
and enemies without, and they penetrated life in the GDR at
every level. In the end, their effect was to ensure that no word
of complaint got through from the grassroots to the leadership,
which, ageing, clinging to its memories of past struggle and
dreaming of the visionary future, became atrophied, increasingly
out of touch with reality, cocooned in its enclave and its
lifestyle. The old men in Wandlitz and the thousands of Stasi
operatives in porkpie hats developed a symbiotic relationship;
the Stasi were effectively the leadership's blinkers. Too much
information turns eventually into none. Back in August 1989,
when Mielke, worried about the number of citizens fleeing the
country, asked about the overall situation in the GDR he was
told it was 'stable, of course'. He then asked was it possible
another 17 June, the 1953 Uprising, might come about, and
assured it would not: 'That's why we're here.' The Stasi supplied
and guaranteed the cloud of unreality in which the leadership
conducted its policies without interference.

According to official GDR government information – never
reliable – 85,000 operatives worked for the Stasi full-time,
probing into every corner, counting the socks in the drawers,

the shoes in the cupboards. Another 109,000 worked as paid informers, *Informelle Mitarbeiter* – IM. There were 33,127 employees in East Berlin. It is likely that many more were employed both full-time and on a casual basis. West German intelligence estimates the true totals much higher, at 100,000 full-time and 500,000 paid informers. This would make them the largest employer in the East. Later estimates double again the number they first thought of. Files were kept on 6 million East Germans, a third of the population. In some cities every letter was opened and every second telephone conversation listened to. Precise Germanic counting records that 1,052 people listened to telephone conversations, many of which were taped and stored, 2,100 opened and read letters and recorded their contents, there were 5,000 agents on special surveillance, 16,000 on permanent action. For weaponry they had 342 anti-aircraft guns, 3,537 anti-tank missiles, 4,499 machine-guns, 76,592 machine pistols, 124,593 pistols and revolvers. At their disposal were 12,903 personnel carriers and 2,531 buses, 2,350 trucks, 230 fast motor boats and four aircraft. Requisitioning at will, they occupied 2,037 flats and houses throughout the GDR, of which 652 were in East Berlin, together with twenty-four holiday homes with 2,058 beds for Stasi members. There were a further 1,000 offices in the Stasi local administration for Berlin, located further along the Frankfurter Allee, a complex scheduled now to become a hospital. There were command posts in underground shelters outside the fourteen district capitals as well as close to the leadership's enclave at Wandlitz. In 1989 their cost to the GDR was 3.6 billion marks. On 17 January there was official confirmation that the Stasi were organized as a paramilitary force, with arms depots, an 'over-dimensional' surveillance system, vast privileges and 1.3 per cent of the national budget at their disposal.

The citizens' control committees, set up to dismantle the Stasi and to trace collaborators and informers, has its work cut out, and the Stasi block and mislead its inquiries. The main committee consists of some 100 people, volunteers on secondment from their regular work, some of them computer and other specialists. Their first task, in co-operation with the Volkspolizei, was to seal Zentrale, and its files. It had not been in anyone's interest, they decided, for the mob to wreck the files; the files would be needed for future prosecutions of Stasi employees. Many of their former victims were planning to go to court. The committee had lists, but many of these were incomplete, and every day they discovered something new. Early in their work computer specialists traced cables out of Zentrale to an underground bunker full of electronic equipment. At the end of January on Köpenicker Allee they discovered Dept VIII (Observation). Everything was fully functioning, although the building was supposed to have been converted to a child care centre two years ago. Everywhere they look they see the Stasi; it is, says Hannelore Köhler of the citizens' committee, 'a Hydra's head. The head is cut off but the body still lives.'

Officially established in February 1950, from 1957 till his recent fall its head was Erich Mielke. The head of internal security was Egon Krenz, till he became General Secretary after Honecker. The Stasi, with the bureaucracy and Party leadership and the army, were the aristocrats of this captive society, the chief beneficiaries of the clampdown that followed the Uprising in 1953. Thereafter the state froze, and through the decades control became more efficient, more absolute. In the years since, they have remained in place, stronger and surer of themselves. It's difficult to believe they will go quietly.

The Stasi operated internally and externally, and was highly active in West Berlin, with a history of intrigue and kidnapping Eastern defectors, and some Westerners, and spiriting them back to the East. Abroad, the GDR's foreign trade apparatus and the diplomatic service was riddled by them. In 1985 Mielke enacted Order No. 2 'to prevent, discover and combat' underground political activities. Dissidents, complainers, critics, all were to be considered criminal; anyone thought to be opposed to the state was checked, followed, documented in the files, regularly updated. The object of Order No. 2 was, Honecker said, 'total information'. Its effect was to create a climate of ever-present fear throughout the land, a substantial contribution to the social and economic stagnation that ultimately did for the GDR itself.

Stasi and the Party leadership were intimately connected. Leading officials of the Stasi and the SED used a telephone network that could not be tapped. Mielke regularly reported to the first and second secretaries of the SED, and SED's security chiefs, and the heads of the police and army. The data collected, the digests of tons of files, came together in Mielke's office in

Stasi-Zentrale. He shared his information with Honecker. There was no parliamentary control over these activities. In the highly centralized and top-heavy bureaucracy of the East, all management personnel decisions involved the Stasi, and anyone recommended to an important appointment had to be checked for reliability. Just as the Party shadowed the administration and the economy through Party organizations at every level, creating a parallel administration, so the Stasi shadowed both. Security checks were implemented on everyone joining the army, requesting a trading licence, or applying to study at a university. Informers would then check out friends, colleagues, neighbours, family. Often security checks extended to close relatives of the applicant as well. Anyone found to have 'a negative political attitude' or 'undefinable contacts with the West' was rejected. There was, of course, no appeal, and reasons for turning down an application were never given. The files remained indefinitely, and could be far-reaching in their influence. A criticism made in the fifties could result in the refusal of a foreign trip thirty years later.

Apparently the Stasi also provided Party and state officials with special services. Western films and pornography were copied in the educational film hire department and shown to selected audiences in Wandlitz. The Stasi photo lab developed the leadership's holiday snaps. The former Prime Minister, Willi Stoph, who had many Western relatives, had his visitors picked up at S-Bahn Friedrichstrasse by a driver. They came in via a special door guarded by a Stasi member, avoiding the checkpoint. Visitors at this door came with a password or the other half of a postcard, and included delegations of the West German Communist Party, spies and high Stasi officials.

To transgress any of the rules, to speak out on any matter however mundane, to stick out one's neck, was to invite attention. Education, housing, work, promotion and thereby standard of living were all centrally controlled, and a negative entry meant effective elimination from any of these. In the Stasi, East Germany evolved an Orwellian system of control: all pervasive, forever watching and listening, controlling through fear of exposure, loss of career, prison.

Sigrid's story begins some ten years ago: when she was a schoolteacher, she had a penfriend in Denmark. Once the penfriend sent her a parcel of goodies – biscuits and sweets for

the children, napkins, and among sundry items a catalogue of
Danish furniture. As a precaution, she separately mailed Sigrid
a list of the parcel's contents. The parcel arrived. Everything
came through but the catalogue. Sigrid was disappointed. She'd
heard about Danish furniture, its simplicity, and her husband
was good with wood, and might be able to make something
from the catalogue. She wanted to read it, dammit, and then she
got angry, and then she went down to the Postkontrolle and
asked to see the official responsible for her postal address. After
a long uncertain wait she got in to see him. She said 'It's only a
catalogue of furniture. It's only pictures of tables and chairs and
corner cupboards.' The official shook his head. No, she could
not have it, and no, he would not explain why he had so
decided, he would not discuss the matter further with her. The
interview was over. She went out of the building, and to the
sentry on duty at the gate vented her spleen on such an idiotoic
decision. A few days later at school the director called her into
his office. She had insulted the People's Police. She had insulted
the Government. She had insulted the socialist system. She's not
a schoolteacher any more.

Stasi Knechte, it says here along the Normannenstrasse side:
slaves, mercenaries. *Stasi rück die Akten raus*: Stasi get the
files out. Fat, comprehensive, they document the private habits
and predilections of each citizen, weaknesses, mistakes, youthful
transgressions, the written-up reports of tales told by informers
who turned out to be workmates, neighbours, teachers, bartenders, and the exhaustive inquiries of the professionals. Their
appetite for information was insatiable, and Stasi informers,
official and unofficial, in and out of uniform, were everywhere:
customs officials, waiters, museum attendants, Jehovah's witnesses, travel guides, chambermaids, stewardesses, railway con-
ductors, prostitutes, anyone with ears. In trouble with the Stasi,
a citizen might be offered a deal to work for them. One officer
described how he became a Stasi: when he was at university
they played football on a Sunday morning. One Sunday there
was no pitch free, except one which everyone knew was the
Stasi pitch. This man led the rest on to the pitch, and play
commenced. But not for long. Arrested, he was offered a deal:
spy on your fellow students. Or else. From that day on he was
Stasi, with a gun in his armpit. There were artists and musicians
who might hear in conversation of someone planning to leave

the country. There were theology students whose studies were paid for, and who informed on other students and, later, on church and opposition groups. They spied on tourists, on GDR citizens, and on each other. Foreigners, transit passengers, soldiers, students, policemen, artists, musicians, clergymen, were all registered in one or other Stasi department. Most public buildings and hotels were monitored and wired. Critics of the regime such as Robert Havemann, Wolf Biermann, Stefan Heym and Wolfgang Templin were spied on exhaustively, their mail opened, their visitors checked and registered. Photographs were taken of their every move, their friends were interrogated, they were followed everywhere. At Havemann's funeral Stasi attended, registering everyone there and having a word with them afterwards. Even in December and into January telephone tapping continued, and mail intercepted, and people were still discovering microphones on their persons or in their apartments.

The army of informants grew every day, like cancer, taking over more and more property and resources and personnel. Mountains of paperwork grew around these activities. They were old-fashioned. For the most part the Stasi distrusted computers, and so their databanks were replicated in several departments, and much of the file work was done by hand. Their files were the outcome of the Party's paranoia, its obsession with enemies within and without. They were a further pressure to conform in an already deeply conformist society, where the individual was encouraged to wave flags on public demonstrations, support Party-sponsored resolutions, work, marry, bear children, and die without one word of complaint. For they were always listening, in bars and restaurants and public places; a comment on a painting in the public gallery might be overheard by one of the attendants, who had a little job on the side. They were everywhere. Advancement in the Stasi depended on recruiting more informers, and only top SED officials were excluded from recruitment. Each employee had to find twenty-five new members each year, or get a negative report, and so the Stasi grew like an obscene chain-letter. Since each potential recruit had to be checked, the paperwork grew, and before an approach was made the investigator knew everything about his subject. A few minor transgressions could always be found, or failing that, concocted. Their method was blackmail. In checking someone out, a list of 101 points was completed, illuminating an individual's character, attitude to work, social position, ability to keep a secret, hobbies, reading matter, body gestures, articulation, moods, intelligence, ability to judge, to memorize, any special knowledge, attitudes to the army, the USSR and other socialist states, differences in official and private views, where they lived, contacts in the GDR, relatives or friends in the West. An individual's sexual behaviour was ticked off as compulsive, unrestrained, insecure, self-controlled, uncontrolled, boastful. Each investigated citizen's details, however private, were on file, ready for instant use, and no corner was too personal for them to poke into.

Internal mail was extensively searched, and letters addressed to the West were opened by department PFZ (*Postzollfahndung*). Their task was to open envelopes, read and evaluate the contents. They opened the letters by steam. According to one former employee, the offices had to be repapered every six months due to the steam. Letters were then sealed once more by the technical department. A letter damaged by this procedure was thrown away. They regularly took money from envelopes. Since there are no arrangements for sending money by cheque or order to the GDR, and since it is technically against international postal law to send cash through the post, they did this with some self-justification. Every two weeks an official from Stasi-Zentrale would collect the money. Even in the smaller post offices they collected up to DM 4,000 each week.

The Stasi's favoured method of uncovering opposition was to search a suspect's flat unofficially while he/she was out. People living in the same house or block were given things to do so that they all left the building for the period. This reveals the extent of their control: one man would be given a doctor's appointment, another an interview with an official, a student kept late at school. With the building secured, a special squad broke into the flat. They first took Polaroid pictures of everything so it could all be put back in place after the search. They looked for Western newspapers, foreign currency, letters, leaflets, anything suspicious. If they found sufficient incriminating material, the team would come back later with a prosecutor.

Arrest and interrogation followed. Suspects were usually arrested at work, to encourage the others. There would be perhaps just a little problem, a matter to be cleared up. In custody and interrogation every attempt was made to make the subject feel helpless; the suspect was told no law, no lawyer, no friend or relative could prevent his/her being kept in custody indefinitely until everything had been admitted and anyone else involved implicated. They were thorough and Germanic, and documented everything. These interrogations were indefinite, and could go on for months, though few were able to withstand them for more than six. The Stasi worked on fear, uncertainty, on psychological terror, ultimately on violence but for preference on the fear of it. In the end confession was the only way out of the routine of interrogation. Held indefinitely, with no particular charge as yet and only questions the direction of which couldn't be seen, in isolation, incommunicado, the suspect eventually broke. Former prisoners and Stasi interrogators concur in this: eventually they got a confession, eventually they found something, and on that basis got a conviction. Their confidence in this lay in the fact that they had all the time in the world, they were doing their job and earning their living, while the suspect languished indefinitely in prison, in suspension. Their methods differed from standard police interrogation procedures perhaps only in their thoroughness, in the amount of time they were prepared to take for a result on the slightest accusation. Interviews appear to have been carried out on a regular basis, to establish routine and dependency, for a definite period of time. They appear to have ranged in degree of formality. Since they were mainly investigating imaginary crime, the Stasi could afford to fuss with details, wait. Contact was regulated presumably to encourage some moment, some possibility of intimacy between investigator and subject. The prisoner got used to a schedule, to a procedure, which might then be abruptly broken, an expected meeting cancelled at a moment's notice. As police and jailers the world over know, the prisoner may dread the moment when the door opens, but it breaks an otherwise interminable time of being banged up. The rest of the time while under investigation the prisoner saw no one, was without news, cut off entirely from the world, even from fellow prisoners. The intention was for the prisoner to come to depend on the interrogator, confide, spill the beans, confess and get it over with. In the end that's what happened: the suspect became convinced that the only light at the end of the tunnel lay through confession, conviction, prison. In the end the victim would be grateful, help the interrogator clear matters up, and sign the confession. There are reports of torture, as yet difficult to confirm, and some ex-prisoners say they heard beatings taking place, but most reports speak of a fairly civilized ritual, imbued with its own sense of gathering certainty of no way out. The victim was eventually brought to understand that only by confessing could the endless business of interrogation be brought to a close. Thereafter the certainty of prison became a nightmare to be got through, and thereafter, marked, the condemned's career in the GDR was finished. Nothing for it then but to try to emigrate to the West, or join the sub-culture of criminality.

In Potsdam the citizens took control of the local Stasi head-quarters, where they found fifty tons of files, some of them shredded paper. The prison there held between fifty and sixty people in fifty cells. Six of its former Stasi officers were questioned by members of New Forum, and one said he had not realized they were a source of so much fear. A former Stasi prison, also in Potsdam, was opened, and is to be turned into a museum of the SED regime. Formerly used by the Gestapo, it held about 140 men and women awaiting trial in eighty prison cells. The cell for a single prisoner was 2.90m × 1.10m, for two 2.90m × 1.40m. In the cells wooden stools were fixed to the ground, cots pulled against the walls during the day. There was a toilet in the corner. At night the lights were switched on every 2–5 minutes. Prisoners were called only by number. Before questioning they were searched and had to put on different underwear. Exercise in the 'free period' of ten minutes took place in a tiny space known as a 'tiger cage', where cameras recorded every move. Most suspects lived in isolation, without association.

In East Berlin there were three Stasi prisons, one in Magdalenenstrasse, part of the Zentrale complex. It housed 200 prisoners. Remand prisoners were two-ed up in cells four metres square, with wooden plank beds and an open toilet. Instead of windows there were glass bricks. Nearby were thirty interrogation rooms, each with a telephone, a safe and a sound-proofed door. The walls were wired, so that touching a wire automatically closed all the doors in the jail. Exercise was taken in tiger cages, walled concrete boxes three metres high, covered in wire mesh, and above them catwalks patrolled by armed guards.

Among the special departments of the Stasi were:

Department I: security of the army and the border guards, monitoring a soldier's every move. At initial interview it was decided whether to send the soldier to the interior or the south, if it was felt he couldn't be trusted, or to the border with West Germany if he could. At the first sign of unreliability he was posted away. This department contained twenty-seven generals, and had its own troops within the army and its own guard batallion of 7,000 men, the Feliks Dzierzynski. Various sub-departments became almost independent secret services.

Department II: counter-intelligence, dealing with the exterior of the GDR, Western journalists, and so forth.

Department III: monitoring telephones. Despite the claims that this department ceased functioning in January, there are persistent suspicions that tapping continued, and that this function has been taken over by the army.

Department VII: police.

Department VIII: observed transit traffic between West Germany and West Berlin on television monitors. A Trabi parking by a Western car was regarded as a potential contact, and might mean the driver's next foreign trip being refused. Petrol pump attendants, waiters and policemen often doubled as Stasi agents on the transit routes. All information was collected at the Michendorf service station.

Department IX: had agents working in holiday resorts in other Eastern block countries, whose task was to prevent contact between East and West Germans.

Department XVIII: responsible for the economy. Directors of combines were checked for political reliability. Those who complained were registered. The careers of many managers ended here.

Department XX: the heart of the Stasi. Here political parties and mass organizations were watched, and the department was responsible for political and ideological subversion and undercover political activities. Its guidelines: everyone represents a security risk, and in order to be safe one must have total information. Here, as throughout the GDR, security took precedence over individual rights.

Special new departments and arms of the Stasi were constantly being established, right to the end. Many of these were so secret that even other Stasi members did not know about them or their functions. One was the *Arbeitsgruppe Minister* near Berlin, responsible for the training of special agents. Another was established around Alexander Schalck-Golodkowski and his foreign currency operations. In the mid-eighties, with the deepening suspicion of the SED leadership, the atmosphere in the Stasi changed. In 1985 came Mielke's Order No. 2. The Stasi machinery was militarized, and every member kept a uniform and combat gear in his office, ready to go. Members, both men and women, underwent military training. They were kept alert to the imminent possibility of a Western invasion. At the same time more emphasis was placed on ideological training. Departments began to cut themselves off, and less and less was publicly discussed. The guideline 'Everyone is a potential enemy of the Party and the State' was now directed against the Stasi itself, who became victims of their own organization. Stasi members were constantly afraid of denunciation by their colleagues, and so they worked with particular zeal. They kept their activities secret even from their families, and were forbidden to watch Western television programmes in their own homes. They themselves were under observation, and were constantly tested on their attitudes to the class enemy. Those employed opening the mail were tested with control letters containing hostile passages; failure to report meant a cut in salary, and exclusion from promotion. When Stasi accompanied delegations to the West, as they always did, there were Stasi members in the same group keeping an eye on their fellow Stasi. On athletic trips abroad, every fourth or fifth person was Stasi.

Only those rated absolutely trustworthy and who were without friends or relatives in the West were employed. Recruits had to sign a statement declaring that they would report even members of their own families. Employees earned about 2,000 marks a month. According to status, a Lada and a driver were assigned; generals got Citroëns, available also off duty and for holiday trips. Most leading officials lived in villas, attended daily by Stasi employees. They sailed yachts, and shopped at the Leiterladen Berlin, purchasing Western goods and generally living the life of Riley.

Such was the sword and shield of the revolution, a vast bureaucracy of fear, blackmail, reports, snooping, threats. Though many of their victims went to 'normal' prisons, they operated their own remand prisons, and so hung on to their suspects till they had a result. In prison, convicted politicals were mixed with criminals, and the latter were encouraged to dominate the former. Those who merited the attentions of the Stasi were far from all being critics of the system, let alone its opponents. In such an atmosphere everyone was suspect, and anyone might fall into the frame. The Stasi, the security arm of the corrupt East German leadership, became an industry running on the perpetual fuel of suspicion. Suspicion bred more suspicion. To break any of the many rules of the GDR was to be marked, kept thereafter in a lowly position, from which promotion would never come, and one did not have to go to prison to achieve this distinction. Other privileges could be denied, permission to travel abroad refused. You, or your children, might not qualify for further education, or for a holiday, a larger flat, a Trabi.

In the end such a system defeated itself, crippling initiative and stifling the imagination, as the army of the disaffected, of those who having fallen lost hope, grew. Forty years of looking over their shoulders became a habit. In the end no one would stick their neck out, for fear of losing it, so when the state shuddered to a halt there was a crisis of indecision everywhere. The Stasi straitjacketed their society, hosing up informers and suspects, processing both, imprisoning the one and moulding the other into its own image. For the GDR the safety valve was always the West, and in recent years the politically disaffected were more frequently allowed to emigrate – some were encouraged to do so. The GDR, which had stressed and encouraged literature and culture, encouraging many exiled writers and artists to settle there in the early days, eventually threw its poets out of the Republic, and turned it over to the thought police.

When the crowds stormed the complex, they broke in and ransacked the files, smashed and carried off equipment, ripped out phone wires and threw furniture through windows, and, finding a portrait of the disgraced leader Honecker still on the wall in the lobby, smashed it. It was they who sprayed the angry graffiti: *Glasnost, SED nee, Besatzer raus, Ich will meine Akte haben* (I want to have my file). But the main object of their interest and their fury were the files, of which as many as they could get hold they scattered and burned. These events, on television and in the newspapers, contrasted the gap between the Stasi and the populace it watched and guarded: in the kitchens smoked salmon on the menu, wines in the wine racks. More orderly citizens of East and West were shocked by the invasion. New Forum and the other opposition groups quickly condemned it.

Two days later, there's little sign of damage. The streets are quiet, and apart from the presence of so many Volkspolizei, normal enough. At the corner of Frankfurter Allee there's a busted file box, the light green colour of military furniture, which has been prised open and left for dead. There's only the writing on the wall, and the heavy police presence at every barred gate, and the question: where are they? Are they, as some believe, back in reserve in the interior, in those vast tracts of military land closed to the public?

After the *Wende* the Stasi were to be reduced. Then in mid-January they were to be abolished, disarmed and disbanded. By the end of the month 25,000 had been dismissed; the process takes time. The German language, moving ponderously from past to present to future, accounts for part of the explanation: *they are being disbanded*. In a centrally planned economy it takes time to shift X operatives from A to B, retraining them to drive trams or ambulances, and the slow-thinking bureaucrats are still in place, with their hierarchies and ideas of orderly progression. Consider their dependants, their function as consumers, and the dependent workforce that served their requirements. Then add the economic effect of the sudden unemployment of the army of informers, people who had grown used to supplementing their income with regular reports on their neighbours.

On 22 January the deposed Egon Krenz, requested to appear before the Round Table in East Berlin, made a personal statement. The Stasi, he said, speaking of the organization he was supposed to control, 'violated every democratic principle', and were completely outside all control. They interfered at every level – instructing officials and delegates in local government, in district and national government, in the army, the Volkspolizei, the Ministries and the Party leadership. They worked through conspiracy. Even high party functionaries were controlled. In forty years, Krenz said, the informer service became 'a hostile power', a state within the state '*Staat im Staat*' – and this produced passivity and resignation, stifling initiative and spontaneity.

Krenz went on to apologize to the citizens of the GDR that 'under the old security doctrine I let this happen', claiming to be as much a prisoner of the Stasi as every other East German.

Krenz's disclaimer was received with contempt. In charge of internal security, he now claimed they had controlled him. What's for sure is that he would have received the intelligence coming in throughout 1989, indicating the growth of the exodus and civil unrest; he was therefore responsible for Honecker's and Mielke's ignorance of the true situation, and therefore in a position, when push came to shove, to replace Honecker, with Gorbachov's blessing and support, in the Politburo. It begins to look at if this is precisely what he did, in a palace revolt designed to keep the Communists in power, but in the end the popular revolt removed him.

But there remains disquiet and suspicion. Where are they, and in what sense have they been disbanded, and can they at some point regroup, as – say – taxi drivers, ambulance drivers, at their disposal a vehicle and a radio that could mobilize them quickly? Paranoia works at the question. Many are now employed driving just such vehicles. Recently there was a taxi-drivers' strike, and the drivers gathered to protest at the city Rathaus, claiming that ex-Stasi drivers were still being paid their old salaries, three times a cab-driver's wage. Some are driving trams and buses, replacing the missing workers who have fled West. Many are reported to have gone West themselves. At any rate from 1 February ex-Stasi were disqualified from drawing a pension in the West; this was a popular decision that may be illegal, since FRG regulations do not specify a pension on the grounds of occupation. Others are reported taking menial jobs in factories, filling boxes, carrying things; no one helps them or communicates with them. Many find it difficult to get work, and are unemployed. Some are hired as security guards. Some are now in the customs service fighting speculation and the black market. None of the ex-Stasi jailers are to be taken into the regular prison service. None of the postal censors are to be hired by the post office. There is a problem: what to do with so many operatives who are trained only to watch, and to interrogate and ensnare? No one knows the answer. Some members of New Forum have suggested that they should employ some of them themselves, to protect and rehabilitate them.

As production workers they replace workers who have gone West, but no one is keen to hire them. Some have secured jobs as teachers and administrators. Interflug has retrained seventy of them as flight attendants. A hundred who were part of a special combat unit have been placed in a new special unit to fight terrorism. Some are miners, some street cleaners. Others go in for security work, anticipating the arrival of Western business. A former Stasi major from Erfurt was found working for the Frankfurt am Main airport police. Twelve former Stasi were hired as guards at East Berlin's national museum. In February the GDR post office published the following advertisement in *Neues Deutschland*:

NOW WE KNOW SOME SECRETS THAT WEREN'T. ASK US ABOUT GETTING RID OF MICROPHONES. WE ARE THE EXPERTS. THIS SERVICE IS AVAILABLE TO PARTIES AND POLITICAL ORGAN- IZATIONS EVEN BEFORE THE ELECTIONS. OUR EXPERIENCE AND MODERN TECHNICAL EQUIPMENT IS AT YOUR DISPOSAL.

Two former Stasi, with a West Berliner, established the GDR's first detective agency in Plonzstrasse, close to Zentrale. They get calls every day from ex-Stasi seeking employment, and expect to hire between twenty and twenty-five of their former colleagues.

The committees began to open the Stasi warehouses of stock-piled goods, where cars and furniture abandoned by those who fled were seized and stored. One building contained some 20,000 articles seized in the post from the West; of these goods the Stasi had first pick, and the rest were sold in state shops. A room in Normannenstrasse was found to contain 20,000 Cyrillic Bibles, collected over the years on behalf of the Soviets, for whom the Bible was subversive literature. In mid-March it was revealed that Alexander Schalck-Golodkowski's firm *KoKo* (*Kommerzielle Koordinierung*) had hoarded 21.2 tons of gold ingots, which had been secured. Schalck-Golodkowski was still in hiding in the West, accused of smuggling arms and drugs. According to the report of a special commission, every year 15 million marks in foreign exchange were spent on the former SED leadership, used to purchase Western goods for them and their relatives. The Wandlitz government housing enclave received 6–8 million marks in foreign exchange every year. By the end of March, 200 completely furnished flats used for clandestine meetings had been discovered in the Berlin Mitte district alone. 100,000 metres of Stasi files were found in East Berlin. All transit registration cards of GDR citizens were collected and recorded on microfiche. 80,000 cassette tapes with recorded telephone conversations were found. These will be destroyed. Seventy tons of forms and more than 100,000 tons of files were discovered in one department alone. There were two rooms lined with copper, to protect the computers from satellite surveillance. It's still not clear how much material was removed between 9 November and mid-January. Mielke's safe was empty.

The department for espionage abroad, excluded from the scrutiny of the citizens' committees, continued operating in the West. In January it was reported in West Berlin that an Eastern agent had been held, charged with attempting to recruit students. On 24 February the head of Hamburg's *Verfassungsschutz*, the Office for the Defence of the Constitution – the West German internal secret service – announced that GDR agents were still operating in the Bundesrepublik. He claimed that 2,000 West Germans were still on the Stasi payroll, and not one had defected. But then, he would say that, wouldn't he? He confirmed that Stasi foreign espionage agents were being taken over by the KGB, and that files and documents had been moved to Soviet military bases for transfer to Russia, in anticipation of the East suspending espionage in the West after the election. Markus Wolf, the former East German spymaster, was in Russia, said to be integrating the GDR spy network in West Germany into the KGB. It then emerged that some agents in the West had turned themselves in. Some had been asked to continue working. Bluff and double bluff. Some operatives, and some important files, were said to have moved to the West to work with the West German secret service. Some are still in their old positions working for a new master, others are freelance. In the past four out of five diplomats were Stasi, and most of them were still in place.

It was claimed that by the middle of February approximately 5,000 Stasi members had gone to the West, and that in the early days some had taken certain files with them. 'They already know who they want,' the man said. Months after the event it was alleged that the storming of Zentrale on 15 January had been organized by Western agents – or infiltrated by them – to get their hands on key files, assisted by new friends inside who had left a window open. In late February the GDR Defence Ministry confirmed a Western report that West German citizens had received secret military training in the GDR. In the mid-seventies Honecker had ordered a Volksarmee facility near Frankfurt an der Oder to be prepared, with army instructors but under overall Stasi supervision. They were stopped in 1988.

Towards the end of March began a spate of arrests of Eastern agents working in the West, many of them operating in the armed forces. One was a printer working for the West German army, who had been passing copies of documents he'd printed on conferences and training exercises since the early seventies, using a pensioner as his courier. A couple who had photographed and passed Bundeswehr and NATO documents were arrested. In early April a West German working for NATO was accused of spying for the GDR since 1969, passing on documents on disarmament negotiations. A cipher officer working in Bonn's permanent mission to NATO was held on suspicion of passing secrets to East Germany for the last twenty years. A man working for the West German foreign service who had passed documents to the Stasi since 1975 was arrested. A computer expert working for the Bundeswehr with access to important data was arrested. By 20 April, seventeen agents had been apprehended since the beginning of the year, and more arrests were to follow.

Lest anyone think such activities were exclusive to the other side, there was a report in *Spiegel* in early March to the effect that the BND, the West German secret service evaluated personal letters from the GDR on a large-scale basis. Every day more than 10,000 letters from Eastern Europe, especially from the GDR, were delivered to a centre in Hamburg-Winterhude. The secret service denies this. But then, they would, wouldn't they? Towards the end of March the secret service announced that it would cease working in the GDR, 'more or less'; it was pointed out there were still 380,000 Soviet troops in the GDR, and groups of former Stasi who would need watching.

Details of prison conditions emerged. Under a harsh regime, prisons are likely to be the harshest. Though the use of torture and severe treatment as a policy has been denied, excesses of zeal have been admitted: bullying, ill-treatment, cruelty and sadism. In the prisons conditions were harsh, and there was minimal contact with the outside world, the windows were covered with steel blinds to prevent prisoners seeing out. Political imprisonment, regarded as an educational process, was naturally counter-productive. The harsher the treatment, the deeper the disaffection. A West German organization has documented conditions in prisons in the GDR. Its report names 2,000 prison staff by name, rank and code-name; among the worst are two sergeants from Cottbus known as 'Red Terror' and 'Arafat', another from Karl-Marx-Stadt called 'Kung Fu', and 'The Cat' in Hohenschönhausen women's prison.

On 23 February Andreas Merten, aged twenty-seven, from Mühlhausen-Erfurt, reported that he was tortured by the Stasi, and his claim was confirmed by a West German doctor who examined him. Merten claimed the Stasi pulled oily threads through his testicles, rammed long needles into his body, and pushed a broken spoon down his gullet into his stomach. Two weeks afterwards he was operated on, and he is now in the West, soon to undergo more operations. In April, according to *Stern*, details emerged of the Stasi's use of psychiatry and psychiatric clinics to detain those it wished to intimidate, and the use of torture and blackmail. In the Waldheim psychiatric clinic in Hochschweitzschen, arrested 'patients' were locked up, sometimes in dark cells, for days and weeks; they were interrogated, kicked, deprived of food, beaten up, they had white foam sprayed in their eyes, were made to sit in ice-cold water, and their feet were burned; women were raped, people were injected with emetics and saline infusions to cause nausea, and threatened with worse. The worst part of the clinic was Ward M1, 'the shelter'. Some were 'pumped', lying on their stomachs with nurses pulling their legs back; the pain was said to be unbearable, and to cause temporary blindness. The same treatments had been discovered in 1974 by Amnesty International in psychiatric clinics in the USSR. The clinic at Hochschweitzschen was presided over by a Dr Poppe, an advisory psychiatrist for Leipzig district, an executive member of the society for psychiatry and neurology, and till October 1989 an SED party member. He has since gone to Switzerland. Nurses working there noticed that (1) the Stasi came and went a lot, and (2) a lot of people admitted to the clinic seemed quite normal. Interviewed by *Stern*, Poppe said that many patients might seem normal, but were obsessed by the belief that they were followed by the Stasi. Belief becomes reality; what matters is what people believe to be happening. Apocrypha and paranoia are the parents of history.

Meanwhile the control commissions, finding their work of investigating the Stasi somewhat formidable, called in ex-officers to help them. This created its own paranoia; by giving ex-Stasi access they could not be sure their activities were not being reported, or how many files were being spirited out under their noses. Blocked by former Stasi members, and infiltrated by them, they decided to check themselves out, called in a prosecutor, and opened the files on themselves gathered by Department XII. Some went so far as to call for a secret service of their own. In the streets demonstrations demanded retribution, and angry citizens continued to attack ex-Stasi, their families and their homes. There were violent threats against committee members from ex-Stasi, phone calls and letters, and the fear persisted that the Stasi were organizing to boycott and sabotage the new government after the elections.

As to the tons of personal files, some said they should be destroyed, others were for sealing them, others for turning them over to the academics; no doubt they'd be a goldmine of statistical research material. Hundreds have gone to the courts asking for compensation, but for this to be figured the files will be required. So the files themselves are difficult to dispose of. Many of them are in disorder, scattered in the invasion of Stasi-Zentrale or destroyed or removed by the Stasi themselves. What isn't known is how many files were removed by the Stasi between October and January. The card indexes themselves are vague, listing agents and victims alike, and sometimes using code-names; they are scattered, and the same person may be listed in several cities. Since the Stasi never trusted data-processing systems, the files aren't centralized, and much of the data is reproduced in various departments around the country. Many files are missing, or what's worse, partially missing; some are in Russia, some have gone West.

Were the Stasi really finished? By early March out of thirty-eight buildings in Normannenstrasse, seventeen had been cleared. A week before the election the Round Table claimed the Stasi was now unable to operate; it no longer monitored telephone calls, checked mail, or observed people. Others begged to differ. The use of surveillance cameras was discovered: 'traffic' cameras all around Alexanderplatz (an area exclusive to pedestrians) and the centre of East Berlin were shown to be linked through the police monitors to the Stasi. But at Zentrale most of the operatives had been dismissed. At the same time the citizens' committee at Normannenstrasse concluded that the Stasi leadership had in reality been paralysed and unable to respond to the political changes in East Germany in 1989, despite its exhaustive inquiries into the lives of the citizens of the GDR. It was well-informed about opposition groups such as New Forum, Initiative for Peace and Human Rights, the SPD, and the atmosphere among the population at large, but though it wanted to know everything it ended up knowing nothing. Nevertheless, it emerged that they had been preparing twenty-four internment camps for dissidents from peace, church and environmental groups. Their names were listed. The Stasi had been prepared to lock up thousands of its people, rather than give way. A crackdown had been planned.

In the first week of March the Feliks Dzierzynski barracks in Hessenwinkel near Berlin were cleared, with other barracks soon to follow. Drunk, the soldiers destroyed most of the barracks before quitting. As time went by former Stasi facilities were released into public use. In April the former Stasi transport department was taken over by BVB, the East Berlin transport authority, and opened for public use. The BVB took over 800 vehicles. Two special trains, one used by the former government, the other by the army, were taken over by the Reichsbahn to be used for tourism. It was a matter of converting the works of the devil to useful purposes; an East Berlin firm in Köpenick that used to manufacture bugs and listening devices for the Stasi announced in April it would convert to the production of hearing aids.

Nevertheless it was widely believed the Stasi were not yet done with. Telephones were still being tapped, and eavesdropping went on well into the new year and even beyond 18 March. Hanna Köhler of the citizens' committee warned against the employment of Stasi in certain areas where they could form Stasi cells. She knew of no such underground activity, but that proved nothing. In March it was reported that the director of VEB Baureparaturen (house repair) in Berlin Hohenschönhausen, a PDS man, had dismissed long-term employees and taken on Stasi, several of whom were immediately given leading positions. Out of 220 employees seventy are former

Stasi, who are not integrated into regular work brigades, but form their own Stasi brigade. Employees feared the Stasi were forming cells. Around the country, citizens' committees reported obstruction and infiltration, missing files, missing pages from files. In early March Stasi informers and employees were released from confidentiality, and were allowed to talk about their former activities, and – if asked – must report everything to the police and prosecution. On 8 March in Erfurt it was reported that even after the official deactivation of the Stasi, secrecy of the post was violated. The committee there reported little success in the three months it had been working, and claimed that many former officers were now in high-ranking positions in state-run enterprises. In that district not a single Stasi member was in prison. Twenty local Stasi officers got jobs in industry and replaced directors who had been dismissed having left the SED. It was claimed that Department 1A of the local Volks-polizei, which used to co-operate with the Stasi, was still compiling information on dissenters, and many unofficial employees of the Stasi were still working. Members of the committee claimed that the local prosecution was not helpful and blocked inquiries, and the committee assumed some prosecution attorneys were former Stasi officials. 'We have to admit we have failed,' they said. 'We are trying to do the impossible.' 4.5 kilometres of files were discovered. Especially tricky for the committee was the Soviet secret service, and whenever any sign of it emerged, investigations were immediately suspended. They confirmed that files had been transferred to the KGB. In one district, local people stormed a house thinking it belonged to the Stasi, only to find it full of Russian soldiers with machine-guns. US intelligence has also expressed interest in the Stasi files.

At the sixteenth and last meeting of East Berlin's Round Table on 5 April, four representatives of the committee responsible for the deactivation of the Stasi complained that forty-three former Stasi employees were on the committee, supposedly assisting in the location of Stasi property. They argued that while it seemed to be deactivated, its inner structure still existed. A former Stasi employee working for the German post office as a departmental head was able to see important paperwork.

There was a popular demand for retribution. At the end of March after the election thousands demonstrated in East Berlin, demanding that all politicians, lawyers and judges be vetted for Stasi involvement. But in a situation where, as it emerged, one third of the population had in one way or another co-operated with the Stasi, the numbers of the guilty were too many, and the line between victim and oppressor often ran thin. In some sense, everyone was culpable.

The past recurs again. After World War II the de-Nazification programme only went so far in both Germanies, though it was more thorough in the East. In the East the determination to punish Nazis was carried out by people who had been their direct victims, Communists and Jews, but one effect of this was to blind the Party to its own excesses. Beyond a certain point, on both sides of post-war Germany the need for administrators, judges, teachers, outbid the lust for revenge. So here again. How much of the detritus is to be carried forward into the future as part of a united Germany is the question. So many are tainted by their involvement.

Some were for amnesty. Kohl endorsed it, though the Bonn Ministry of Justice said an amnesty for former Stasi was speculative. Members of New Forum spoke of forgiveness; there were suggestions that hearings and trials be held without passing sentence. On the streets protestors demonstrated that that would not be sufficient. Attacks on Stasi members continued. Some foresaw the suspicion and flow of accusation going on for years. What was needed was a house clearing, a cleansing of the dirty stables. But it was claimed Stasi cells were forming in safe havens, in the army, in the police, in the customs.

Many of the new politicians were pastors, lawyers, people with a history of resistance and dissent. Excluded from government, they had no experience of power, but plenty of the dirty tricks brigade. Ibrahim Böhme, leader of the SPD, suggested rehabilitation for the *Mitläufer* – those who were only fellow travellers. Lothar de Maizière of the CDU suggested amnesty for Stasi members after the election. Their suggestions of leniency later looked suspicious when they were themselves accused of Stasi involvement. Through March several politicians were accused of having worked for the Stasi, including Wolfgang Schnur of Democratic Awakening, Martin Kirchner (CDU), Lothar de Maizière and Ibrahim Böhme. On 17 March, members of the commission responsible for the de-activation of the Stasi in Erfurt claimed to have evidence that twenty-seven top candidates of various parties were former Stasi members.

With Schnur they were on target. Schnur we have met before; he was the forty-five-year-old Rostock lawyer with a reputation for defending civil rights cases, who had proclaimed his life's work fulfilled by the December amnesty for political prisoners. More recently he had demanded that 'lawyers, judges, everybody involved must be removed. Justice means they must acknowledge they were guilty.' Schnur hotly denied the charge that he had been an informer for years. Then in the Rostock Stasi offices the local citizens' committee discovered four sheets of paper with Schnur's name. Schnur continued to deny involvement. He issued a declaration of honour, a most solemn public statement for a German to make, from which no retreat is possible, denying any Stasi connections. Then Eppelmann, his deputy in Democratic Awakening, a man of great integrity and a priest, looked into his file. When he came out he said nothing, which was a nod as good as a wink. There was a signed receipt for a medal for long service with the *Staatssicherheit*, dated 7 October 1989, that auspicious date of the fortieth anniversary that brought down first the leadership, then the Party and its police apparatus, then the whole state. Schnur was obliged to admit it. Two former Stasi officers confirmed that they had paid him for his services. He had worked for the Stasi since the early seventies, delivering information on opposition and church groups, and met Stasi officers in Rostock and East Berlin every 6–8 weeks. His last code-name had been Dr Schirmer; when he began working for them in Rostock he was known as Thorsten. A few years later he was Heuchler (hypocrite) because the Stasi assumed he was working for the West as a double agent. He was. More than thirty files on his Stasi activities were discovered in Rostock. So much for his honour. On the 14th, four days before the election, he resigned and was replaced by Eppelmann, but the electoral damage to his party, Democratic Awakening, had been done. Having resigned, he went into hospital with a *Kreislaufkollaps*. The one with egg on his krenz was Kohl; thinking to cover him Bonn had issued a statement claiming that Schnur worked for them, and had passed information for years. So he was a double agent, doubly damned. Goodbye Wolfgang Schnur. I think we will not meet again.

Through March the charges continued. The secretary general of the CDU admitted having had occasional contact with the Stasi in the eighties. He and Schnur were said to have been named on a list of twenty-three politicians suspected of intelligence activities. On 18 March the election came and went, resulting in a landslide for the parties of the right, led by the CDU, a vote for rapid unification. Then on the 22nd Eppelmann claimed that 10 per cent of the newly elected members of the Volkskammer were former Stasi. The accusations against Böhme and de Maizière came days after the election. The charge against de Maizière, including his alleged code-name, Czerni, came from the same ex-Stasi source as Schnur's, so when the one proved true the other looked authentic, though it wasn't. Same old mix. De Maizière's response was to demand his file, and have himself cleared, and his attitude from the start was one of dignified outrage; he was clearly not implicated. In Böhme's case the allegations came from two ex-Stasi officers, one of whom claimed to have been his controller, that he had spied on church groups and authors since the late 1960s. Böhme demanded his file, but when examined the file had only three index cards, with a fourth missing, presumably removed by the Stasi. The case was not proven; Böhme was not clear. He claimed that in the file he was listed not as an informer or an operator, but as a subject. Maybe he panicked; to resign looked like an admission. In any case, since the procedures to clear him would take a long time, for the sake of his party he resigned the leadership. At the time there was a lynching atmosphere; the people were angry. It was enough for the accusations to be made. Mud sticks. Rumour runs his hosts ragged, and the revolution devours its parents.

In hindsight the pattern clarifies. On 12 April in an interview in *Die Welt*, Ottfried Hennig, CDU parliamentary secretary, accused Modrow of having allowed the Stasi to continue its work while he was still in power. He complained that all those responsible for the economy and the repression were too old to be tried, too sick, senile or unfit to be kept in prison. Krenz was reported to be getting high fees for appearances and signing copies of his books in West German bookshops. Hennig continued: the Stasi were still with us, still listening in, still looking at the mail, they just had different assignments. In a ZDF Studio 1 interview, a former high-ranking Stasi officer confirmed these remarks: parts of the Stasi were still functioning, he said. According to him, three weeks after the elections, telecommunications reconnaissance was still being carried out in West

Germany. Secret files were still compiled and smuggled out of rooms guarded by members of the citizens' committees. The old ties between Stasi hardliners and the PDS were still active. Central areas of the Stasi were now integrated into ministries, the army, and various branches of the Soviet secret service.

So was this it? Former Stasi were accusing politicians of involvement in itself, leaking documents to the press, to discredit the other parties and create confusion. Some charges were true, some false. The Stasi, what survived of it, was believed to be still working on behalf of the PDS. With Schnur they were right. Both he and Böhme they had eliminated. The deadly mix of some truth and some lies was working.

Still the accusations flowed: all over the country officials, factory managers, priests, were being accused, and suspicion thickened the air. Whether motivated by Stasi mischief, or foreign espionage interest in creating instability, the damage done to the struggling movement for renewal was formidable. Eppelmann's claim that forty of the 400 newly elected members of the Volkskammer were Stasi was substantiated by other sources, and a committee of the Volkskammer set up to vet each member. But which forty? It was unconstitutional to name anyone in the legislature. In a *Spiegel* interview Eppelmann called for a general pardon, to exclude the crimes of murder, manslaughter and deprivation of liberty, aware that thousands in the streets were demanding justice. But since no one could be named, it was a matter of the suspect admitting, and resigning. In a lynch atmosphere, who is going to own up, he asked? No one would accuse himself, and the liars will remain silent. *Spiegel* quoted an unnamed PDS official's claim that an internal party directive existed to discredit politicians of other parties by publishing prepared Stasi documents. At the same time Werner Fischer, head of the government commission investigating the Stasi, together with members of Bündnis 90, claimed that a number of deputies were working for West Germany's BND, and had already started passing information. He based this information on letters received from former East German intelligence officers. A week later Fischer claimed there were attempts to delay checking out the representatives, and confirmed that some files had disappeared. He claimed that people involved in the de-activation committees were receiving more and more threatening letters and phone calls. He himself had been threatened with death on several occasions.

Staat im Staat. After the election, with unification a certainty, the house-cleaning goes on. As do the rumour mills. The problem is to know who to trust. Most of them are presumably running for their skins, but the opportunists and the intelligent will take some files with them. Most of the essential information is in any case in their heads. It doesn't take a lot of intelligence or experience of history to know that, even identified, accused, punished, the Stasi will not go away. They will defend themselves with such information as they have.

Two tales from Sophie: in one, when the crowd stormed Stasi-Zentrale on 15 January, one of their number was the son of the head of the Eastern association of butchers, printers, or haberdashers – she won't say for fear of breaking a confidence. Inside the buildings, the son thinks he'll look for his old man's file. He looks for it. He finds it. Towards the end of the year, the head of the trade association of butchers, printers or haberdashers in West Berlin, given *Wende* and *Durchbruch* and impending *Vereinigung*, at any rate between the two cities, had invited his opposite number, the head of the corresponding trade association in the East, to their annual end of year beanfeast. The invitation was duly issued and sent, on 6 December. When the young man finds the file on 15 January, there on the top is a copy of the invitation. Sophie's other story comes from one of her visits to Potsdam, to which she now returns again and again after an absence of forty years. She met a young man at Sanssouci and they got talking. He was, he said, a student of law at the Freie in West Berlin, or about to become so. He had his student loan, his place, he was mature, he would become a lawyer, he was from the East. What did he do before? she asked. He was an officer. In the Volksarmee? she asked. *Nein*. In the Volkspolizei? *Nein*. And not in the customs or the navy or the air force. In the Stasi.

They were pervasive, they saturated the life of the GDR, and they will not vanish overnight. Their stain persists, like the trails left by Nazi administrators and operatives and agents years ago, into the future, which will become the present. They too are coming into Europe, their skills will be available, and many of them are difficult or impossible to retrain. Because of East Germany's ready entry into Europe, we will hear of them, or members of them, again. There are too many of them simply to disappear, too many who depended on them: the

Mitläufer, the hangers-on, the people who co-operated with blackmail or took a little stipend, who went along and didn't feel – don't feel – any guilt. How will the East absorb them, the *Mitläufertum*, and how the West? Evil has a way of not going away, once introduced. The Stasi aren't dead and they won't lie down.

15

THE DOOMSDAY REPUBLIC

All day it has rained heavily and steadily from a lead sky, a downpour to drown the whole earth. About midnight it stops, the wind gets up – the *Berliner Luft* – air blown through trees across open land and water, that seems fresh enough. But the rain is full of sulphur, nitrogen, dioxins. Sulphur burns through the dead leaves and stabs the soured land: acid rain.

The world is dying and we're why. Here in the centre of Europe it's intense, visible, the figures daunting; the number-crunching stuns the brain. The socialist countries, in their drive for heavy industry, cut corners and left the lids off the boilers, largely ignoring pollution controls. They spilled their waste into the air and the water, darkening both; their soils and forests are dying. The poison cloud is thickest here at the centre, in the vast industrialized belt that includes south-western Poland, south-eastern Germany, and northern Czechoslovakia, between the rivers Oder and Mulde and south into their tributaries, and for which the Elbe is the main drain. Now in towns like Nova Huta and Erfurt and Bitterfeld the human life-span is demonstrably shorter, respiratory diseases are rising curves on the graphs, and the air is acrid and thick most days. It is all one huge disaster zone.

After the war the territory that became the GDR found itself without heavy industry and with few energy resources, and what it had was wrecked or expropriated by the Russians. The Russian Zone paid a high price in reparations, in machinery and industrial equipment, dismantled and shipped off to Russia. The traditional German industrial base lay in the West, on the Ruhr and the Rhine. The East had virtually to start from scratch. The object of the exercise was to recover from defeat and ruin, harness the pumps to the Russian donkeys, and work to develop heavy industry. This promised exports and hard currency and a better life for the workers; by 1971, when Erich Honecker took over, the GDR had risen to tenth place in the league of industrialized nations, and second behind Russia in the Eastern bloc, and though living standards were poor compared with the West, they were high compared with the rest of the East. The rest is a tale of forty years of central state planning by a leadership without a critic, and the suppression of all questions.

In the West too the message in the early fifties was clear: recovery equals heavy industry. The dismantling of the Krupp empire was halted. As both halves of Germany were enrolled on separate sides of the Cold War, the two rival Germanies rolled up their sleeves and went to work, each developing industry without notice of the environmental or social cost. In the West the Greens emerged in protest, and it is significant that they appeared there first, response to cause. Now in the West the Greens are called the Greys, but in the East environmental issues are only just emerging, with figures for damage of staggering proportions. On both sides of the border vast tracts of land are laid waste, dead earth, soils full of poisons on which new houses are built, in which people develop mysterious tumours. The Rhine is a dead river, said to be a fire hazard. Around Mainz are vast tracts of dead forest, stumps without leaves or birdsong, the corpses of trees through which on a Sunday the Germans still tramp in their walking boots, following old trails through the ruins, imagining themselves still *Wandervögel* – wandering birds.

In the East protest was difficult, data unobtainable and usually a state secret, any comment likely to be taken for treason. Nevertheless, environmental issues became woven into protest. Officially nothing was admitted. Official statistics either didn't exist or were liberally invented, and most of the little that is known is the result of local initiatives. In East Germany's 1989 statistical yearbook the only pollution entry is an annual sulphur dioxide emission of 5 million tonnes. Until the *Wende*, environmental groups worked with peace and civil rights groups, often through the protection of the church. In East Berlin members of the Environmental Library were imprisoned in 1987, and in the Rosa Luxemburg demonstration in January 1988 it was members of this group, among others, who were arrested. The Society for Nature and the Environment, founded in 1980, has joined the Green League, an umbrella organization, and a Green Party was established, fielding candidates in the March election.

The country the West is taking over lock, stock and barrel is a blighted land. Much of the structure is pre-war and suffers from lack of maintenance and renewal, and most of the machinery likewise. Work is labour-intensive. In the East there were controls, with laws and regulations to protect the environment, there was an environmental protection department, but none of the rules were enforced. There were only 500 water inspectors for the whole country. In the last ten years there has been little investment in the East German infrastructure. Its industrial plant is ageing, its housing in bad repair, its roads and railways in poor condition. It will cost approximately DM 85 billion to renovate the GDR's canal system. There's no technology for cleaning up the mess, and what technology there is is in a state of terminal decay.

In Leipzig the air is so filthy that statistically there ought to be a smog alert every day. In the Halle–Leipzig area a high proportion of people suffer from asthma, bronchitis, cancer, circulation and heart problems. Environmental damage is worst around Cottbus, and towards the Polish border, and south of Leipzig towards the Czech frontier, with all three economies pumping into the same poisoned space, passing the parcel down wind and down river. Around Cottbus since 1984 a steady increase in malignant tumours has been reported, and among men the mortality rate from bronchitis, asthma and lung diseases is the highest in Europe, double the European average. In Brandenburg it was recently revealed that the steelworks has been pouring 9,000 tonnes of heavy metal dust into the atmosphere each year, including 4 tonnes of toxic cadmium. Scientists claim that since the steel plant, opened after the war, 36,000 tonnes of zinc, 12,000 tonnes of lead, 5,000 tonnes of copper, 2,000 tonnes of chrome, 100 tonnes of cadmium, and 60 tonnes of nickel have been deposited on the city. In Bitterfeld life expectancy is reported to be five years below the national average for men, eight below for women, with a noticeable increase in cancers and lung diseases. Bitterfeld, 'dirtiest place in Europe', is the centre of East German chemical production. Here the Spittelwasser is one of the most heavily polluted rivers in the GDR; it is dark brown and stinks, and contains salts and toxic substances. In Bitterfeld and other towns plants date back to the nineteenth century, the towns are covered in soot and almost derelict, waste is discharged direct into the rivers. As a result, some parts of the GDR have become unfit for human habitation. Matthias Voigt of the Environmental Library includes among the 1989 exodus a category of 'environmental refugee', and claims that in the south some people left for their health.

Reports suggest that in the GDR 66 per cent of the rivers and 23 per cent of still waters need cleaning. Rivers and streams are heavily polluted; 9,000 lakes are dying. Experts estimate it would take DM 100 billion to clean up the rivers, lakes and canals. In many cases the degree of contamination is not yet known. There is a shortage of technical equipment, and a chronic shortage of water purification plants. Experts estimate that 10,000 kilometres of all rivers in the GDR are dead and only 3 per cent of all lakes contain water fit to drink. Waterworks do not work, the sewage system is inadequate and extensively damaged, and organic waste is said to be responsible for more pollution (80 per cent) than metals (3 per cent). The cost of bringing the GDR's waterworks up to Western standards is reckoned at DM 25 billion. Most of the filth ends up in the Elbe and then in the North Sea. The Elbe arrives in Dresden already polluted from Czechoslovakia, and collects mercury levels 250 times higher than EC limits; it is polluted locally by cellulose and pharmaceutical factories and by 50 million tonnes of fertilizer used annually in farming; on its way through East Germany it collects ten times the mercury and heavy metals dumped by West Germany into the Rhine. At the end of February Greenpeace established a GDR section, and termed the situation in the GDR 'dramatic'. It sent the Greenpeace ship *Beluga* up the Elbe to determine the precise contamination of the river, as a result of which in April it declared the Elbe the most heavily polluted river in Europe, if not in the world.

Almost 10 per cent of agricultural land is contaminated, mainly from industrial emissions and pesticides. It is said that the soil is so polluted that the worms are dying. Heavy fertilizer use has reduced the area of farmland and weakened what remains. Passing through the GDR, you see great fields with huge bald patches, areas of country that look exhausted. Large tracts are heavily polluted with nitrates, phosphates, potassium and pesticides used in the last two decades of industrialized farming. On the other hand, still in good shape are the state hunting forests reserved for the leadership's shooting parties. But over 50 per cent of forests are said to be damaged, and Western experts claim that only 14 per cent of the trees are free of pollution. Around Leipzig, three-quarters of the trees are heavily damaged. In 1980 a UN report claimed that 12 per cent of the trees were damaged, and in 1988 that 37 per cent were dying. A recent report suggests that 83 per cent are affected, and that as a consequence almost every second tree is damaged. One-third of plants and animals are affected. With 291 per cent sulphur dioxide emissions per inhabitant for 1988, the GDR has the highest count in the world. In the East air pollution is five times that of the West.

In March a formerly suppressed report by the Health Ministry was published, reporting that environmentally related illnesses were commoner than was believed. In East Berlin the Secretary for the Environment said that if people had known about it, they would have left immediately. In some places, every second child suffers from asthma, and 30 per cent of children living near chemical plants suffer from eczema. Over 40 per cent of the population live and breathe a high concentration of sulphur dioxide. People fall ill more often with gastrointestinal diseases attributed to insufficient hygiene and bad water quality. At the same time, 50 per cent of the homes and hospitals in the GDR are in disrepair.

From the air, in the Hannover air corridor, looking down on the district of Magdeburg, the eye as far as it can see takes in only devastation, the earth scoured in long ridges and circles for its single harvest of brown coal. Open-cast mining has laid waste 60,000 acres. At the heart of the problem is lignite, soft brown coal, the GDR's only natural energy source. Lignite has a high sulphur dioxide content. Everywhere in the East a thick brown dust coats buildings and monuments, the smoky detritus of lignite. Often found in surface deposits, vast tracts of the country's landscape have been scraped out for it by huge surface mining machines, and they don't put the soil back. The trains run continually to the ageing power stations. The GDR, the world's largest producer of lignite, derives 70 per cent of its energy from this source for use domestically and in power stations, but it's said that three-quarters of it goes up in smoke. Its twenty-six lignite power stations run at 26 per cent efficiency. Largely pre-war, they themselves use 10 per cent of the energy they produce. The power station at Jänschwalde produces one-seventh of the GDR's energy, but emits sulphur dioxide and other pollutants equivalent to half the acid rain pollutants produced by all the power stations in the West. In November the East German government published figures for sulphur dioxide emissions at 6 million tonnes per year, three times that of West Germany. The government has promised to reduce sulphur dioxide emission by 30 per cent, and lignite production by a third from the present 300 million tonnes annually. But the problem is to find an alternative. The oil supply from Russia is drying up. One possibility is the import of natural gas.

One possibility is not nuclear power. In the south-west, towards and across the Czech frontier, lie uranium mines that supply Russian and East European nuclear programmes. Here again, safety is at a minimum: highly contaminated waste is dumped in open slag heaps and slurry ponds, used as building materials and road gravel. As to nuclear power itself, four reactors are under construction at Stendal to the West of Berlin, and there are working reactors at Rheinsberg to the south, and at Greifswald on the Baltic coast. It is this latter station that is the source of much anxiety, especially in Berlin. Opened in 1973, the Bruno Leuschner nuclear power station at Lubmin near Greifswald was intended to produce a fifth of the GDR's electricity. Eight reactors were planned, of which four are working, one at the turn of the year was under test and by the end of 1990 will be on the grid, and the other three are still under construction. But Greifswald doesn't conform to Western safety standards, and is known as the Chernobyl of the north. The reactors there are type WWER 440, Soviet models of which forty-one are working in the Eastern bloc. Like Chernobyl they lack containment, and until Chernobyl, fighter planes from the Peenemünde base regularly overflew the Greifswald complex. In 1986 a Soviet fighter crashed only seconds away. All four reactors are permanently under repair, and were constructed badly. Nos. 1 and 3 were built on poor ground and tip slightly. For financial reasons no emergency system was installed. Slipshod work practices mean that contaminated overalls are simply washed and reworn. Residents of the area were kept uninformed, and did not know that in 1988 160,000 cubic metres of contaminated waste were dumped into the Baltic.

At Greifswald a long record of incidents and accidents from 1974 to the present was rigorously suppressed. Until the end of 1989, few people knew that in 1976 there had been almost a total meltdown of Chernobyl proportions there, which would have contaminated north Germany and Scandinavia. In reactor No. 1 a cable caught fire and safety protection devices and the cooling system did not work. Five out of six pumps did not function, and all important indicators were out of order. It was pure coincidence that the sixth pump was attached and prevented a meltdown. The accident was kept secret and four months later No. 1 was functioning again. In 1988 there were 242 'unplanned events', and eighteen fast shut-downs, and the complex was shut down for 231 days. To keep things quiet forty full-time Stasi were employed, employees were intimidated, and SED members occupied all leading positions.

A West German safety commission examined it in January, concluding that it was 'an unbelievable security risk' and that all four reactors should be shut down immediately. But they produce 10 per cent of the GDR's electricity. When the West German environment minister visited Greifswald, the construction site at Stendal and the waste disposal site at Morsleben, he concluded that it would be impossible to bring the stations up to Western safety standards. It would cost up to DM 500 million per reactor. In response to the reports of Western experts in February, reactor No. 2 was shut down. In April Greenpeace called for a complete shutdown of the whole plant and a thorough inspection of all other nuclear facilities in the GDR. A Round Table initiative in January resulted in a report in May condemning the security systems and emergency equipment in all four reactor blocks. Pipes could burst at any moment, they said, claiming that the whole complex should be closed immediately to avoid a similar disaster to Chernobyl. A joint East–West commission has been set up, looking first at safety in the GDR's nuclear industry. Reactors 1 and 3 have been shut down, and 4 will remain on the grid only till the end of the year.

But fears continue for the safety of Greifswald. Berlin is 180 kilometres away, as is Copenhagen. In April a report by the ecological institute in Darmstadt made on behalf of the Berlin Senate concluded that Berlin would be totally contaminated by a meltdown at Greifswald, or at Rheinsberg. An accident at Stendal, still under construction, would also contaminate Berlin. Berlin's Senator for the Interior said it would be impossible to evacuate the 4 million inhabitants of the city, even with open borders. A spokesman for the Darmstadt institute said that if it rains and the cloud comes from Rheinsberg or Greifswald, people in Berlin would die immediately. From Stendal in March came a report that construction regulations had been violated in August 1989. Pipes did not pass quality control, the quality control officer who discovered faults was expelled from the site; the director ordered the pipes used and asked another control officer to forge the documentation; when he refused he was subject to disciplinary proceedings and his salary was cut.

So this is the end of the dream of Marx and Engels and Lenin, and of all those who struggled and studied and worked and intrigued and fought for social justice through social owner-ship, all their lives, many who went to prison, many who were shot and brutally murdered for their efforts and beliefs. It's over. What is left is a badly used country, and for much of it the damage may be irreversible. There is a touching naïvety in Eastern beliefs in the infallibility of Western remedies; we our-selves aren't yet ready to accept that some problems may be without a cure, some decay too far gone. A new environmental law is being drafted, reports *Spiegel*, incorporating most of the standards of West Germany. The problem is that, when this law is applied, more than half the enterprises in the East will have to shut down.

A joint East–West environmental commission has been estab-lished. The GDR is willing to close down 400 enterprises that cannot be redeveloped, and approximately 10 per cent of the factories and power stations in the Bitterfeld region are to be closed down. East Germany has also agreed to install air and water filtering systems, financed by the West. Estimates put the cost of recapitalizing of the GDR's industrial base at DM 800 billion, and the country will need capital injection of DM 100 billion per year for the next twenty years. The cost of cleaning up the East is put at DM 200 billion. The Ministry of the Environment estimated in early March that of the funds needed, DM 45 billion was for clean air, 50 billion for clean water, and

5 billion for the redevelopment of waste disposal, all this to be completed by the year 2000.

As if in anticipation of the Wall's collapse, last July West Germany signed the first comprehensive environmental agreement with the East, whereby, of DM 300 million, the West was to pay a third to reduce pollution in the Elbe. In December there were promises of further large amounts, with East Germany to spend twice that. Already there are cross-border agreements and commissions attempting, if nothing else, to estimate the scale of the damage. The GDR has identified what it calls environmental disaster areas: the Bitterfeld–Wolfen area, the area south of Karl-Marx-Stadt, around Frankfurt an der Oder, and areas near Leipzig, Halle, and Zwickau. That's about half the country.

Here in Berlin the problems were confounded by the presence of two cities in the space available for one. Neither side felt responsible for the other, and since waste is no respecter of frontiers, West Berlin found itself trapped within the East's mess. Berlin's air is therefore polluted, and the huge areas of woodland in the west of the city are under attack from acid rain and visibly dying. Its lakes are polluted to varying degrees. West Berlin under its ruling and abrasive Red/Green coalition is acutely conscious of the problems, and has made corrective efforts. Catalytic converters and lead-free petrol are compulsory, rules which the Trabi has challenged. There are stringent emissions controls. On some of its lakes and rivers, huge cleaning machines sieve the water and inject oxygen, bringing them back to life.

For its part West Berlin was content to dump its garbage, some of it toxic, in the East, and one direct result of the opening of the Wall was an end to the garbage traffic through the border, and a garbage crisis in West Berlin for a while. Ten days after the opening of the Wall there was a demonstration outside West Berlin city hall by environmentalists from East and West Berlin, demanding an end to the contract by which, since the early seventies, West Berlin had dumped its garbage in the East. In January the GDR's environmental department began negotiating for an end to it. West Berlin complained breach of contract, then gave in, and limited its export of waste to the East to 1,000 tons a month. Then the garbage piled up.

A landlocked island without an ocean, West Berlin produces

1.4 million tons of garbage a year. 400,000 tons of that it burns, and the rest is transported to East Germany, under a twenty-year contract signed in 1974. In addition, 40,000 tons of 'special waste' (dangerous to health, air, water, pathogenic, explosive or inflammable) is sent East every year. The East stores dangerous toxic substances for the West. In addition, private manufacturers have been paying East Germany to dispose of industrial waste, at about a tenth of what they would have paid to ship it to West Germany.

The East, Deutschmark-happy, bought and dumped the capitalist West's exotic garbage at sites at Schöneiche, south of Berlin, and Vorketzin and Deetz, near Potsdam. Guarding the dumps from garbage-pickers eager for anything from the West was just another little job for the Stasi. All three sites accepted special waste in addition to garbage, and at all three the ground water is polluted. All of them are in bad condition and fall well below Western safety standards. No matter, said the old leadership, if it earned hard currency. In the East the garbage contract was part of Schalck-Golodkowski's foreign money machine, and was organized through INTRAC, the foreign trade organization. In the last ten years Schalck-Golodkowski managed to make between DM 1 and 2 billion profit on the garbage.

When the disposal of special waste at Vorketzin stopped on 15 February, it was feared some West Berlin firms might have to close; especially affected were paint, electroplating, printing workshops and photographic laboratories. Here the special waste is the lethal by-products of industries developed to get around the transport problem, producing small and complex items like drugs and electronics. Meanwhile the special waste was kept in two temporary storage areas in West Berlin, expected to be full by the middle of May. Firms in West Germany that had offered to dispose of it by incineration were refused authorization to transport it; there were state elections on the way, and no one wanted Berlin's garbage. By the end of March, however, the garbage crisis had been temporarily resolved. It would go to West Germany, and meantime the Senate would look into refurbishing the incineration plant at Vorketzin. That would mean it would become much more expensive to dispose of toxic waste there, and the Senate feared the costs would encourage firms to avoid proper disposal. Toxic chemicals were already being poured down the drains in large quantities, despite heavy fines and imprisonment. Greenpeace agreed, and claimed that West German firms were proposing schemes in the East that had already been rejected in the West, such as incineration of garbage and toxic waste to produce energy as a substitute for lignite.

In Berlin, on environmental as on other issues, a new dawn broke. Both halves of the city agreed on joint smog-regulation, including restrictions on East Berlin cars. In the event of a smog alert, forty East Berlin enterprises will cut production, and it is planned to install fifteen new measuring stations in the East. Data will be exchanged via fax. In March West and East began the merger of their inspection associations, regulating both car emissions and environmental protection. It emerged that 1.2 million East Berliners use as much water as 2.1 million West Berliners, put down to the low cost of water in the East. But the problem is that East Berlin's water isn't chlorinated, and the West's is, and there was some concern as to what happens once the two systems are rejoined.

With the Wall open, West Berliners began exploring the hinterland of their city, denied them for so long. The GDR, though much of it is ruined, is in many areas beautiful, old, like the past they say, unhamburgered. The affluent hitched their trailers and boats, and set off in search of recreation. With the spring the East expected invasion, and there was concern expressed by residents of East Berlin's Müggelsee, afraid of the damage tourists will do to the area. 20,000 motor boats are expected from West Berlin, and a citizens' initiative is demanding that boats be banned from the lake. The lake supplies the Friedrichshagen waterworks with 60,000 cubic metres of water a day. The quality of the water began to deteriorate at the beginning of the seventies, and today there are twice as many algae as twenty years ago. The lake is about to die.

Here at the old border the stars, when you can see them, still form the same constellations. Around here the birds are few. Sparrows, scrapping over roosts, and the sinister two-tone hooded crows, grey above black, that seem to be everywhere, like the police. The cold sour rain begins again, acid rain.

16

ZUKUNFTSMUSIK

Zukunftsmusik: future music, wishful thinking, pipedreams. The Stasi and the old guard dreaming of a comeback, their victims of revenge, the intellectuals of renewal in a separate GDR, what's left of the Party imagining defeat, the fascists dreaming of chaos and power, millions of Easterners of the Deutschmark. And in the West, fast buck dreams. February.

Grunts: up from the lakeside past the station a squad of sweaty American soldiers labour with heavy packs, guns, ammunition, water-cans clanking against their backsides. The Ossis between bus and train don't seem to notice. The army is on exercise, still keeping up appearances, still fighting the enemy. With the Wall there was an edge to the world. Now there's none. If there are no edges, where is the centre? Saith the *I Ching*: 'Unlimited possibilities are not given to man. If they were his life would dissolve in the boundless.' They've taken away the world's edge.

Gorbachov: 'I am going to deprive you of your enemy.' History is idiosyncratic, serendipitous, a jumble of facts and fictions, odds and ends that don't necessarily fit. Tony reports that coffee at the offices of New Forum is best ersatz; at the headquarters of the SPD it's the best from the West. The taxi drivers of East and West are learning each others' streets, wondering which will change; Marx-Engels-Platz is already reverting to its old familiar name, the Lustgarten. A sign of the times is the *perestroika* display in the Aeroflot offices along Unter den Linden: news photographs of demonstrations, protests, troops in Tbilisi, the admission of trouble. Gorbachov is being open in a place newly opened. *Urbi et Gorbi* says fresh graffiti opposite the House of Ministers, but on the streets Gorbi badges have almost disappeared from lapels and caps. They are no longer looking towards Moscow, but to Bonn, and the new father figure is Helmut Kohl. The PDS still pursues Gorbi's image, in Modrow the Prime Minister, in Gregor Gysi the Chairman of the party. Krenz tried and fumbled it. In Moscow, Shevardnadze says East Germany has wasted a lot of time since November. In East Berlin the thinkers of the Bündnis group around the Round Table are still talking.

Some dreams are nightmares. On the evening of 19 February they began taking the Wall down at the Brandenburger Tor: trucks, troops, lights, jib crane, police, crowds impatient to see the slabs lifted away at last, the Wall further opened: 'Take it down, take it down.' There was a festival air about it all, peckers frantically chipping, townsfolk and tourists, soldiers showing off leaping over barriers. Along the Wall a young man, drunk, sang *'Nieder nieder nieder, nieder mit der Mauer.'* In the Tiergarten the crows, disturbed by it all, raised their own ruckus. By the Reichstag through openings between the slabs the crowds wandered the old death strip and down to the river, where young marine *Grenztruppen* hung about by a fast boat moored at the bank, fraternized, tried to look knowing, chain-smoked. A transformer buzzed. Beside it people inspected the remains of the watchtower dismantled that day, the first to go, from which most of the shooting must have come that accounted for so many crosses just here on the Wall's Western side. Its slabs stood neatly stacked to one side – window frames and panels of wire mesh, a scramble of old wiring, the only keepsake no one wanted a raggy looking toilet brush. People went up along the river bank to the bridge, where a loose piece of corrugated iron opened on to Otto-Grotewohl-Strasse. The Western adventurers ripped their way through here, among them a young man carrying a huge West German flag over his shoulder, who kept circling through the opening and down to Unter den Linden and right and out at the Tor again, and round again along the river. Later as the first slabs lifted away, he was on the Wall with a crowd of as many as could hold on there, waving his flag. People cheered and clapped, someone blew bubbles that drifted over the machinery, and (I kid you not) a white goose flew east over the Gate. Framed in its arches the swift malignant blink of the television tower at Alexanderplatz. The demolition got serious, the crowd excited, pressing in beside the trucks, television camera crews darting in under the jib. Inside the Wall at the second wall, others were already busy with coal hammers. On the other side, through the Gate, sightseers from East and West stepped down through the arches of the Tor, come to join the festivities. Among them, bowling through at a swift lick, came a man in a wheelchair, with but one leg and the other in plaster, wearing a white plastic safety helmet and with a six-pack of beer strung in a net, one hand batting his wheel, the other – the right – in spasm in the air as he yelled repeatedly '*Juden raus, Juden raus; Sieg heil, Sieg heil.*'

Two stories about drills and two jokes about Honecker. In the first drill story it's summer 1989 in Berlin, hot, long, dry and dusty. A man who lives by the Wall goes crazy. He flips, and takes his electric drill on a long cable and starts drilling a hole in the Wall. They hear him of course, and suddenly where no door was known to be a little iron door opens in the Wall, and they come out and grab him. They take him in, question him, confiscate the drill, and chuck him out. In the second drill story, which is about survival in the GDR, a man who has a garage to rent out puts up a sign saying to let, for hard currency. Dollars or Deutschmarks, he doesn't mind. The Stasi come to visit: take the sign down, or change it to read marks, East German marks. What can he do? he says, he needs the foreign currency to buy an electric drill for his work. He's a carpenter, and the only way he can get a drill is for hard money. The Stasi think it over. Here's the deal: they will supply him with a drill from their stores, and they will rent the garage, for Ostmarks. He takes it. That's what he wanted all the time.

The first Honecker joke goes like this: God is sick and tired of the way the world is run, and calls Gorbachov, Bush, and Honecker into his office. 'You've got two weeks,' he says, 'to sort it out. Otherwise I'm sending a flood to drown the world, and this time there'll be no Noah.' Bush goes home and speaks on nation-wide TV: 'My fellow Americans, I have good news and bad news. For one, God exists, that's the good news. The bad news is he's going to send a flood and drown us all.' Gorbachov goes back to Moscow and speaks before the Presidium: 'Comrades, I have bad news and only more bad news.

In the first place God exists, and this for us is bad news. In the second place he's going to drown the whole world.' Honecker goes back to Berlin and addresses the Volkskammer: 'Comrades, I bring only good news and yet more good news. For one, God recognizes the GDR. For another, he's going to send a flood and drown all the other countries.' In the second joke, adapted from the Russian, Honecker gets up early in the morning and goes out on to the verandah of his villa in Wandlitz to watch the sunrise. 'Good morning comrade sun,' he says, 'shining on our land, growing the corn for our bread.' The sun replies, 'Good morning comrade Honecker. What a pleasure it is to shine on your wonderful country, so progressive, so peaceful, so content.' Honi has his breakfast, gets in the limousine, goes to work, does a full day's work with meetings and appearances, goes back to Wandlitz for his supper. It's sunset. 'Goodnight comrade sun,' he says. 'Thank you for shining on the GDR bringing wholesomeness and pleasure to all.' 'Bugger you,' says the sun. 'I'm off to the West.'

At the Zoo: in the locker recesses the drunk, the stoned, the weary, sleepers and mumblers among the vomit and old newspapers. In the lobby people wait, drink, queue, squabble, hustle, sleep, wait some more, long lines of patient Africans sitting on huge boxes of electronics. Outside on the money market: Germans, Turks, Poles, some Asians, some Arabs. The police are disinterested. The only offence being committed here is trading without a licence. There's no haggling: the rate is 1/5. Most deals are small – DM 20 for 100 Ostmark, and there's not much profit, they are working the edges between the Wechsel rate, the official rate, and the future. An Easterner caught going back at Friedrichstrasse with 45,000 Ostmarks explained to customs that the exchange rate at the Zoo had been lousy, and he'd decided not to bother. In February GDR customs confiscated approximately 5 million Ostmarks on the East/West border, 4.2 million of it in Berlin. An East Berliner was caught trying to smuggle out 205,000 Ostmarks, and a foreigner smuggling 130,000 Ostmarks in, planning to bank it and eventually end up with Deutschmarks. At the end of February GDR customs found 2.5 kg of gold, worth more than 450,000 Ostmarks, on two Easterners who were part of a black market ring. They had smuggled gold worth 1.1 million purchased in Luxemburg or other EC countries where they didn't have to pay VAT. They sold it in the GDR, and brought their profits to West Berlin or put it in GDR savings accounts, hoping to make on the currency exchange. The East has expanded its customs; this is where many ex-Stasi now work. In the mail about 5,000 packets and parcels per day are sent across the border; these are X-rayed to look for drugs or weapons. Packets containing newspapers and books are always opened. Fascist publications are regularly confiscated. About 5 per cent of all packets coming from West Germany and West Berlin are opened, while from 12 to 15 per cent of those leaving the GDR are opened. Customs are watching for antiques, which if discovered are returned to sender. They keep nothing. Letters containing money are still opened, as international law requires, and identified with a stamp. Soon there is to be a postal money order system. Through such trivia life begins again across the old fault line of Europe.

But the cabaret has turned serious: here almost everyone is tainted to some degree, almost everyone and everything undermined by the past, and this poisonous music now proposes to enter West Germany and Europe. As Havel said of Czechoslovakia, totalitarianism isn't black and white, but includes everyone: 'everyone carries a piece of it; everyone is both oppressor and victim.' Modrow, working now with a coalition of all parties, is clearly looking for the best deal for what's left of his country. He confirms what Kohl has been dragging his feet over, the Oder/Neisse line at the Eastern border, and apologizes to the Jews for the Holocaust. But the Stasi still lurk, and rumour still runs, and suspicion clouds the mind. After the first flush of drunken freedom, the customary caution has caught up with people. No one really trusts anyone. People who smoke Kenton cigarettes are said to be Party members: they *ken* the *tone*, they know what's going on. The poisoned intellectual climate is matched by the poisoned environment.

The Memorial to Socialist Heroes by Friedrichsfelde Ost is a great natural boulder anchoring a circle of graves, some *ermordet vom Faschismus* (murdered by Fascism), or *hingerichtet*, many quite young, and a great iron plaque listing all the murdered heroes. The graves of Karl Liebknecht, Rosa Luxemburg: 'the dead warn us'. On the red brick semi-circle of wall at the next radius from the stone, in bushy seclusion the identical plaques of the dead founders of the Republic, Ernst Thallmann and Wilhelm Pieck and Anton Ackermann and the others, some who suffered in prison, some who came like Ulbricht in the baggage of the Russians, their war worked out in Moscow. They are numbered as they died, in order, without distinction. More wall awaits their successors, who will not come here now. Beyond, in little plots, squads of small polished red marble slabs in neat rows, carefully tended, bearing names and dates and nothing more: Party faithful, the rank and file brought to their orderly ends, their struggles over, their banners laid down at last. Elsewhere a large stone has had the letters of the name and dates removed – someone perhaps after their death fallen from grace with the regime. Another bears the names of three men, their dates of birth and death, all in 1943, the word *ermordet*. And a large stone, tantalizing in its mystery, bearing some twenty names: the Memorial to the Dead of 5 July 1951, but no hint, and no mention in any history and no answer to any question, of what happened on that date.

Elsewhere it is the ordinary graveyard of ordinary citizens, the recent dead husbanded and tended, the distant overgrown and marked by abandoned monuments, greying angels, the word *nicht* (not) obliterated by ivy leaving only the word *vergessen* (forgotten), on a black stone the name and dates of a young man and the one word *warum?* (why?). The widows rake the loose sandy soil around their men's graves, weeding, tidying, in such housewifery as is left them. The style here is simple: trees, flowers, monosyllabic memorials spelling out only the name, the word *Ruhestätte*, resting place, *Familie*. Some graves bear the addition of a cross, others, the graves of the materialists, an ear of corn. Most bear only the surname. Silence broken by birdsong, small animals raking in the leaves. Then a trumpet breaks out, a solemn golden last salute in the sunshine, and then a long line of old people in assorted blacks bearing flowers. The line stops. A man at the front of the line begins an oration as the trumpet falls into silence. The trumpeter puts his instrument into its case and strides off across the graves, lighting a cigarette. The birdsong resumes.

Day X is coming: the day of the conversion of the Ostmark to the Deutschmark. The West is buying out the East's currency, but the question is when and at what rate. The president of the Eastern Sparkasse suggests a 1/1 rate for money put into savings before the deadline of 9 November, to cut out the speculators. Most would like a straight 1 for 1, but beggars will not be choosers. At 1 to 1, all savings would treble into Deutschmarks, but so would all debts. Maybe some savings will be changed at 1/1, perhaps the first 2,000 marks, so Ossis go on dividing up their savings. By March an East–West currency commission is doing the groundwork on monetary union. On the black market the rate improves with the news, holding a steady 1/5. The election is coming, but that doesn't generate as much anxiety as Day X. It's assumed that whoever wins, the PDS is finished, and with it the centralized economy, and most likely the GDR too. When Day X comes the Ostmark will cease, East and West Germany will enter economic union, and political union will follow. The East will be dismantled, the market economy introduced, and massive subsidies on food, rent, consumer goods, to the tune of 50 billion Ostmarks a year, will be withdrawn, and prices will shoot up. For this reason the queues form at the savings banks in the East, and the money runs West and comes back as black market Deutschmarks. Meanwhile big business from the West, represented mostly in its West German formations, is beginning its buyout of the East, though there's a lot no one wants. Old and overmanned and spewing pollution, industry can't compete, the rotting infrastructure must be rebuilt, replaced, reinvented. All the same, they're saying they did it before in the West after the war, and they'll do it again, and reproduce the economic miracle, the *Wirtschaftswunder* of the fifties. The GDR's 300 *Kombinate* producing 80 per cent of its gross national product will be broken up into smaller pieces, slimmed down for profitability. Everyone knows that means unemployment. Many organizations will simply close down, and the result will be massive job losses in the East, and the tidal wave of the West will slam through here, especially in Berlin. When the West turns out not to be Superman with all the answers, and when East and West figure out the real costs of unification, there's going to be a lot of anger hereabouts, and who will the Ossis turn to then?

News from a country gone rotten in the rain: the East is collapsing into the arms of the West. Strikes, sitdowns, demonstrations, resignations. The workforce is demanding 40 billion marks in wage rises, a figure Modrow says is 'beyond the resources of the state'. Everything is disrupted; Volksarmee and Volkspolizei stores are being opened as food stockpiles run out. At the beginning of February the entire town council of Magdeburg resigns; at the end of February the East Berlin mayor, Erhard Krack, resigns charged with corruption, but the suggestion that Momper be mayor of all Berlin isn't taken up. On the 9th, reports of a chemical factory explosion in Halle. The firm that makes shirts for the Stasi is to cease production, and it's reported that 15,000 border guards have been made redundant. The new slimmed-down force of 25,000 will all be redundant soon: no borders to guard, no one left to leave. On the 19th the Monday night demonstration in Leipzig is as usual, massive, a sea of black, gold and red flags, as Peter describes it. Up on a balcony a bunch of skinheads were shouting 'We are not fascists.' There is fierce hostility to any mention of socialism.

The rate of emigration still runs at 2,000 a day, many of them skilled workers, but the more that come West the fewer skills they bring, the more strain they put on Western resources. And on their own. This year up to 24 February 100,000 have gone West: in January 63,000, in February 41,800. Few go back home again. Hopes for improvement after the election are low; resentment at the rich West is growing. There's a feeling among Ossis that they are becoming second-class citizens in their own country. In the West resentment at the incomers, and their pull on the social welfare systems, grows. At the beginning of 1989, 128,000 resettlers were unemployed. In the East, hospitals and schools and public services, especially the health service, are undermined by the exodus. They never did function efficiently; hospitals are all-equipped and have low technical standards. Of the 340,000 who left last year, 2,000 were doctors, 1,500 dentists, and many thousands more nurses. Forty-five formerly unemployed doctors from West Berlin are working in East Berlin, and West Berlin's emergency doctor service is now extended to East Berlin. Other doctors are working on one- and two-year contracts in the East. About 2,000 Eastern doctors have applied to establish private practice. The West is supplying beds and medical equipment. An estimated DM 500 million will be needed to bail out the GDR health service this year, 170 million to save the eighteen city hospitals in East Berlin from collapsing.

With thousands of other immigrants of German origin, West Germany is groaning under the impact. 'In a year that will be a million more over here,' says Herr K. He has hired some of them at his firm, but he says they work too slowly, they have no sense of hard work. Otherwise they are welcome to what the West has to offer, provided they work for it. He speculates: West Germany will exploit the East's connections with Russia to expand its trade East. It needs the Russian speakers in the GDR. Possibly, he says, they will use the GDR to leapfrog their way eastward. But then he snorts at his own argument: do they need to? Look at the trade figures.

The Möbius strip: in early February Helge Möbius, manager of Limex, the Eastern state company marketing the Wall, went to the US to establish contact with bidders. To date, he claimed, there had been about 300 offers. A commemorative group wants to buy sections and set them up in the approximately forty places in the US named after Berlin. Many museums and galleries, and Sotheby's, are said to be interested. Limex sells only complete slabs. Before they took over, an American businessman had offered to buy the entire Wall for $50 million. The latest on offer are the watchtowers, 6 metres high, at DM 100,000. Disney is said to be interested in watchtowers and Wall sections. The Wall training area near Neu-Zittau, a complete section of wall out in the woods for border guard training, is under offer to an American film director who wants to buy it, watchtowers and barbed wire and all, and ship it to the US to use as film background. At the end of the month parts of the Wall went to Paris to be put up in the La Defense district.

4,000 Wall dogs, Alsations, Rottweilers and Schnauzers, are out of work. Strangely, many people are interested in them, and after an initial press report that they were to be slaughtered in some canine holocaust, the animal protection society in the West took up their cause. An American proposed to sell them as souvenirs, a Spanish firm proposed to use them for animal experiments, and the Koreans proposed to eat them. 1,500 of them found homes with East German families, and 2,500 were brought to West Germany for placing with homes and as security guard dogs. In February three went off to Majorca to guard hotels. The dogs, for all their reputations as fierce guardians of the death strip, turned out to be quite soft. Some that went West as guard dogs were returned as too timid. Many failed the tests for entry to the West German police, and turned out to be scared of gunshots and ran off when attacked. By March only one had passed the test.

Talking with Friedemann it's as if there had been a death in his family. His Party is finished, its membership down to 1.2 million, about half its 1989 figure. His country is finished. It doesn't help that his Party, and therefore he, is responsible for the collapse of his country. He reports the threatened end of free school meals and child care centres, the resignation of the minister who said it, and says that in Prenzlauer Berg there has already been a meeting of parents and teachers about drugs. The Wall had its uses. The West is coming, with its poverty, home-lessness, crack, guns, squalor and random violence. Here they lived in a poisoned cocoon, safe from everything but themselves. Now they are out in the light, totally unprepared, and everyone is looking. Here the truth, when they get to it, begins to look like mirror speech, always the opposite: statistics jiggered, trade figures notional, the news fictional, the Stasi with its fingers in everything, and all for nothing; for the interests of Russia and the banquets of the *Nomenklatura*. In 1953 Beria, after the suppression of the Uprising and before his own downfall, had exclaimed at a Moscow Politburo meeting 'The GDR? It's only kept going by Soviet troops.' It all went wrong years ago, the wrong model, the wrong leadership, bent to Stalin's will. Honecker wasn't the only prisoner of the Nazis in Brandenburg, and was by no means the most interesting. Ackermann, who had come back with the Moscow group, had other ideas for a socialism modelled on post-war German circumstance, but he was put aside by Ulbricht and in due course assigned to his slot in the wall in the graveyard of socialist heroes.

Friedemann reports his evening Party meeting: more resignations. An old man, a life-long Marxist, had stood up and said he could take no more of the Party's hypocrisy, put down his Party card and walked out. At the Writers' Union there were Stasi, of course. Friedemann now knows who they were, and is surprised to learn they carried guns at all times, even in meetings and seminars. He says there was a great fear of writers and intellectuals, and anybody who was involved in artistic work, who was in any way connected with the arts, writers, actors, anybody, had a file. A man he'd known for years turned out to be one of them. His story was that after the war, when he was a young man, eighteen years old, he was jailed for six weeks by the Russians and then for four weeks by the German police in 1945. They told him if he wouldn't work for them he would be jailed for six years. So he had worked for them ever since.

Friedemann sighs, laughs. 'I love the people but I hate the crowd,' he says. He resents living in a zoo, the focus of Western curiosity. In the bars around Chausseestrasse on a Saturday afternoon they come over in droves, walk about a bit, drink cheap Eastern booze and go back and say they've seen East Berlin. 'There's nothing there,' they'll say, and some: 'It's just like here.' **They came, they saw, they did a little shopping.** The West has won, and comes to gloat, and Friedemann is of the party of the culprits in the country of the beaten. He knows defeat brings ruin, and already his work with television is drying up, old projects shelved, contracts cancelled. No one wants to make a film any more about a young artist who came to Communism in the twenties, fought in Spain, was wounded and interned in France, fought in the underground there and returned at last to the land of his birth, freed from the chains of history at the naissance of the GDR. He says. No chance.

Scenting victory, the SPD claims 70,000 members, and is at this stage in the game, early February, tipped to win. In the West, Oskar Lafontaine, who only weeks before had said Ossi subsidies should be stopped, is being talked of as the next leader of the SPD West, and with the SPD in power in the East and perhaps an electoral win in the West German elections in December, he could be the next Chancellor of a united Germany, a distinction coveted by Kohl. *Zukunftsmusik*. At this stage in the East a poll shows 54 per cent for the SPD, 12 per cent for the PDS, 11 per cent for the CDU, and for New Forum, in at the beginning of the *Wende* and now a political party forming part of the Bündnis group, a mere 4 per cent. As in all revolutionary upheavals, what the thinkers think and what the people want diverge, but at this stage it still looks possible: a separate GDR, socialist and democratic, the third way. In the polls the Liberals, like the Christian Democrats tainted by their past record of co-operation with the Communists, trail with 3 per cent. Behind them smaller groups and parties are setting up –

the Greens, two Women's parties, left wing purists, the Pink Carnation, the German Beer Drinkers' Union, campaigning against the country's absolute ban on drinking and driving. Not everything about Communism was mad.

Then in early February the CDU (East) formed an electoral alliance, the Alliance for Germany, with the right-wing DSU and Democratic Awakening. Then Kohl and the CDU (West) formed an alliance with the Alliance, and began to pour in assistance, opening a campaign headquarters in East Berlin and stage-managing the election campaign. Likewise the SPD (West) began printing election posters and leaflets for the Eastern SPD, and the flow of computers and software and strategies and money sped East across the border. Interference from a foreign state, complained the PDS. No one took any notice of them.

And then the fortunes of the Eastern CDU began rapidly to change, as if by magic, with appearances and rallies by Kohl all over the GDR till the election, riding the unification train: 'We are one people.' Kohl caught the popular demand, and implied that the currency would change at par, or left it vague enough for people to think that's what he said. Hey presto. Through February and into March the Eastern election became visibly an extension of West German politics.

The Brandenburg worm: beneath the Brandenburg Gate, a *Deutsche Post* van is parked. Workmen have opened a trapdoor in the road beneath the central arch of the Tor, and from it they have winched a long dark worm. It is rusty, damp and shiny from the sandy earth, where it has slept for decades. They yank it out by one severed end and slowly pull it on a hawser by its gaping neck down into the Pariser Platz, ten, fifteen, twenty, thirty metres. There they rest it, while one man with a hacksaw begins cutting a clean end from the mess of chopped cable, blue, yellow, red, a spaghetti of telephone intestines. The end has been hacked through with an axe, crudely, years ago when communications were abruptly cut back in 1952, and now they are going to rejoin it to the system. They resume pulling, dragging the worm from its long winter sleep beneath the Brandenburg Gate.

We have to buy the next product up, Wessis complain, because the Ossis come over and buy all the cheapest stuff. They're sick of their poor relatives, who just keep coming. 'They don't see us,' they complain. They bump into people on the pavement, they drive all over the road. They pay traffic fines in large Ostmark notes and take the change in Deutschmarks. 'They're just after what they can get,' they say.

And the Wessis have their own dodges, and the Ossis their complaints. From living in mutual prisons, Berliners now live in mutual zoos, with fiddles to be worked both ways. Books, records, shoes, are very cheap in the East. West Berliners fill their cars up in the East, where the gas is cheap. Small businesses mail their letters from the East, at a sixth of the rate. Westerners buy rail tickets through friends in East Berlin at a fraction of the cost. West Berliners are opening savings accounts through friends or relatives in the East, and sitting back waiting for currency reform. It all contributes to the ruin of the Eastern economy. Westerners now have to pay restaurant bills in Deutschmarks if they cannot prove they have exchanged the money officially at 1/3, and waiters are authorized to ask guests for passports and bank slips. This hardly improves their user-friendliness. Before the *Wende*, the waiter was king; now, after the *Wende*, the difference is the waiter is still king. But the good news is that business has gone up more than 100 per cent.

And crime is on the up. On 12 February East and West Berlin police chiefs met for the first time in forty-two years. They agreed to meet regularly and to co-operate in the exchange of traffic information, security at U-Bahn and S-Bahn stations, and the prevention of threats and events near the border. In East Berlin the number of bomb threats is increasing. There is a deep fear in the East of terrorist activity, and of fascists, and a recognition that there are those interested in further destabilizing the country: an unspecified foreign power, the neo-Nazis, the old guard, remnants of the Stasi, the Revolutionary Armed Factions which the West fears may be using the East as a hideout. With the Wall open, many GDR criminals went West, where the GDR authorities couldn't reach them, and the pickings are richer. Between the two cities, as between the two states, there are no law enforcement or extradition treaties, and police and prosecution co-operation is difficult. According to West German law the GDR isn't a foreign country and its citizenship isn't recognized, and therefore no such treaty was ever negotiated. Bonn and East Berlin are currently drafting such a law, but meanwhile the villains are busy, and the crime figures in the West are rising. In the first quarter of the year thefts from cars were up 45 per cent, burglary 60 per cent, theft of cash 113 per cent, robbery 80 per cent. At the same time the number of young West Berliners involved in crime in East Berlin went up, and there was growing violence with skinheads attacking foreigners, and West Berliners coming through to attack skinheads. Fascism had made a rapid recovery. In February customs found twice as many neo-fascist publications on the border as in January.

The Wall is down along the length of one side of the road to Steinstücken, revealing a wide strip of tracked sand without vegetation, poisoned land, with ditches and bunkers, and beyond it trees. From here a piece of Wall was taken off by the US Army, to be erected in front of the Berlin Commanding Officer's office. On a Sunday all along the southern border the woods are full of earnest walkers, the traffic heavy towards Glienicke. The Wall through the woods hereabouts is broken through in several places, cracked, slabs missing, lengths of coping fallen. Slabs have been taken for garden fencing, or paving, or souvenirs. All through here are unofficial crossing points, Westerners dodging through to walk about on the other side, in the village of old people trusted to live here beside the Wall. There, the Wall and the strip between divides up the village into sections separated from each other by more walls. The patrol comes, two soldiers in a light car. Everyone slips behind the Wall, and the patrol sees what it wants to see: nothing, and drives on. People come out and cross, some on bicycles, claiming back the old lost territory.

The city comes together, because it has to. By mid-February West Berlin had given DM 2 million in direct aid to East Berlin, with a DM 40 million loan for tourist facilities. By February's end there are twenty-four new crossing points. But traffic to and from the border crossings at Chausseestrasse, Friedrichstrasse/Charlie and Invalidenstrasse collapses almost every day, and in the East the transport system is regularly halted in the rush hour. At Potsdamer Platz, used by approximately 80,000 cars each weekday, there are constant jams. The crossing is to be widened to three lanes of traffic in each direction and, from Easter, public transport will run all the way to it on both sides. East Berlin has agreed to remove the underground bars that prevented escape and divide the city's sewer system, and block the drains. The East is inviting artists to paint their side of the Wall, presumably as part of their strategy for marketing it. Posters in the West show a collapsing wall and the words LET US BUILD BRIDGES FROM THESE STONES. But the wall in the poster is a brick wall, not the Wall. Formerly in the East the attitude in shops was 'We don't know, we can't do it, we won't'; now they try. In February, East German newspapers became available in West Berlin. The West Berlin *Tagesspiegel* opened an office in East Berlin, *Tageszeitung* began to produce an East Berlin edition, *Volksblatt Berlin* went on sale in the East, and the West German news agency dpa offered its services in the GDR.

In GDR schools there is a shortage of teaching material without ideological content, and West Berliners are asked to donate old school books. Teachers, especially of history and political science, are desperately trying to catch up with literature in their own field; suddenly teachers are expected to have ideas of their own. Curriculum reform is happening in schools and universities, and all twenty-nine sections of Marxist–Leninist studies in universities have closed down, making 1,000 teachers redundant, departments of economics and history are regarded as steeped in ideology. Teachers, formerly secure in their posts (if politically clean), are anxious, many of them opposed to change. With the changes in the school system many parents are anxious; working parents rely on the schools to take care of their children after school, and aren't willing to give up day care centres, kindergartens and free school meals.

10,000 East Germans have already inquired about studying in the West, where they will be eligible for a student loan. In Berlin the Freie and the Humboldt have established first contacts. John, who went to the first meeting at Humboldt, described a three-hour meeting of fifteen people from each side making speeches in a small room without windows or ventilation, a language lab consisting of ancient Czech tape recorders and teaching videos of people making phone calls. When they went to lunch there was no food left, but no one wanted to say so. Out of such beginnings will come a proposal to link Humboldt, the Freie and the Technische Universität into one huge University of Berlin. At present, many Easterners want to study in

West Berlin; with a Western loan they can live in the East and study in the West. Agreements have been reached to fund joint research projects in areas of environmental protection, ecology and information, together with exchange of personnel.

In the East in the golden windows of the Volkskammer the city is reflected, broken up, distorted into dream shapes. At Lenin-platz the huge red statue of its namesake stares Westward into the sunset, flat capped against the sky, still sure of his purpose. In the parks the bronze statues in the dried fountains are rust-stained. Everywhere paint peels, shingles fall, stucco peels off, bricks and concrete rot, gutterings block and rain seeps into the structure. Public areas are scruffy, untended, adrift with rubbish, and everything here is down at heel, unrenewed, looking fam-iliarly like much of London, parts of New York and Detroit, as do the inhabitants, who look like the West's underfed. Every-where scaffolding, piles of materials, walls half built, half started, half finished. It is the landscape of sameness, falling apart: wide streets, blocks of flats, concrete, pavements holed and cracked, buildings with grey faces peeling away. Everywhere Trabis in grey, blue, beige, the pastels of the doomed republic.

Ingrid: her parents are having trouble. They may be evicted from their house. Her father, retired now, was formerly high up in the SED, and the resentment of his neighbours threatens to dispossess them. All this has happened before, she says. Years ago her father, evidently an opportunist, was in the Nazi Party. After the war when the SED came to power he was threatened with eviction. At that point she, Ingrid, a young girl, was told to join the Pioneers, and through that they managed to hang on to the house they had then. Now, having worked himself upward through the SED, he is threatened again. Their house is claimed by someone in the West from whom it was confiscated forty years ago. No one has any sympathy for him, except Ingrid.

The carnival along the Wall goes on, tourists still arriving, still chipping. Towards Charlie the activity increases, pitches selling chippings, badges and epaulets and medals, presided over by one noisy Scotsman, with drink taken. 'Roll up roll up,' he cries, pointing his finger repeatedly at a small pudgy woman hammering at the Wall. 'Spot the Russian at the Wall. Spot the

Russian.' The traffic heavy as ever, the same stream in and out, Trabis, BMWs, Ladas, cars with CD plates, battered Polish bangers. More tourists, more Berolina tour buses, tours now from the East of the West. Two ageing men on foot with a television set wrapped in a blanket and roped into a parcel, carried short of breath between them. Two young women with plastic bags from Nana Nanu. Tourists around the Escape Museum, the Imbiss, the shops selling postcards and T-shirts and souvenir mugs. The protesters who were permanently camped here demanding exit for their relatives have long ago met them and gone home. Otherwise it's the same, French, US and British military posts, flags, signs, West German customs, who are interested in the Poles; the barriers, the upraised booms, the East. What was once the focus of so much fear and fury is banal now, an exhausted cliché.

Further up the Wall business thins out, collecting again at Potsdamer Platz and the Brandenburg Gate, where a regular market has developed along both sides of the Reichstag. This is a free trade zone, on the strip of GDR territory where a West Berlin trader's licence isn't needed, and where the East has not so far interfered. Stalls sell drinks and snacks, photographs and paintings of the Wall, some framed, some made into clocks. It's busy, with the excitement and comfort of markets, click of coin on the move, gaslamps and a radio tuned to a music station: 'Ain't gonna work on Maggie's farm no more.' Eastern guards are said to be selling their hats for DM 25, complete uniforms for DM 45, steel helmets for DM 60, pins, buttons and badges for DM 10. There are *ad hoc* stalls selling bits of Wall, chips made into earrings, keyrings, there are T-shirts, posters, army medals, pins, badges, buttons, boots, epaulets, jackets, hats, gloves, obscure bits of soldierly gear, the abandoned baggage of an army without a purpose. One stall is a market for uniform freaks; a West Berlin cop buys an Eastern army steel helmet.

At seven in the evening a group of soldiers comes out. They bang around the metal fences to cordon off the work area, and lean on them, smoking, chatting with the stall-holders. They are getting ready to dismantle tonight's section of Wall, behind the Reichstag and down to the river. They await orders, used to military life, which turns out to be waiting for something to happen before being moved somewhere else to wait for something to happen there. At eight there's a whistle and a loudspeaker, and the West Berlin police cordon off their part of the area and clear it of sightseers. Now people must walk around the Reichstag to see what's on the other side, as is the nature of barriers. On the other side, more stalls, some traders moving to where the action will be. By the Spree the last of the Wall slabs still stand, awaiting dismantling. The work is slow, done at night. Here, where the slabs have been removed, you can see how they were mounted on the old tram-tracks that ran around the Gate. The slabs that remain are gnarled and chipped away; one eaten through in the middle has collapsed under its own weight, keeled over on its rods. Behind new wire fencing the transformer still sings its one-note song, and along the sandy track along the river, now fenced off, the green army lifting gear sits, as if sleeping, waiting to be wakened to rip down more Wall. At the river bank people wander the space, remarking on its history of bullets and silence, as if inspecting the ruins of an old civilization. There are lights along the other shore, the Charité, the Japanese Trade Building, the trains to and from Friedrichstrasse rolling along the embankment. Buildings here have suddenly become neighbours again, like the inhabitants of opposite sides of a frozen lake meeting in midwinter. From one of them a woman's voice, a sharp contralto, bursts into an aria. In another through the ground-floor window are the lights of an office, a telephone exchange with miles of bound cables, files, desks, consoles, at one of which a very beautiful blonde young woman dressed in brightest red is picking up the telephone, her red lips forming into an O.

From the past old claims resurface. Many West Berliners and banks and insurance companies are discovering they own property in the East, taken over or abandoned years ago, to which they claim title. Many small businesses, long ago taken over for derisory compensation and incorporated into state organizations, may be difficult to trace. East Berlin expects about 10,000 such claims. By mid-February 1,500 West Berliners had applied to the Senate for funds to research their claims to property in the East, and it is estimated that over 150,000 West Berliners own land in East Berlin. Half the site on which the television tower stands is owned by a Western insurance company, and the GDR Foreign Ministry stands on land belonging to a West Berlin lawyer. One West Berliner claims eight pieces of land in

East Berlin worth DM 37.5 million, including the site of the Hotel Metropol on Friedrichstrasse. Western claims may apply to one-third of the dwellings in the GDR. It all adds to the insecurity. A family in Köpenick were told to move out by a West German who entered the house, claiming it was his property. The tenant of a house in Potsdam was told by his new West German landlord to move out by 15 May, as he wanted the house for himself. More unease. Resettlers who left houses behind are now claiming them back. There are reports of shady housing renovation deals by West Berlin companies. East Berlin tenants have established a tenant protection agency. Many who invested work and money in property taken over by the state twenty to thirty years ago face eviction, or large rent hikes. This is all currently subject to GDR regulations, but how long will they last, and the law of which state do we think will prevail? To counteract this the state building authority in the East is asking West Berliners owning houses in the East to sell them. Where a property is in need of repair – and most are – the owner must put up the money within a month, or sell.

Western companies are negotiating with the East; there are plans already for four McDonald's hamburger outlets in Alexanderplatz. Bad news for the rain forests. Lawyers from East and West have been getting together, unofficially, forming informal partnerships, sitting in on each other's meetings. The legal disparities between East and West create tricky possibilities, as do the many questions of ownership and title. So there must be lawyers present, arbitrators for the disputed jurisdictions of the future. They are negotiating the ground rules for selling off the battlefield. With the announcement in the East of the open market in place of a centrally planned economy, many West German firms moved quickly. Up to the third week of February 7,000 firms had expressed interest, and the first contracts were being signed. Everywhere the buzz phrase is *joint venture*, as East and West seek each other as partners. It's a carpet-bag situation, as the managers of state organizations sign contracts with Western firms, and are taken over. For 25 per cent recapitation they put in telephones and computers, retrain the staff, and do an inventory. They'd have to do that anyway. They're snapping up bargains, as if the GDR were a pile of old jumble. Trouble is, much of it is.

Volkswagen will replace the Trabi with the Polo. Opel

(General Motors) will replace the Wartburg, building 150,000 cars annually in the East in a similar deal. Daimler-Benz will build trucks. Thyssen and Krupp are talking heavy engineering. Hotels and department stores are planned. Siemens are linking with Robotron. The power company Veba is already supplying electricity to the East. Deutsche Bank, Dresdner and Commerzbank have opened branches in the East. Insurance, hotel chains, retail chains, electrical and engineering groups are negotiating deals, investing mighty sums. About a half of West German business is on the move East.

With the announcement of freedom of trade, GDR firms were allowed to deliver goods and services to the West and charge in Deutschmarks. Western goods became available in East Berlin: exotic fruit and veg and Coca Cola at the Centrum department store, electronics and household appliances, usually too expensive for Easterners. For now profits are deposited in Eastern banks, pending legislation. In the East the plan seems to be the build-up of small business; in February 20,000 East Berliners applied for trading licences to open their own stores. A Small Business Association was founded, and rapidly attracted membership. But the likelihood is that local efforts, under financed and lacking experience, will be swamped by incoming Western firms, who will soon have the lion's share of the East. State monopolies will be replaced by corporate monopolies. The East is a freefire zone; in the West the cartel office would restrict them, but as yet they have no jurisdiction in the East. By the time they do, big business will be in place, *fait accompli*. Hence the hurry.

Now again we have a German colony, Tomas says, meaning the East. He is being ironic. 'In the past we had colonies and lost them.' A young man from Bavaria, he explains the advantages, till now, of living in West Berlin, where his travel costs are subsidized, there is an 8 per cent tax advantage, and no conscription. Unification, he shrugs, what does it mean? It means the rise of the right in Germany again. The Easterners are Germans, so they join us. And what happens when the German Poles in Poland say, 'We are German too?'

'*What is happening now is too fast and chaotic for me*,' says Gregor Gysi, Chairman of the PDS. The GDR is running fast to unification, and all the talk of a gradual coming together, in timed and worked out phases, is being stampeded by the collapse of the East and the rush for the border. Modrow's proposal in early February for a confederation and gradual unification, with the eventual capital in Berlin, was ignored by Kohl, and like Kohl's own plan, soon outdated. In proposing a neutral unified Germany, Modrow's was essentially the same used plan the West wouldn't buy years ago from Stalin and Khrushchev. In any case the GDR is distintegrating rapidly, collapsing into the arms of the West, its government without authority. West Germany, with little choice in the matter, is stepping in to take over the management, but Bonn refused a request for DM 15 billion in emergency aid. Not till after the election, and the demise of the PDS. Technically it can all be done quite simply, under Article 23 of the West German constitution by which the five *Länder* of the East, first having reconstituted themselves from the fifteen districts the SED dissolved them into in 1952, collectively or individually apply to join Federal Germany. The election is only to decide the pace of unification, and to formally kick out the Communists for ever, and for a say in it all. That's the easy part. The problem is clearing up the mess.

They want the shark without his pearly teeth. Some are beginning to realize that in return for their surrender, the West is promising nothing; the terms of currency reform are waved about, but not decided. Of those who are to vote in the GDR's first free election in fifty-seven years, some are reconsidering what they are about to lose, and this accounts for some renewed interest in the PDS. Most people say they'd like unification with the West, but for the East to retain some distinction, and most of all its social net, which is considerable. They want the shark without the teeth. Some are already nostalgic: in the GDR till now everyone had a job however unpromising, a place to live however small, food to eat, if low quality. They had a regular expectation of promotion if nose-clean, within their trade, within their cadre, and if not a lot of anything, a basic subsistence, an education. Basic needs were heavily subsidized. They had a net beneath them that, in being there, may have become invisible. All employees had a national insurance scheme costing 10 per cent of earnings, 12 per cent paid by the employer, that guaranteed a pension of 300–470 marks a month, and sickness benefit to 90 per cent of pay, child benefit doubling with each child, and mothers a year off work at 70 per cent of income. There is welfare for those who cannot work. In the GDR, where there had been till now officially none, unemployment is a new phenomenon. As of 26 February an earnings related benefit up to 1,000 marks a month, or 70 per cent of net pay, became available. By the end of February thirty-two state-owned enterprises had dismissed approximately 38,000 employees, of whom 11,000 were still looking for work.

But in all this socialist security there were no surprises, so no incentives: the GDR died of boredom. The monotony of the music must be why Ossis go for any sort of lottery, in West Berlin betting on the black Queen or the disappearing dice along Stuttgarter Platz by the Import/Export, or in the East crowding round a booth selling bunches of wild flowers and a bowl of folded tickets, betting crazy. In a rigorously planned society, chance, the random ticket to a prize, provided one of the few diversions from routine. In a planned society everything must be planned, including laughter; cabaret in the East was close to the bone, though still tightly controlled, an outlet for frustration. When the Wall came down all the routines and all the jokes were suddenly out of date. Spontaneity was discouraged, hence Ossi reserve. They are a serious folk, though they laugh and are mischievous. But for a Westerner they are characterized by an unimaginable poverty of spirit, the imagination habitually suppressed. They are institutionalized. Heaven grew boring, with nothing to look forward to. Now the 'socialist German state', without socialism, ceases to have a reason to exist, and the majority of its people demand the experiment be ended. Now there's a general air of anxiety and despair, with half the population sitting on their suitcases, in *Torschlusspanik*, door-closing-panic, defined as the fear of losing your turn in the line. Friends, neighbours, relatives, workmates, your doctor or your children's teacher or your spouse or your lover or even your parents suddenly disappear into the legendary West. Everyone is on the edge of movement; even the guards are leaving. Most people who stay are holding their breath till the elections, praying if they pray with their fingers crossed. The exodus disrupts everything; there is a shortage of blood, because donors who were formerly paid for regular contributions go West and swap their blood for Deutschmarks.

*

West Berlin is full of holes, through which the proletarians come. In the West they are discovering that many of them are unreconstructed Germans, 'too German' they say, raw and crude, asking the way to the Sex-Kino, slagging off the Turks, taking little interest in the other half of their city but to covet its glitz. They come from a long way back, many of these Ossis, from forty years of theoretical tolerance of the rest of humanity but little encounter with it, and before that Nazism. And before that the Prussian sneer. The Government's ideology designated racism a Western and a fascist phenomenon, and dismissed the matter. Their now open racism is raw and shocking. They have been mentally on ice for forty years. That they have not shared our history is one excuse. What we call the sixties and the seventies and the eighties has passed them by. Their history has done nothing to temper their intolerance of the *Untermensch*, and their assumption that as Germans they're superior. So they're unreconstructed, let's say. At Marchlewskistrasse U-Bahn station an elderly woman is shelter-ing behind a pillar, drunk, tired, sorting out her shopping bags, muttering about the Jews, and that Hitler didn't gas enough of them. On the left, beyond the fringes of the Party, apartheid was one of the faces of acceptable protest, and there were those who compared the GDR to South Africa's institu-tionalized oppression, a comparison difficult to sustain, given that East Germans are with very few exceptions, and those shunned, universally white, Teutonic. And with that they are provincial, still Saxons and Thuringians and Prussians rivalling each other. As to the Jews, Schalck-Golodkowski is Jewish, Gregor Gysi is Jewish. Nazi repression meant that Jews who survived the Holocaust were often Party members. This makes them targets again. Otherwise here, there were few foreigners, most of them from the Eastern bloc, and few opportunities to meet any. The theory of human equality was never tested. And the influx means a charge to the racist lobby in the West, provoking insecurity; everything seems to be moving to the right, whatever the SPD may believe. In the West in education all innovation and experiment is out, and it's back to the old Germanic learning by rote system, obeying orders.

'The night train is coming. The baker man is baking bread. The

baker man is baking bread. The night train is coming.' DDR1
has turned itself into a music station, listened to with RIAS and
BFBO in the East, taking requests, communicating, playing
songs that say '*relax, don't worry, take it easy, relax*'. Tom
Waits: '*no one speaks English and everything's broken*'. The DJ
comes on, speaking English. 'This is for you Lucky: *Broken
English.*' When he says it he makes it sound like the 'German
Democrapic Republic'. Over on DDR2 they're playing the
'Kyrie Eleison'.

In collapsing Kreuzberg, opened now to its neighbours across
the river in Friedrichshain, business is picking up. Derelict
streets are suddenly alive again, with deliveries and customers,
with electronics, Export/Import. From Warschauer Strasse on
the other side it's a cat's jump across the bridge to do business
in Kreuzberg, without the hassle of the city. But not everyone's
happy. A proposal to open a new crossing at Kohlhasenbrück,
down in the south-west, angers the local residents, in their quiet
leafy suburb beside the Wall. They insist it be only for pedestrians, and win. And other relationships are changed. What
now of love affairs across the Wall? Once, with a Wall in
between and little communication, the East was the perfect
place for a West Berliner to keep a mistress. Relationships were
often confused by the Wall, by flight. There's this tale: some
years ago he dumped wife and two children, and fled West.
Under the law for reuniting families, she applied for an exit
visa. Years went by, as they do, and meanwhile she met another
man, also married. Eventually she got out, and joined her
husband. It didn't work, and three months later they split, and
divorced. So then she was in the same position as before,
wanting a man beyond the Wall. Over on his side, he got
divorced. She got permission to go East for a day, and married
him. He had to wait six weeks before coming to join her. When
he did, that marriage didn't last long either. She divorced him.
He now turned to getting his ex-wife and kids out, and while
the paperwork was in process the Wall came down. They all
moved across the city to join him, living in his flat, where they
are reported miserable.

The old fear: one afternoon in late February John drives over
from the West. We drive about the city, scouting the locations

of a movie in our minds, the cameras in the boot, glimpsing down streets and bouncing across roofs the black flashing glimpse of the television tower. We stand on the bridge at Warschauer Strasse and survey the city and its tracks. Just to see we drive around Stasi-Zentrale, once around the block, speculating how many of them are still in there. Still 15,000 Werner says. More of the cameras have been taken down, but some are still there. A woman on a balcony notices us, sees our West Berlin plates. Minutes later re-entering the Frankfurter Allee a cop steps out into the road, his hand up: 'Why are you here? What were you doing down Magdalenenstrasse? Where are you from? Get out of here.'

The two Berlins move closer, announcing more openings, more links, more transport connections. By the election on 18 March there are thirty-four crossing points. Plans are announced for the extension of tram-lines into West Berlin to link Easterners to the U-Bahn system. No one's sure who's to pay for it: it's at the convenience of Easterners, but it's on Western territory. In the East the tram network is to be extended. DM 1 billion per year will have to be invested in the public transport system of Greater Berlin during the next ten to fifteen years, or traffic will collapse, it's predicted. East and West transport authorities are reactivating the old S-Bahn ring system around Berlin, projected to be completed by 1994, and the Senate is to spend DM 50 million this year to reactivate four S-Bahn lines severed by the Wall. The broken lines will be healed again. In the East ghostly long-abandoned stations at Potsdamer Platz and around the Mitte are being reopened. The autobahn ring systems of both cities are to be joined up. On the roads an avalanche of cars is expected to hit Berlin. In East Berlin, where 80 per cent of the population use public transport, this is expected to change, resulting in rapid growth in the number of cars in the city. By the end of February ship connections had been re-established between Wannsee and Potsdam, and the Weisse Flotte (White Fleet) sailed between. The BVG and the BVB, West and East Berlin traffic authorities, agreed to co-operate and eventually to become one authority. In February the Western allies were already negotiating away the ADIZ, the Air Defence Identification Zone, which had prevented direct East–West flights, and on 10 March the first scheduled German flight across the ADIZ took place.

On the railways, crews and locomotives are still being exchanged at the border. The two state-run systems aren't compatible. The cost of renewing the East's rail network is put at DM 100 billion. Of the GDR rail network of over 14,000 kilometres, more than half needs extensive repair, and at any one time a third of it is out of service. By nature of the long frost between the two countries, connections East and West are minimal and slow, and not a single line is electrified, and this has long isolated Berlin. In the East north–south routes between the Baltic and the industrialized south are electrified, but not modernized, and trains move sluggishly across the landscape. In February both authorities, DB and DR, agree to build a fast train connection between Hannover and Berlin; starting on 27 May inter-city connections would run between Leipzig and Berlin, Frankfurt am Main, Cologne, Munich and Nuremberg. By the summer of 1991 Berlin will be connected to the Inter-city network, with direct trains between Bonn and Berlin. Eventually DR and DB will become one company. The energy companies of both states will co-operate, and power lines are to be linked.

West Berlin is acutely short of housing. Before the opening a quarter of a million were looking for an apartment. Employees of both housing administrations are now exchanging posts to experience the other side's problems. In West Berlin the housing situation began to change dramatically in 1988, and in the last two years rents rose 50 per cent. The situation in East Berlin is equally bad. 94,000 East Berliners are looking for accommodation. Flats are very cheap, but very small. They are also scarce, and while there are many empty properties, as many as a million homes in the East it's said, most are in need of extensive repair. Only 3 million were built in the last two decades, most of them *Betonsilos*, concrete silos, looming in the distance called Marzahn. These are small, but have central heating and warm water. While the housing authority concentrated on modern flats, the older housing stock of the city, half of it pre-1918 tenement buildings, rotted away. Tenants were rarely interested in repairs, labour and materials often in short supply, the bureaucracy slow and unresponsive. In the first quarter of the year there was a big drop in the number of buildings renovated and built, due to the emigration of 18,000 building workers moving to the West. There's a poetic justice in this; for years before the opening the GDR hired out construction gangs to West Berlin, neglecting their own sites and undercutting the rates in the West, part of the Schalck-Golodkowski hard currency business. For this reason much of East Berlin looks like a permanent building site. Out of 631,000 dwellings in East Berlin 32,800 don't have an inside toilet, 25,000 are unoccupied, 3,000 are condemned, 16,500 are severely damaged. It would take 200 billion marks to renovate all housing in the GDR. The West Berlin Senate recently promised East Berlin DM 25 million to renovate buildings in Prenzlauer Berg and Thälmann Park. The situation is confused by the exodus. Many flats are left vacant by those fleeing West. Since the opening 23,000 East Berliners have left, and thousands of flats stand vacant, but it's a problem to know when a flat has been abandoned. In the East flats were assigned by the state, according to family size. One or two people were assigned a one-room flat, a family three rooms or even two. As a result an unofficial exchange system was set up, whereby people swapped their flats without informing the housing authority, so in the East many people don't live at the address where they're registered. To protect tenants, the East Berlin housing authority announced at the beginning of April that it would take over the 375,000 nationally owned dwellings in the city, which would not be put on the free housing market. At the end of April they announced that rents would be doubled.

Berlin the capital: at the beginning of the month the cancellation of a new DM 12 million press centre in Bonn encouraged speculation that the government might be planning to move to Berlin. Then came an announcement from Daimler-Benz on 13 February that it would build its new headquarters in Berlin at Potsdamer Platz. On the opposite side of the Wall apartment houses under construction in the Mitte were stopped. Daimler-Benz were coming to town. That seemed to clinch it. At the same time a fall in property prices in Bonn encouraged the guesswork. By now in West Berlin property prices had risen 20 per cent since the opening, and many national and international companies were planning to set up offices in the city. Siemens was reported looking for property. The Hertie company were thinking of building an administration complex on the Lenné Triangle. The US World Trade Centre Association was also interested in the site. There are disadvantages to Berlin: energy costs are 20 per cent higher than in the Federal Republic, and the city involves long transportation from the West, and high property costs. On the other hand there is the East, with land and empty buildings, and in a united Germany transportation would hardly be the problem. There's all the East beyond, and all those markets, and Berlin is ideally placed to be at any rate the commercial capital of the new economic empire forming there. If it becomes the political and economic capital, Germany may well be centralized again, the antithesis of the Allies' federalizing of the West after the war. As to the future development of the city, two rival schemes are emerging: business wants to put up skyscrapers, creating a focal point for itself. Another group wants to preserve the old city and the green areas around it, and build housing, arguing that the city will attract poor immigrants from the East. They see an opportunity to correct mistakes made in the cities' development in the past. The Greens suggest that the area of the Wall and the death strip should be developed as a walkway and cycle track, a green band through the city. Some want to keep a section of the Wall as a memorial. Some suggest the new M-Bahn (magnetic railway) should be run along its path. Others suggest it would make a fine motorway.

In the storm Peter's house beside the Wall has been damaged, and his roof has come apart – slates and rotten beams are falling in front of his house on to the pavement, and a young woman was hit on the head by a beam and taken to hospital. The police came from both sides, and couldn't agree on how to block the walkway off, or which side's barriers to use. Since the pavement is Eastern territory, it was decided to use their barriers, flimsy candy-striped fences and no sign saying 'Danger'. Today people push aside the fences and walk on; it seems the lesson of the Wall has not yet sunk in. Peter's problem is how to get the roof fixed. It is an international problem. A Western firm cannot erect scaffolding in front of the house on Eastern territory; nor can an Eastern firm put up scaffolding against a Western building. As a problem that cannot be resolved by the two sides, it then becomes a matter for resolution by the four

Occupying Powers, who have larger fish to fry just now. Peter's roof has become a matter for the six countries involved, the four plus two. Meanwhile the roof is leaking and the alleyway is dangerous.

17

THE WINDS OF MARCH

Five months from *Wende* to Wahl, from Honecker's fall to the election of a conservative alliance dedicated to unification with the West and abolition of the GDR. 'Look on my works, ye mighty.' Not long ago the GDR was still its awkward nettled self, firm in the conviction of its own rightness and inevitability, fierce in denunciation and opposition to the West, thoroughly German in its orthodoxy. Since then its long captive population has been through the Wall to the West. Now the GDR is collapsing into its mirror image, so far more or less in good order. People are talked out of recklessness; they are orderly and German, and forty years of *Marxismus–Leninismus* have muted their behaviour, so there's little violence so far. Less than a year ago Honecker was saying the Wall would last 100 years. Now he's in Lobetal, north of Berlin, living with his once estranged wife Margot in the house of the pastor in a village for mentally and physically handicapped people: the old atheist at bay, charged with high treason, conspiracy, abuse of power, and dying from cancer. Krenz has been and gone. Modrow and the last of the Party are on the way out.

Even in retrospect it's hard to grasp the pace and scale of such change. Behind the lattices of information, the accusations, statistics, agreements, the new formalities of an open border, statements by politician and announcements by departments, there form the patterns of the coming together of these two divided cities (and states), in the confluences of transport and energy and effluent. Buses and trains cross the border again. In East Berlin the police complain of lack of discipline on the streets, and there's a rise in traffic accidents. There are about 60–80,000 visitors in the city each day. The Eastern city map now has the West on it, where formerly it was white terra incognita with some woods. By the 18th, election day, there were thirty-four crossing points between the cities. Fearing an invasion from the West, the Müggelsee is put off limits for motorboats, and tight regulations introduced to control the expected environmental damage from the influx of 15,000 West Berlin motorboat owners. Museums in East and West Berlin agree to co-operate in mounting exhibitions and exchanging works. Sections of the Museum of German History in the East are shut, awaiting reinterpretation. On the *perestroika* front, for the first time the Eastern police announced the actual penalties for traffic violations in the GDR; till now, it had been a lucrative little state secret.

Day to day there's high politics and low, the doings of the ambitious and the scared with their schemes and combinations and their secret dreams, the intrigues of the Stasi, manipulations from Bonn, the refreshing presence of the occasional honest broker from some other department of life in the East, the nitty gritty statistics of emigration, unemployment, rates of exchange and bills of lading – these fill the air with facts, but behind it all what's happening through March is that the Eastern election is being bought by Kohl, the GDR is becoming an extension – a colony – of West Germany, and big business is driving a big bus down the middle of the road. Between the March election and the currency union, rumoured – accurately, again – by *Bild* in March as 1 July, and of course denied, there are deals to be made. When unification comes, the conglomerates will be in place. The speed with which they are moving suggests that there were always contingency plans for just such an event. Whatever else is happening, and whatever the price of bananas, this is the future coming into shape: a united if distorted Germany, Berlin the effective capital; the rich richer, the taxpayers pay for all, there are a few lucky chickens and a lot of carpet-bags piled up in the lobby. There's fortunes to be made in such a moment. Eyes down, look in.

Nie wieder Nazi Terror, scrawled across a railway bridge, in black; never again. *Nazi Skins*. The spray-can comes to East Berlin. *Bundis go home. Faschis raus. Nazis Stasis und Sozis raus. SPD nee. PDS = Partei der Stasi. PDS = Parasiten, Diktatur, Stalinismus. Wir hören nur Kohl* (All we hear is Kohl). GYSI-STASI-NASI-NAZI. Along Mühlenstrasse, where the long inner wall divides the city from the Spree and the rest of the universe, painters are at work on the Eastern side, beginning what they term the East Side Gallery. *Zukunft kein Beton für solche Mauern* (No more concrete for such walls). *Wer das Geld hat, hat die Macht* (Who has the money has the power). At Warschauer Strasse, by the Oberbaumbrücke crossing, graffiti demanding no compensation for settlers, people who have left and who are now returning to reclaim the property they abandoned. Getting off her train, an elderly woman puts up an umbrella designed as the map of the world she has seen little of. From the S-Bahn, somewhere in the muddle of factories and flats and heating pipes and yards of used materials, a half-built building with a banner proclaiming *Besetzt gegen Spekulanten* (Occupied against speculators).

Sunday, Friedrichshain, around Samariter: long dusty streets, most of them permanent building sites. Down side streets, rubble, piles of building materials, pipes, planks, bricks, roadstones, paving slabs, scaffolding, cranes, battered cement mixers, and everywhere crumbling buildings, some inhabited, some not, indistinguishable from each other. Everywhere holes in the road, the pavements slippery with dust. And rubbish, islands of skips piled with carpets and old TV sets recently replaced, furniture dumped from the apartments of those who have gone. Efforts to sheer it all up seem constantly outflanked by shortages of materials and labour and lack of enthusiasm. Entropy has got the upper hand here, amid the detritus of a society that lost interest in itself. On every corner it seems there's a broken toilet bowl. On the batterd doorway of a shop someone has hand-lettered a sign: *nicht KaDeWe*. Wind and sunshine, the city an afternoon haze down long wide avenues, trams clanking down the central strip. Traffic: Trabi Mercedes VW Opel BMW Trabi Trabi Wartburg Lada, taxi, one fat Zil with East Berlin plates. They say the Trabis are piling up at the factories; no one wants them any more, and their price is falling through the floor. They want second-hand Western cars, and a market has opened in Marzahn selling them in Ostmarks. On either side of the Frankfurter Allee, great blocks, the same the workers walked off in 1953, tall, concrete, grey, ugly. At street level shops: the butcher's and the baker's, the empty-looking little supermarket with its line of trolleys, Apotheke, Delikat, Post, shoe store, clothes store, their names repeating along the Allee in ageing neon and faded paint. Everything here needs a good brushing down and a coat of colour. In the green strip between pavement and traffic new flowers have been planted, and the bushes trimmed. The wide pavements are filled with people out strolling in the sun, mostly families, couples, people with children, push-chairs, mothers with new babies in wickerwork prams, not many old people. Sunday is almost everyone's day off at the same time. The town's shut tight, save for the occasional ice-cream outlet, the rare Imbiss on a corner where the long patient queues form, a lone restaurant flooded out with customers, a *Kneipe* where sullen men lean over tall glasses of surly Eastern beer. Up Bersarinstrasse the buses, bearing posters on their sides for *Die Morgenpost*, on sale here now. Along the Leninallee the trams, clanking. At the sports centre a long long line snakes round the building, where those who wait patiently in the abrasive muggy air outside can watch through the glass those who got here early, swimming in the cool green interior of rubber plants. Then around the Volkspark Friedrichshain, which is crowded, the paths full, the park planned not as a place of relaxation but a site of many activities. Relaxation is a serious business, both sides of the border, more so here. The paths are for walking on, and wind through the activities, which are not much taken up, the spaces quartered for tennis, table tennis, soccer, hockey, adventure playground, swimming pool with benches, duck feeding, sitting, tea or coffee subject to avail-ability. At the head of the queue at last, both run out: *Tor-schlusspanik*. The queue disperses, patient, docile, used to it. Once more around the park, to the memorial to the Polish war dead, to the memorial to the dead of the Spanish Civil War. They all end in admonishments to be vigilant in the guarding of social-ism and freedom from fascism. Here and there odd lengths and projections of thick heating pipes, barely distinguishable from what, west of here, would be sculpture. In one corner of the park a collection of cement statuary – cement stags, sheep, rams, lions, giant frogs in the waterless pool; around the outside the cement figures of idealized peasants at peace with nature, small and childlike: the farmer leads his pig to market, a girl gathers doves to her chaste breast, another straddles a duck, the seamstress has fallen asleep at her work. Then up the Bunker-berg. The view west across the city includes the line of cranes that mark the border, the distant West Berlin television tower, and the nearer eye of Darth Vader glittering through the budding trees and the afternoon haze, as ever. From the Tiergarten the distant sound of the carillon: bells from the other country.

It's two weeks before the election, and forty years of history will go out with the tea-leaves. No one seems over-excited, though conversations buzz with acronyms: PDS, CDU, SPD, DDR, BRD, EC. *Helmut* they say, meaning Kohl or Schmidt. '*Wir sind ein Volk*,' they chant at the demonstrations, now transformed into election rallies for Kohl: '*Wir sind ein Volk, Wir sind ein Volk*,' a cry that pleases Germans but a chant that pricks needles of old terror in all their neighbours. It is a phrase changing with emphasis and tone; its meaning has perceptibly shifted in these months. Back in the autumn it meant they were *a* people, *the* people, with a voice and a power their own to say 'no' and 'no more' to the petty empire of their oppressors, that they were the people of the GDR who by virtue of their endurance and their suffering for forty years had earned an identity of their own. Now spring has followed autumn and the winter was brief, and the cry has come to mean in a language that fails to distinguish between *a* and *one* that they are one people with the Germans of the Federal Republic. So they will be. Nothing can stop them.

The exchange rate settles at 1/5, dropping in early March to 1/4, as speculators buy up Ostmarks against the promise of currency union, anticipating a final rate at 1/2 or 1/3 that will still see them in profit. Customs report an increase in smuggling, a boom in black market activity around banks and railway stations in East and West Berlin. The scale of the loss to the Eastern mark is itself threatening the eventual exchange rate. At stake are personal savings in the GDR now estimated at 170 billion Ostmarks.

Membership of the Party is down to 650,000. Many have left to join the SPD, where they are not trusted. Too many old names, they say. Old *Genossen*.

Through March the emigration rate begins falling. In the first two months almost 133,000 went West, and in West Berlin some 250 a day are still reporting to the reception centre. In the second week of March there were less, and the numbers declined from 1,700 to 1,500 per day. A few GDR citizens were returning to the East, even, it's said, one or two adventurous Westerners, weary of being on the dole. After the election the emigrants dropped further, and in the week following only 5,000 left as opposed to 12,000 the week before. But West German officials were still expecting many more to leave for the West before 1 July, the fabled Day X. At the end of March 13,000 out of 85,000 unemployed in West Berlin were resettlers, an increase of 250 per cent from 1989. The expected rate of unemployment for Greater Berlin was put at about 15 per cent. And the city cannot take any more, settlers or commuters; the labour market and the housing market are saturated. To discourage resettlers from staying on in temporary accommodation, West Berlin has put up the rents. Bonn is reported to be attempting to make it more difficult for people to come.

In the East, ghosts in the wiring, the old guard persist. At the end of January Honecker, Mielke, Mittag, and Hermann (media/propaganda) were charged with treason and conspiracy and abuse of power. Many more senior officials and 212 local officials faced charges of misrule, corruption, and abuse of power. Honecker was released from the Charité on 29 January after cancer surgery and imprisoned. The arresting officer named the charges against him. 'Ignore him,' Honi said. 'He's only covering his tracks.' He spent a day and a night in jail, claiming he was too ill to stay in prison. Offered a state flat, he refused, fearing reprisals from the neighbours. Then he was offered two attic rooms in an Evangelical pastor's house in Lobetal, sharing kitchen and bathroom. The priest reasoned we're all human, but the neighbours complained, there were nasty phone calls and threats, people left the church, and there were bomb threats. At the end of March a crowd of people stopped Honi and his wife's motorcade taking them to the state villa they had been assigned. They had to go back to Lobetal. He's said to be numb and totally exhausted, and though he thinks he made a few mistakes he can't accept that everything he stood for was wrong. He blames Krenz. Krenz blames him. He says he won't vote in the election. Then at the end of March the East Berlin prosecutor's office said there were no grounds to charge him, or Mittag or Mielke, with high treason or conspiracy. Honi was under medical examination to decide whether he could stand up to a trial on lesser charges of corruption and abuse of power.

In the first week of April he was admitted to a Soviet army hospital. Faced, some of them, with accusations of Stasi involvement, the new politicians were less eager to prosecute the former leadership. Mielke was released from prison in March, on health grounds, pronounced senile by the doctors, unable to stand trial. His pension, over 5,000 marks a month as a former army general, was restored. Cynics, and there were many, claimed it was all a trick. In an April interview with his son, Frank, in *Stern*, Frank admitted that loyal Stasi were organizing hiding places for him. In April Schalck-Golodkowski popped up from hiding in the West to say that at the end Mielke, senile or not, had been fed false information, and misled by the Kremlin to expect Russian support last October.

Scraps of news of Schalck-Golodkowski's operations dribbled out, the pattern of an empire reconstructed from its ruins. Known as Big Alex, he built a complex network of state companies dedicated to earning hard currency, and made billions of Deutschmarks for the GDR through them. He controlled a network of secret SED firms in Western Europe, and operated through the Stasi. Profits financed the West German Communist Party, the Stasi, the leadership's lifestyle, and some third world guerrilla movements. The web of firms were vaguely connected, mostly under the aegis of department *KoKo*, which also organized the arms trade. In March Luxemburg's CARGOLUX confirmed that in April 1988 they had refused a request from the GDR to ship 1,100 tons of arms from Schönefeld to Addis Ababa. The weapons came from the Stasi, the army, and the Ministry of the Interior. Arms were transported from Schönefeld every Tuesday and Thursday, and until 1988 transport planes from both Iraq and Iran regularly collected machine-guns and pistols. In early April, in *Die Welt*, Schalck-Golodkowski emerged in a lengthy interview; he revealed that *KoKo* had made an annual profit of about 3 million marks in foreign currency, of which 1.5 million went directly to the state; the rest was put into foreign investments or bank accounts in the GDR, Switzerland, Austria, and Luxemburg. None was deposited in West Germany. There were accounts for the exclusive use of members of the leadership; Stoph had about DM 250 million in his personal account, Honecker DM 100 million at his disposal. It was with some of this money he had bought the bananas, back in October. Schalck-Golodkowski also admitted the export of arms, to Iran and Iraq, and to Egypt and Jordan, pointing out that this was no more than other countries East and West do as a matter of course. They made about DM 40 million a year out of the sale of works of art, DM 10 million from the sales of stamp collections. He denied any involvement with drugs, and defended his actions against his accusers; he was, he said, providing gold and currency reserves against a financial collapse.

That's in the past, but here the past won't lie down; there's a keen thirst for revenge on the old men of the Party, and anger that they're all too old or too sick to be tried. The citizens of this rotted country have little else to do but worry as the West moves in. On all sides deals are being struck: Kaiser's food chain will open thirty-eight shops in East Berlin, the Drospa drugstore chain plans to open 100 outlets there. Suhrkamp Verlag is taking over Aufbau Verlag, which turned out to be the property not of the state or the people but of the Party; now the list is being stripped, new editions of Heym and Wolf brought hurriedly forward, Western authors are in. On the newspapers of the East, Springer and Maxwell and the rest are surely moving. The four major West German houses, Springer, Burda, Bauer, and Gruner & Jahr, controlling 75 per cent of the media in the West, have set up a joint distribution network for their magazines and newspapers, creating a monopoly outside the range of the West German monopolies commission. This was before the Government abolished the state monopoly on distribution, a *fait accompli*. Soon Springer will have bought into *Der Morgen*, Bauer into *Junge Welt*, the former FDJ newspaper, Maxwell's Mirror Group are negotiating with *Berliner Verlag*, East Germany's largest publisher and the property of the PDS, and Murdoch's News International has agreed with Burda to set up a joint publishing plant in Berlin. Many of the new titles that appeared after the *Wende* are threatened, as are jobs. The chairman of the Eastern Union of Journalists protested, referring to 'quasi-colonialist tactics' to carve up the markets. Everywhere the property is rapidly being assessed, the contracts drawn, the area surveyed. Till the election, however, many contracts are only pending; at the Leipzig Trade Fair over 12–13 March, many deals were clinched, but the volume of business was down on previous years.

*

Here in the East in March the new cold is beginning to bite: in the first ten days of earnings related benefit 3,000 East Berliners applied for it, more than half of them skilled workers, and there were 15,000 vacancies. By the end of March 40,000 Easterners were unemployed. Unemployment was especially high in East Berlin. Unsurprisingly, the new job centres reported difficulties finding work for former Stasi lawyers, social scientists, and economists. On 6 March the Volkskammer adopted a new labour law giving workers the right to strike for the first time in forty years. Some workers were forming links with trade unions in the West. On the dodgy front, some people are believed to be working in West Berlin while drawing unemployment in the East. Knowing what's coming, everyone is insecure: jobs, houses, cost of living. Pensioners worry over their pensions, savers over their savings; it all depends on what the Bundesbank agrees with Kohl over the exchange rate. In early March the East Berlin Round Table endorsed the adoption of a social charter proposed by two members of Modrow's caretaker cabinet as part of the unification package to maintain the East German social net: the right to work, trade union rights, gender equality, free health and education, retention of state subsidized rents, a better charter they claimed than the West German Basic Law. And will the shark please remove his dentures? On the third, a Saturday, there was a huge demonstration in East Berlin against the impending surge in rents, and against the activities of West German property speculators. They gathered before the Rote Rathaus and blocked the streets, one noisy contingent demanding 'no more *Betonsilos*', speakers took it in turn to speak, and the police diverted the traffic and sat in their cars. Everyone was getting used to this by now.

At the beginning of March, Kohl and the three Alliance leaders called for the quickest possible unification, and agreed that the best course was Article 23, by which the West German constitution, legal, economic and social systems would be adopted. By contrast the SPD, mindful of the differences between the two states, called for negotiations under Article 146, by which both Germanies would jointly work out a new constitution. Since this promised to be a drawn-out process, the SPD began to lose support. Kohl's appearances at East German electoral rallies drew the masses. On the 2nd he addressed a rally in Karl-Marx-

Stadt, which he insisted on calling by its old name, Chemnitz. A week later he was in Magdeburg speaking to 100,000: 'We need each other,' he said, projecting the image of the Father of the Fatherland. At the same time the campaign turned dirty, the Alliance hinting that the SPD was full of Communists who had deserted the SED to masquerade as social democrats. Some were accused of Stasi connections. There were smear tactics, hate mail, attacks on the offices of rival parties and attempts to disrupt rallies. The SPD and CDU accused each other of complicity in the former regime. Then the opinion polls that in February had given the SPD 53 per cent of the vote began swinging; a new poll in the first week of March gave the SPD 34 per cent, the Alliance 30 per cent, the PDS 17 per cent.

At Magdalenenstrasse, at Stasi-Zentrale, most of the graffiti has been painted out, leaving *Glasnost* and *Ich will meine Akte haben* pasted over to read: I will have my PDS. On balconies flags rival each other in the March breeze, East German, West German, some the black Berlin bear flag, along windows the frieze of red, gold and black. Everywhere on walls and windows and boarded-up doorways election posters are pasted over each other, overlapping, ripped, some written over, some with eyes or faces scratched out, constantly changing. Some are home-made jobs. What's evident is the virulence with which they are ripped down and defaced. All the same they bring some colour to the otherwise colourless world of the East: the colours of Germany on the Alliance posters, the greens of the Greens, blue of Bündnis, red and white of the PDS, red and white of the SPD, starred blue Euroflags of the SPD proclaiming *Ein Europäisches Deutschland*. Everywhere the posters and slogans supporting one or other of the groups and parties that in sundry combinations and alliances present a twenty-four ballot choice. *Für die Schwachen eine starke Opposition* (For the weak a strong opposition), says the PDS. *Don't worry take Gysi*. There's one that looks like an octagonal traffic sign, lettered white on red, exploiting the similar acronyms of the two parties under attack:

STOP
PDSPDSPDS
STOP

The passion lies in opposition, in the energy applied to daubing over and ripping down other parties' posters. Everywhere they compete for space, mostly trying to block the others out, relying on the repetition of simple messages. *Wir sind die neuen PDS*. The CDU: *Wir sind ein Volk*. The DBD (Farmers): *Brot für das Volk*. Bündnis 90: *Bürger für Bürger*. And from the NDPD, the new Nazis: *Für die Deutsche Zukunft*.

Another day of wandering, down into the city: the usual wind across the great wide spaces, the television tower leaning into the sky, shoppers, lunchers, tourists, people queuing at a bookshop, crowding the Imbiss stalls, walking in the sunshine, Vietnamese shivering in their thin clothes, exotic groups of Africans, Chinese, plain Russians. Over from the West, the Hare Krishnas in their robes, offering their own brand of monotony. Yesterday it was the Sally Army. On the Marx and Engels statues there are stickers: *Der Bär ist rot* (The bear is red), meaning Berlin is red, and will vote red. Elsewhere, everywhere: *Don't worry, take Gysi*. By the S-Bahn entrance a stall is selling fruit and salad vegetables for Westmarks, expensive, but there are buyers, who choose carefully and examine their goods and their change. A man is giving away copies of *Horizont*. Inside the S-Bahn a couple of stalls have set up, each selling the same goods – balloons, the West *Berliner Morgenpost*, rub-off lottery tickets. People crowd around, cutting from one stall to the other as if expecting some difference in either, inspecting the *Morgenpost*, but at 3 Ostmarks they don't buy. There's more interest in the lottery.

Towards the border the road runs out of ideas, ending in Wall, broken through. In the strip by Kommandantenstrasse they're laying sewer pipes. The border is abandoned by its guards, the watchtowers vandalized, everything broken, light-bulbs, search-light, windows, wiring ripped out. Inside the watchtower, metal ladders go straight up the four flights, four concrete boxes one on top of another. The ruins of a metal desk and chair, broken glass, the angry leavings of thirty years watching the border, cold in winter, hot in summer, boring in every season. On the wall in pencil a soldier has written *Heinz von Rostock 23/5/86*.

At Potsdamer Platz they're digging ditches and laying drains in the death strip, preparing the ground for the coming of

Daimler-Benz. Teams of workmen from East and West are at work, the Easterners Vietnamese, the Westerners Turks, both supervised by Germans. On the Eastern side of the Wall fresh graffiti has sprouted:

> We met inside this tomb.
> We kissed first here.
> I thought we would never part.
> I thought it would never fall.

It is quickly painted out. People wander over from the Western side and into the old death strip, where Coca-Cola cans and broken bottles mark the high water mark of Western invasion. They inspect the mound that's all that's visible of Hitler's bunker, beneath a concrete grille a hole lined with bricks, going down into the ground, the whole of it covered in rabbit droppings. Twilight of the Gods. That's all she wrote.

On Saturday, a week before the election, the party workers made a few brief appearances in Alexanderplatz and at other points around the city, flying pickets of the faithful getting up the vote. It was all low key, without much enthusiasm on anyone's part, almost as if everyone were embarrassed that this was the first free election their country had ever had, and probably the last. At the Frankfurter Tor for about an hour, coloured umbrellas, stalls, papers, literature, pennants, stickers, flags, muzak, quiet speeches on loudspeakers, but no big guns, no hoopla. The CDU's heavy artillery is concentrated on the heartland, ignoring Berlin, where it doesn't expect to make much headway. Through the morning Alliance, SPD and PDS shadowed each other around the town. It was cool, almost half-hearted, a bearded man handing out leaflets for the Liberals to the passing crowds by the U-Bahn entrance, almost surreptitiously, as if he still expected to be pulled for it. The CDU paper is dominated by BMW ads: *the BMW Party*, someone jokes. By noon it is all over, and the tents and umbrellas have been folded for the weekend, and most of East Berlin has clocked off.

It's as if they'd not yet got the hang of it, as if no one could believe that in a week there really was to be a free election, the first in this part of the universe since 1933, that would vote for unification, as if the fundamental changes that would bring were somewhere far away, across the Wall perhaps. Russia says no united Germany in NATO. It's all remote, here. Over there, Kohl is still embroiled in a row over the Polish border, refusing to acknowledge the Oder/Neisse line, insisting that legally only an all German government can give such an undertaking. Genscher, his Foreign Minister, publicly disagrees. Genscher wants the matter sorted now; Kohl is placating his own right wing, and in particular the *Bund der Vertriebenen*, the Federation of the Expelled. The Bund, a highly vocal and effective pressure group formed in 1950, represents the 12 million-plus Germans who were expelled from the eastern provinces after the war, mainly from Silesia, Pomerania and East Prussia, now part of Poland and Russia. Zbigniev Herbert: 'The dictators wheeled my country west on a wheelbarrow.' Of those expelled, 3 million went to the East, 9 million to the West, where they are vociferous in demanding the return of their lost lands in the East. In the West the Bund overlaps with the Republican Party, the neo-Nazis, whom Kohl fears may cross the magic threshold of 5 per cent of the vote in the December elections, giving them representation in the Bundestag. The Poles protest. In reply, Kohl demands they give up all claim to reparations, which they did back in 1953, and guarantee the rights of Polish citizens of German descent, already guaranteed by treaty. Eventually the rest of Europe, alarmed by the prospect of renewed German territorial ambitions, Poland, Czechoslovakia, Russia and America and especially Genscher, get him to back down. The Bundestag says the borders aren't in question, and up there in the distant May of the future Weizsäcker will go to Poland to do what clumsy Kohl couldn't and say sorry about the war, and say it again on the site of the Warsaw Ghetto. Here in March, Modrow attacks Bonn's ambiguity over Poland.

But here in the street they don't much care about Poland, and just want to be part of the West. They're worried about their own future. They can't see that everyone else in Europe gets anxious when the border posts of the debatable place we call Germany start moving. East and West they say they'll be safe inside Europe, and they won't go crazy and declare war on everyone again, they know better now, schooled in the democratic procedures of the Federal Republic. And what is the East schooled in? Here they say: why not? But there's the imponderable to ponder: the critical mass of 80 million

Germans. No one around here is predicting the future. Here people are anxious about other issues: jobs, homes, cost of living, the impact of the West. They're trying to unravel it from its TV images. They don't know yet what to be afraid of but the West is coming, and there's a sense of foreboding about. The heavy totalitarian ice has left people numb; most of them, the majority of the population under forty years old, have never known anything else, were educated in the traditions of privation and struggle, acceptance that those on high knew best and weren't to be questioned. They're trained to keep their heads down. Many express resentment at the West: why did they have to pay so hard for World War II? Many complain they feel like second-class citizens in their own country: 'Everything is for Westerners.' They feel looked down on by West Germans, and looked down on by their Eastern neighbours, who regarded them through the years as the poor Germans, the inferior Germans. They know their country is disintegrating quickly, and they feel impotent to do anything about it. Everyone has to start looking out for themselves, they shrug. It's a hard world. They feel they can't do much about their fate, and they're right: their fate is being decided elsewhere.

Out on the streets everyone seems young, married or about to be, young parents with their children wearing their Sunday best. Their styles are relentlessly proletarian, blue-jeaned or formally old-fashioned: men in suits, women in ruffles and flounced skirts, their hair up, rouged and heavily made up. They are tender and attentive with their children, holding them, hugging them, touching them. Yet it's as if everyone here were from some vast council estate on the outskirts of Hull or Bolton or Gateshead, the people who used to shop at the Co-op and went on coach trips to Morecambe Bay. They have been reared in proletarian traditions, and excluded from bourgeois influence. They are the workers of the GDR, unambitious, content with a small circle of acquaintances, with simple sports and pleasures, with alcohol, with a gamble. Or not content, as it turned out. The place has the feel of a toytown turned hideous, an anti-Disneyland with the same child-centred, childlike mentality. Anyone else, managers, administrators, go to different recreations elsewhere. The old appear to live somewhere else. All the others, with any aspiration to escape conformity and poverty, have fled. Those left have a pallor, a thin pinched look from lack of vitamins, the look of people underfed and overburdened.

They seem beaten and weary, and if they're not visibly excited about their election, that may be old habit, or just that they don't know how to behave on such an occasion. Politics has been poisoned here; everyone talks about freedom, but that's what the old regime talked about for forty years, forever moving the carrot of prosperity up the stick. Everyone here is careworn – not the new flashy working class of the West who have what these people covet, but the old and permanently impoverished proletariat of the big cities forever hovering on the edge of oblivion. Theirs is an older tradition, by-passed by the winds of change and the *Wirtschaftswunder*, led down a side alley into one of evolution's dead ends. Their tradition, reflected by the ruling ideology and the regime whom it suited, has concentrated them on domestic life and the family, and where all public life was *terra incognita*, and dangerous, people turned inward, did carpentry and tended tomatoes on their balconies. On every flat, by the window or on the balcony, a little six-inch pipe in which to stick the flagstaff on days of great speeches and parades. Getting married and having babies was how you got a better flat, and bigger benefits, so you worked with your work brigade, stayed in your cadre, lived at home with your family, and didn't have much of a neighbour-hood, producing the next generation to be nurtured in socialism. The tradition of early marriage was matched by a high divorce rate; there was also a high suicide rate and high rates of mental illness. It didn't work out. Now there's a new generation that takes the struggles of the past for granted, and wants what the West has, can't see why it should sacrifice and struggle any more.

Ossis, they're called over there, who go West with little money and disrupt the orderly lives of West Berliners, blocking the pavements, staring at the shops, filling the trains and the buses. The West is a great supermarket, a glitter of expensive lights along the Ku'damm, everything they can't afford. In the KaDeWe they blink at the heaps of food, the delicacies, the cheeses, lobsters, crabs, tanks of live fish, sides of beef, crates of wine. West Berliners will say, now they've made up their minds how they feel about them, that those left behind are those without the gumption to get out, the dumb and the daft and the backward and the scared, forming a great inert mass, the residue, the lumpen, and the Party faithful. Here the intellectuals talk of what might have been, but the workers have voted with their feet.

From here the West looks distant, unbelievably rich and wasteful, with an over-abundance of choices that no one here can afford. 'What's wrong with my Trabi?' Friedemann asks. 'It gets me there.' In the centre of town every day a Western firm delivers fruit and vegetables to the Centrum store, pineapples and bananas and oranges and Fanta and Coca-Cola for sale at Western prices in Ostmarks, but it is all unbearably expensive. Here there's too little, and too little choice, the same shops selling the same products: one kind of everything, and not always that, a pile of battered apples, tasteful arrangements of whatever is in. This week it's lemons and kiwi fruit. There's not much point going further down the road in hope of choice; there the choice will be the same, and by the time you get there there won't be any left. Only at the Delikat, more expensive and therefore for a higher class of earner, is there imported tinned fruit, Polish Krakus, imported sausage, more choice of cheese.

Over in the other half of the city crime is reported up by 8 per cent in the first quarter of the year. Shoplifting is up 50 per cent, and shoplifters are now prosecuted straight away to prevent their disappearance back East. In mid-April the new head of the West German Federal Criminal Office, the BKA, reported that while criminal activity had never been much in the East because there was little to steal, since the *Durchbruch* it had come down by a third. He said drug use was on the rise, and that the East was already a transit station for stolen vehicles between West Germany and Poland. And spying continued as before; in Bonn as he spoke another Stasi operative was arrested, a month beyond the elections. Berlin, he said, could easily become a crime centre, with crime spreading to Eastern Europe and the GDR – with Berlin the transit station – in the middle. In West Berlin work on the side was increasing, with more and more illegal employment of foreigners. The main activity continued to be smuggling. In March GDR customs confiscated 4.5 million Ostmarks being smuggled into the country. In the same month GDR customs prevented the smuggling out of 1.5 tons of herbs, 5 tons of meat, 3.8 tons of chocolates and sweets,

3,040 pairs of shoes, 3,822 pieces of underwear, and 5,218 cosmetic items. Items smuggled in to the GDR include cigarettes, pocket calculators, pullovers and scrap copper.

Over there the number of refugees coming from countries other than the GDR is still increasing, from Poland, Romania, Czechoslovakia, Russia. In the first three months of the year over 43,000 arrived, and it's estimated that between 160,000 and 180,000 will have arrived by the end of the year. As it gets more difficult to get in to West Germany, large sums of money are being paid to escape organizations: false documents and organization cost up to DM 20,000. More than a million Poles have visited this year. 26,000 of them were caught smuggling goods in, and this was considered a small proportion. They bring furs, caviar, alcohol, cigarettes, black market currency. More and more are coming by charter bus, and these now include Russians who fly to Warsaw and take the bus to Berlin. Other Russians arrive in cars, stocking them up and going back. Behind the state library the Polenmarkt still flourishes; over one weekend at the end of March the police arrested more than 200 Poles for illegal trading, and confiscated 200,000 cigarettes, alcohol, and hundreds of 20-zloty coins. About the same size as one Deutschmark, they fit West German slot machines. Police counted 30,000 people on the market, and claimed 25,000 of them were traders. The Polish influx is heavy around Savignyplatz, along Kantstrasse and Joachimstaler Strasse, where shopkeepers are complaining of the emergence of a second Polish market, with much Import/Export concentrating on Polish customers. They mostly buy electronics, video recorders and television sets; the assumption is that having taken them through to East Berlin, where 14 per cent VAT plus customs duty are refunded leaving the country, they bring a lot of them back for resale. In April the Berlin Senate called for the reimposition of visa conditions on Polish citizens, and the Justice department began sentencing illegal traders immediately, confiscating the goods, and stamping their passports to prevent re-entry to West Berlin.

In the West there are more and more demands for changes in policy towards settlers and the closure of the emergency refugee camps. But the government doesn't want to close them, because at least this way they regulate the flow of resettlers and distribute them throughout the country. Berlin's Senator for Social Affairs said she would not build a new wall and leave the settlers waiting outside it, and that she won't close the transit camps. In mid-March Bonn was talking cuts in welfare and social services for resettlers. Oskar Lafontaine wanted to close the camps and stop all benefit, and there was support from various provincial governments in the West, and from Democracy Now and other groups in the East. On 20 March they announced the end of benefits for refugees from the GDR and the closure of the reception centres by 1 July.

So that was to be Day X.

On both sides of the border attitudes to foreigners are hardening. Now that fundamental changes have taken place in Eastern Europe, Bonn wants to re-examine the status of refugees from those countries. In the West about 700,000 refugees would be affected and might lose their status. The Government in the East announced that there would be a new law on refugees and foreigners. Both sides are tightening the bolts. This year so far almost 2,000 non-German refugees have come to West Berlin. In West Berlin there are 270,000 foreigners living in the city. Many fear the future, and fear that once Germany is united they will be deported. Many have noticed a change in attitudes towards foreigners since 9 November, a new hostility, especially from Easterners. In West Berlin 40 per cent of refugees are Vietnamese, plus Romanians, Angolans, Poles, Libyans and Indians. In the East a ministry report concluded that a large number of young people in the GDR are hostile to foreigners and are right-wing radicals. A quarter of all students and apprentices are opposed to foreigners, and one fifth want the Germany of 1937, though in the same study 60 per cent express fear of fascism. In the East the stereotypes are: Poles buy everything, Africans take our jobs and Cubans molest our women. In April Hanoi announced it would send no more workers to Eastern Europe this year. It's estimated that the 60,000 Vietnamese workers in the GDR support about a million Vietnamese back home. The government announced that there will be no more foreign workers this year, and GDR firms were said to be trying to get rid of those they have. Most of them will work out their contracts and be sent home.

Refugees who fail to get in to West Germany end up in East Berlin, where they try to get an immigration visa for the GDR, in anticipation of its incorporation into the FRG. Many Romanian gypsies, entire families, began living in the station at

Lichtenberg. Eastern Europeans who have been living in the GDR are applying for citizenship in growing numbers. Many who have been living there for years now want to become East Germans, so they will then become citizens of the Federal Republic.

Meanwhile in the GDR army morale was collapsing, and there was a wave of desertions. Many conscripts were applying to do alternative community service, under a new law, making it optional to work in hospitals or old people's homes as an alternative to military service. The Volksarmee was to be cut from 170,000 to 70,000, and might even be disbanded. The West German Bundeswehr announced they would accept no officers or NCOs from the Volksarmee. Stasi secrets were still unravelling. And dark graves from the past began to open: on 26 March the *Berliner Zeitung* reported the discovery of a mass grave near Neubrandenburg where thousands of Nazi collaborators, SS and army were massacred by the NKVD after World War II. Days later a second mass grave was uncovered in woods near Oranienburg, then a third in woods north of Berlin, and then another near Bautzen, a former Nazi prison taken over by the Russians. It was estimated that up to 96,000 former Wehrmacht and SS, together with civilians including children, had died in these camps, of hunger, sickness, on forced marches, or by execution, in the immediate post-war years. At Buchenwald and Sachsenhausen the NKVD had simply moved in behind the Nazis. Stalin's terror was intended to cow the rest of the population, and at the same time eliminate former Nazis, Hitler Youth, anti-Communists, priests, intellectuals, and anyone suspected of hostile sentiments. The net was wide, and many were swept up in it, including many young people. This then was the condition on which the GDR was founded: terror. In some relief from direct terror, the GDR's own system of security and intimidation seemed milder, but the Stasi simply took over where the Russians left off. From Dresden came reports that between 1952 and 1960 Ulbricht's regime had secretly guillotined sixty-two political prisoners in the former Nazi execution chamber there, false death certificates were made out, and the remains cremated.

Don't worry, take Gysi, the sticker says, as if he were Alka

Seltzer. His face is everywhere, in the newspaper parachuting from a plane, on the flywork on the walls, staring out of a poster at the street's end, frank, challenging, arms folded, in steel-rimmed glasses, a business suit, a man who looks as if he means business: the Gorbachov model. The bankruptcy manager, *Bild* calls him. Gregor Gysi, Chairman of the PDS, successors to the SED, the former bleak mean-minded masters of the GDR, invites the voters to vote for him. Another version of him is a cartoon drawing of his face, cheeky, daring, in red scarf and black peaked cap, round glasses, a direct look: the face of a clown, a Groucho Marx without the moustache, and not at all the face of a man expecting defeat. The polls give his party 17 per cent, but his face in the posters wears an endearing sort of look, as if daring voters to trust him after all, with his brown eyes and receding dark hairline: the human face of socialism here at last, perhaps. At the end of the street someone has added a Hitler moustache to his poster, arms folded, staring out at the passing citizenry. It doesn't suit him.

Gysi sees rents, pensions and the workplace in danger, the West moving in fast, and points to the achievements of the GDR. What he wants is a party *mit Idealen*, with ideals. A laywer, he has a long record of defending dissidents and conscientious objectors, and was instrumental in getting New Forum legalized. He also breeds cattle. He has no political background, and is not part of the party apparatus. In public he is sharp, witty, ironic. What he wants is to retain the sovereignty of the GDR, and its main industries in public ownership, and hang on to the welfare net, and he warns that the East may lose everything it has gained since October to the West. He accepts the inevitability of unification, but wants it to evolve slowly. And with great care. He sees the party's role in opposition to force the SPD to pursue social democratic policies, and says good riddance to the careerists who have left the party. By all accounts he is a shrewd politician, who foresees a role for himself in a united Germany; he has an eye on Bonn and beyond it Strasbourg. For Gysi the party isn't over.

The party turned out to be in a bar, Petra's Bierbar, in Gubener Strasse behind Marchelewskistrasse. It was a pleasant bar, stereo good enough to sing to, dance to, talk through. In a small room to one side was food: sausage, ham, pork, cheese, bread. At the bar the booze was free to members of the wedding party, mostly young working folks, friends of bride or groom or both. At the back a large room where people sat at tables, drinking. About two-thirds of the bar were regulars, though the borders between were blurred and there was a lot of mixing, a lot of good humour. The general object of the evening was to get drunk, and having got drunk, sad. 'We rely on this,' Tim says, waving his glass. 'Mud in your eye, Tim.' The bar was full. And there he was: Gysi, perched on a high stool at the bar's end, jammed in the long corner with his back to the wall, with a steady drink supply coming, not looking worried at all. He was talking, listening, using his hands, face, shoulders, the whole of his short stumpy body listening, his ears cocked, his dark eyes making contact. Tonight he was Dad, out at his son's wedding party, some weeks after the event, with his own father and other members of his family, relaxing, exactly one week before the election. As on the posters it was a big square face that dealt chin out with the world it encountered; the blue stubbled outthrust jaw and receding hairline was a Bob Hope sort of face, a Hubert Humphrey or a Jack Lemmon. It was a face always in motion, talking animatedly with whoever got to him, argumentative, attentive, sharp. When listening his wide mouth curved upwards in a boomerang of a smile. It was the face of a man who found pleasure in argument, in talk, in people, in interaction. He was relaxed, out in the world, with no security, no minder. He was still a politician. No apparatchik, he moved like a boxer, like a Chicago bar-room politico.

The bar filled some more. To drink there was wine, beer on tap or by bottle, for other choices a row of bottles labelled with their prices on the top shelf beyond the row of red shaded lights: sundry liquors, several Korns, Stolichnaya, Cinzano, Kirsch, Korona Sekt, Rotkäppchen. On the stainless steel bar top, stickers from Dubai, the Karachi Sheraton Hilton. Flowers, a pile of wrapped presents. On the pine-clad wall behind the bar a selection of beer mats, mostly from West Berlin and West Germany, some from Bavaria. Presiding over all, Petra. She poured drinks where she would, efficiently and rapidly, between chain-smoked cigarettes, favouring whom she chose with glances from her deep dark long-lashed eyes, sparkling under heavy camouflage, and moving sinuously between her two young bartenders. From time to time she entered into long confabs with Gysi across the bar in his corner, touching, patting his shoulder. Whatever she was saying to him, it mattered to her. And to him.

She was a large woman, Petra: what men call generous, ample in the hills and valleys of her body. Perhaps fifty, she was clearly *eine lustige Frau* who enjoyed all the pleasures life had afforded her. She moved like a great snake, like an anaconda, the blue silk of her mighty brassière flashing when she raised her arms as she did, from time to time, to some section of the music, twisting her body in a belly dance, the promise of total sensual eclipse. Her long hair up in combs, Cleopatra in her make-up and with much cheap jewellery about her, in her leather apron she was the captain of her ship, no man's woman, a Mother Courage under whose direction the evening proceeded noisily towards oblivion.

From time to time cameras flashed, some for the family occasion, some to be seen with Gysi, who hammed it up, posed, put on a toothy mock smile, twinkled his fingers. Perhaps one of the cameras was his, perhaps one was hired by the bar. The hired photographer was having a hard time of it. His girlfriend, a tiny girl in black wearing black stockings that laddered into shreds as the evening went on, was getting fighting drunk. From time to time she went off into the side room to sulk or weep, where he would try to humour her, kneeling at her feet, appealing, pointing out that he was working. But then, in time, he was drunk too. People danced in the small space available. For the regulars, Gysi was in important visitor, his trips to the toilet through the bar and the backroom a long detour of handshakes, argument, drinks, autographs. Some were for him, some against him, but he was popular, unafraid, diving into his objectors. Engrossed in listening, he was about to light a cigarette the wrong way round, but he spotted that too. Petra put up more drink, and then Gysi was talking across the bar to his father, whom Petra had brought round the bar for just such a purpose, to the corner Gysi had jammed himself into. Someone was saying the old man, Klaus, had been ambassador to Rome, a Minister for Culture, for Education, Under-Secretary for Church Matters, high in the Party once, but had fallen from grace with Honecker years ago. Nothing further. Hans wanted to talk, to say 'Now we are free. Now we can speak what we want, write what we want.' His flat in Köpenick has four rooms, for himself, his wife, two children, he says. 'Four persons, four rooms. Not enough.' As a skilled typesetter he earns 1,250 marks a month on *Neues Deutschland*. Divide by three for Deutschmarks at the official rate. Divide by three again for pounds, by two for dollars. 'Not enough.' Then, suddenly, he said, 'The Wall is open, so is the CIA,' and turned away and said no more, and proceeded to get morosely drunk.

Then Gysi was bartender behind the bar, Petra and the barmen leaving him to it as he put up beers, poured Sekt, cracked jokes, pressed more flesh, more points, dropping his hands flat on the bar top, hunched forward, listening, like a baker, like a tradesman, bargaining. The cameras were out again, Petra retired to some corner of her own to smoke, and then she was back as he went into a signing session, with the flash bulbs popping. Underneath was a shy man, who'd taught himself courage. Or a joker, out at the end of his rope, but with still a trick or two up his sleeve. And then he was through clowning and had had enough politicking, and he was out on the floor dancing with Lucky, with whom he was clearly enamoured. What Gysi wanted to do now was dance.

The evening closed as everywhere, with tears from the girl in the shredded black stockings, her boyfriend going off in a huff with his equipment, and a couple of fights in the backroom, sudden eruptions of broken glass and toppled furniture that in the end came to nothing. Gysi's son was the centre of one of them, but whether the row was over politics or women was never clear. The words were the same by this side of the *betrunken* evening. The cellarman came up from below to double as referee, a tough young tiger whose head jerked back and forth between each accusation. And there was Petra, circling, circling, staring them down, patting them gently towards the door and out into the night. Her look said it was time for everyone to go, with one more drink, one more tape, before everyone staggered off into the night. Outside the town was quiet, with little traffic, most of it taxis, the rarest of night buses. And dark. The East is dark, and goes to bed early. Down in Alexanderplatz there's no one about, just the nightingales beginning to sing, calling to each other across the great spaces, from the dark trees and the roofs of the sleeping apartments.

Then came the election, a breezy warm Sunday, with everyone out about the city centre, Easterners, Westerners, tourists,

Russians, Asians, Africans, Vietnamese looking puzzled by it all, a Western yuppie with a portable phone calling Earth. For sale ice-cream, *Bratwurst*, beer, balloons, lottery tickets. By the PDS building the faithful, attending the speeches relayed outside, pressing into the building. More sausage, beer, the air of an impromptu beer garden, with music, an incongruous stall selling glassware and vases. At the House of Democracy on Friedrich-strasse, offices to the other parties, supporters came and went. More music, Sekt in reserve. Whatever else, the GDR is on holiday, celebrating its demise. On Karl-Liebknecht-Strasse a couple bearing rough hewn wooden crosses, their faces painted with ashes, their clothing covered in assorted election posters, dragging rattling chains from their ankles, walk through the press. By the Neue Wache under the noses of the still goosestep-ping sentries two men argue fiercely, one for, one against unification; 'Intelligentsia' says the man who's all for it and spits. Under the television tower a harmonica band playing popular airs, a face painter, a group in the costumes of jugglers and clowns waiting to do their act. In Alexanderplatz a rock concert given by Stuyvesant: *Come Together*, heavy metal, leather and chains, the crowd not visibly moved, at the front a few fists raised, some feet stamping, scattered applause when the set's over. *We are the children, the ones left behind.* That evening, all over town, parties awaiting the count, supporters preparing for victory or drowning the sorrows of defeat.

Then it was over, and the vote counted a victory for the Alliance, with 48 per cent of the vote on over 90 per cent turnout in an electorate of 12 million. The SPD took 21 per cent, and went into a massive sulk; the PDS polled 16 per cent, and were quite pleased. The CDU with 42.5 per cent was the largest party in the Volkskammer. In Berlin, where the CDU had little following, the vote was for the SPD and PDS. Through-out the GDR only 10 per cent of the workers voted for the PDS, and 59 per cent for the Alliance. In retrospect the landslide looked inevitable, the result almost an anti-climax, given Kohl's capture of the popular cry for unification, and the sense, day by day, that the GDR had no future. After the election German–German talks on unity and aid and currency union went swiftly forward. The pending contracts were swiftly signed. The vote had been for a quick unification, and for the early demise of the GDR.

The Alliance immediately began seeking a coalition with the SPD, but the SPD wasn't having any of the third Alliance partner, the DSU; there had been electoral punch-ups and dirty play in the campaign. The Alliance parties refused Kohl's demand that they form a parliamentary bloc based on their electoral alliance. They were seeking coalition, for while they had enough votes together to form a government, what they were after was a 66 per cent majority in the Volkskammer to carry out constitutional changes, and so effect unification. Many of the new politicians were without experience, most of them formerly branded dissidents, priests, lawyers, doctors, farmers. After the election Kohl appeared to want to slow the pace down, and hedged on the exchange rate. For two weeks, till 3 April, the haggling continued, till the SPD changed its mind and agreed to talk coalition; by then its leader Ibrahim Böhme had resigned, firmly denying Stasi involvement. For three weeks after the election the horse-trading between the parties continued, hindered by accusations against Lothar de Maizière and others. Finally a cabinet was announced on 11 April, formed of a coalition of the Alliance parties, the SPD, and the Liberals. De Maizière was Prime Minister. The new government announced it would pursue speedy reunification under Article 23. By now the exodus to the West had slowed to some 700 a day. As to Day X, in early April the Bundesbank proposed an exchange rate of 1/2, with only personal savings to 2,000 marks at 1/1. As the Volkskammer met for its first session a massive demonstration took place outside, of Berliners demanding 1/1. People protested that Kohl had promised in the campaign a straight exchange of all money at par; when it came to it, no one could point to where he'd actually said it, though somehow that impression had been reached. Insecurity increased. Protective measures were being taken on both sides. Before its demise the Modrow Government had passed a law giving Easterners the right to buy the houses they lived in; on the other side, because of overcrowding, entry to West Berlin universities was restricted for GDR citizens, and student loans for those studying in the West but living in the East were halved. The lines were drawn.

Lucky stirs her coffee. 'Poor Deutschland,' she says. '*Armes Deutschland. Die Deutschen sind dumm; eine Wahl für Coca-Cola, für Bananen.*' She herself voted Green. She straightens out the wrappers from her sugar cubes. They advertise the zoo: *Paradies für Tiere* (Paradise for animals). She is gloomy at the prospects. Now there will be no alternative to the West. It's all over. Across the street a man is patiently scraping off election posters, flaking the strips into the wind. '*Tschüss*,' Lucky says, leaving for work. '*Tschüss*.' It sounds like a kiss.

18

ENDS, BEGINNINGS

By late March at Checkpoint Charlie they were dismantling the section of Wall dividing Zimmerstrasse from its pavement, working their way up towards the team working down by night from the Brandenburg Gate. Peter will have a few disturbed nights as the machinery grinds down the Wall, and then a new view of the world: the sandy death strip, riddled with malice and poison, and the pockmarked grey buildings opposite, on the other side, that will soon be no more than they ever were: the other side of the street.

At the end of March Momper and Krack, the mayors of the two cities of Berlin, were to have planted thirty trees along the Wall between Otto-Grotewohl-Strasse and the Brandenburg Gate. By then Krack had resigned, accused of corruption, and in the event the first trees were planted by East and West Berlin police. In April East Berlin demanded a stop to the tree-planting, pointing out that the use of the land had not yet been determined: it was still their territory. The East was negotiating on its own behalf with West German and foreign firms wanting to build in the border areas in the centre. In West Berlin plans for green areas and an autobahn along the Wall were shelved; on the Western side the border area was to be divided into fifty sections, and planning suggestions worked out independently.

The trade in the Wall continued, continues, by the peckers along it, and overall by Limex, its distribution in little pieces around the planet, and maybe, maybe not, they'll keep a bit here for a memento of the bitter years. At Christmas, President Bush had quipped that the hammer and sickle had been replaced by the hammer and chisel. On 17 March the first three of more than 200 segments of Wall were auctioned in West Berlin at the

Hotel Intercontinental; the rest were to be auctioned at Easter in Monte Carlo, the profits to the GDR health service. In what a Senate spokesman termed an unparalleled lack of taste, an Eastern advertising agency proposed keeping a 1,000-metre stretch to put billboards on. Soon after the formation of a government, de Maizière announced that the Wall would be levelled completely in the next months, and at the end of May announced the complete opening of the city by 2 July and invited Western firms to help demolish the Wall in return for the sections they took down. Goodbye Wall. It was now a matter of time, a disposal problem. The West's traffic authority anticipated rejoining some 150 roads within the city; fifteen new bridges would have to be built. As of the beginning of the summer vacation, passports would no longer be checked and the border guards would become redundant. Goodbye border guards. By July the border was to be completely open. Down in the south the fence was ripped down, mostly by children; at first the East posted guards, then gave up, and then the fence was flat. Just beyond the perimeter of the city, suburban West Berliners began encountering their new neighbours in quiet farming villages, out in the country.

And goodbye death strip. In April ten tons of lupin seeds were distributed on it, covering about 50 kilometres; yellow lupins are said to improve the quality of the soil, and decontaminate it. A Marlborough hoarding appeared on the Eastern wall at Checkpoint Charlie. A border guard's booth at the Brandenburg Gate was converted to a postcard stall. Plans were announced to open Hitler's bunker in the death strip at Potsdamer Platz to historians from East and West. A two-storey underground shelter built during World War II and partly blown up after, much of it was believed to be underwater. It turned out that the rabbit warren mound visible in the death strip was all that remained not of the bunker itself, but of its laundry. There was anxiety that the bunker might become a place of fascist pilgrimage, and from the East came a proposal for a historic mile between the former Gestapo HQ on Prinz-Albrecht-Strasse and Voss Strasse, incorporating the bunker. Others wanted it levelled. As with the Wall, the past is difficult to come to terms with hereabouts. In preparations for a performance of Pink Floyd's *The Wall* in the death strip in late July, another bunker was discovered nearby, said to be that of Hitler's bodyguards, four low rooms containing rotting wooden benches, empty bottles, gas masks, a wooden leg, and three large wall paintings, depicting the SS in heroic poses, with eagles, lightning flashing from their eyes.

Old traumas surfacing in the torchlight. And new ones: widespread insecurity in the East as to unemployment, the final rate of currency exchange, the switch to Western levels of social welfare benefits, the end of subsidies, jerking the GDR suddenly into the late twentieth century from 1952, where it and its prices had been frozen. East Berliners continued to feel like the poor cousins of West Berliners, who for their part felt they were being made to pay the costs of Kohl's rhetoric. On both sides, growing crime rates, growing violence. The new Nazis were making their presence known, performing much like old Nazis, long latent nightmares resurfacing, violent atavistic dreams. After forty years the same symbols and the same slogans re-appeared. After so many years of hope and struggle and separa-tion, after the drama of the opening, came anti-climax.

With some urgency both cities were developing future scenar-ios, anticipating the city's rapid growth, forced suddenly to deal with many urgent problems. The focus of attention on both sides was the central land of the border, the death strip and its environs. In the West the Senator for Construction said there would be no Manhattan on the Spree; the Ku'damm and Tau-entzienstrasse were out. The areas for development were Kreuz-berg and Wedding. In the city the prime locations were to be Potsdamer Platz, Potsdamer Strasse, Kurfürstenstrasse, Friedrich-strasse, Kochstrasse and Stresemannstrasse. Momper announced that Potsdamer Platz was to become the centre of the city again, and outlined a city planning competition for the development of the area around it and into Leipziger Strasse in the East, construction to begin in 1992. Daimler-Benz would be written into it. They were likely to become the dominant factor in the area, the heart of the heart of the new Germany, and East Berlin complained they had not been consulted when, after the opening, Daimler-Benz had begun negotiating for the site. *Carpe diem.* In the Senate the coalition was split, the Alternative List pressing for more concessions from the company.

The city rejoined itself. In March plans were announced to reopen all the closed U-Bahn stations in the centre of Berlin by the end of September, the first at Bernauer Strasse on 12 April.

In their years of separation the two parts of the city had developed different standards. In East Berlin, where the policy was to house workers close to factories, drawing heat and hot water from them, and never mind the pollution, the zoning laws were incompatible with the West's. Building regulations weren't standardized in both parts of the city. The guidelines for traffic, sewage, electricity and telephone lines were different. Between East and West Berlin there were only 460 lines West to East, seventy-two East to West.

In March the formation of a postal union was announced, with a DM 5 million investment to double the number of telephones in the GDR, and to improve communications between East and West Berlin. The West Berlin authority installed more telephone boxes near border crossings. But by the end of June plans were confidently announced that a computerized telephone system would be worked out for the whole of Berlin by the end of the year. Letter traffic was to be speeded up, and in May the postal services of West and East began savings and giro services, transactions in Deutschmarks. Talks began between East and West on merging their police forces and abolishing all border controls. In the East Marx-Engels-Platz changed its name back to the Lustgarten, and the future of Ho-Chi-Minh-Strasse lay in some doubt. There was a long list of such names to be changed; in Karl-Marx-Stadt a referendum in April voted to change its name back to Chemnitz. The past was rapidly being wiped out, the maps redrawn, and in the East each new innovation came as a novelty. The newspapers quadrupled their prices, their ads and job vacancies by now familiar. On 17 April DDR TV, now called Deutscher Fernsehfunk – DFF – broadcast its first commercials. In mid-June the station's independence ceased, and it was absorbed into the two Western stations. Friedemann was out of work.

In March the Berlin Senate proposed a new *Land Berlin-Brandenburg* with its capital in Potsdam, as part of discussions to reorganize the conurban area. Others proposed Berlin as *Land* and Federal capital. There were now 'Capital scenarios', and speculation as to Berlin again becoming the capital of a unified Germany. The project director of West Berlin's Institute for City Research and Structural Policy looked into his crystal ball and produced a scenario predicting rapid growth over the next twenty years. By 2010, he said, the population would increase by 25 per cent as traditional patterns of immigration from the East, interrupted by forty years of the Cold War, resumed. Within the GDR Berlin would be comparatively richer, a magnet for the many unemployed to be. The housing shortage would continue to be chronic. Traffic would increase, forcing industry and housing development out into the suburbs; side by side with high unemployment there would be a lack of skilled workers, but Berlin would be the only place in Germany where Western technology and Eastern skills could be quickly matched. The city, a key waiting in a locked door for forty years, was the forward base of the hoped-for second economic miracle, destined to become industrially and financially significant due to its position in relation to the whole of Eastern Europe. The plan envisaged Berlin becoming the capital; otherwise it would not survive, and would be swamped and absorbed into the East, shorn of its privileges as a Cold War fortress. There were those who wanted to retain Bonn, especially those in Bonn, and there were those who wanted to split federal institutions between Berlin and Bonn; there were proposals to put the President's office and diplomatic missions in Berlin, or the upper house in Berlin and the lower in Bonn, with other government agencies split. By the end of June the mayors of the two cities had begun a campaign to have Berlin declared the capital, with the presidency, the parliament and all the ministries. And there were those who foresaw what Berlin as a capital would imply – the huge security apparatus presently concentrated on Bonn would descend, and with it all a new solemnity and gravitas in a place otherwise still pleasant to be. And there were those in the East who pointed to the Stasi buildings and shrugged: here was office space. Others, mindful of the past, speculated that with the re-establishment of the five *Länder* in the East, and their integration into Germany, there would then be sixteen separate assemblies and state administrations, providing a persuasive argument for centralism. In West Berlin Michaele Schreyer, Senator for city planning, announced plans to develop the city, retaining green belts running into the centre, developing industry along the ring roads. She said Berlin must be integrated into the rest of Germany, and not again become a centralist capital, dominating every important political, economic and cultural function.

But the CDU in Bonn and big business had their own ideas;

since 9 November property prices and rents in West Berlin had risen by some 30 per cent. After the election unification went into top gear. All the same, in early March an opinion poll in *Die Zeit* showed two-thirds of West Germans would like to slow the reunification process down, and by May a poll by Western television revealed that 86 per cent of their audiences were bored stiff with news about the East. There were many who felt the pace was too fast, and there were too many unknowns in the equation. Truth was, it was all a massive gamble, fraught with the dangers of economic collapse in the East and the resurgence of fascism, and in the West of inflation and a renewed exodus (it had not ceased); to say the least, there would be tax increases. At the end of the gamble there was Kohl, planning to be the first Chancellor of a united Germany, but just now everything hinged on the eventual exchange rate of Ostmarks for Deutschmarks, its effect on the Eastern economy, and the effects of that on the Western. After a period of haggling, offers of 1/2 by Bonn, protests and demonstrations in the East, the rate was finally agreed at the end of April at 1/1 for salaries and pensions and the first 4,000 Ostmarks in savings. Company debts were halved at 1/2. This flew in the face of advice by the Bundesbank, which had favoured 1/2 across the board. Its head, Pöhl, was overruled, and predicted inflation, and said tax increases to fund the regeneration of the East were not ruled out. The Government said they were. Kohl's Finance Minister expressed reservations, but bowed to the imperative of maintaining stability in East Germany. The exchange rate was set, clearly a political decision. Kohl, with an eye to the December elections, was gambling against time and in a hurry, though it was difficult to see how he might have slowed things down in the face of the Eastern economy's collapse. Lafontaine, when asked what he would do, had little practical to suggest. The Government's stated thesis was that the industrial regeneration of the East would come from private investment. Bonds were to be issued 50/50 between *Länder* and Federal Governments to provide DM 95 billion; with savings of DM 20 billion by the withdrawal of subsidies from Berlin and the frontier areas, that would provide DM 115 billion, and DM 12 billion to set up the pensions and unemployment schemes, and beyond lay the unknown costs of cleaning up the Eastern industrial environment. But the huge costs of regenerating the East were still unknown factors in an open equation. To do nothing would be more expensive if not disastrous. In July the total costs were put at DM 120 billion; in July a further DM 10 billion was provided. In present conditions it was believed the Eastern economy would add about 5 per cent to the West German economy, and if it reached the same level of efficiency it would be worth 25 per cent of the whole. With a West German trade surplus in 1989 of DM 115 billion, it was assumed the sums worked out.

And the date was set: Sunday 1 July: *Day X*. When the banks opened that day GDR citizens would have one week to swap their money, and then the Ostmark would cease. The *Staats-vertrag*, the treaty between the FRG and the GDR, was initialled on 18 May, to be ratified by both parliaments, and pass into law on 1 July. There was some haggling, and objections from the SPD East and West, but the terms were set. The treaty determined political relations between the two states, and was the foundation of the currency, social and economic union between them, the first step towards unity under Article 23. It established the market economy in the GDR. Under its provisions as of 1 July the Deutschmark became the official currency, and the GDR gave up financial and economic sovereignty to the Bundesbank. The West German national insurance and pension schemes would be introduced. In effect pensions would go up and net wages down, with an increase of 10 per cent in contributions to pension, unemployment and health schemes. In the exchange of currencies, wages, salaries, student loans, rents, leasings, pensions and maintenance payments would be changed 1/1; all other claims and liabilities at 1/2. The savings of citizens resident in the GDR were set at 1/1 the first 4,000 marks (children up to fourteen, 2,000 marks; citizens over sixty, 6,000 marks) and all further amounts at 1/2.

Thereafter: anybody's guess. In West Berlin speculators bought up Ostmarks and drove the rate firmly from 1/5 to 1/4. The exchange issue would add 14 per cent to the amount of money in circulation; experts disagreed, some predicting a spending boom, fuelling inflation, leading to a rise in interest rates. Others issued bland assurances that the Easterners wouldn't spend all their money at once. Many would buy property. West Berliners groaned at the prospect of a renewed invasion. By now they were inundated not by Ossis, but by Poles flooding in on buses to buy up wholesale the contents of the cheaper supermarkets, Penny Markt and Aldi. Queues stretched round the block, all day, and the shelves were constantly stripped. Berliners at the cheaper end of the market couldn't shop, and Aldi threatened to close down its Berlin outlets. Still supplied from West Germany, they were unable to keep up with the demands. In addition there were other Easterners, Czechs, Romanians, and Russians in fat cars, all hungry. In late May the end of subsidies to West Berlin was announced; they were to be phased out over seven years, the tax advantage, the travel subsidies, the budget deficit, amounting in all to some DM 20 billion per annum. And West Germans were not pleased to discover that as another effect of 1 July, the result of an offer from Kohl to sweeten the Russians, they were to pay DM 1.25 billion for the half year for the upkeep of Soviet forces in the East.

In the GDR unemployment had arrived. The Government itself reckoned that 20 per cent of its industries were non-viable, and with the introduction of West German standards on factory emissions and nuclear safety to come into effect on 1 July, further closures were inevitable. It was estimated that two-thirds of East German industry would collapse, 40 per cent of its businesses. The introduction of a Western economy would bring redundancies, and the preference for Western goods meant Eastern factories were stockpiling and closing down. Goods were piling up in the factories: shoes, Trabis, clothes, electronics, foodstuffs. No one wanted any of it. They wanted the Western variety. So production lines stalled, firms closed, workers were laid off. Various independent institutes forecast that in a workforce of 9 million, unemployment would rise (conservatively) to 1 million, (radically) to 3–4 million. The fact was no one knew what to expect. When the Ossis changed their money into Deutschmarks, would they embark on a great spending spree in the West? Aid of DM 1.2 billion had been granted to help smaller firms, and some might invest their savings and open businesses, but the giants of the West were by now in place. By the end of June, on the eve of monetary union, Berlin's Institute for Economic Research was forecasting unemployment rising to 1.4 million, with a further million on short time, and beyond those figures lay only more question marks. By the end of June it was 142,000: in another two weeks it had risen 70 per cent. The possibility arose of a new exodus, with thousands commuting to work across the border, and up to 400,000 leaving for the West by the end of the year. It was estimated that up to 500,000 had already left this year.

Everywhere in the East there were demonstrations, by farmers whose products were being replaced by slicker Western packaging and variety, by factory workers, by teachers and nursery staff knowing their jobs would go with cuts in child care and welfare services. At the end of May, when the Government announced the end of price subsidies by 2 July, retaining only till the year's end subsidies on rents, energy and transport, the fuse was set to a spiral of huge price rises and wage demands and unemployment. Pay demands were being made for rises of 50 and 100 per cent. With wages in the East one-third of Western levels in the first place, no one was hopeful, and in Berlin the problems were acute.

The easy option was as ever to blame foreigners; the guest workers and new immigrants of the East bore the brunt of it. In the West in late April, amendments to the law for foreigners placed them on a legal footing but made them subject to more supervision and restriction and deportation. A law designed to reassure them made them more vulnerable. In the East the guest workers were first in line for redundancy. The Government began negotiating repatriation with the countries of origin, Mozambique, Angola, Cuba and Vietnam, looking for what it termed a 'humane solution'. But between the idealism of the new politicians and politics as expressed on the street there was a deep gulf. By the end of April 150 firms in the East had applied to lay off 9,000 foreign workers. By now some 3,500 Vietnamese had fled to West Berlin. With refugees now coming in from Eastern Europe and especially Romania, the problem was exacerbated. By the end of May, Romanian Germans were fleeing at the rate of 20,000 a month, many via East Berlin to West Berlin, and 3,000 were now in the GDR. Then the Government barred Romanians without relatives to invite them, and imposed visa controls. But chauvinism, xenophobia and anti-semitism were on the rise.

The events of the *Wende*, which had dramatically changed everything, had passed virtually without violence; now violence was on the streets as insecurity manifested itself in the activities of the right, in organized and random violence. The targets were foreigners, Jews, homosexuals, the left, anyone considered different and 'un-German'; the perpetrators were neo-Nazis, Republicans, skinheads, fascists. Soccer violence was suddenly a new phenomenon. At the end of March four youths walked across a closed bridge into West Berlin, and when challenged by a guard sprayed him with green paint, hit him with chains and ran off into the West. In early April two border guards were attacked and injured near the Brandenburg Gate. The Republicans opened an office and began organizing in Prenzlauer Berg. On 20 April, Hitler's birthday, there were riots in East Berlin following a football game, and in Kreuzberg on the Western side. Skinheads attacked a house occupied by squatters in Prenzlauer Berg, and in Alexanderplatz they attacked police, foreigners, and a café known as a meeting point for homosexuals. Later about 300 people on the Western side tried to cross at Oberbaumbrücke, but were prevented by East and West police; frustrated at not being able to get at the Eastern right, the Western left attacked supermarkets and a petrol station. Kreuzberg, home of the West Berlin riot, was stiffening in response to right-wing threats from across the river; Turkish youths were organizing themselves, and going on the offensive. On both sides riots were becoming more frequent and more frequently violent. Attacks on foreigners and places used by them became commonplace, as did disruption of rallies and demonstrations. On the 28th, following another football game, about 300 neo-Nazis rampaged through central East Berlin. On May Day, though East Berlin was peaceful, there were violent clashes in Leipzig between left-wing and right-wing demonstrators, and twenty-one were detained. At the end of May some 200 skinheads wearing Nazi insignia formed themselves into a human *Hakenkreuz* – a swastika – in Marx-Engels-Platz. At the beginning of June a multinational arts centre, recently opened in empty buildings on the Eastern side of the Wall, was twice attacked by between 100 and 150 neo-Nazis with petrol bombs and iron bars, to cries of *'Ausländer raus'* (Foreigners out). By this time Schönhuber, chairman of the Republican party, had resigned; even for him the party was heading too far to the right and falling into the hands of extremists, he said. In fact in the West German local elections their share of the vote had dropped dramatically. With reunification, much of the Republican thunder had been spent. What was emerging in the East was to the right even further. The Volkspolizei, reported on some occasions to have stood by as foreigners and homo-sexuals were attacked, said East Berlin was the hub of a right-wing renaissance, with a hard core of some 500 and up to 3,000 sympathizers, and back-up from neo-Nazis from the West. There were attacks on Jewish cemeteries. In May the graves of Brecht and Helene Weigel were daubed with anti-semitic slogans. In late June police used tear gas and water cannon to break up a violent anti-fascist demonstration, hurling stones and petrol bombs, outside the offices of the extreme right National Alternative movement. A black Easterner was beaten to death by skinheads because he would not say he was 'not German'.

Tales of the Stasi persisted. The cry for revenge remained strong. Victims surfaced to confront their tormentors and in-formers. In June, *Tageszeitung* published a list of almost 10,000 addresses where the Stasi had spied or recruited. It was rapidly snapped up. The questions remained as to what to do about former Stasi, which to prosecute, where to begin, and what to do with the bulk of them, who must either be reintegrated into the new world or would remain dangerously outside it, exploit-ing its weaknesses. Generally, it was felt they were finished, and what they were up to was smoke across the tracks, but it was widely accepted that Stasi cells had formed in the police and customs, and that they had developed self-help networks. The work of the citizens' control commissions continued; in some cases where they had co-opted former Stasi members to assist them, they still didn't know whether or not files were being smuggled out or tampered with, or whether their activities weren't still being noted. There were still reports of telephone tapping. The atmosphere of suspicion and mistrust persisted. Even as late as July the new mayors of the eleven Berlin districts discovered listening centres in each of their town halls, and telexes still being sent to the Interior Ministry.

In East and West the local elections in May weakened the CDU and Kohl's position, indicating some reservation about the headlong flight to unification. In the East the CDU con-firmed its March victory, though all parties lost ground to smaller groups and specific local issues; there was strong support for the farmers' parties, indicating concern over imports; in East Berlin the CDU came third behind the SPD and PDS. Two weeks later in the West German local and state elections, Kohl lost his majority in the upper house, and Lower Saxony, a former border state, fell to the SPD. Kohl's response was to become more bullish. He announced that the timetable stood, and that the CDU was in favour of early all-German elections, the scheduled West German elections on 2 December to be supplemented by elections in the Eastern *Länder*. De Maizière warned against taking too hasty an approach, but in June the Eastern CDU and the Liberals also called for December all-German elections, with elections to the new *Länder* on 23 September. In acceptance of its inevitability, the Western and Eastern SPD were to unite in the autumn, as were the two CDU and the two Free Democrat parties. There was division on the pace, on both sides, but not much and not for long. In mid-June Eppelmann, GDR Minister for Defence and Disarmament, called for brakes, saying unity should not come till September 1992. But two days later the Volkskammer voted by a large majority to consider merging with West Germany under Article 23, and on the 19th all Government parties East and West agreed to hold all-German elections in December, followed as the polls closed by immediate unification under Article 23. Both governments committed themselves to an Eastern border at the Oder/Neisse. The treaty between the states was ratified by both parliaments. End of June. End of the end.

The major sticking point was Russia, which maintained its objection to the GDR's proposed incorporation into NATO. Russia not being able to do much about it, it seemed unlikely the objection would stand for long, and Kohl was beginning to offer huge loans to buy off Russian objections. Eppelmann, a former conscientious objector who had served time in a military prison, had declared in late April in a joint statement with his Bonn opposite number a commitment to a united Germany, with membership of NATO without troops or equipment on the former territory of the GDR. By then the Volksarmee had fallen from 170,000 to 135,000, with further cuts planned, and possible abolition. However, as one of the four occupying powers, Russia's right to be consulted, and her security, were clear to Eppelmann. The four plus two talks on German unification got under way in early May. There were proposals and offers and a flurry of meetings of NATO and the Warsaw Pact and at the Summit, but these were ducks flapping round a pool. Unification was *de facto*, nowhere more so than in Berlin. As a result of the four plus two, West Berliners were for the first time to be allowed to vote in Federal elections; it was conceded that East Berliners having been enfranchised by the new electoral law to vote for the Volkskammer, the same right should be granted to the Western part of the city. From the end of the year the four-power agreement on Berlin was to come to an end, though Allied troops would remain, not as occupiers and not as part of NATO, so long as Soviet troops remained in the East. In July Gorbachov backed down, agreeing to a united Germany in NATO.

In reality, unification was already in place. By the end of May almost all the planning staffs of East Berlin ministries were experts from West Germany; West Germany loaned some 200 judges to the East to implement legal reform, as well as tax inspectors and unemployment specialists. Much of what happened now was clearing the stables: the arrests of Eastern agents in the West, cipher clerks, military, Federal and Unesco employees; still some 5,000 were said to be lying low, some recruited by the KGB. Markus Wolf, the former Eastern spy-master, proposed an amnesty, but he himself had a West German warrant against him. In Paris a physicist admitted passing microfilmed documents to the Stasi, some hidden in a plastic dog turd, as part of his desire to share scientific knowledge; he got twelve years. In April the government requested the extradition from Syria of Alois Brunner, Eichmann's deputy, for trial on Nazi war crimes. And the more recent past surfaced with the arrest in East Germany of several alleged RAF terrorists wanted in the West, together with Palestinian terrorists alleged to be responsible for the killing of eleven Israeli athletes at the 1972 Olympics, and the bombing of a West Berlin disco in 1986. The RAF had been in the GDR since at least 1980, and the Stasi had provided them with new identities, using them for information and as contacts with other terrorist groups in the Middle East. This was said to have been a personal interest of Honecker and Mielke, reminding the former of his underground activities against the Nazis: the daydreams of the powerful become flesh and blood, car bombs and Kalashnikovs. Whether they had been allowed to continue terrorist activities in West Germany while under Stasi patronage was not yet clear. More arrests were expected, and reprisals promised from the RAF. At the beginning of June the Volkskammer passed a law expropriating the considerable property of the Communist Party. West and East agreed on the return of property expropriated by the East, with the possibility of compensation for Western claimants on property expropriated since 1949. So far a million claims on land and property in the East had been filed. As the last days of the GDR ticked out, fears were expressed that Western firms had not taken up much investment in the East; the problems were the environment and the confused issue of the property laws, promising a legal labyrinth of claims and counterclaims. The West, it seemed, had picked cautiously over the ruins, and taken only what was viable. The prognosis was not, is not, good. The hammer and compass symbol of the GDR was to be removed from public buildings. When removed from the flag, where for the time being it remained, the flag would be the flag of West Germany.

In mid-June Checkpoint Charlie closed and was removed, jibbed on to the back of a truck and sent to sit in a nearby traffic jam. There were speeches by the mayors of both Berlins and by the Foreign Ministers of the four powers in town for the four plus two talks, and tears in the eyes of Willy Brandt, Mayor of West Berlin when the Wall went up. It was confirmed that all border controls at the fifty-plus crossing points would be removed, and thirty-nine previously blocked streets reopened. The two cities became one. At midnight on 30 June the border between East and West, and all border controls, ceased.

In West Berlin they grumble at the disruptions. Once they lived in a quiet corner of Europe, and now again they are in the middle of the traffic. For them unification began on 9 November, and life won't ever be the same again. Since then property prices and rents have risen, accommodation and jobs are harder to find, Ossi moonlighting and falling subsidies have cut wages, theft and street violence and drug use are up. Parking meters are to be introduced, and the battalions of traffic wardens expanded. Berlin has turned into a supermarket for the whole of Eastern Europe. Whatever the future, it won't be as manageable; it will be more expensive, more crowded, more violent, more competitive. Kohl's bid for rapid unification and the terms of the currency buyout were a historic gamble, but it's not his way of life that's altered by the huddled masses from the East. At whatever cost to his own economy, which is part of ours in

Europe, he has pushed ahead in a hurry, and only the future will prove him right or wrong. It may be it will judge that he could not have done other, or slower. Kohl was complaining West German investment in the East was 'in no way sufficient'.

For Berliners, it's all a pain. There are those who will find work in all this, and those that will prosper, and those who will find chances for mischief. Everyone else will pay for it, one way or another, is how they feel. It's obvious, they say now: unification means a commonwealth, a sharing of the West's wealth with the East's poverty. *Das ist klar*. All's clear.

A great slice of history is over. Even so, in the East it's still cold, windier, greyer, just as ever, back when the ice of hostility hissed in the air through here. The old cold is replaced by the new cold of the social market. The border's open, but it's still grim here. The fact is they were just scared, all those maintenance staff on the border, who are now normal folk with their normal insecurities, customs and immigration personnel now so many supernumeraries. What they were afraid of was their own world, but they were taught to be afraid of ours. And they were right about that. In the beginning, despite the Russians and their models and methods, there was socialism, and there were many in this country who chose to be here, chose to stay, and genuinely believed in a historic purpose, scorning the abundance of the West as irrelevant and wasteful, counting the restrictions on freedom necessary to defend their world from the West. That the West is aggressive and expansionist is part of the current demonstration. The Wall, Shevardnadze said at Checkpoint Charlie's close, was a deformed response to an already deformed situation, the existence of the outpost of West Berlin in the heart of the GDR, a foot forever in the door, alluring, undermining, finally triumphant. The Wall defended the East from the West with some reason, though its logic only follows from a mad proposition that a country can be arbitrarily and indefinitely divided by a sealed frontier. The hypocrisy was that the leadership were not restricted by it, and could pass in and out, importing Western luxuries denied to everyone else, living in their own KaDeWe. Behind the Wall the leadership, locked in on itself and finally deserted by its Soviet mentors, decayed, forgot its purpose, turned over the running of the state to the Stasi, and betrayed its history and ideals. They'll not be forgiven by either side for that.

A wounded country, the GDR will enter greater Germany, and Europe, scarred and suspicious, bearing along a sharp dose of fascist venom. And the remnants of the Stasi. And the PDS; in late March PDS West parties were founded in Hamburg and Bremen, and in West Berlin a branch was said to be forming in Kreuzberg. In East Berlin the PDS made no comment. As to Honecker, he denies everything, including the charges of harbouring RAF terrorists. At the end of June investigations were opened into the possibility of trying him for murder, as former head of the armed forces, for the shoot-to-kill policy of the border guards. Mielke is back in custody, where as last heard of he has so tormented his jailers with real or pretended senility that they gave him a telephone, unconnected, on which he rages all day in his cell, screaming that the class enemies are coming.

There's barely been time on the calendar for such rapid history, the sudden outcome of forty years of stasis. The cold that fastened over the East, slowly dissolving over the years in response to Ostpolitik, Western blandishments, Deutschmarks, the commercials on the TV night after night, broke suddenly; quantitative change goes on a long time, then hits a threshold, and becomes qualitative change. Eight months from the Wall's opening, nine since the fall of Honecker, and the GDR is effectively history, its currency a collector's item; by the end of 1990 it will be done with, and the Federal Republic will be 77 million strong.

Here in July this book ends; in the time it takes to transmit this record more months will have passed: stockpiled goods, unemployment rising, exports to Eastern Europe falling now the GDR is a hard currency area, the economy collapsing as Easterners reject their own products for the West's, the possibility of unrest and a new exodus. Anticipating an electoral backlash and growing demands for cash, Kohl proposes bringing the elections forward to October; the SPD refuses to agree, accusing Kohl of concealing the true costs of unification. Elections for the Eastern *Länder* are set for 14 October, with political unification likely at the same time. The collapse of the Eastern economy is swift; CDU and SPD are gambling on its timing. For his part Pöhl, head of the Bundesbank, whose reservations on the exchange rate were overruled by Kohl, predicts eventual success, 'after a difficult, perhaps even turbulent initial phase'.

On Sunday 1 July Easterners begin queuing to convert 180 billion Ostmarks into Deutschmarks; they can draw out from their accounts up to DM 2,000 each. Whether they'll put it back or spend it is anyone's guess; given the likelihood of unemployment, and their Eastern reserve, they're initially cautious, leaving their money in savings, enjoying the novelty of earning interest. They've been spending the last of their Ostmarks, and over the weekend the store shelves emptied of GDR goods: shoes, clothes, electronics, sold off at 80 and 90 per cent reductions, or withdrawn. When the stores open on Monday they stock Western goods in Western marks. The 11 per cent short-term premium on Western goods won't stop the Easterners rejecting their own products; the factory stockpiles and the dole queues get larger and longer. What they're buying is food, and household appliances. But unemployment is up 50 per cent on the previous month, and rising rapidly, and no one knows what figures to predict. There are wildcat strikes and stoppages. On the Monday morning of monetary union 28,000 workers staged walkouts in factories in East Berlin. The signs don't look good.

The 800-mile border between the Germanies is no more, and Berlin is one city. The money changers are out of business. The S-Bahn runs all the way from Erkner to Wannsee, on one ticket, and Friedrichstrasse is just another stop, just another interchange that was once the frozen border, the hall of tears. At midnight on the last of June at Zimmerstrasse, which used to be Checkpoint Charlie, the guards stamp the last of the passports and ID cards, lock up and leave.

In East Berlin the billboards are up. The euphoria of the opening has given way to fear and insecurity, and cigarette ads: *Test the West, Come to Marlboro Country*. Alexanderplatz has turned into a market place. Everywhere there are used car lots selling Western cars. Cowboys and car lots. At the banks they're queuing again for the paperwork, handing in the redundant flimsy notes with combine harvesters and chemical plants and a telephone exchange on one side and Münzer and Marx and Engels and Clara Zeitken on the other. All's over, all begins again. The mighty are properly dismayed.

CHRONOLOGY

1945	End of World War II. Berlin and Germany divided into occupation zones by the Allies.
1948	Currency reform in East and West. City administration splits into E. and W. Berlin.
1948–9	Berlin Blockade and Airlift.
1949	Inception of GDR (E. Germany) with its capital in E. Berlin. President Walter Ulbricht. Inception of FRG (W. Germany, including W. Berlin), capital Bonn. Chancellor Konrad Adenauer.
1952	Stalin offers peace treaty with united and neutral Germany. West turns it down.
1953	Uprising in E. Berlin.
1955	E. Germany in the Warsaw Pact. W. Germany in NATO. Diplomatic relations open between Khrushchev and Adenauer.
1958 November	Berlin Ultimatum. Khrushchev orders Allies out.
1961 13 August October	Berlin Wall built. E. Berlin sealed from W. Berlin. E. Germans stop Allied military vehicles to Berlin, and tanks move to Checkpoint Charlie.
1963 December	W. Berliners obtain passes to visit relatives in East.
1970	Ostpolitik. First German–German summit.
1971	Four-power agreement guarantees W. Berlin's status. Honecker takes over from Ulbricht as General Secretary of the Party.

1972	Berlin Agreement. W. Berliners again allowed East, and transit to West eased.
1973	GDR joins UN.
1974	Permanent missions set up in Bonn and E. Berlin. Treaty between the states easing relations.

1989

2 May	Hungarians open part of their border with Austria. E. Germans flee West via Hungary.
5 June	Polish Communist Party defeated in elections by Solidarity.
1 July	In Hungary 25,000 E. Germans in camps waiting to cross the border.
4 August	W. German embassy in Budapest occupied by E. Germans. Closed 13 August.
8 August	W. German legation in E. Berlin occupied and closed.
19 August	Hundreds in mass escape over Hungarian border with Austria. Honecker proclaims the Wall will last 100 years. Solidarity win Polish elections.
22 August	W. German embassy in Prague occupied and closed.
24 August	E. Germans in Budapest embassy allowed to leave.
11 September	Hungary waives all border controls. About 7,000 flee West. In next three days 15,000 more flee via Hungary.
24 September	Prague embassy occupied.
1 October	Thousands more E. Germans flee through Czechoslovakia and Poland.
2–4 October	Demonstrations in Leipzig etc., riots in Dresden.
3 October	4,500 in Prague embassy. Embassy closed. GDR bans visa free travel to Czechoslovakia.
5 October	7,000 allowed to leave Prague, 600 from Warsaw.
7 October	Fortieth anniversary of GDR, Gorbachov guest of honour. He says who ignores history will be devoured by it. Demos in E. Berlin, Leipzig, Dresden, etc.
8 October	Hungarian Party repudiates Communism. Parliament endorses multi-Party system and free elections in 1990.
11 October	Another 600 in Warsaw embassy.
18 October	Honecker resigns, replaced by Krenz.
31 October	Krenz meets Gorbachov and says *perestroika* and reform for the GDR.
2 November	Harry Tisch (Trade Unions) and Margot Honecker (Education) resign.
3 November	Liberal Democrats call on Government to resign. Five Politburo members purged. Czechoslovakia opens its borders.

4 November	Huge demonstrations in E. Berlin and other cities.
7 November	Government resigns.
8 November	Kohl promises aid on condition of free elections. Politburo resigns. Modrow PM. Exodus and demos continue.
9 November	Wall opens. GDR opens borders. Thousands cross to W. Berlin. In 1989 1.8 million applied to leave. Between May and October 50,000 left. By the end of 1989 343,000 had left for the West.
10 November	Zhivkov, 35 years in power in Bulgaria, ousted.
17 November	Prague, 50,000 in Wenceslas Square; police beat up students. Demos elsewhere, up to 300,000.
17 November	New cabinet in E. Berlin, pledges reform.
22 November	Communists propose talks with opposition.
24 November	Czechoslovak presidium and secretariat, including Milos Jakes, resigns.
28 November	Kohl calls for German confederation.
1 December	End of Communist monopoly of power.
3 December	Krenz resigns.
23 December	Ceaușescu falls in Romania.

1990

29 January	Modrow forms coalition government of all parties and brings forward elections.
18 March	Elections produce landslide for conservative Alliance in the East and for Kohl in the West, effectively a vote for unification.
1 July	Buyout of Eastern currency by West. End of refugee status. Start of social, economic and monetary integration.

EPILOGUE:
GOODBYE TO BERLIN

At the end, tears and fireworks. After July's monetary and economic union political unity speedily followed. Accepted by Gorbachov (in exchange for Deutschmarks), and by the four Occupying Powers, the four-plus-two talks concluded in a treaty restoring a united Germany to full sovereignty within its existing borders. The Soviets would withdraw their troops from the East by 1994, and Bonn would come up with 12 billion Deutschmarks to maintain them till then. In August the unification date was agreed by all parties: 3 October. The politicians haggled and the parties manoeuvred for their places in the new Germany, Easterners worried and grumbled and Westerners grew bored and grumbled, but the unification train sped on at a pace no one could have predicted. Within a year of the Wall's opening Germany was united, and the GDR with its internal border and all its works entered the museums.

In the odd space between unions economic and political, *de facto* and *de jure*, authority in the last of the GDR was administered through Western officials and by the Bundesbank and the *Treuhandanstalt*, the commission organizing the restructuring and disposal, through either privatization or closure, of 8,000 former state concerns. The East was being wound up, its assets such as they were sold off; even Praktika camera of Dresden failed to survive. While the rules of the East applied, the West's cartel office still had no jurisdiction; the media and their distribution networks were the targets for new monopolies. There were problem areas: education, property. In the one the old Marxist-oriented education was to be rooted out – Civic Studies removed from the school curriculum, English substituted for Russian as a second language, and whole departments of law, education, philosophy and economics eliminated from the universities. In protest there were student strikes and occupations; Humboldt was occupied for Christmas. The West's strict abortion law would replace the East's more generous arrangements after a two-year period of grace. As to property, the vexed question as to who owned what in the East, a question that inhibited investment, 13 October was set as the deadline for the registration of all claims on property nationalized in the East: claims would be honoured, property restored or compensated, but it would all take years to sort out. And with unification would come the Church Tax, 8 per cent of income, and the onus would lie on the citizen to prove non-affiliation and exemption.

The costs, debatable, piecemeal, incalculable, much concerned the West that would pay in taxes and the East that would pay in human terms, in job losses, in falling subsidies and rising prices, in insecurity. Estimates, constantly revised upwards, ran from DM30 billion through 100 billion and beyond per year for the next five years. It would take at least ten years to bring the East up to the standards of the West. In place of a 1989 surplus there would be deficits for years to come, according to the Bonn Ministry of Finance, revising its budget estimates for the third time in the year. By the year's end the full costs were being put at DM2,000 billion. Kohl, at any rate, was saying nothing. There were elections coming – in October to recreate the five Eastern *Länder*, in December to elect an all-German Federal Government and state governments – and discussion of the costs was postponed. The CDU was still riding the unification train, and, as expected and subsequently confirmed, the winners in both elections were Kohl and the CDU. Everywhere in Germany the left lost out to unification. Electorally, the Greens disappeared. The PDS hung on by the skin of its teeth, hounded and devious, Gysi boxing clever all the way to Bonn. The SPD, harping on about the costs, had been the moaners at the party, telling the electorate what it didn't want to know. In the East the activists of *Neues Forum* and those who, by trying to change their state for the better, had precipitated its demise were virtually forgotten.

Through the last months of its existence the East staggered on, its government falling apart as first the Liberals and then the SPD withdrew from the coalition. At the end of September, at the last session of the Volkskammer, four Ministers and sixty-five MPs were exposed as former Stasi, and the last Parliament of the GDR broke up in disarray. By now they were no longer meeting in the Palast der Republik, which had been declared ridden with asbestos dust and closed, perhaps to be demolished. Nevertheless, by the year's end the Palast was open again for concerts, discos, bowling, restaurants, and all talk of asbestos in the air had been forgotten.

The East's decline continued; unemployment doubled by the month, till by the year's end it stood at half a million, with almost 2 million of the 9 million workforce on short time. Production and retail sales had fallen by a half. The universal rejection of Eastern goods in the shops hit farmers and producers in the East. More firms closed. Those with jobs expected to lose them; effectively many were earning less and paying more. There were widespread strikes and protests by farmers, factory workers, railway and postal workers, even the East Berlin Volkspolizei. In the city itself some 150,000 people were commuting to jobs in the West. But the overall mood was of deepening gloom. The East's loss of identity was not made up for by the promise of West German citizenship; the sense of being second-class persisted; the sense of being suspended in a vacuum was real. Easterners seemed to be keeping their heads down, renting videos, taking a crash course in Western movies, while the smell of brown coal was still in the air, and nothing much had changed in the broken streets. The East remained distinctly apart culturally and socially, half a century of silence a habit difficult to break. And the demoralized East was being told what to do by the increasingly impatient West, which now perceived the East as the FOB, the *Fass ohne Boden*, the bottomless barrel. When the country was no more, citizens of the former GDR were still known semi-officially as DDR-Burghers, an identity that earned them cheaper travel. To call them anything else was a mouthful of gutterals, *the former citizens of the former GDR*. Outwardly they remained shy, withdrawn, unforthcoming, cold with strangers, numb. Everywhere crime rose rapidly, both violent and otherwise; bank robbers in Western cars outran the police in their Ladas and Wartburgs. Road accidents soared. In the vacuum violence, football hooliganism and racism flourished, and right-wing violence. At the beginning of November in Leipzig, at the Leipzig–Berlin Dynamo game, nervous Vopos, unused to such indiscipline, opened fire on rioting fans, killing one. On the last Saturday of September, four days before unification, I sat at the end of Bernauerstrasse outside the Sportspark in the East, where Darmastadt were the visitors, listening to the sea-roar of the crowd, the wind bearing the blasts of the referee's whistle, the periodic banging of a drum and the intermittent roaring of *Sieg heil*, *Sieg heil*, *Sieg heil*, as if from some old black-and-white film, the chant in the nightmare, surfacing again: the definition of atavism. *Sieg heil*.

When it came, unification in Berlin was a grand bash of bands and sausages, beer and flags and fireworks, though elsewhere in Germany, West and East, the event passed virtually unmarked. The Easterners were mostly spectators at the feast. In the city there were bells and speeches, orchestras and military and jazz bands, Beethoven's Ninth at the Schauspielhaus and Britten's *War Requiem* at the Gethsemane-Kirche in Prenzlauer Berg. At midnight the flags changed. And by midnight there were fierce riots in Alexanderplatz between anarchists and riot police, both sides imported from the West, resulting in 150 arrests.

Thereafter more of the same: counting the costs, the growth of the right, *Ali raus* among the black graffiti, *Links stinks*, *Rechts voran*. Immediately after unification there were arrests of former spies. The West put it about that they had a list of 3,000 former Stasi, only some of whom they would detain. The PDS was raided and accused of smuggling funds to Russia, and accusations flowed against the other, tainted, former bloc parties of the East. A string of wanted Red Army Faction terrorists and spies were found to be living in the East, set up by the Stasi with new identities. Revelations of the inner workings of the Stasi continued; they were, it seems, the agents of their own destruction, paranoia devouring itself until they 'choked to death'. There were stories that they had instructed the Iraqis, among others, in terrorism and in chemical and biological techniques. In any case they were still about, some taken over by the KGB, others teaching, working in the police or at the post office, opening restaurants, still trading on their secrets. A new map of East Berlin appeared, replacing former maps that had distorted streets and excluded the locations of government and military buildings; it had been stolen from the files by a former Stasi officer and sold for DM29,000. Days after unification it was discovered that a Western spy had received funding in East Berlin only days before. An arrest warrant was issued for Honecker, still languishing in a Soviet military hospital where, for the time being, he remained, protected by his Soviet mentors.

By now the Wall was gone from Berlin, much of it distributed in slabs and chips around the planet, the evil thinly spread at last. At what was once Checkpoint Charlie a single slab stood as a memorial, along with other exhibits from the Cold War museum. Another memorial slab was unveiled at the Bornholmerstrasse Bridge, and the Museum of German History exhibited another three. Along Zimmerstrasse, alongside the former Gestapo headquarters at Prinz-Albrecht Strasse, a length of it remained, scarred and scribbled over to its metal rods, survivor of an abandoned plan to create a memorial way that would include Nazi and Cold War sites and buildings. No one missed the Wall, despite the slash of colour and wit and fear it had carried through the city. **One day this will only be art.** In the East a kilometre and a half of its length along Mühlenstrasse became the East Side Gallery, a huge outdoor exhibition of paintings – handsome, but lacking the spontaneity of the Wall's old artwork and graffiti, its attraction a traffic hazard. Bits of the Wall were still on sale, or, at least, painted concrete chips of doubtful provenance, and the great bazaars at the Brandenburger Tor and elsewhere were still piled high with caps, flags, uniforms, belts, badges and medals, helmets, gas masks, Red Army knives, watches, torches, German and Russian gear sold off by the soldiery hungry for Deutschmarks. From the same sources there were many cheap firearms on the market. At the unification junket tourists were stumbling about the city dressed in NVA helmets and the discarded outfits of Russian generals. More cabaret. Zimmerstrasse, across which the tanks had faced each other, was now to be a real street again, and the trees planted by the East back in March were ripped out immediately after unification. The West wanted nothing to remain of the GDR. Checkpoint Charlie itself stood ghostly and abandoned, a tangle of vandalized wiring and broken glass stinking of urine, the backdrop for cigarette ads, one a handshake under the *Come Together* motto precisely mimicking the old Grotewohl–Pieck handshake that forty years ago had united the Eastern SPD and KPD in the SED. There is a symmetry to these events, to all these images. Here the traffic flowed straight through now and, beyond, Benetton had opened up in the old Intershop. Beyond the abandoned building sites along the old border there are newly opened U-Bahn stations, Western banks and businesses, the Dresdener Bank with its windows smashed in someone's fury.

In East Berlin the Deutschmark prices were higher for the same goods, higher still further east. As the year ran out, around Alexanderplatz fewer gamblers were betting on peas under matchboxes, but there were dozens of stalls selling tatty market goods – scarves, belts, bags, jackets, fruit, groceries, and around the corner and across the great square more of the same, selling the same goods. And everywhere there were people selling cigarettes, by carton or by pack, the newly poor. Up around Prenzlauer Berg most were Vietnamese, shivering in their thin jackets, though here in the grey centre of the city most were solid citizens, soberly dressed late employees of the state that died under them. Up around the Frankfurter Allee S-Bahn new shops were opening, boutiques and hairdressers and small restaurants, a kitchen and bathroom supplier, and everywhere video rentals, and further down towards Samariterstrasse and Mainzer the ruins of the squats evicted by the police in three days of violence in November, when 350 were arrested. Renovation of these blocks went on under police guard and in a hurry, as the old graffiti of the revolutionary Berlin left vanished: *Don't cry, work*; *Learn to Burn*; *Factories don't burn themselves, they need your help*. In protest the Alternative List resigned from the Red–Green coalition, but it was now less than a month to 2 December and the elections beyond which Germany, and Berlin, would elect a government. In Bonn the riots were seized on as further reasons for not moving the Federal government to Berlin.

By the year's end, the celebrations and excitement over, despondency reigned. De Maizière, Kohl's deputy in the CDU who had just been elected to Bonn, resigned his party and government posts, again accused of involvement with the Stasi. The future of Berlin still lay in doubt; it was a capital in name only. Few in Bonn wanted to move to Berlin, and the old arguments against the revival of a centralized Germany continued. The end of showcase Berlin found the city with too many state orchestras and operas and theatres and zoos, and the subsidies were dwindling. The former Nazi film studios at Babelsberg near Potsdam, taken over by the GDR, closed.

In any case Berliners found new concerns to worry over; their isolation at an end, the German border with Poland and Czechoslovakia now lay not far away, collapsing Russia one country over. Estimates of massive Eastern immigration, especially from Russia, reached alarming proportions: Berlin, the old target of the migrants, lay on the old transit routes. There was much fear of upheaval in the East, with plans for investment there to forestall chaos. Berlin's vast stockpiles of supplies, laid down since the Berlin Blockade, were sent to Russia, along with food parcels and donations. Help for Russia ads appeared in newspapers, and it was said that the former Stalingrad was reduced to rations sparser than those imposed during its World War II siege by the Wehrmacht. New fences were going up to the East, along the Austrian border, along the Polish border, and it was now harder than before the revolutions for Easterners to get into Germany and harder still for hopefuls from the Third World, displaced now to the Fourth. The metal sheds and furniture of Checkpoint Charlie were being dismantled, to be re-erected on the Oder-Neisse.

As to the ebullient West, confident and expansive, a joke may illustrate: Bush and Gorbachov take the cybergenic treatment and are frozen for a couple of hundred years. Brought round together, they're both sitting in the recovery room drinking coffee and reading the papers. 'I see the dollar's now worth 30 Pfennig,' says Gorbi. 'And I see there's trouble on the German–Chinese border,' says Bush.

But the tale ends in bangs and whimpers. While Berliners, with Germans and the rest of Europe, had been staring at their navels, at the Wall and its rupture, a new war was forming in the Gulf, and under its cover the old repression was returning to the European East. With the new year, as the Red Army's Black Berets opened fire in Vilnius and Riga, it was clear that Gorbachov was abandoning *perestroika* and reverting to control by the army and the KGB. The West had abandoned him for the sake of a costly war in the Middle East and thrown him to the wolves and the hardliners. *He will become a dictator*, some said, *without even knowing it*. And meanwhile, others pointed out, the Soviet Army remained in what had been East Germany, demoralized and deserting, denied transit rights by the Poles rumours of the death of the Cold War had been grossly exaggerated after all. I recall it was but months ago that there was talk of Nato becoming redundant, that there was a short season when we thought the long cold was over and the borders were open, and we and our children might live unthreatened lives in otherwise uninteresting times for the first time in all our lives. That season was soon over. *History*, as Friedemann says, quoting Hegel, *is what nobody wanted.*